PERSPECTIVES

Series Editors: Colin MacCabe and Paul Willemen

THE SCORSESE
CONNECTION

Lesley Stern

INDIANA UNIVERSITY PRESS
Bloomington and Indianapolis

BFI PUBLISHING

First published in 1995 by the
British Film Institute
21 Stephen Street, London W1P 2LN
and the
Indiana University Press
601 North Morton Street, Bloomington, Indiana 47404

The British Film Institute exists to promote appreciation, protection and
development of moving image culture in and throughout the whole of the
United Kingdom. Its activities include the National Film and Television Archive;
the National Film Theatre; the London Film Festival; the Museum of the Moving
Image; the production and distribution of film and video; funding and support for
regional activities; Library and Information Services; Stills, Posters and Designs;
Research; Publishing and Education; and the monthly *Sight and Sound* magazine.

British Library Cataloguing in Publication Data
A catalogue record for this book is available from the British Library

ISBN   0-85170-512-X
       0-85170-513-8 pbk

US Cataloguing data available from the Library of Congress
A CIP catalog record for this book is available from the Library of Congress

ISBN   0-253-32952-3 (clothbound)
       0-253-21011-9 (paperbound)

Cover design: Romas Foord
Front cover stills from *Taxi Driver* and *Mean Streets*
Back cover: Scorsese filming *Taxi Driver*

Typeset by
D R Bungay Associates, Burghfield, Berks

Printed in Great Britain by
St Edmundsbury Press Ltd, Bury St Edmunds, Suffolk

Contents

Acknowledgments

During the slow writing of this book, John Frow, Laleen Jayamanne and Jodi Brooks have been a constant inspiration through their own work and through the kind of provocative criticism that is sometimes alarming, always enlivening. Many other people have contributed by reading parts of the book in draft form and providing invaluable feedback. I would particularly like to thank Christine Alavi, Lizbeth During, Anne Freadman, Ann Game, Ross Gibson, Jane Goodall, Bill Green, Liz Jacka, Noel King, Sylvia Lawson and Ross Poole. Others have generously given information and ideas, helped me to work out particular problems or provided very practical assistance: Eleanor Frow, Jan McKemmish, June McGowan, Carlos Calero, Bruce Hodsdon, Lynne Tillman, Mike Gampi, Glenn d'Cruz, Tracey Moffat, Jan Rowden and Ken Kruikshank.

Paul Karkkainen, Jennifer Kitchener and Genevieve Lloyd have made much possible. Helen Barnes, the best of friends and neighbours, has been an enormous help and encouragement. I have been fortunate in the last few years to belong to a seriously lucid writing group: thank you to Ruark Lewis, Diane Losche, Martin Harrison, Ian Maxwell, Cathie Payne and Martin Thomas.

The ideas for this book, and its shape, have been developed whilst teaching in the School of Theatre and Film Studies at the University of New South Wales. I am particularly grateful to the many students who have participated in the course on Contemporary Approaches to the Cinema and to the few who have participated in Histrionics. Their enthusiasm, curiosity and weird perspectives have pushed me to refine many hazy propositions. Their questions and insights are manifested in the book in various ways, sometimes, no doubt, as unconscious appropriation. I hope that they will take this as a sign of life. My colleagues in the School have provided a rare atmosphere of intellectual generosity, for which I am more thankful than I usually let on.

I have received two research grants from the Faculty of Arts and Social Science, University of New South Wales. Paul Garcia provided excellent research assistance in the initial stages of the project; Jennifer Harris did so in the latter stages when her calmness and lucidity were invaluable.

Early versions of chapters were delivered at the following events and venues: 'Kiss Me Deadly: Feminism and Cinema Now' at The Power Institute, Sydney University (1991); 'Cinema and the Perversions' at The Brisbane Centre for Psychoanalytic Studies (1991); the Institute of Modern Art, Brisbane (1992); The Ultimo Seminars, University of Technology, Sydney (1993); Film and History Conference, La Trobe University (1993); 'Sexuality in Cinema: East and West', University of Newcastle (1994). I am grateful to the organisers for inviting me and to the participants for their responses. Parts of Chapter 4 originally appeared as 'The Oblivious Transfer: Analysing *Blue Velvet*', in *Camera Obscura*, no. 30, 1994.

Paul Willemen, long ago it now seems, astonished me by suggesting that I write about the cinema of Martin Scorsese. The idea brewed and took possession. What eventuated may not be what he had in mind, but I am nevertheless very grateful to him for seeing something that I could not see, and for his encouragement and patience as an editor. In addition, I would also like to thank Colin MacCabe and the British Film Institute's publishing crew for their support.

Chapter 1

Life Is Fraught with Peril

It's a pitiful ending. The high-flying gangster, who lived in splendour like a king, is now consigned to suburbia and an endless vista of empty time. Henry King (Ray Liotta) stands in his desultory bath robe on the footpath, picking up the newspaper, while in voice-over he tells us: 'Can't even get decent food. Right after I got here I ordered some spaghetti with marinara sauce and I got egg noodles and ketchup. I'm an average nobody. I get to live the rest of my life like a schnook.'

But then an extraordinary image flashes up, sears the blandness of the *mise en scène*, and it hits us: this isn't really an ending at all. Joe Pesci (as Tommy, a character who is well and truly dead), in medium-close-up, unloads his gun directly at the camera. He grins at us as he fires, and as the frame fills with smoke another scene is called to mind – remember that famous image from silent cinema, the concluding shot of Porter's *The Great Train Robbery*, where the leader of the outlaw band shoots straight at the audience?

The end of *GoodFellas* is at once assaulting and exhilarating. This shot, which comes at us from out of the blue, is – like Porter's ending – somehow enlivening and curiously engaging for an ending, where we expect resolution (rather than a new engagement in the mystery of cinematic genesis and annihilation). In discussing 'the history of the ending' in early cinema, Noël Burch refers to this particular image as the best-known example of the emblematic shot.[1] Although this kind of shot could serve a narrative purpose – could, that is, be stitched into a sequential structure – it retained some of the force of the autonomous medium-close-up from which it derived. This force is partly generated by the establishment of eye contact between actors and spectators, but it can also be located in the very autonomy of the shot, in a presentational or monstrative, rather than primarily narrative, aspect. The most fascinating evidence of such autonomy lies in the fact that this shot was actually delivered to exhibition venues as a separate reel which could be shown either at the beginning or end of the film.[2]

In *GoodFellas*, it would seem, 'this shot' has to come at the end where it serves to suggest a kind of non-closure: in plot terms Tommy is dead and his explosive appearance here represents a return of the irrepressible, forebodes not a conclusion but a long night ahead – a night of the living dead, a night at the movies. Or perhaps a comic-book resurrection with deadly intent.[3] But its emblematic status means that it could conceivably have been placed at the beginning where, although its function of course would be somewhat different, it would still probably register an affective charge, elicit a kind of engagement more typical of so-called primitive cinema, or the cinema of attractions.[4]

If this shot of Tommy provokes a memory of another image then we might also say that it represents the return not just of a character or an idea but of a certain kind of cinema. But the past never returns unadulterated, the cinematic process always works upon the material of 'screen memories'. The concatenation of Tommy's machine gun is accompanied by the sounds of punk, sounds which develop into the Sid Vicious version of 'My Way', a kind of anthem associated with Paul Anka and Frank Sinatra, here ironically overhauled.

> 'This is my way; where is yours?' thus I answered those
> who asked me 'the way'.
> For the way – that does not exist. (Nietzsche)[5]

And as we hear Sid Vicious, so another (virtual) image materialises out of the murky mists of auditory memory, an image of the Sex Pistol himself in that bizarrely staged documentary, *The Great Rock 'n' Roll Swindle*. In this film he performs 'My Way' on stage and at the end, as the sequence turns (perhaps?) into fantasy, he pulls a gun and fires 'point-blank', as the Edison catalogue said of the outlaw in *The Great Train Robbery*, 'at each individual in the

The Great Rock and Roll Swindle (Julian Temple, 1979)

audience',[6] actually killling a number of people in the diegetic audience (blood sprays and the sound of applause turns to howls of horror) and then, in closer shot, he aims directly at us. Tommy returns as the ghost of the outlaw, a reincarnation of Sid Vicious.

Life Is Fraught with Peril

At the end of Raul Ruiz's *Life Is a Dream* (a long drawn-out, endlessly deferred, repeatedly rehearsed ending) the hero faces his assassin:

> Will this bullet ever come?
> Wanna read while you wait?
> What've you got?
> *OK Magazine*
> Too late
> Lenin's *State and Revolution*
> Too early
> Here's the bullet.

Endings in Scorsese seem also to come too early or too late (*Age of Innocence*), to be almost elided, arguably evaded (*Taxi Driver* and *King of Comedy*) or operatically inflated (*New York, New York* and *Cape Fear*). Almost always they are very cinematic endings – they remind us of other films, of other cinematic moments and gestures, and they remind us not just that we are watching a film (we know this), but that watching films is fraught with wonder and peril.

Scorsese's first short film, *What's a Nice Girl Like You Doing in a Place Like This?* (made in 1963 on 16mm, 9 minutes, black and white) ends with a seascape and a tiny figure, just head and arms emerging out of the ocean, shouting 'Life is fraught with peril!' The film is a zany mélange of New Wave stylistics, Ernie Kovacs gags, and the monstrous magic of silent cinema. Scorsese: 'I decided that there would be not one match cut. Each cut would be a surprise. I'd cut to a shot that's moving, or to a still or animated shot, stopmotion photography.'[7] Algernon, the protagonist, becomes obsessed with a painting (first it is of a man in a boat on a lake, and then it becomes a painting of the empty sea shore). At the end of the film he disappears into it (or alternatively, the painting becomes the film, fills the screen with swooping gulls and crashing waves), with a tiny figure in the distance, shouting.

> Literally, I have the image of myself always keeping my nose right above the water, the waves always getting to me and about to sink me'. (Scorsese)[8]

It ends in the water but only in order that it may begin and end again in water – in *Cape Fear* in 1992. But before *Cape Fear* some of these ideas, these imagistic fantasies, recur elsewhere: in Michael Snow's *Wavelength* (1967), where a long zoom disappears, in the end, into a painting of the sea, and *Barton Fink* (1991), where the hero also disappears into a painting (or the painting becomes the film). Although Scorsese has described *What's a Nice Girl* as a tale of 'pure paranoia',[9] it is also a a joyful demonstration of the generative power of images and the mobility of spectatorial imagination. The very cinematic nature of this ending will be echoed in later endings. *The Last Temptation of Christ*, for instance, cuts from Christ's death on the cross to abstract colour flashes from the end of camera reels, evoking the ending of Monte Hellman's *Two-Lane Blacktop* (1971).[10]

> *What do you see? Red, green, yellow lights. I wanted to show these elements but without necessarily placing them as they are in reality. Rather, as they remain in the memory – splashes of red and green, flashes of yellow passing by. I wanted to recreate a sensation through the elements that constitute it.*
> (Jean-Luc Godard)[11]

The ending of *Life Lessons* might also be thought of as cinematically ostentatious. The camera irises in to a circle in the centre of a black frame, and in the circle there is an image out of focus, simply a sense of various shades of white; on the soundtrack is Procul Harum's 'Whiter Shade of Pale'. The image sharpens and we see Lionel Dobie (Nick Nolte), in long shot, at the opening of his big one-man show, picking up a very young woman by offering her life lessons – a process which strongly suggests that the whole story is about to begin all over again. And then the iris closes right down and the credits roll. This is not, as in *GoodFellas*, a surprise ending. We can recognise the 'revelation' as part of a system that was inaugurated with the very first shot. The film begins with 'Whiter Shade of Pale' and a series of irises opening onto a number of discrete objects or scenes: a paint palette of vivid primary colours in thick, oily, tactile close-up; paintbrushes; Nolte's restless pacing body tracked closely by an equally restless camera; a glass of brandy on the floor. This could have been presented as a montage sequence, the images cut together; but then it would have been a different sort of sequence and a different sort of film. Scorsese has said that he wanted to use theatrical lighting and so he 'used an iris shot to do what a spotlight would do.'[12] The iris differentiates images, marks them out, presents them to us – on a palette, as it were, full-frontally. They work as autonomous close-ups do in early cinema, they 'do not use enlargement for narrative punctuation, but as an attraction in its own right'.[13]

The exaggerated formality of the opening and closing sets in place a structure for charting obsession. Lionel Dobie is fixated, in the grip of a purposeful pursuit. His painting and his obsession with Paulette, the Rosanna Arquette character (or whoever can replace her), are intimately bound up. His obsession with the woman is cathected in painting: paint becomes the medium of possession and the woman is in a sense conjured into existence by his restless, driven desire to experience feeling (and if he cannot literally touch or feel her he is propelled all the more urgently to paint). *Life Lessons* strings a cinematic tightrope between stillness and movement, between the still-life (those distilled moments of close, almost fixated, scrutiny of objects isolated in space) and the liveliness of movement (movement of bodies, stories, desires). In this tension the still may be animated – invested, that is, with a peculiar force of attraction – and movement may be stilled; the propulsion of obsession conceived as repetitive motion, the movement towards conclusion as reiteration of the beginning.

> *A still photograph is concerned with the isolation of a moment or second of time. The wealth of detail which usually escapes our attention as each moment passes is here arrested for our leisurely scrutiny and examination. The moment is stayed, is composed within a stable frame. But in films the problem is directly opposite, for films are concerned with the way in which the moment passes and becomes the next one. This metamorphosis cannot be composed within a frame, but only through frames, from one frame to the next. Such movement concerns itself not with details of space, but with details of movement in time.* (Maya Deren)[14]

What *Life Lessons*, through its very theatricality, makes cinematic, is that obsessive quality, the ability of the film medium itself to conjure obsessions and desires into being, to engender bodies and dreams, and to tear them asunder. Bits of bodies, etiolated obsessions, turn up later, in other guises (after being churned around in the garbage compacter in *GoodFellas*, to the gruesomely sublime accompaniment of 'Layla'), in other films, other dreams and nightmares.

The Word Flew into his Head as Fast and Clear as the Flash and Whistle of its Breath

If the ending of *Life Lessons* is more cinematic than diegetic, this is not to say that it is tacked on or superciliously self-reflexive. If the irising effect, like the freeze frame which is systematically deployed in *GoodFellas*, works in an almost anachronistic way to attract the viewer, to focus attention, and intensify dramatic engagement, this is not to say that Scorsese's cinema is quintessentially primitive. Rather, it is to propose that the ending, or more generally what we might call the Scorsesian indefinite ending, is imbricated in a more thoroughly sustained textual modality (and cinematic genealogy). This modality is characterised by a shift of climactic affect from the ending to a variety of points within the film, so that any element of the structure may, for various reasons, become acutely (even if ephemerally) significant. Dramatic intensity is dispersed (spread mosaically, *not* evenly like margarine) through the body of the text, so that individual scenes, moments, gestures, are invested with sensate significance. Of course this is a tendency, not an absolute mode, and as a tendency it is evident even in the most classic of Hollywood movies. It is also a pronounced tendency in many feature films made during the era that Deleuze characterises in terms of a crisis – a crisis of the action-image.[15] Scorsese's cinema, however, is a particularly generative instance, both for illustrating this tendency with tenacious persistence, and for doing so in a way that provokes some intriguing difficulties, riddles revolving around that perennially perplexing issue of how films make sense.

David Malouf, in his novel *Remembering Babylon*, describes a scene where a man who has been cut off from his own language for many years is suddenly apprehended by an image:

> *He looked up into a clearing, all raw timber and scattered leaves, and saw a bearded fellow in a blue shirt and braces who spat on his hands, took up a long-handled, bladed instrument, and stood, preparing to swing it. He was amazed. A kind of meaning clung to the image in the same way that the clothes he was wearing clung to the man, and when the blade flashed and jarred against wood, it struck home in him. Axe. The word flew into his head as fast and clear as the flash and whistle of its breath. Axe. Axe. Circles of meaning rippled away from the mark it blazed in the dark of his skull.*[16]

The image works not simply as something seen; it is felt, its meaning is felt, or rather, it comes to signify in the process of bodily apprehension. The cutting work of memory is conveyed here, rather than simple recognition. Malouf's writing does more than describe; it actually enacts the work of memory, the way in which memory can be provoked, the way in which, in the cut, a connection can be made, and a new understanding can emerge. This is what we might call 'embodied knowing'.[17] Although Malouf is not talking about cinema at all, I find this to be a marvellous and inspiring piece of writing for evoking the way that cinema works, thoughtfully, through mobilising a range of senses. It also provokes a reflection: if the cinematic experience is not exclusively about looking or the sense of sight, so it is not exclusively, or hermetically, about cinema. A space opens up – a space which I will call 'Scorsese' – where a variety of texts, and memories, intersect and reverberate.

Sappy Endings

When it comes to the end of a Scorsese film you can usually expect a degree of critical consternation, or even downright hostility. *Taxi Driver* was seen by some critics as either unbelievable or irresponsible, and *King of Comedy* – where Rupert Pupkin emerges from gaol as a celebrity – was seen by some as a heinous reiteration of the original crime ('the most irresponsible film to hit the screen since Scorsese's *Taxi Driver* – perhaps more dangerous than the 1976 film that reportedly served as an inspiration for John Hinkley Jr's attempt on the life of President Reagan').[18]

> *Some people wanted a more 'ending' ending.*
> (Paul Newman about *The Colour of Money*)[19]

> The Wizard of Oz *reminds me of the frightening power of movies to move. I'm glad it has a happy ending.* (Derek Jarman)[20]

New York, New York caused much consternation because of its failure to deliver a happy ending within the format of a happy genre – the musical. '*New*

York, New York', argued a typical review, 'ends on a dying fall that is positively Chekhovian, still not having made up its mind whether it was a musical romance or a drama about musicians.'[21] The film originally ran for over four hours, and in the first released version (136 minutes) the 'Happy Endings' sequence was not included. Featuring Francine (Liza Minnelli) in a triumphant star-is-born routine, it was subsequently reinstated as the grand finale in a re-release (163 minutes). 'Happy Endings', as well as being a lengthy and gorgeously extravagant song-and-dance number (going on and on as though to infinity like the grand finale of *An American in Paris*), is also the title of the film that Francine is starring in, a film about a girl becoming a film star. So the Chinese box effect, not unusual in the genre, is here exploited and considerably amplified. Jimmy Doyle (Robert De Niro), Francine's estranged husband, comes to the opening and when he visits Francine afterwards generic expectations suggest a reunion. But Jimmy makes a slip and refers to the film as 'Sappy Endings', and so we know at this moment, deep down, that neither of them will show for the stage-door meeting.

This invocation of sappy endings is telling. It points to the way in which Scorsese negotiates the parameters which delineate Hollywood genres, and it tends to foreground the fact that endings, like beginnings, are always provisional (of course, the 'textual' always bears traces of various negotiations – often at studio level, to do with budget, technology, censorship, and so on). Although it may be the case that beginnings and endings are always provisional, it is equally true that the majority of films, Hollywood films anyway, make a virtue and indeed a rule of such contingencies, to such an extent that the framework (as a discernible structuring device) often tends to disappear or at least to become transparent. There have, however, always been film-makers in Hollywood who are aware of the constraints and deploy them ironically, parodically, or overtly as a device. Douglas Sirk, for instance, talks of his use of the happy ending as a 'deus ex machina' and Sturges of his invocation of the 'miracle ending'.[22] For such film-makers the very contingency and generic formality of 'the ending' allows for resonance and allusion to other films, and also incites the viewer to make allusions and connections. The viewer, in other words, is invited to open the film out just as it formally closes down. In this moment the intertextual conundrum is made visible: where does one text end and another begin?

In its endless finale *New York, New York* proliferates a number of contesting endings. Scorsese: ' "Happy Endings" made one side of the film complete and whole – the part connected to all the old Hollywood musicals that I adored. The real ending made complete the other side of the film – the Cassavetes-like story about creative people in romantic relationships.'[23] It can possibly be considered as akin to *Falling in Love*, the end of which, Slavoj Zizek argues,[24]

Enacts, in a condensed form, the entire gamut of possible denouements of extramarital affairs in cinema history . . . the charm of the film consists in this playing with different codes, so that the viewer can never be sure if what he/she sees is already the final denouement . . . What makes *Falling in Love* a 'postmodern' film is this reflected relationship to the history of cinema, that is to say, its playing over of the different variants of the narrative closure.

7

But where *Falling in Love* is excruciatingly parsimonious in its doling out of narrative variants, *New York, New York* generates a breathtaking audacity that I also experience in the ending of *Cape Fear* and in many Hong Kong movies, but especially in John Woo's *The Killer*. *The Killer* has the most extraordinarily drawn-out ending – a kinetic and dazzlingly choreographed shoot-out – which alludes to such films as *Duel in the Sun* as the wounded lovers crawl towards one another, and *Magnificent Obsession* as we wait in suspense to see if the blinded heroine will, in this moment of trauma, regain her sight.

> I couldn't watch the end, it was all so frightening – the sun beating down, the woman's hands bleeding and these two people who were so much in love they had to kill each other. I think the music by Dmitri Tiomkin also made it all seem like a horror film, but my mother kept yelling:

> 'Look at it, you took me here to see it, now watch it!' (Scorsese)[25]

Endings always have the capacity to provoke this ambivalence or tension, this desire to see it through to the end, conjoined with a simultaneous drive to look away, to refuse or defer the conclusion. This tension is focused most acutely in those films where 'the end' is marked not just as the end of the story but as a cutting edge between different regimes of reality, between different registers of the fantastic. If movies have the capacity for incarnation and disembodiment, the capacity to bring worlds into being, to engender bodies and transubstantiate matter, the question is (and it is a question that films like *King of Comedy* and *New York, New York* both ask): what are the connections between those worlds willed into cinematic being and other worlds, histories, social milieus? This is the acute question of intertextuality, the import of asking where one text ends and another begins. It is in the insertion of this question that Scorsese represents a variance from the *Falling in Love* trajectory, from a 'nice' postmodernism cleansed of vituperative yearning. The dilemma that his films so often present is this: what happens when you fall out of love, when the dream ends, when the world you've created so intricately begins to implode? Or, to inflect this slightly differently: how do you sustain the fantasies that inspire energy, action and transformative insights?

And Now It's All Over

> *The boundaries which divide life from death are at best shadowy and vague. Who shall say where one ends and the other begins?* (Edgar Allan Poe quoted at the end of Roger Corman's *Tomb of Ligeia*).

The most shocking moment in *GoodFellas* occurs a bit before the very end. We find ourselves, with our 'hero', suddenly located in an FBI office. Everything is flat – the colours, the décor, the characters, all are leached of intensity; a cold clammy sensation infiltrates the atmosphere. What is shocking is the sense of disorientation effected by this location shift as we are catapulted into alien territory, and then brutally reminded that this is 'normality', and normality is terrifying. Without realising it we have been transported, and utterly immersed, for over two hours, in the particularities of a vibrantly rarefied world. And then we're dumped.

GoodFellas is a sort of life story, not so much the life of an individual as the evocation of a way of life. It does, however, centre on a particular character, charting his childhood initiation into and subsequent life in the neighbourhood Mafia. In voice-over Henry reminisces about his boyhood in the world of the GoodFellas. One of the great attractions of belonging to this world, for a boy, was the possibility of 'going anywhere' and 'doing anything'. This dream come true, as he enters manhood and acquires some status as a Good-Fella, is manifested in two awesome instances of camera movement. The first introduces all the 'wiseguys' in the local bar in a continuous weaving camera movement, pausing at each guy as he turns and responds to the camera, to Henry's voice-over introduction. This scene is reminiscent of the delirious track through the red bar in *Mean Streets*, and indeed there are ways in which *GoodFellas* is a remake of the earlier film. But there are differences too, primarily in the rendition of fantasy. The reflexivity in this scene from *GoodFellas* aligns Henry's fantasy, of going anywhere, with a camera that can move unhindered through an impossible space. Later, when Henry is wooing the woman he will eventually marry, they go to the Copacabana club where there are queues waiting to get in so he takes her round the back to the service entrance. The camera follows them as he leads her into an alley, down stairs and through passageways in the building, as he weaves through the kitchen area greeting people as he goes and at last enters the club where a table is instantly set up for them in the front row and champagne sent over. She's impressed. And so are we. It's as though you can't believe this is happening and you don't want it ever to end, and when it does end so spectacularly with champagne and everyone's attention it's like pure ecstatic wish fulfilment. It's a marvellous cinematic acting-out of power and seduction. Where Karen is impressed by Henry, we, the viewers, are impressed by the camera movement, but in both cases there is an affect, the exhilaration is tangible, we are moved, transported – we feel it bodily and are moved outside our bodies.

This is seduction. Yet the very virtuosity of the camera foregrounds the fantastic nature of the movement. As the camera carves up, delineates, composes space, it makes its world. This is power – to delineate a space, control a world. The fantasy is that it is the whole world, that the world is your oyster, that you can go 'anywhere'.

At the end Henry's voice tells us that what he misses most is 'the life'. On one level this way of life refers to the Mafia; but on another level it's more general. The film is about a world willed into being by obsessive desire, it's about the reality of fantasy, about carving out a place by cutting up space. So too it is about the dangers of cinema. We witness, and perhaps are implicated in, the enactment of an obsession. All obsessions involve a theatricalisation of desire, an impulse to create a world, to carve up space, to compose the elements of existence according to the measure of desire. This impulse corresponds to the fictional enterprise because it involves the creation of a world that is delusional and yet vividly coherent. In a phrase apposite to the Scorsesian universe (though his concerns are with literature) Leo Bersani sees in this impulse 'the factitious coherence of all obsessions'.[26] The cinema, too, involves the creation of 'other' worlds, the carving up of space, a *mise en scène* of desire. Of course, not all movies are engendered in an obsessive dynamic; but Scorsese's cinema frequently makes a connection between fictional protagonists driven by obsessive desires and the cinematic process itself.

In the court room, when he's turned state witness, Henry speaks directly to the camera: 'And now it's all over.' But is it? When that weird unmotivated shot of Tommy firing directly at us flashes up, there is a kind of reprieve. It represents vitality, offers a respite from the blandness of the FBI office and the housing estate; but it also represents the dangers of cinema. *GoodFellas*, in the way that it creates a totally self-contained world and immerses us in it, echoes many of those Powell and Pressburger movies that Scorsese so admires. But when I leave the theatre what reverberates most strongly is a movie to which it seems to bear little resemblance: *The Tales of Hoffmann*. I'm not sure why, perhaps because they both insist – not overtly but through whispers that return, bodies that turn up again – that the cinema might be lethal, even when we love it most. Cinematic desire, in Scorsese, can't be easily extricated from the desire to be a gangster.

Chapter 2

Meditation on Violence

> *We had to delay if not avoid what we thought of as the moment*
> *of castration in the editing suite. That was 1968, editing became*
> *a byword for a reformist moment which attempted to contain the*
> *revolutionary one we lived in the streets where we shot. Editing*
> *tended to block and freeze material that was vital and came*
> *to us 'red hot' from the laboratories. For me, the editing room*
> *was a cross between a slaughterhouse and an autopsy room;*
> *it was the closest moment I could think of (in the process of*
> *film-making) to death and embalming.* (Bernardo Bertolucci)[1]

The blood is leached from *Raging Bull* and yet it comes to us 'red hot', too hot to handle, still too red for a body slashed, excessively, and bled to black and white.

A woman twirls, flies through space, compelled by the red shoes she wears to dance for ever. A newspaper flutters into the air, into her arms, transforming there into a human shape. The couple dance together and in the circulation of desire there is a transference: her dress is slowly imprinted, assumes the texture of windblown newspaper. Like the woman dancing, *Raging Bull* bears an imprint, can be read in terms of *The Red Shoes*; it is as though *The Red Shoes* has bled subliminally into *Raging Bull*.

Too Hot to Handle

There is a film I often show. I load this film onto the projector and tell the students to watch carefully, they are about to see a film about the cinema. There's a moment of blackness when the lights in the room are switched off, then, for a moment, the beam from the projector illuminates the screen and I hold my breath. Then there is redness, flesh, butchered corpses. Or so it seems. I try, every time, to watch. Part of me, indeed, is fascinated and attracted by these images, but they also repel. I have to look away, close my

11

eyes. Sometimes I have to leave the room. Later they say: how can you talk about this film, how can you claim to have seen it, presume to teach it, when your eyes are closed? 'But I am watching,' I say. And it's true. The images are insistent, even when my eyes are closed the images seem somehow imprinted on my retina. And although I tell myself, 'These are only images of bloody bodies, only images embalmed that you are seeing; you aren't seeing – with your own eyes, for yourself – real bodies truly bleeding', it makes no difference. But, of course, this Brakhage knows. There is a documentary quality to *The Act of Seeing with One's Own Eyes*. Set in a mortuary and documenting autopsy procedures it is uncannily reminiscent of Bertolucci's 'cross between a slaughterhouse and an autopsy room', but the documentary dimension is almost a pretext for fictionality. It is a film about the way the cinema engages the imagination, about a dynamic of repulsion and attraction, about the imbrication of images and imagination (and seems to me one of the most interesting manifestations of his theory of 'closed-eye vision').[2]

In the quotation that opens this chapter, Bertolucci is talking primarily about the way editing, in the heady days of 1968, was experienced as an act of violation, interfering with the primacy of the real and deadening all vital impulses. When I read this the film that first came to mind was *The Act of Seeing with One's Own Eyes*, which is odd because, although it thematises and depicts a version of death and embalmment, it is hardly an instance of cinematic 'still life'. On the contrary, it never fails to disturb, to bring images and fantasies alive. To then superimpose *Raging Bull* and *The Red Shoes* over *The Act of Seeing with One's Own Eyes* might seem at first simply to exacerbate that oddness, in so far as these are films characterised by a virtuoso editing which is hardly 'reformist', which certainly does not 'block and freeze'. But Bertolucci speaks not only of editing; he is articulating something more general about the cinema, using editing to focus a particular fear and thrill involved in film-making. He conveys an excitement about cinema's ability to transmit something that is 'red hot', and also a fear of cinema's capacity to deaden and embalm. But despite arguments about the tendency of any representational mode, and of continuity editing in particular, to contain disturbance and literally 'reform' the castration threat, editing is not intrinsically deadening. Though it might be, and there is the danger. It might be deadening not exactly in the sense suggested by Bertolucci (a numbing) but in another, though related, sense: it might articulate a death threat, enact a death drive.

If cinema does not simply reconstitute a presence of bodies, but if it participates in a genesis of 'the bodily', then it can also dismember bodies, disperse bodily fragments like Acteaon, torn limb from limb by his hounds and scattered in pieces through time and space. Moreover, the film itself can materialise as a body of sorts, a body that bleeds – metaphorically, but with sensible affects, producing, for instance, sensations of illness, fear, ecstasy. Making a film, then (and making it up as a viewer, in the act of seeing with your own eyes), involves the risk that in generating the thrilling and the ecstatic you will go beyond the pleasure principle and encounter a death threat. Bertolucci says as much – to a large degree through editing – in

Before the Revolution, especially in the famous jump-cut sequences and in the opera sequence, where the force of desire between the young protagonist, Fabrizio, and his beautiful aunt is conveyed through a dizzyingly ecstatic orchestration of camera movements and cuts. But it is double-edged, this desire, razor sharp; the other side of ecstasy is danger, the threat of annihilation and death, a fate intimated by the operatic setting.

Raging Bull and *The Red Shoes* were provoked into being for me, I suspect, by these words of Bertolucci's not because they deaden but rather because they also pose a death threat, and in that very posture they invoke the ecstatic. The association with *The Act of Seeing with One's Own Eyes* pivots around the notion of slaughter, cutting as dismemberment and bleeding; but also (and this is part of it, crucially so) they are all films obliquely – through enactment one might say, rather than through direct discursive means – about cinematic experience. Just as the pivotal sequence of *Before the Revolution* takes place at the opera, thus enticing us into a heightened dramatic mode as it simultaneously foregrounds our place as audience, so *Raging Bull* and *The Red Shoes* are also about performance and viewing. The former is about a spectator sport, boxing, and the latter about ballet. In both the viewing position is doubly articulated as we occupy the position of the audience both within and outside the diegesis. But such thematic concerns are merely an indication. It is in their enactments that both films explore the act of seeing in cinema.

> *For more than anything else, cinema consists of the eye for magic – that which perceives and reveals the marvelous in whatsoever it looks upon.* (Maya Deren)[3]

The question of what makes a film 'red hot' is related, though not reducible, to cutting. Cutting carries threatening connotations. However, this is not all that cutting implies, and when the relationship between editing and motion is emphasised, new issues arise. In both films editing itself is used almost magically to create sensations of velocity; but more particularly I am interested in the way editing is frequently combined with the speed of filming (employing both resolute slowness and rapidity) to enact a compulsive drive. Second: the question of what makes a film 'red hot'. In so far as the phrase 'red hot' implies 'too hot to handle' there is an evocation of touch. Bertolucci is speaking, literally, about handling celluloid in the editing room; but I intend to deploy the phrase as a figure of speech to explore the relation between what it is that makes it difficult to get a handle on these films and the way in which the films themselves obsessively enact a drama around the taboo on touch.

In *Totem and Taboo* Freud argues that the principal prohibition is against touching.[4] The totemic object, which is simultaneously sacred and unclean, inspiring veneration and horror, must not be touched for fear of its capacity for contagion and transference. The offender who touches runs the danger of being possessed. Many critics, in whom a greedy cinephiliac tendency lurks, actually yearn to be possessed, and in much writing on Scorsese there is a kind of mimicking of the films in a critical discourse that obsessively repeats terms such as 'immediacy', 'intensity', 'danger', 'excess', as though repetition in itself constitutes evidence and validation. It is as though contact with the films produces a kind of adjectival delirium tantamount to possession. It is a phenomenon that intrigues and irritates me, no doubt because I find myself implicated, compelled to repeat. So it is that the notion, or rather, the question, of immediacy – the immediacy of touch – constitutes the starting point for this work on Scorsese.

Raging Bull and *The Red Shoes* themselves enact, in an obsessive mode, a death drive and thus implicate the viewer or would-be critic in a dangerously mimetic relation. Both films, moreover, dramatise the relation between obsession and the totemic object. Freud stressed the relation between obsessive behaviour and forms of behaviour instituted by the totem-and-taboo dynamic by locating both the prohibitions of neurotics and taboos in touching, and extended the sense of this to include the notion of coming 'in contact with'.[5] This chapter will focus, then, on a series of totemic objects – boxing gloves, red shoes, *Raging Bull* and *The Red Shoes*.

That's Entertainment

The totemic object, in so far as it implies an ordinary object invested with extraordinary qualities, summons a context of ritual, of ceremony, of theatre – a context realised in sharp opposition to the everyday. The gloves and the shoes both indicate an arena of performance, an arena in which the ordinary body is transformed. On the stage, in the ring – boxing, dancing – for an audience, the body is ceremonialised. Both films revolve round the relationship between art and life, as has frequently been discussed; but what interests me is the way in which their enactment (rather than simply their theme) renders familiar distinctions between artifice and naturalism, for instance, or between public and private, perilously uncertain. In both cases it is the body, the 'decided body', to borrow a term from the language of performance, that paradoxically becomes the site of radical uncertainty. But before going further into this notion of the decided body, a reminder of what these films are 'about'.

The Red Shoes, made by Michael Powell and Emeric Pressburger in 1948, opens with a crowd waiting outside a stage door. As the doors are opened the crowd turns into a mob, literally storming the theatre. Tension builds as we anticipate the performance. In the audience, that is as spectators, are the three main protagonists of the film, who do not yet know one another, but who are destined to become entwined in a drama of desire, ambition, creativity and possession. There is Boris Lermontov (played by Anton Walbrook in a steely mode of restrained stylisation), the impresario who presides over a prestigious ballet company and who incites the young composer Julian Craster (Marius Goring) to write a ballet called 'The Red Shoes' for an equally young and unknown dancer, Victoria Page, whom he intends to make into a great star. Vicky was played by a ballet dancer (Norma Shearer), not an actress, which creates a fascinating performative tension in *The Red Shoes* itself,[6] and across the energy field mapped by both films (there is a kind of inversion in *Raging Bull* where the main protagonist

14

is played by an actor (Robert De Niro), not a boxer, but one who learnt how to box and literally reshaped his body to an extraordinary degree in order to play the part – a rite of passage that has now entered the annals of Hollywood legend). The ballet of 'The Red Shoes' within the film *The Red Shoes* dramatises a girl's desire: she yearns for a pair of red shoes but when she gets them they take her over, body and soul, so that she can neither take them off nor stop dancing. This tale is mirrored in Vicky's 'everyday' life, in the framing story. In their first meeting Lermontov asks her, 'What do you want from life? To live?' 'To dance,' she replies. Dancing is her life, but it is also a compulsion that poses a threat to 'ordinary' happiness and in the end it drives her literally over the edge – to her death.

Raging Bull, made by Martin Scorsese in 1980, is encapsulated in its opening shots. It begins in a dressing room in New York City, where Jake La Motta, ex-middleweight boxing champion now grossly overweight, is reciting his lines in preparation for a performance, in a night-club (it is from her dressing room that Vicky flees at the end of *The Red Shoes*, to avoid having to perform). The words are faded in before we see him: 'I remember those cheers. They still ring in my ears.' The poem, with its stumbling repetitions, lasts the length of a single take, in medium-long shot, with La Motta puffing on a fat cigar. It ends: 'So give me a stage/Where this bull here can rage/And though I can fight/I'd much rather recite/That's entertainment.' Cut to a medium-close-up with a title over – JAKE LA MOTTA 1964. Cut to a shot of a much younger, sinewy La Motta, in the ring (also in medium-close-up, but from the opposite diagonal). Over the image of him at the ready, gloved hands poised, is the title: JAKE LA MOTTA 1941. On the soundtrack we hear, softly, the line repeated: 'That's entertainment.' Then there is an explosion of sound and movement, blows, flashlights, the crowd roaring. At the end of the fight the ring is mobbed (as the theatre is stormed in *The Red Shoes*), people trampled underfoot, chairs sent flying through the air. *Raging Bull* is a film based on the life of boxer Jake La Motta, but more accurately, I think, it is a fiction about a man who lives in order to fight, just as Vicky lives in order to dance. In fact only about fifteen minutes of the film are devoted to boxing. Violence, however, is dispersed into the everyday, into the way that Jake lives out his closest relationships, enacts his paranoid delusions and jealous obsessions.

These are the opening scenes, but in fact both films have significant credit sequences, prior to them: *The Red Shoes* depicts a series of painted flats culminating in flames emerging out of a pair of red satin ballet slippers. The credits of *Raging Bull* are laid over a scene of a lone boxer (in long shot) in cloak and hood rehearsing his moves, shadow boxing in extreme slow motion, accompanied by a hauntingly elegiac soundtrack. The film title itself – *RAGING BULL* – appears, over the black-and-white, in scarlet. The music is the Intermezzo from the opera *Cavalleria Rusticana*, played with the curtains up but revealing a set devoid of characters, so that the audience can reflect and imagine. It is usually performed in conjunction with *I Pagliacci*, an opera which stages a confusion between the everyday and the theatrical in a plot concerning a jealous actor who murders his wife and her lover during the performance of a comedy.

15

> *There exists in many European languages an expression which*
> *might be chosen to epitomise what is essential for the actor's*
> *life. It is a grammatically paradoxical expression, in which a*
> *passive form comes to assume an active meaning, and in which*
> *the indication of an availability for action is couched in a form*
> *of passivity. It is not an ambiguous expression, but a hermaph-*
> *roditic one, combining within it action and passivity, and in*
> *spite of its strange-ness it is an expression found in common*
> *speech. One says in fact, 'essere deciso', 'être décidé', 'to be*
> *decided'. And it does not mean that someone or something*
> *decides us or that we undergo decision, nor that we are the*
> *object of decision. It doesn't even mean that we are deciding,*
> *nor that we are carrying out the action of deciding.*
> *Between these opposing conditions flows a current of life*
> *which language does not seem to represent and around which*
> *it dances with images.[7]*

Eugenio Barba, discussing the 'decided body', points to a paradox: this body performs by virtue of training, discipline, yet in the act of performing it appears as possessed, almost as an involuntary presence. There is something hard to grasp, something other than technique even though it includes technique (thought of as a repertoire of acquired skills), that differentiates this body from the everyday body. It is to do with the particular way of deploying energy, and includes a context: the presence of an audience, the marking out of a quasi-ceremonial or ritualistic space. 'The actor gives himself [*sic*] form and gives form to his message through fiction, by modelling his energy.'[8] The performing (non-quotidian) body is distinguished from the daily body by the kind and range of such techniques, and the ways in which they are used. The distinction is *not* made on the basis of whether the non-quotidian body has or lacks technique, the daily body being somehow 'without' them, or 'natural'. On the contrary, quotidian techniques are profoundly cultural, but usually learned and acted out on an unconscious and habitual level. What is interesting to performance theorists[9] is that within the Occident the distance which separates daily body techniques from extra-daily ones is often neither evident nor consciously considered (unlike in India, Bali, China or Japan, for instance).

Boxing and ballet provide us with two instances of clear theatrical differentiation within a Western context – sites for a particular modelling of energy. Hence it seems useful to draw on an understanding of acting (using the term broadly to include a range of performance modes) that focuses on the way energy is deployed by and through the body, rather than privileging psychological or mimetic principles. But there is another reason for this detour, this allusion to a tendency within performance studies that is peculiarly attentive to cultural constraints and conventions. *Raging Bull* and *The Red Shoes* are about performance, about the way in which bodies are transformed and 'possessed' by performing – in the ring, on the stage. The red shoes and the gloves, as totemic objects, derive their force from this performative, quasi-ritualistic context. But the films also, it seems to me, enact a dilemma that is peculiarly cultural, that has precisely to do with the fact that in the Occident the distance which separates daily body techniques from extra-daily ones is often neither evident nor consciously considered. If we think of performance as a way of converting and transforming energy, then it seems that in these films there is a demonstrable excess: energy that is not contained by the performance arena is transformed differently in the quotidian, ecstasy is repeated, but with ruinous reverberations.

Faced with *Raging Bull* and *The Red Shoes*, let us contemplate the fiction of a decided body. What is interesting in Barba's discussion is the peculiar combination of passive and active, voluntary and involuntary. The decisiveness of the performing body, carried over into the daily by Vicky and Jake, is transformed into a catastrophic indecision or inability to contain a compulsive and deadly drive. Although they are extremely active, they are also gripped by passivity, in the thrall of obsession, which is, by its nature, involuntary. But we are not just speaking of the protagonists: the films themselves are textual bodies, at once decided and potentially out of control.

> *There exists a primary level of the actor's dramaticness which has nothing to do with intellectual categories but which relates uniquely to the way in which the actor manipulates his or her energy. The way he/she exploits and composes the weight–balance relationship and the opposition between different movements, their duration, their rhythms, permits him/her to give to the audience not only a different perception of the body but also a different perception of time and space: not a 'time in space,' but a 'space-time'.*[10]

Raging Bull and *The Red Shoes* both articulate this 'space-time', not just thematically, as films about performers often do, but through their modes of staging different movements, their duration, their rhythms. They permit the viewer a different perception of the body – cinematically spaced out. There are other films whose techniques are similarly extra-ordinary, such as Cassavetes' *Opening Night* and Rivette's *L'Amour fou*. Deleuze, in discussing 'the cinema of the body', cites both these directors and says that sometimes this cinema 'mounts a ceremony, takes on an initiatory and liturgical aspect, and attempts to summon all the metallic and liquid powers of a sacred body, to the point of honour or revulsion'.[11] Remember that vivid and painfully sensational scene in *Opening Night* in which Gena Rowlands, caught between the arena of the stage and the everyday, bangs her head repeatedly against a door frame – a focusing of energy at once voluntary and involuntary, not dissimilar to the scene in which La Motta enacts a similar gestus in the prison cell. *The Specter of the Rose* is in a slightly different register (in a weird and wonderful register all of its own), but it is also about bodies cinematically spaced out by dancing and death. Demonic possession is enacted in this tale about a ballet dancer, a psychopath who murders his wives. 'I'd like to pick you up', he says to a new love, 'and hold you

17

till you were tattooed on me.' Of *L'Amour fou,* Deleuze writes: 'Rivette invents a theatricality of cinema totally distinct from the theatricality of the theatre (even when cinema uses it as a reference).'[12] We might say the same of Scorsese, and Powell and Pressburger.

But the Gloves Are Red

It all begins with the telling of a story, with several stories and various beginnings. And in every beginning there is an ending (or two). One of the stories goes like this: whilst preparing for *Raging Bull* Marty shot some 8mm while Bobby was training in a gym, and he showed this footage to Michael Powell. As the film ended, Powell turned to Scorsese and said, 'But the gloves are red.'[13]

When, in *The Red Shoes,* Boris Lermontov, the impresario played by Anton Walbrook, tells the story of Hans Christian Andersen's 'The Red Shoes' (to Julian Craster the young composer), he fondles a statuette of a pointed foot in a ballet slipper. It is a severed foot, set on a pedestal. Julian asks, 'What happens in the end?' Lermontov shrugs the question off, tosses his answer into the wind: 'Oh, in the end she dies.'

Scorsese's version of watching the 8mm footage goes like this: [14]

> I remember we were looking at this, projected on the back of a door in my apartment on 57th Street, and Michael Powell was sitting on the floor watching it with us. Suddenly Michael said, 'There's something wrong: the gloves shouldn't be red.' Back in 1975, he'd written to me after first seeing *Mean Streets* to say that he liked it, but I used too much red – this from the man who had red all over his own films, which was where I'd got it from in the first place! But he was right about the boxing footage, and our cinematographer Michael Chapman also pointed out how colour was detracting from the images.

There is a generic underpinning to these explanations of how *Raging Bull* came to be shot in black-and-white. Today's fighters usually wear red gloves and pastel-coloured trunks, but our memories of boxing in the 40s and 50s are in black-and-white, partly because of grainy documentary footage and newspaper photographs and films like *Body and Soul* (1947) and *Champion* (1949). But in these anecdotes there is something in excess of genre explanation. 'But the gloves are red' coming from Michael Powell immediately evokes the red shoes. There is an intimation of the relation between the shoes and the gloves, realised through redness. The identity between these two objects cannot be reduced simply to a question of colour, but the decision to repress colour in *Raging Bull* produces a ripple of reverberations and dispersals. The black-and-white film seems to vibrate with colour, most especially with red, though it is not the gloves that we see as coloured, but rather the redness of blood that we see spurting through the cuts and slashes, dripping off the rope, seeping through the black-and-white images (literally so in the title). The boxing gloves echo the red shoes as agents of compulsion, compelling and even seducing us to look even whilst forcing us to look away, to avert our gaze from intolerable mutilation. Both films are at once exhilaratingly magical and cruelly violent; they enact cinematically both balletic and pugilistic impulses.

They Had, It Seemed, Grown on to Her Feet

To begin then: a pair of shoes, a pair of boxing gloves. At the heart of *The Red Shoes* there is a ballet, also entitled 'The Red Shoes'. In this ballet a woman in white dances, in a spotlight, past a shoemaker's shop where her attention is caught by a pair of crimson ballet slippers. She is transported by a reverie; imagining herself in them, she dances beseechingly for the shoes as though at a shrine, until at last she pulls away and tries to forget by dancing with a lover. But the shoes remain, attracting her back into their orbit. In an extraordinarily audacious and breathtaking shot the woman runs headlong towards the camera, leaps in mid-flight into the shoes and continues dancing without interruption, although the mood and quality of her dancing suddenly become more vivacious and joyful, as though she is absorbing into her being the nature of the red shoes. A sense of the red shoes as magical is strongly conveyed in this scene, but as the ballet progresses the magical dimension takes on a more sinister cast, for it becomes apparent that she cannot take off these shoes which have a will of their own, which keep dancing and dancing and dancing. She is driven inexorably – through episodes of frenzy, exhaustion, hysteria, despair – to death. The Hans Christian Andersen fairy tale on which the ballet is based, puts it thus:

> She was very much frightened, and tried to throw off her red shoes, but could not unclasp them. She hastily tore off her stockings; but the shoes she could not get rid of – they had, it seemed, grown on to her feet. Dance she did, and dance she must, over field and meadow, in rain and in sunshine, by night and by day.

At the end of the ballet she tries to cut off the shoes, cut off her feet with a large and lethal-looking knife, but the knife turns into leaves on a vine wrapped around her ankle; when it turns back into a knife in her hand she throws it, like a dagger, point first, into the wooden floor. There is nothing left for her then but to dance until she dies, and so the ballet ends.

> *The key in her hand turns into a knife; a flashed image, almost subliminal, haunting – a knife in the bed; her face reflected in the blade; her throat slit.* (Maya Deren, *Meshes of the Afternoon*)

At the end of the film, the heroine, Vicky, who has played the lead role in the ballet, also dies. In a headlong rush towards the camera she plunges to her death, flying over a balcony and onto the train tracks below. This event takes place a few moments before the curtains are about to open on a production of 'The Red Shoes' in which she was to have repeated the performance that made her famous. The ballet goes ahead without her, an empty spotlight dancing over the stage, illuminating her absence. She lies on the railway track, her legs gashed and bloody, bound by the scarlet ribbons of the ballet shoes, wrapped up in ribbons of blood. 'Take off the red shoes,' she says and as they are lifted from her feet she dies. Meanwhile on stage the ballet is ending, the spotlight is still, centre stage, and in the centre of the spot, a pair of red shoes. Thus the ending of the ballet is the end of the film.

The shoes appear initially as ordinary, recognisable objects. But before long their supernatural dimension becomes apparent. They are intensely desirable but once taken up, put on, there's no stopping and no going back; they have a life of their own, compulsive and all-consuming, so that ultimately they destroy, through a kind of contagion, that which they touch. Attainment of the object of desire simply provokes further desire and sets in motion a pattern of compulsive repetition. At the end of the Tale of Olympia in *The Tales of Hoff-mann*, the mechanical toy winds down and disintegrates into pieces, but a single leg, invested with a life of its own, keeps dancing. What is so extraordinary here is the disturbance of boundaries between animate and inanimate, between human and cinematic bodies and desires. The 'puppet' Olympia is played by Norma Shearer, who remarkably denaturalises the dancing body, but the moment when she 'dies', when the mechanical springs leap out of her head, is immensely horrifying.[15]

> Cinematic techniques are employed to give a malevolent vitality to inanimate objects. (Maya Deren)[16]

Once Jake La Motta dons boxing gloves he is doomed to a cycle of obsessive repetition, playing out round after round, in the boxing ring. In the end he does not die, but still has to repeat his performance compulsively, although in the end it is lines he repeats and not blows. In the night-club that masquerades as a theatre he plays out atonement and expiation. De Niro repeats the words of the young Brando in *On the Waterfront* ('I coulda been a contender') and in doing so he repeats the fate of Brando – that is, to become old and bloated. 'The obsessional act is ostensibly a protection against the prohibited act; but actually in our view, it is a repetition of it,' says Freud.[17]

In both films the shoes and the gloves clearly figure as supercharged objects, almost magical in their effects. However, the very fact that they are so apparently significant might alert us to the fact that they mean too much and thus, paradoxically, rather than containing meaning they indicate a process of signification whereby excess (of various sorts: excessive desire, ambition, pleasure, colour, speed) is made manifest. Another way of saying this is that they do not, in and of themselves, mean anything; rather, they function as cinematic tropes. In rhetoric a trope is a figure of speech, and by 'cinematic trope' I mean to imply a specifically cinematic articulation (thus, a process in excess of representation: the shoes don't simply stand for or in place of something else, but are a form of process, of cinematic energy). Although they are both objects of attachment, attaching to the body, to hands and feet, we need to guard against the temptation to attach them too closely to the characters who possess and wear them. For one thing, it is quite clear that this is a double-edged process: to possess these objects is to be possessed and ultimately it will be more rewarding to pay attention to this dynamic, and its operation through the filmic texts, than to try to read the objects in terms of individual characters. This is not to exclude the fact that in some instances and on certain levels they might well serve to articulate something about both Jake La Motta and Vicky, but the point is that this is not their only function. Driving desires and rampant ambitions are dispersed through the body of the text, and this means that on the narrative level a variety of characters are implicated (this is particularly the case in *The Red Shoes*). But it is not simply in terms of characters (one or many) and narrative *raison d'être* that these objects function; they are objects of investment *par excellence* – that is, they provide an anchor or point of crystallisation for various unattached and often excessive energies, and by doing so they provide a psychic safeguard against madness.[18]

An objection could be raised here. It could be pointed out that neither Vicky nor Jake is saved from madness or at least tragedy. But this is just it: although the characters are not saved, in some senses the films *are*; they don't disintegrate into the madness and death of eternal repetition. Although the films engage us in a death drive they actually release us from the logic of their own perversity and restore us to an economy of pleasure. I would argue that this is partly because the energies (both ecstatic and destructive) unleashed by the films are invested through these tropes. This means that we too, watching the film, are exposed to the death threat but also offered the possibility of investment via these objects or tropes. We can objectify what we experience as the emotional, but might also think of as psychic drives. Put like this, the object status of the shoes and the gloves is clearly cast in terms of the figurative. That is to say, it is not simply as functional and denotative objects that they exist, but as totemic.

The charm and mystery of *The Red Shoes* is surely derived from its basis as a fairy tale. The ballet itself, lasting a full fifteen minutes or so, is an extraordinarily fantastical *tour de force*. The heroine, propelled by her red shoes, seems to fly through space, passing from night to day, encountering characters who dissolve into one another in landscapes that merge and transform before our very eyes. The cinematic momentum produces a sense of exhilaration that is way in excess of the narrative drive; it is as though we are being swept along, literally propelled by the movie. This of course is a familiar 'move' in the musical genre, a move that we might refer to as a flight of fancy; but what makes the difference here is that the fantasy mobilised by this flight goes on too long, incorporating paranoiac projections, repeating the movements to an excruciating degree, such that extreme perturbation is registered. This reverberates beyond the ballet and into the framing story, but already the reverse is also operating: the ballet is permeated by 'the everyday life' that surrounds it diegetically, by the desires of the three protagonists (for each other and for their 'art', as dancer, composer and impresario). If, for a moment, we superimpose *The Red Shoes* over *Raging Bull* the perturbation that we have registered comes into focus as perversity. *Raging Bull* is much more clearly driven by perversity, the imbrication of pleasure and pain is foregrounded more directly, but the circulation of energies is not so different – compulsive repetition is still the dominant motif in both films. If, then, the reflection of *Raging Bull* inflects the fairy-tale fantasy of *The Red Shoes* with an element of perversion, so the reverse process superimposes over the perversion of boxing a fairy-story fantasy. Both the extremely lyrical slow-motion balletic sequences of *Raging Bull* and the terrifying speed and violence of some of the *Red Shoes* sequences can be conceived as flights of (furious) fancy. The 'masculine' world of boxing is a fairy story; the 'feminine' world of ballet is refracted in a boxing ring (a boxing ring that Alain Masson likens to a magic circle).[19]

A Young Girl's Hands

The boxing gloves both protect and conceal the boxer's hands and they take the place of bare hands, in the process becoming weapons, actually enabling the man who wears them to fight. Fairly early in the movie Jake confides to Joey as the two men sit at the kitchen table, 'What's the matter with me? My hands. I got these small hands . . . a young girl's hands.' This involves him in a paradox: it means he can't ever be the best because he will always remain smaller – 'I'm never gonna get a chance to fight the best there is' – but it also means he *has* to box, is driven to somehow negate and conceal, by wearing gloves, these 'young girl's hands'. He has to use the component of femininity as a weapon, a missile. Immediately after he has confessed (his 'problem', his weakness, his secret) he asks Joey to hit him in the face. Joey is reluctant and has to be cajoled and eventually bullied into complying. Eventually, with a tea towel wrapped around his hand in lieu of a glove, he hits him, repeatedly, in the face in a series of tight shot-reverse-shots. It is here as though Jake is expiating his sins, inviting and enduring punishment for having 'girl's hands'. But there is also a substitution of face for hands. Later (after an early defeat by Sugar Ray Robinson) we see him flex his hand in a bucket of iced water (echoing the scene where he pours cold water down the front of his pants to douse desire and preserve energy for fighting). Ostensibly an act of protection and preservation, the slow clenching of his fist in the water (depicted in close-up, the camera very slowly and slightly zooming in) suggests a massive effort of repression, an effort to negate these 'young girl's hands'. The repression and the expiation go together. 'I done a lot of bad things Joey. Maybe it's coming back to me,' he says, his hand in the water (Freud: 'The obsessional act is ostensibly a protection against the prohibited act, but actually, in our view, it is a repetition of it'). If there is a fear of castration in *Raging Bull*, there is also (and these drives are not incompatible) a will to self-destruction, or at least a will to negate and destroy that part of the self that suggests femininity.

> *The room is lit by lamps. It is an elegant room of wine-red tones and deep blues. In the middle of it a figure reclines on a chaise-longue. A man's hands are clasped tightly together, fingers intertwined, forming a rigid steeple. But the thumbs escape, dancing in agitation. It is Lermontov and he has just received news of Vicky's marriage. He crumples the telegram in his right fist, thumping it several times into his other hand.*

*The sound of the blow reverberates, as do the groans of pain, issuing
in a staccato manner from this body held so stiffly, so restrained.
He walks towards the camera into medium-close-up, pulls his arm back
and then lunges violently forward, his fist coming straight at us. A quick
cut registers the fist smashing violently into glass. Now, with the camera
behind his head, we can situate the previous shot as a mirror image. He
holds his fist still for a few moments, clenched in the posture of impact.
The glass is shattered. As he drops his arm the fragmented image of a
man's face looks back at us.*

Gloves figure elsewhere, in another movie. Remember that famous scene
from *On the Waterfront* where Brando is walking with Eva Marie Saint, to
whom he is very attracted; but he's nervous, shy, doesn't know what to do
or say. She drops one of her gloves – tight-fitting and of the thinnest white
leather – and he picks it up and fondles it, fiddling absent-mindedly, slipping his own hand into it. It is as though, through this gesture, he conveys
an intimacy not apparent in his halting speech. Or this is how it is usually
read, celebrated as a great moment of method improvisation in Hollywood
cinema.[20] But something else besides naturalism is conveyed here. Within
the context of this scene the glove is a very felicitous object. Its circulation
transforms the relations between inside and outside, renders boundaries uncertain. The glove functions within the diegetic space as a magical object,
enabling Brando – as Terry Malloy, as character – to invest undirected energy. But it also functions for Brando the actor as a kind of supernatural device; in the very process of investment (enabling the audience too to focus
energy and disperse tension) the ordinariness of the object and the gesture is
transformed, to some degree ceremonialised.

*She takes his gloved hand in hers. There is a dissolve and in close-up
the gesture, the slightness and gravity of the movement, is played again.
Through a series of dissolves he takes one of his gloves off and touches
a pearl button on her wrist. The buttons are undone. Prising apart the
glove's opening he sinks his face into the inside of her wrist. A ceremonial.*
(Age of Innocence)

A ballet shoe is put on, over the foot, just as a boxing glove is put on, over
the hand. But once the red shoes are put on they can never be taken off.
They conceal and cover but also become one with the body; indeed they
come to 'possess' the moving body. There is no way of saying where the
body ends and the shoe begins, no way of distinguishing between inside and
out. Derrida,[21] after Heidegger, spends a long time pondering Van Gogh's
shoes, noticing the tongue of the shoe, the traces of a body, of labour, of
cultural inscription, teasing out this relation of inside and outside.[22] Here
too there is a problematic of inside and outside, but also of daemonic possession, and the shoes and gloves of which we speak fall within a different
lineage: that of cartoons and fairy tales. And, as with those objects invested
with magical properties in cartoons and fairy tales, they draw attention to
the mystery and instability of sexual identity.

23

> *The gloves which Camille wished to try on were of the thinnest*
> *white leather and tight-fitting. The woman . . . brought one of the*
> *gloves to her mouth and breathed into it before handing it across*
> *the counter to Camille . . . Filled with her breath, the glove took*
> *on the form of a hand which suddenly and deeply frightened*
> *Camille. It was a languid boneless hand, a hand without a will, a*
> *hand floating in the air like a dead fish with its white stomach*
> *uppermost. It was a hand she did not want. It was a hand that*
> *could not clench itself. It was a hand which in caressing would*
> *in no way be a hand and would not caress; it would lead away.*
> *At that moment she knew what he was offering her. He was*
> *offering her the possibility of being what she pretended to be . . .*
> *The gloves fitted her perfectly. The leather across her tiny bony*
> knuckles was so tight that it shone as if it were wet. (John Berger)[23]

If we understand this confession scene (confessing to 'girl's hands') as an attempt
to articulate a sense of subjectivity or experience of the self, then clearly it is also
about a sense of self as inadequate, requiring confession (of a culpability for
something that is lacking – that is, masculinity and power as embodied in powerful hands) and punishment. Subjectivisation, for Jake, coincides with the experience of his own powerlessness, of his own position as that of a victim of destiny:
'No matter how big I get no matter who I fight no matter what I do I aint never
gonna fight Joe Louis. I'm never gonna get a chance to fight the best there is. And
you know something? I'm better than them.'

In the face of this natural deformity he is powerless, there is nothing he can do.
We could say that Jake blames the feminine in himself (as embodied by his hands)
for preventing him from realising his ambitions of greatness. But it's not quite as
simple. For one thing Jake as character is not so self-conscious; but more to the
point, the film text never posits masculinity as simply dependent on repressed
femininity. This film, along with other Scorsese films, exhibits an obsessive fascination with as well as a repulsion for the problem and experience of masculinity,
and whilst it mobilises a variety of masculine fantasies it is most fascinating in exploring masculinity *as* fantasy. Puzzling over how this happens (why the fascination? Or rather, why the intersecting fascinations, mine, Scorsese's, that of
intradiegetic characters), my mind wandered to another instance of ambivalent
fascination conventionalised in the cinema: the *femme fatale* figure most familiar
in the film noir genre. This might seem like an odd place to start (insinuating a
connection between Jake la Motta and the *femme fatale*), but I think now that
the reverberation was not accidental. Though the connections might seem ab-
struse they will lead us back with utter simplicity to Jake's request to Joey, after
his confession: 'Do me a favour. I want you to hit me in the face.'

The Game that Can Never Be Mastered
Slavoj Zizek discusses the coincidence of subjectivisation with the experience of
one's own powerlessness in terms of the *femme fatale* in the hard-boiled detective

novel (but he interestingly illustrates his point by an example from elsewhere: Adorno's discussion of *Carmen*, specifically of that moment where Carmen as 'bad-fatal object' is subjectivised, felt as victim of her own game): [24]

> In the best novels of this genre, a certain reversal happens when the *femme fatale* as 'a bad object' is subjectivized. . . . What gives her power of fascination to the *femme fatale* is exclusively her place in masculine fantasy. She is only 'mastering the game' as an object of masculine fantasy. The theoretical lesson that one should get from this is that subjectivisation coincides with the experience of one's own powerlessness, of one's own position as that of a victim of destiny.

What exactly is this theoretical lesson, and how is it arrived at? It is fairly clear how a conception of subjectivity as powerlessness is derived from the instance of the *femme fatale*. We can illustrate repeatedly the fact that when she thinks she masters the game she is in fact as much a victim as her victims. However, Zizek makes the point that this form of subjectivity (the woman's realisation of her own powerlessness) is part and parcel of male fantasy. In other words, the threat posed by the *femme fatale* (she devours men, uses her sexuality to gain power over them), which also elicits fascination, is neutralised for the masculine subject when he casts her in the position of experiencing herself as powerless, when a particular form of subjectivity is ascribed to her. Now this implies a certain form of contorted identification. He (the male subject), in the process of protecting himself, places himself in the perspective which is hers; or, to put it another way, he realises her position. This identification must involve him, paradoxically, in experiencing himself as powerless. From this can be derived the theoretical lesson of, as Adorno puts it, 'the original passivity of the subject'. That is to say, we can extrapolate from the particular to note that in general the experience of subjectivity coincides with the experience of powerlessness.

What interests me here is what Zizek implies, but doesn't explore, about masculinity. Many critics have noted that if there is within the film noir genre a compulsion to punish the *femme fatale* (through killing her off or neutralising her), there is also a partial exposure of that compulsion. This is why feminists have been so interested, or indeed fascinated, by the genre, arguing that it disturbs the filmic ordering and containment of sexual difference. The personification process (bad-object personified in *femme fatale* exerts fascination and simultaneously threatens hero) means that the focus has been primarily on the figure of the woman as site for examining the construction of sexual difference. The men in film noir tend to be pale in comparison (classically, the detective who becomes caught up in the investigation and thus undone). This focus means that some of the questions implied in Zizek's argument have not really been examined. What, for instance, happens when the male subject experiences himself as powerless? The film noir genre generally resolves this question narratively, in terms of characters. The woman is punished or saved, that is, the bad-object is negated or reformed. But what are the general theoretical implications of the aporia which is opened up when a system posited on mastery – masculinity – is exposed as, in fact experienced as, illusory; when 'mastering the game' is posited on a fundamental condition of powerlessness?

How, under these conditions, does masculinity continue? What fantastic structures are necessary to sustain it?

I suspect that it is the process of personification itself that has deflected these questions. They surface, however, precisely in those filmic texts where the bad-object figures as a strong presence, but unattached so to speak, not personified in the person of the *femme fatale*, not invested. They surface particularly in a film like *Raging Bull* and other Scorsese films revolving round protagonists frequently unreconciled; on the edge of psychosis they play out, obsessively, a game of mastering the threat, of mastering masculinity. The *femme fatale* might not be much in evidence in Scorsese films, but an understanding of the way she figures in masculine fantasy can very usefully illuminate the Scorsese dynamic. And, conversely, these films provide a useful way into developing issues around masculinity that might have been raised initially by an analysis of the *femme fatale*. There might not, in Scorsese, be a *femme fatale* to serve as bad-object before whom the masculine subject feels fascination and fear, but it might be that the bad-object is internalised in the Scorsese hero (think particularly of J.R. in *Who's That Knocking at my Door?*, Travis Bickle in *Taxi Driver*, Jimmy Doyle in *New York, New York*, Paul Hackett in *After Hours*, Lionel Dobie in *Life Lessons*, Max Cady in *Cape Fear*, as well as Jake La Motta). This is not quite as simple as saying that the Scorsese hero is fascinated by and simultaneously fears his own repressed femininity (or homosexuality), though this might not be inaccurate.[25] Rather, it is to argue that he is involved, still, in a fantastical construction of the bad-object, but one that exacerbates and foregrounds the problem of masculinity precisely because there is no external 'other' to be 'objectified', to be the bad-object.

In the case of the *femme fatale*, identification with the bad-object allows structurally for resolution. Identification as a process here involves transformation and rehabilitation: either she is turned into a good object, or she is punished, but either way the masculine subject is confirmed as subject. However, it's a precarious project and just how precarious can be seen when the bad-object is integral to the self. Rather than rehabilitation (under the guise of acting upon the other) there is the threat of being undermined from within. If she is me, then masculinity must be experienced as a double inscription of powerlessness or passivity. But this experience totally contradicts the knowledge of masculinity posited on self-possession and the exercise of power. The contradiction opened up here cannot be easily resolved through projection, through a rehabilitation of the self in terms of (through differentiation from) an other. Nevertheless, there is of course a drive to reclaim subjectivity and what this means, paradoxically, is a desperate, obsessive and frequently violent 'acting out' of masculinity in a repetitive attempt to negate the horror opened up by this internalised bad-object. The desperation, obsession and violence are born of engagement in a game that can never be mastered.

> *At bottom everything stands still – against this the*
> *thawing wind preaches.*
> *The thawing wind, a bull that is no ploughing bull, a raging bull,*
> *a destroyer who breaks the ice with wrathful horns.* (Nietzsche)

This is the real force of masculinity as fantasy. It is not simply that the associ-ation of masculinity with power is illusory; it is rather that masculinity itself corresponds to the structure of a game that can never be mastered but must be played out, a game in which each manoeuvre is provoked by the force of a bad-object, the annihilation of which would amount to an annihilation of self. The force of the bad object is registered through fear and fascination, and through a punitive dynamic that frequently mimics what we too often assume to be the masochism of femininity.

And so we are returned to the scene of 'domestic intimacy' between the broth-ers, the confessional 'hit me' scene. Before passing on to *The Red Shoes* I want to pause for a moment to note the way in which the scene is diegetically framed. Joey arrives in the midst of a violent marital quarrel, the wife is ejected from the room and before the men sit down at the table Jake yells at her through the closed door, 'I'm gonna kill ya!' She is then out of the scene (obscene?) but returns at the end. The sequence ends with a fleeting shot of her watching and listening secretly. Her absence is secured through a violent threat and yet she returns, like the repressed, is present as a silent witness. Later, in his second marriage, Jake – jealously obsessed about his wife Vickie's absence – interrogates her about her movements. She tells him she's been to see (has witnessed) *Father of the Bride*, another film, as we know, about troubled and suspicious masculinity.

Like a Girl Committing Suicide or Like a Ballerina?
That masochistic inflection of femininity is manifested in *The Red Shoes* in the logic of Vicky's suicide flight. I say logic because the dynamic of the film has set up a pattern of repetition that seems thematically to revolve round choice (will she choose dancing or living an ordinary 'everyday' life? Which man will she choose? And so on), but in fact the psychic logic (which is what propels and drives the film) actually enacts the impossibility of choice. Compulsion cannot be helped; obsession precludes choice and culminates in death and ecstasy.

The Red Shoes and *Raging Bull* both spin intricate tensile fictions in which ob-session and ecstasy are enmeshed. In *Raging Bull* the connection is enacted most particularly in the fight sequences, but the overall narrative is structured like a classical tragedy in which the rhythm of rise and fall (of the hero) opens up, in the end, an elegiac space for mourning (the loss of male beauty? of ecstasy itself?).[26] The man himself, however, doesn't die. *The Red Shoes* is much more explicit about the imbrication of ecstasy and obsession and death.

Just before the curtains are about to open for the first time on the ballet of 'The Red Shoes' Lermontov holds Vicky's hands to his chest, as though in sup-plication, confession or declaration. He wants from her ecstasy – 'ecstasy I've seen in you only once before'. He admits to having seen her at the Mercury Theatre on a wet afternoon, dancing Odette in *Swan Lake*. She might not have been aware of him in the audience on that occasion, but we as the film audi-ence are hardly likely to have forgotten a sequence so charged with the energy and dangerous desire of dance. It is the first time in the film that we see a body

The Red Shoes (Michael Powell/Emeric Pressburger, 1948)

transformed from the daily, a spectacularly 'decided body'; and it is the first time that we witness balleto-cinematic effects. The scene in the Mercury Theatre lasts for a few minutes, but the crucial sequence – for the way it introduces and prefigures the action of the film – lasts only 28 seconds and is composed of a dozen shots.[27] After setting the scene – a poster outside the theatre, the gramophone playing, the small audience – we are shown the stage. In long shot Vicky, as Odette, in her white swan's costume, enters screen left (stage right), dances across the stage and begins to pirouette back. This is almost a 'proscenium' shot: respectful of the stage, it is full frontal and almost static. Cut to a medium-close-up moving shot as she twirls twice; and then there is a whirl of abstract colours and shapes interspersed with flashes of the audience. This is clearly a subjective series, but what matters is not what she sees, or even primarily the perspective (it is not set up as a point-of-view shot), but the sensation, a vertiginous experience of 'space-time'. We are drawn into this sensationalism, but also drawn, albeit imperceptibly, into an exchange of energy between actants on the stage and in the auditorium. From the audience we cut to a medium-close-up of Vicky twirling, and then a close-up – her head slightly back, spinning, a smile of bliss appearing in the movement. There is another subjective shot, with flashing lights and colours, which eventually settles and comes into focus on Lermontov in the audience. In long shot, static, she holds her pose, back where she began. Cut from this to a close-up of Lermontov watching intensely, and then an abrupt cut to Vicky in extreme close-up. This shot always evokes for me the shocking experience of the

28

close-up in so-called 'primitive cinema'. It is as though all the intensity, the flagrant momentum that has been generated, is here distilled, precariously. Her lips are vividly scarlet (prefiguring the red shoes), her mouth like a wound, and her elaborately painted eyes are wide and wild (a look that will reappear in the suicide flight). She appears possessed, transported, ecstatic. Possessed by the obsession that is dancing or the desire that is Lermontov's? There is no answer, or rather, it is impossible to give an answer that opts for one or the other. And this is the impossibility that kills. There is something curiously frightening in this shot (although not purely 'in' it; the effect is also derived from its placement in the sequence, the way it is cut in), an intimation of the deadly aspect of ecstasy.[28]

> Shots are held together not by the constant identity of an individual performer, but by the emotional integrity of the movement itself, independent of its performer. (Maya Deren)[29]

The cutting in this sequence, the spacing of shots, the rhythm and timing are reminiscent of many sequences of *Raging Bull* where the viewer is drawn into the ring, implicated in the subjectivity of the shots, in the sensation of deadly ecstasy. In fact nothing could be more repetitious and circular (and therefore potentially tedious) than boxing, round after round after round; nothing, that is, except classical ballet, pirouette after pirouette after pirouette. Indeed, it is partly the aspect of obsession that renders this material interesting (that gives a charge to the endless repetition); but it is the cinematic rendering of obsession that engenders ecstasy.

This cinematic rendering involves a rhythm and timing partly effected through editing, but also through slight variations of camera speed. The use of slow motion is particularly intriguing; although it is deployed for various effects and isn't systematic, nevertheless it is often associated with Jake's paranoid consciousness, his obsession and jealousy. Sometimes, in the ring, its use is precisely temporal: to suggest something like the unreal duration of those moments in a car crash, the moments before death; but other times the effect is not purely temporal – the very slight variations (running the camera at 36 or 48 frames per second, say), particularly when combined with the sound dropping out, serve to render Jake's opponents in a heightened, almost imperceptibly transfigured way. The cinematic effect functions like an act of will, a theatricalisation of desire; it is as though he (we) are bringing a world into being, composing the elements of existence according to the measure of desire. To put it simply, it means slowing the enemy down, in order to focus and hit. But this mode of transfiguration isn't only deployed in the ring: it is often used for rendering Vickie from Jake's point of view (and the men of whom he's jealous). Initially she appears like a vision, imperceptibly floating; later as an image of infidelity and betrayal. This cinematic attraction is double-edged.

The scene in the Mercury Theatre anticipates Vicky's suicide flight. She is in her dressing room where she has been practising in her new red shoes. Her dresser hands her the normal peach-coloured slippers that she is to wear for the opening of 'The Red Shoes'.

> *So much for realism. I now brought the Red Shoes into play as a*
> *magical image with a power over their wearer, exactly as in the*
> *fairy tale. I went close on the Red Shoes with the camera and*
> *worked out with Jack Cardiff a high intensity of colour and*
> *light, which seemed to give the shoes life. So I invented the*
> *action where Moira takes a step towards the camera and the*
> *shoes stop her dead and then turn her round exactly as if they*
> *were the masters. The flashing light and the flaring colour get*
> *more and more intense, and she starts to run in the opposite*
> *direction to the stage.* (Michael Powell)[30]

She rushes along the corridor, round a corner, down stairs, into the sunshine, down more steps, and over a balustrade. In order to capture the sense of continuous movement as Vicky runs down the stairs, of compulsive dancing (and to ensure that her feet stayed in view), Powell mounted a 25-foot-high spiral staircase on a turntable which was turned slowly as she ran down. Two takes were shot and edited together almost invisibly.

This rush to death is extraordinarily fluid, exhilarating and balletic, but it is also – or at least I find it so – nauseating. Perhaps this is because of the anticipation, because the ending is so strongly inscribed in the flight itself, as, precisely, a repetition (many contemporary reviewers chastised the film-makers for the 'bad taste' of this bloody ending, but I wonder if their troubled response doesn't register this very tension – between artifice and naturalism, public and private). In this flight, just as in the ballet of 'The Red Shoes', we witness the traversing of an imaginary space, the charting of 'a geography that never was',[31] and it is this cinematic rendering of 'space-time' that is at once so magical and catastrophic.

> *'Mr Powell! Shall I jump like a girl committing suicide,*
> *or like a ballerina?'*
> *I thought. 'Like a ballerina.'*
> *She is only in the air for about eight frames, but it is one of*
> *the most beautiful cuts in the film.* (Michael Powell)[32]

It *is* thrilling, this flight through the air, but there's a risk: that in going beyond the pleasure principle you will fly in the face of death.

Varieties and Waves of Intensity

> *The protagonist does not suffer some subjective delusion, of*
> *which the world outside remains independent,*
> *if not oblivious; on the contrary she is, in actuality,*
> *destroyed by an imaginative action.* (Maya Deren)[33]

Throughout this writing a voice has whispered, ghostly images have hovered, flitting between the lines, shadowing the text. The ghost of Maya Deren, for whom 'the condition of the ecstatic' was 'the incandescence of obsession'.[34] The title of this chapter has been taken from a twelve-minute film she made in 1948, *Meditation on Violence*. Like most of her projects it explores and stretches the relation between dance and film, but what makes it particularly pertinent is that it is derived from boxing (Chinese boxing). In reflecting upon the film she pointed out that in so far as the film is a meditation its location is an inner space, and its concerns are more with the idea of violence, rather than with the act. 'However,' she writes, 'meditations investigate extremes, and life, while ongoing and non-climactic in the infinite sense, contains within it varieties and waves of intensity.'[35]

The gloves and the shoes, then, serve to focus and crystallise unattached energy. They also indicate, as in totemic rituals, an aspect crucial to spectatorship and performance – that is, the ceremonial. Both gloves and shoes mark out the body and an arena of performance, the stage and the ring. They imply a trained and disciplined body, an extra-daily body. But when techniques of the body appropriate to the stage and the ring disperse into the quotidian there are no boundaries to contain these single-minded desiring bodies. Hence, the perverse logic of ecstasy. It is dangerous, and the danger for us is that we might be infected by coming into contact with the ecstasy, by touching what is 'red hot'. Going to the movies is an event, a way of ceremonialising. But as part of life we take movies away with us, project after-images elsewhere, and onto the movies we project scenes and memories and forgotten sensations. Or should I say: we use the movies as objects of investment, like the red shoes and the boxing gloves. And that might save us from madness, but it might also open up glimpses of horror, moments when the cutting is palpable and we must avert our gaze. I am reminded, while not looking, that looking – at the screen – constitutes an activity, a performance, a potentially dangerous encounter. In the movie theatre the act of seeing with one's own eyes is always more than it seems.

Chapter 3

A Glitter of Putrescence

It is dark. There is a clash of cymbals, and the film begins. From centre screen steam gushes, swirling like light out of a manhole, polluted light, glitteringly opaque.

It is dark. A subtitle reads TEXAS 1868. From within the darkness a door is opened outwards. Light spills in. The immensity of a desert landscape is framed by the doorway, by the domestic. The camera moves us forward, through the frame, following a woman onto the verandah; in the distance a figure on horseback rides slowly, inexorably, towards the homestead.

The bumper of a yellow checker cab moves in slow motion through the steam, coloured neon lights are refracted by the rain, the urban landscape is rendered almost abstract, overcrowded, electric. Through the cab window, a sign we can decipher: *Texas Chainsaw Massacre*.

Home and Away

The Searchers opens in a contradictory manner. A man rides in, out of the desert, returning home, but on the soundtrack the film's theme song reiterates a different trajectory: 'Ride Away, Ride Away'. This tension between 'home' and 'away' inaugurates a restless cinematic mapping of obsession. As Brian Henderson has pointed out, the question 'What makes a man to wander . . . and turn his back on home?' that initiates *The Searchers*' quest is never answered.[1] As Ethan Edwards (John Wayne) walks away at the end of the film in a scene that rhymes with the opening (the door, framing the figure of Ethan in a desert landscape, is pulled closed, returning us to darkness) the soundtrack picks up the opening refrain:

> A man will search in heart and soul
> Go searching way out there.
> His peace of mind he knows he'll find
> But where, Oh Lord, oh where?

The Searchers (John Ford, 1956)

The posing, or opening out, of this question strains against the elegant symmetry of closure. The question that has no answer reverberates, threading a nomadic passage through Hollywood cinema (and it reverberates precisely because it is unanswered, because it suggests a troubling scenario of irresolution).[2] *Taxi Driver* remakes *The Searchers* in part through 'resurrecting' the character of Ethan Edwards in the figure of Travis Bickle, but also through its filmic exploration of pathological narrative. It 'remakes' not in the sense of producing a simulation of the original, but rather by recasting, or acting out a scenario that simmers within the classical constraints of the Fordian text. The burning question isn't really 'What makes a man to wander?' What burns is the question of what troubles a man. It burns the filmic text – and therefore the spectator too – to such a degree that the wandering becomes obsessive, dangerously restless, pathologically violent.

Of both *The Searchers* and *Taxi Driver* we might say that it is not simply the hero's problematic relation to home that fuels the fire; it is the way in which an oscillation between 'home' and 'away' is modulated (and the destabilising effect exacerbated) through a dynamic of pursuit-and-salvation. Central to both films is an impulse to rescue – to 'return home' – a woman who does not want to be saved. For seven years Ethan Edwards searches for his niece Debbie, captured as a young girl by the Indian Chief Scar during a massacre of the Edwards family. One way or another he aims to save Debbie and take his revenge on Scar. Travis Bickle becomes obsessed with the idea of saving a twelve-year-old prostitute from her life on the streets and from her pimp, Sport, against whom he nurses vengeful desires.[3] The perversity of this impulse to save, to return 'home', is manifested in an increasingly compulsive, irrationally 'driven' pursuit. But what, I am driven to ask (in writing), is compulsive about the films themselves? What makes them compelling to watch? Why am I caught up, again and again, in viewing after viewing, in these jagged trajectories? It is not, I think, simply as character studies that they compel, though certainly both Ethan Edwards (or John Wayne) and Travis Bickle (or Robert De Niro) are disturbingly mesmeric. No, it is something to do with movement. I am moved (touched, chillingly, somewhere) each time, but it never feels as though I have moved closer to a destination. The repetition of this movement (aimless yet compulsive), this being moved, perhaps signals an enactment, in the process of viewing, of the obsessive structure of the films themselves.

Taxi Driver, made under the sign of *The Searchers*, might be expected to offer a reading and in so doing to answer those questions which *The Searchers* leaves open. In fact, it reiterates, though with a different intonation, and exacerbates the irresolution; it exaggerates the violence. But this very intensification, when read back into *The Searchers*, woven through it, generates new textual patterns. Just as the ending of *The Searchers* reflects back on the opening, through the formality of the rhyming coupled with the straining against classical symmetry, so *Taxi Driver* reflects back and stands in relation to *The Searchers* – in a relation of fearful symmetry.

John Wayne lifts and holds her at arm's length. I hold my breath. No matter how often I've seen *The Searchers* before, I do not know, at this very moment and for a split second, whether he will kill her or fuck her. The odds are even. Then he sweeps her into his arms and says, 'Let's go home Debbie.' In the midst of carnage, Iris, or Easy as she is called on the street ('Easy to remember'), weeps. She has no option but to watch this massacre

Out of the Past (Jacques Tourneur, 1947)

undertaken supposedly for her, for her salvation. We do not see her again, but we see the word of her father – in the form of a letter he writes to thank Travis – and we hear his voice expressing gratitude that Iris, through the agency of Travis, has returned home. The Avenging Angel, Travis, has acted in the Name of the Father.

'Let's go home.' This phrase is echoed with a bitter twist in Scorsese's first feature, *Who's that Knocking at My Door?* At the end of the film the girl (played by Zina Bethune, she has no name and in the credits is simply designated as 'the girl') tells J.R., the hero (a young Harvey Keitel): 'Go home, go home.' J.R. is an Italian boy, hangs out with his friends on the mean streets of Little Italy, messes around with girls who are 'easy', but won't sleep with the Wasp girl he is having a relationship with because of Catholic guilt or fear. When she reveals that prior to meeting him she had been raped, he leaves her. After a while he returns, seeking a reconciliation. They are momentarily happy, until J.R. says 'I understand now. I forgive you. And I'm going to marry you anyway.' He offers her forgiveness for the fact that she is sexually impure, or contaminated, as he sees it. She is astounded and seems to realise for the first time that he will always consider this a matter for forgiveness, that he will never forget, that his memory will be relentless and pernicious. 'Go home. Go home.' At this moment, sitting motionless in her dressing gown, isolated in long shot in a large dimly-lit room, she is a figure of extreme stillness, of quiet resolution; J.R., hurtling down the stairs, kicks and shouts, all hysteria and solipsistic violence.

'Go home. Go home,' she says, echoing words that J.R. himself quoted to her earlier in the movie. In their first meeting, a chance encounter whilst they are both waiting for the Staten Island ferry, he tells her about *The Searchers*. She is reading *Paris Match* and J.R.'s eye is caught by a couple of stills from the movie. He assumes that she's familiar with it – 'You know, with John Wayne' – but she can't remember having seen it. So *The Searchers* turns out to be a perfect pretext for seduction. Though Scorsese's scene is a homage to Ford it is shot in a style much closer to the French New Wave than to classic Hollywood. The sequence-shot lasts six minutes, including two brief cutaways of John Wayne. He cajoles her, trying to get her to remember, evoking the film through details: 'It was in colour! That guy was in it who played Christ . . .' 'Jeffrey Hunter?' she asks. 'Oh yes, and Natalie Wood was in it,' he reminds her, 'she had a big scene at the end there . . . "Unnt-meah, unnt-meah. Go away! Go away!" She's trying to get him to go you know.' Eventually the girl remembers ('Oh wait a minute, was that the picture where Jeffrey Hunter is supposed to be trading Indian rugs and he winds up trading for an Indian bride, and he doesn't know what to do with her?'). 'I'm not used to admitting I like Westerns,' she confesses. J.R. is confident: 'Everybody should like Westerns. Solve everybody's problems if they liked Westerns.' She laughs, a little embarrassed (I imagine) by this generic certainty, but enjoying the exchange: 'Okay, I like Westerns.'

Okay, I Like Westerns

She is caught in a beam of light. Blinded. The projector illuminates her panic, throws images onto her body – horses rearing into the air, hooves kicking, corpses rolling. Judy Garland as Esther Blodgett has just been signed up as a singing star to one of the major studios. This is her introduction to the studio head. She is ushered unceremoniously into a darkened theatrette where he is viewing the rushes of a Western. Her back against the screen, she can see nothing and is getting in the way of the picture. Their meeting is brief: 'I see you dear. Good to have you with us.' In the dark she stumbles back and forth trying to find her way out of the theatre, but again and again she is drawn back into the line of light, into the path of warring Indians.(A Star is Born)

I know what it's like, to be Esther Blodgett in the dark, I know it writing this chapter. And with 'the girl', too, I feel empathy, the girl in *Who's that Knocking at my Door?*. The Western: it's a genre that's troubling for us girls, its pleasures perplexing.

It was a long trip from the farm to Harare, or Salisbury as it then was, always an exciting journey, but particularly so on this occasion, for we were to stay overnight and see for the first time a marvellous new spectacle, television. Anticipation, which had been seething for weeks, encompassed curiosity about a tantalising phenomenon called the 'TV dinner'. The prospect of eating and watching simultaneously seemed sheer bliss. And it was. *Wagon Train* was enthralling, and only the beginning of years of television Westerns: series like *Rawhide, Maverick, Bonanza*, and movies all weekend. My father was a farmer and we rode horses and read Zane Grey and detective novels and watched Westerns on TV. When I was a teenager the farm went bust, we moved to town, and I earned a crust at weekends teaching white Rhodesian cops to ride. The sensation of power was exhilarating, it was easy money – but a shameful secret. It felt, in a colonial country where the police constituted a racist and virtual paramilitary force, like an act of treachery. For a long time I never told anyone. For years I didn't watch Westerns, not one.

> *You forget that this master* [Brezhnev-Mosfilm/Nixon-Paramount] *has been demanding the same film for fifty years.*
> *You forget that this film has one name: The Western, and that this is not by chance.* (J. -L. Godard, *Weekend*)

In the pub, in another country, the men asked what I thought of Westerns. I had by now left home, it was my first interview for a job teaching film, and this was the informal, friendly part of the ordeal. I had to confess it wasn't my favourite genre. 'Why?' they asked, eyebrows raised. I had no good reasons. Since I never saw any Westerns, I was quite unable to talk in an informed and critical fashion about the genre. At a loss for words, acutely embarrassed, I offered a feeble explanation: I told them I had watched so many Westerns with my father as a child that I just got sick of them. Under their eyebrows the men exchanged glances. One of them, a little kinder than the others, suggested that I might have some memories of those childhood

viewings. But my mind was blank; I couldn't remember a single Western. At the time I felt mortified by my own stupidity (and shocked into watching Westerns again); some years later it seemed to me a surprisingly accurate (albeit unknowing) answer. The Western is indeed a genre of the Father. And now, via *Taxi Driver*, I remember, reflect again – in part about a film that itself, in 1956, reflects back on the Western – and wonder if the forms of immersion and resistance mightn't be quite complex, or more complex than I was once prepared to admit.

> The first image that I remember seeing on a cinema screen was a
> Trucolor trailer for a Roy Rogers movie, in which he was wearing
> fringes and jumped from a tree onto his horse. My father asked me
> if I knew who Trigger was and I imitated firing a gun. 'No,' he said,
> 'it's the horse's name. I'll take you to see it next week.'
> (Scorsese)[4]

A Minute Freed from the Order of Time

It is a famous moment in Hollywood cinema, the moment in the desert when John Wayne lifts Debbie. Or, rather, it is the moment between, the fractional pause while he holds her at arm's length, before he says, 'Let's go home.' Seven years have passed since her family were killed and she was captured. The little girl is now a young woman. Her father was Ethan's brother and her mother, Martha, was the woman whom Ethan loved, silently. Debbie by now, it is implied (but never shown), has found another home, and replaced her father with a lover, Scar. In his searching, Ethan becomes obsessed by the idea of revenge, fixated on Scar, and it becomes increasingly unclear whether, when he finds Debbie, he will kill her or rescue her. In either case he conceives of himself as saviour (he will kill her because she has been contaminated, because she has been rendered impure). He had on an earlier occasion – when she urged her 'saviours' to leave her alone, declaring 'these are my people' – attempted to shoot her. In his obsessive searching (during which there are several returns to a surrogate home, to a neighbouring homestead), he is accompanied by Martin Pawley, who had been adopted by the Edwards when his own family had been massacred. Martin (who is one-eighth Cherokee) considers himself to be Debbie's brother, a relation disputed by Ethan. The search is represented in a highly elliptical manner, so that even after repeated viewings it is very hard to grasp the time-frame of the comings and goings.

John Wayne's gesture is often interpreted in terms of the physicality of memory. It is as though in holding Debbie his body remembers and in the moment of memory he recognises her:

> It is not just the physical contact that prevents Ethan from killing the last of his family; there is also a sense of the profound memories which are flooding back into his consciousness as he touches her. The lifting gesture, which seems almost involuntary, recalls the moment inside the home long ago when he lifted the child Debbie into his arms.[5]

Godard also remembers: 'In *The Searchers*, when John Wayne finds Natalie Wood and suddenly holds her up at arm's length, we pass from stylized gesture to feeling, from John Wayne suddenly petrified to Ulysses being reunited with Telemachus.'[6] And in the context of discussing the 'mystery and fascination of this American cinema', he asks: 'How can I hate John Wayne upholding Goldwater and yet love him tenderly when, abruptly, he takes Natalie Wood into his arms in the last reel of *The Searchers*?'[7] It is true, we are not prepared to be moved so suddenly. We have not been warned, as it were. There is no plotting of psychological motivation. Andrew Sarris puts it laconically: 'A man picks up a girl in his arms and is miraculously delivered of all the racist, revenge-seeking furies that have seared his soul.'[8]

Already the tears are trickling down her neck in anticipation of this scene. She stares at the screen. One moment he's going to kill her, and then suddenly, without warning, he bends and lifts her into his arms. 'Let's go home Debbie.' For whom does she cry? Is it for Debbie that she cries? For Ethan Edwards, or Scar? Or for the man she left at the airport? She thinks: am I the child-woman who doesn't want to be saved, and at the same time wants to be scooped up in strong arms and taken home, no questions asked? Or am I him? Relentless, always returning. That movement, the gesture, the way he scoops her up in his arms, the way the camera tilts, is charged. Something inside you moves. She can't tell why but remembers another inflection of this movement, an image from *The Tomb of Ligeia*. Who is he, this man who rides in from nowhere and will ride away; is he the figure of paternal protection or is he the vampire incarnate? He's driven by some obsessive pathology, but what does he want? She'll never know this, what it is that men want.

Early in the film, on his arrival home, Ethan lifts the little girl, Debbie; clutching her by the shoulders he holds her aloft at arm's length. In the desert at the end of the film, Ford invokes our memory of this domestic scene, and it is in the duration, or sensation, of the echo that we are moved.[9] We may not consciously recall the earlier scene when watching the later one, but the repetitions work upon us cinematically; various elements – framing, the deployment of gesture, the tableau effect and, crucially, timing – all come together to activate a response. McBride and Wilmington are right to draw a connection between the physical contact and the 'memories which come flooding back as he touches her'. But the interesting question, I think, is this: who remembers what, and how? As viewers we experience a kind of 'physical contact' though it is not necessarily or exclusively an identification with the protagonist's act of touching. It is more like the return of the image, its registering in our body. What takes place is something like the cinematic equivalent of Proustian 'involuntary memory', and it is crucially dependent on an associational register, on a relation between sensations, between images (it is not about the affect an image may induce in isolation). It 'takes place', of course, in time, but here time is contracted, two different instants are superimposed, so that we move out of the logic of narrative.[10] For Ethan Edwards there might be a collapse of seven years' searching. For us, some other distance contracts, startling us by a sensation of immediacy.

> *But let a noise or a scent, once heard or once smelt, be heard or melt again in the present and at the same time in the past, real without being actual, ideal without being abstract . . . A minute freed from the order of time . . . one can understand that the word 'death' should have no meaning for him; situated outside time, why should he fear the future?* (Marcel Proust)[11]

It is as though, for a moment, we have been delivered from death. Perhaps our tears signify joy and relief. But, as memory ripples through us, there is also a sensation of loss, the opening up of a void, a whispering fear of the future.

Time Lost and Time Regained

Involuntary memory pertains to sensation – the sense of touch, sight, smell, hearing – rather than intellectual recognition. Some sensation in the present, and the most familiar example is Proust's account of the taste of madeleines, summons an experience of the past. In the case of the madeleines it is the 'flavour' of Combray, Proust's childhood home. The repetitions that spark off involuntary memory so often return us to home (Proust's memory of waiting in agony as a child for a goodnight kiss from his mother, which in turn generates the story *In Search of Lost Time*), but simultaneously they are almost posited on the impossibility of recovery, of returning home. This is perhaps why, although the revelations of involuntary memory are usually marked by an experience of extreme joy, of overwhelming plenitude, they might sometimes evoke pain. 'Why does the involuntary recollection [in some instances], instead of an image of eternity, afford the acute sentiment of death?' asks Deleuze.[12] He speculates that in the sensuous image itself there is an essential ambivalence, a contradiction between time lost and time regained.

In the cinema it is not uncommon to experience involuntary memory. It can happen that we are suddenly and unexpectedly seized, in the midst of the most seemingly mundane film, by an overwhelming sensation of sensuous reminiscence. It occurs within and across a constellation of largely personal and idiosyncratic associations. But as a phenomenon it is not insignificant, for surely it is as much for these startling moments as for the stories, or the stars, say, that we go to the movies. I suspect it is one of the reasons why people do indeed continue to 'go to the movies' instead of just watching videos, for the physical conditions are well disposed to the activation of involuntary memory and receptivity to sensuous images.[13] For the moment, though, I am less concerned with these more idiosyncratic instances and more concerned with those instances where films play in a quasi-structured way upon the memory of the viewer (the viewer's memory of the film, that is, but also of 'film' as a history of cinematic images). Somewhere between voluntary and involuntary: a zone of acute memorial indeterminacy.

39

Let's Go Home, Debbie

She is touched, albeit for a brief and intense moment.

I am touched in various ways, possessed at this moment by a spiralling range of sensuous images. Not all benign. The stab of recognition (it is like a ghostly knifing, palpable but hard to locate) stirs an incipient sensation of horror.

The lineaments of this image are familiar; it is an icon of the horror film and we've caught a glimpse of it often before in that recurring moment when a mon-ster-man gathers a woman up in his arms and carries her over the threshold, in macabre parody of a wedding scenario.[14]

A latent image materialises, then, as the present image – Ethan lifting Debbie – evokes an experience of the past, the past of the movies (my experience, my history of the cinema, images embedded now in my bodily unconscious, folded or scrunched up in memory tissue). Before seeing, however, there is a sensation: of horror. Then the image (*Bride of Franken-stein, The Tomb of Ligeia*) materialises. Not only horror, though. As Ethan lifts Debbie I am (virtually) touched – a sense of time regained that is evoked by a rhyming with that earlier image (where he lifts Debbie the child). This ambivalence – call it horror and home-coming – is inscribed in the process of involuntary memory; in the sensuous image itself there is an essential ambivalence, a contradiction between time lost and time regained.

But can the 'acute invocation of death' that accompanies these sensations be fully attributed to involuntary memory? The viewer also deploys voluntary memory to read and interpret the signs and work of the film. As viewers we read the film (any narrative film) backwards, we make sense retrospectively, we remember what has gone before. Voluntary memory 'doesn't apprehend the past directly: it recomposes it with different presents'.[15] Remember the first time Ethan picks Debbie up. There is something significant about that encounter that the critics often forget. It is marked by misrecognition. Ethan addresses the girl as Lucy, but she tells him 'I'm not Lucy, I'm Deborah.' This moment of misrecognition indicates, on the most obvious level, the passing of time, the fact that Ethan has been away so long (has lost track of time) and the children have grown so much that he mistakes their identities. But it also suggests that his links with home are extremely tenuous, so that he is literally 'out of touch'; even when holding the girl in his arms he does not know who she is. And though he recognises Martin's kinship ('Someone could mistake you for a half-breed,' he sneers), he cannot recognise his own family. Jean-Louis Leutrat argues that when Ethan lifts Debbie up in his arms the second time he rectifies the misrecognition by an act of recognition.[16] For me, remembering the other signs, this scene (though it has resonances of the sentimental, a yearning for resolution) repeats, or doubles, the misrecognition. Ethan comes and goes, he repeats movements, he takes his time like all obsessives, but he is driven by a fundamental misrecognition. And this misrecognition remains murderous, drives him, at the end, to continue his search.

Well, Then Again, John Wayne . . .

The notion of repetition (as a structuring of time) is crucial here; but there are different kinds of repetition in play. I want to distinguish two. First there is the repetition associated with narrative itself and then there is the kind of repetition associated with obsessive behaviour. Narrative, like the pleasure principle, is economical. The opening up of difference always incorporates an implied promise that there will be a return to the same, a closing down, a healing of the breach. Thus every narrative needs a disruption, an introduction of disequilibrium, to get things going. Equally, it requires a restoration of equilibrium in order to end. If the narrative opens with a murder and the question of 'whodunnit?' it will close with the answer; if it begins with the departure of an old king it will end with the arrival of a new one (typically, through birth or marriage). This rhyming pattern which gives overall shape to the narrative is echoed in smaller units and sequencing so that most narratives tend to proceed according to a structure of question-and-answer or opening up and closing down or losing-finding. For the viewer or reader the narrative pleasure is in part derived from this very process of repetition – pleasure is derived not just from the story, what the narrative is about, but from the process, how the story goes about its telling. The process of narrative has been compared to the childish game of *fort-da* as described by Freud: a child gains control over a potentially distressing situation – the absence of the mother – by making up a game, where it throws and retrieves an object simultaneously repeating the phrase *fort-da* (gone-here), over and over again, thus, in a ludic scenario, controlling the process of coming and going, of absence and presence.[17] This structure is economical in that it contains and accounts for everything.

The kind of repetition associated with obsessive behaviour is similarly, though more desperately, to do with mastery and control. The obsessive has displaced an original affect on to an idea which has acquired the status of a fixation. Although his behaviour indicates an attempt to recapture, in so far as he is fixated he is fixed, unable to move, doomed to repeat (in symptomatically compulsive behaviour) rather than resolve. Obsession is crucially to do with time, with stretching time out (through rituals of repetition such as washing hands, avoiding cracks in the pavement, counting words, making lists), making time matter (or count). All of this is in the service of putting off the moment of action, of decision, so in a sense it is also about losing track of, and effectively wasting, time. It has to do with putting off an ending, deferring a resolution. Narrative patterning plays on repetition and difference, whereas obsessive behaviour suppresses difference. Narrative proceeds towards closure (the opening up, of a landscape, say, or of a crime, is repeated in the closure through formal symmetry, but hermeneutically it is completed), whereas obsessive behaviour defers closure through repetition of the same.

The Searchers is at once the most classic of narratives and a limit case. Through its elliptical and aimlessly compulsive narrative, which literally loses track of time, it mimics the obsessive disposition and gestures towards the obsessive strain that runs, in a subterranean thread, through all narrative. In Ethan Edwards we are presented with a 'hero' who is clearly an obsessive neurotic,[18] but whose neurosis verges on the pathological (presented in such a way that the horrific dimension of ordinary heroism, of the 'Western' formula, is

41

brought to the surface, as it were). In a later genre, sometimes referred to as the Street Western,[19] Travis Bickle emerges as a fully fledged psychotic. Both Ethan and Travis do act in the end, but their actions do not signal closure. Ethan neither finds Debbie nor kills Scar. His actions consist of not-shooting Debbie and of scalping-Scar. Although these two actions might seem to strain in different directions they are intricately bound up together and can be thought of as a single act, one that is inscribed as an obsessive repetition rather than a resolution (thus signalling future re-enactment). The narrative itself reverberates with the affects of both the obsessive and the incipiently psychotic. *Taxi Driver* presents a hero who definitively acts, perpetrating single-handedly an extremely bloody massacre. But this is not presented narratively as a resolution; rather, it too is inscribed as an obsessive repetition, in a narrative that is profoundly disturbed in its frequent veering into aimlessly compulsive trajectories. Doubling the misrecognition over and over again, Travis Bickle, the hero as psychotic, has risen like a double-headed King Kong from the ashes of *The Searchers*.

Martin: Debbie!

Debbie: Unnt-meah!

Martin: Debbie, don't you remember? I'm Martin, I'm Martin, your brother. Remember? Debbie, remember back. Do you remember how I used to let you ride my horse and tell you stories? Don't you remember me Debbie?

Debbie: I remember, from always. At first, I prayed to you: come and get me, take me home. You didn't come.

Martin: But I've come now Debbie.

Debbie: These are my people. Unnt-meah! Go! Go, Martin, please.

J.R.'s cajoling of the girl in *Who's that Knocking at my Door?*, his attempt to make her remember, curiously mimics the exchange between Martin and Debbie. Martin is an apprentice searcher, and a kind of apprentice obsessive to Ethan, but in the end he is reconciled as a hero – he kills the villain, and returns home to marry and take his place as future father. J.R. is less reconciled, in a lineage with Martin but destined to repeat some of the moves of an Ethan in a narrative that is dispersed and far from conservative (his anxiety that the girl remember *The Searchers* persists in his use of another paradigmatic Western, *Rio Bravo*, to explain the difference between 'broads' whom you sleep with and 'girls' whom you marry). The exchange between J.R. and the girl has the wonderful ebullience of movie-talk; it captures a kind of crazy cinephilic patois and evokes the pleasure of shorthand communication, the way we toss back and forth colours, stars, moments, fragments of narrative, in an attempt to remember, to recapture the filmic experience. But it also foreshadows a sinister unravelling of time and memory. J.R. says Scar was really nasty, 'but then again he was a bad guy', and almost as an afterthought he adds: 'Well, then again, John Wayne could get pretty nasty when he wanted to be.' Travis Bickle also enacts the compulsion to make someone else (a woman) remember, but by now such a move is clearly implicated in a psychotic acting out of murderous obsessions. Travis becomes obsessed with the idea that Iris, when she got into his cab, was trying to get away from Sport, and he insists on trying to get her to remember: 'Don't you remember any of it? Well that's alright, I'm gonna get you out of here.' Travis's mission to save her is posited, like Ethan's, on a fundamental misrecognition.

Oh he was more nasty than Wayne could ever get, but then again he was a bad guy. There were a lot of nasty Comanches in that picture. Well then again John Wayne could get pretty nasty when he wanted to be.

Recapture (or The Economy of Salvation)

Consider the motif of capture and recapture. Debbie has been captured. Ethan will recapture her. There is a temporal dimension to this motif: he searches to recover what is lost and to regain time. For seven years Ethan goes round in circles, searching: to rescue Debbie or to take his revenge on Scar? As the narrative progresses it becomes clear that the initial objective – salvation (to save Debbie) – is displaced by that of revenge. In terms of plot he is driven to take revenge against Scar, first for his violation and murder of Martha, and second because, presumably, in taking Debbie captive he has 'taken' her sexually. Ethan becomes fixated, focusing his hatred on Scar's racial otherness associated with sexual menace. But perhaps it isn't a matter simply of displacement, or of a privileging of one objective over another. It could be that the relation between salvation and revenge is more entwined and devious than common sense would assume.

In trying to grasp what might be the relation between Ethan's two objectives, involving Debbie and Scar respectively, it is useful to look at a series of relations between the characters, putting the stress, however, on relations rather than characters *per se*, so that we are talking more about figurative (and deviously entwined) relations. To do this will necessitate the introduction of another figure and temporal term – Martha, who is associated with time past. Martha, in her absence, is the figure who signifies recapture, and serves to complicate all other pairings. In addition to the pairings of characters there are couplets: revenge and salvation, sex and race, incest and violence. I shall look briefly at the way in which these are threaded through three sets of relations: between Martha and Ethan; between Debbie, Martha and Ethan; and between Debbie, Ethan and Scar.

1. Martha and Ethan

Martha is a forbidden love object. She is married to Ethan's brother and therefore 'in law' his sister, and she figuratively echoes the original forbidden love object, the mother. Their love, initially unspoken, is soon figured as unspeakable, a transition represented in two scenes, a farewell and a homecoming. In the first instance, Ethan, having just arrived home at the opening of the film, is leaving again to join a search for cattle thieves. The Reverend Clayton witnesses Martha tenderly stroking Ethan's coat whilst she thinks no one is watching. In the foreground he looks away as, behind him, Ethan briefly holds Martha by the shoulders and kisses her on the head. The Reverend's averted gaze acknowledges and conserves an unspoken love or desire as, precisely, unspoken. On their return home Ethan and Martin discover the homestead burning. Ethan finds Martha's dress and stumbles into the blackened house (framed as in the opening and closing), calling her name. He emerges shocked, refuses to let Martin look and will not speak of what he has seen – her body, murdered and scalped. Martha is thus construed as an unspeakable sight. In seeking to avenge her, Ethan, a sexually abstemious hero, is fuelled by a fixation on the sexual monstrosity of the Indian Chief, his own libidinal drive channelled into an obsessive search. In plot terms Ethan's revenge is plausibly motivated: the massacre, abduction and/or violation of white women provides the catalyst for the action of innumerable Westerns. *The Searchers*, however, maps out a series of configurations that undermines the temporal explanation of cause and effect. As the film unfolds it becomes increasingly clear that it is not the unspoken that precedes and explains the unspeakable, but rather that there is something unspeakable (repressed) that motivates Ethan's every action.

2. Debbie, Martha and Ethan

Debbie is a substitute for the dead Martha, not only as her daughter but because she is positioned (in Ethan's eyes) in the same way in relation to Scar, as object of sexual violation. When Martin at one stage says 'We're beat and you know it', Ethan swears to find them 'as sure as the turning of the earth'. The reason he gives is that Scar will rear her 'till she's of an age to . . .' – at which point he chokes on the unspeakable. Debbie is also the child he might have had with Martha. As substitute Martha, and as Martha's daughter, she is able to occupy the place of lover and daughter to Ethan. The idea of substitution is underscored by the film in a series of looks. First, there is the Reverend Clayton's averted gaze, marking the unspoken; second, there is Ethan's shadowed face registering the unspeakable sight of Martha's body; and third, there is his look at the young girls recaptured from the Indians by the army, who have lost their minds presumably as a result of contamination and violation. This look (it is an extraordinarily discordant shot – an abrupt cut and zoom in to a low-angled, shadowed view of Ethan in which he appears in an extremely sinister cast) is not unlike the gaze turned away from Martha's body except this time it is a look at the girls and if looks could kill this one would. The girls stand in an intermediate position. They represent an intimation of what happened to Martha and what could happen to Debbie. We are forewarned that for Ethan, albeit unconsciously, there is an identity between Martha and Debbie (mediated by these mad girls); and when he finds her he will be disposed to kill. Now if Debbie is a substitute Martha then Ethan not only desires to kill her, but desires her sexually. In fact, we might say that his desire to kill her is an effect of his disavowal of sexual desire. To recapture Debbie is to recapture the past (Martha, time lost), but recapture constitutes violence – sexual violence, moreover.

3. Debbie, Ethan and Scar

Scar has Debbie/Martha; he has what Ethan lacks. In some sense the struggle between the two men is over possession: over women as possessions, and over the question of who possesses sexual power. Ethan's concern to conserve the purity of his race and his family ('his' women) situates him as a fairly normal Western hero, a figure that the movies inherit from a literary tradition stretching back as far as the Puritan occupation of North America.[20] This 'concern' with saving white womanhood from the sexual attacks of black (i.e. non-white) men has been frequently analysed as sexual anxiety and jealousy manifested in a racist projection onto the other. What makes of Ethan an abnormal Western hero is the degree to which *The Searchers* exposes his concern as an obsessive and potentially pathological fixation, and the degree to which it explores the way this fixation involves simultaneously a projection onto Scar of Ethan's own unspeakable and repressed desires and a disavowal. There is a mirroring effect in the relation of Ethan and Scar: in answer to Scar's capture Ethan will re-capture, ostensibly to bring Debbie home, but perhaps 'to capture [her] again'. In response to Scar's scalping Ethan will scalp, and in response to Scar's killing Ethan threatens murder (the massacre is in turn Scar's revenge for the murder of his own children by white men, and he explains this when showing his acquired scalps to Martin and Ethan). To recapture is to re-enact Scar's action, effecting a displacement and re-placement of Scar. When Ethan scalps Scar after he has been killed by Martin he assumes the mantle of rapist, and simultaneously effects the symbolic castration of Scar. In castrating him Ethan can take his place, take possession of his family, 'take' his woman. That is – Debbie. But, it might be objected, in the end Ethan saves Debbie, he does not kill or rape her. My argument is that salvation and revenge have been intimately entwined by the film, so that the act of salvation is steeped in incipient (and sexual) violence. On this point *Who's that Knocking at My Door?* reaches back into *The Searchers*: the only way J.R. can assimilate the idea that 'his' woman has been sexually possessed (in fact raped) by another man is to convert the sense of jealousy and sexual anxiety into 'forgiveness' and salvation (just as Ethan relents, refrains from killing Debbie at the last minute, in effect forgiving her for her impurity and contamination). But the obsessive does not forget; for him to forgive is to punish, and to save is to take revenge. His memory will be relentless and pernicious, dedicated to the futile task of recapturing time lost.

> *Thus the will, the liberator, took to hurting; and on all who*
> *can suffer he wreaks revenge for his inability to go backwards.*
> *This, indeed this alone, is what revenge is: the will's ill will*
> *against time and its 'it was' . . . The spirit of revenge, my*
> *friends, has so far been the subject of man's best reflection; and*
> *where there was suffering, one always wanted punishment too.*
> (Nietzsche)

So, when Ethan picks Debbie up and says, 'Let's go home', although there is a flash of involuntary memory that summons an association of home, of originary plenitude, there is also a memory of the film's gradual charting of violence and salvation within the same economy. This, I think, is what I experience as a stab of recognition, an iconic ghosting over the image, registered as an intimation of horror. Certainly I am moved, by the intensity of this moment of tenderness, but by something else too, by a recognition of the implacability of paternal misrecognition. And so I cannot, like Godard, 'love him tenderly'. The sensation of sexual menace that emanates from this image is not easily separated from the desire for (and impossibility of) home as a safe refuge. The oscillation between home and away continues.[21]

One day there'll be a knock at the door and it'll be me. Love Travis.[22]

A Kind of Scar Has Been Formed in the Shape of Piety

Freud reminds us that the principal prohibition is against touching, since touching has the capacity for contagion and transference.[23] This is in the context of expounding similarities between the prohibitions erected around taboo objects and prohibitions erected by obsessional neurotics. Clearly it is the touching between an Indian man and a white woman that horrifies and obsesses Ethan Edwards, stirring up fantasies of contagion and transference (he both desires and abhors Debbie because she has been touched by the other). His fixation with purity (sexual and racial) leads him to murderous intentions presented in the form of piety: he will save Debbie either by killing her or bringing her home. Piety, according to Freud, is a way of responding to ambivalent feelings that survivors nurse against the dead. He argues that this ambivalence (between hostility and pained affection) which once expressed itself in open warring has, down through the course of ages, diminished (though it persists on an unconscious level) so that 'we now find that a kind of scar has been formed in the shape of piety, which declares "De mortuis nil nisi bonum"[Speak no ill of the dead].' 'Only neurotics', he adds 'are obliged to reproduce the struggle and the taboo resulting from it.'[24]

Viewed from a high angle: Travis Bickle, naked from the waist up, doing press ups. His back is slashed by a long, jagged scar.

A scar is formed on the surface of the skin, the place where touch, and race, is registered. It is the sign of a wound which, although it has closed over, has inadequately sutured. In *The Searchers* Scar is not simply a name; it is a sign of exchange.[25] Scar, the man, exists as a projection of all that Ethan desires and fears, and in their mirroring there is a transference, a contagion manifested as bodily inscription. Ethan, in mourning for Martha, in his attempts to recapture her, has acquired his own scar formed in the shape of piety. Clearly it is not the death of Martha that initiates Ethan as an obsessive neurotic (when he rides in out of the desert he is already marked), but this event comes to serve as a condensation of all that is unspeakable in his psyche. In Ethan the wound has not quite closed. He is 'obliged to reproduce the struggle and the taboo resulting from it'; he remains, in some sense and at the heart of this almost perfectly measured and classical film, festering.[26]

Repetition takes place across cinematic landscapes too: across films, genres, periods. Sometimes the repetitions echo as quotation; at other times it may be simply the framing of a gesture, a movement of the camera, three notes on the soundtrack – moments in which memory stirs.[27] Ethan Edwards returns: at the end of *The Searchers* he returns home, only to leave again, to repeat obsessively the moves of his mission. And like the return of the repressed he returns again and again in the cinema of Martin Scorsese. Across time, over cinematic bodies, the scar is transferred.

I Once Had a Horse

Taxi Driver *reopens an old wound.*

Where Ethan Edwards rode on horseback through Monument Valley Travis Bickle drives in a yellow cab through the streets of New York City. In its transposition to an urban environment the Western undergoes some changes. 'I once had a horse,' says Sport, 'she got hit by a car.' Ford composes desert landscapes that play on the relation between figure and ground to suggest a sense of immensity, a framing of the unknowable. Scorsese's frame is crowded with detail; his camera circles, tilts and shudders, capturing and captured by the milieu. The distance between figure and ground is reduced; instead of immensity there is a sense of compressed space, of a supercharged atmosphere; the steam that billows out from centre frame in the opening shot exudes a sense of the uncontainable that will pervade the film.

Out of the night the bumper of a yellow cab emerges like the snout of a huge beast rising up out of some subterranean lair. It edges into shot filling the frame, accompanied by a dramatic soundtrack. This curiously oblique introduction inaugurates a sequence of restless images, a sequence that signifies compulsive aimlessness. The cab glides out of view, steam rising in its wake and in the steam a title: TAXI DRIVER. Then a big close-up of a pair of eyes, suspiciously scanning. Lights, shadows, colours move over these eyes; these eyes move through textures of the city.

> He is native to night; it is the eyes for day which are closed.
> He sees perfectly the dimensions of night with his eyes of night.
> (Maya Deren)[28]

A dissolve from the eyes to a view of a car window from the interior, rain falls heavily on the glass, through the rain the world seems ultra-close, utterly abstract shapes and colours crowding onto the screen. Suddenly the wipers flash, focus is pulled and we are through the window, through the frame of the windscreen, witness to what is just recognisable as a cityscape, a neon vista stretching before us into the distance. The image breaks up, prismatically dissolving to a street scene. We are cruising, gliding in a lateral track next to the pavement; people on the street move in slow motion, like the living dead. A burst of red steam gushes into the frame infiltrating the scene, dispersing. The eyes are framed again, restless, looking this way and that, bathed in a red filter. The image is bleached out.

> *When you drive in Paris at night, what do you see? Red, green, yellow lights. I wanted to show these elements but without necessarily placing them as they are in reality. Rather, as the remain in the memory – splashes of red and green, flashes of yellow passing by. I wanted to recreate a sensation through the elements that constitute it.* (J.-L. Godard)[29]

This sequence consists of only five shots. It is descriptive and evocative rather than narratively functional. In some senses it tells us nothing. It is not the beginning of the story, it does not situate us, and, rather than introducing the main protagonist, it represents him by a pair of eyes, eyes that burn through the screen, intensely focused, but, as with the satanic Robert Helpmann in *The Tales of Hoffmann*, we cannot tell what sinister intentions are focused there.[30] But it works as a concise and effective introduction to the film, alerting us to several key elements. *Taxi Driver* will be about looking, framing, perspective; and as viewers we will not be given a clear vantage-point. In this coda we both see from someone's point of view (in the car, behind the wheel) and we see him seeing, but what he sees is out of focus, in slow motion, dissolving into abstraction. We are moved through space, through shots, but without a sense of continuity or destination. Somehow we are drawn very immediately into the experience of a vivid restlessness. Where *The Searchers* begins at the beginning, ostensibly, and frames the hero in a serenely composed long shot, *Taxi Driver* immerses us *in medias res* thrusting the hero upon us in extreme close-up. In fact it is not really *in medias res* (just as *The Searchers* does not really begin at the beginning), it is not a section of the story, not a narrative syntagm, but in suggesting a hero who searches (looking, restlessly looking, this way and that), and a restless moving around, *Taxi Driver* economically recapitulates concerns of *The Searchers* and simultaneously heralds its quite different *modus operandi*.[31]

> *There is a texture for torture, it builds through whiplash colour and speed of lights.* (Carolee Schneeman)[32]

There is a beauty that entices, but also a sense of incipient violence. The steam rising out of manholes hints at a rotting universe beneath the streets, a decay that is barely contained. I am apprehended by this opening, apprehensive and yet attracted by this 'glitter of putrescence'. Out of the past, from another genre, this phrase resonates. Near the beginning of *I Walked with a Zombie* the innocent heroine is warned that all that glitters is not human; on board the ship carrying her to the West Indies she is told that what awaits her will seem as the water through which they move – beautiful, glittering in the moonlight – but she should beware seduction, for what she sees is a 'glitter of putrescence'. The phrase is apt, and the echo is not, I think, entirely arbitrary. *I Walked with a Zombie* takes place mostly at night and unfolds as a tale of the living dead, of the vindictive 'resurrected'. 'I like looking at old Val Lewton films a lot,' Scorsese says, rattling off a list of Lewton films that include *I Walked With a Zombie*, *Cat People* and *Isle of the Dead*. 'I just like the look of them; they're so beautiful.'[33]

Travis Bickle is a kind of resurrected Ethan Edwards, but he is also a zombie-like figure who roams the streets by night. And he will not die; at the end he lives again and will be reborn in other Scorsese characterisations, most notably as Max Cady in *Cape Fear*. But it is not just characters who are reincarnated: ideas persist, questions that are not answered, anomalies that drive by night through a variety of cinematic landscapes.

Clean Like My Conscience

Putrescence, pollution, the impulse to purification: in the next five minutes of the film (during which we see Travis getting a job with a taxi company, driving around in his cab, and in his room writing in his diary) these concepts are vividly dramatised. When applying for the job Travis is asked about his driving record: 'It's clean like my conscience,' he says, smiling at the witticism. After the job interview there is a slow pan around his room – disordered, filthy, rotting leftover food, unmade camp bed, magazines strewn around – whilst his voice-over intones: 'May 10th. Thank God for the rain which has helped wash away the garbage and trash off the sidewalks.' The camera hovers momentarily on him writing and then cuts to the bumper of the cab gliding pneumatically past the neon sign for *Texas Chainsaw Massacre* and the flashing pink lights advertising *Fascination*. In the taxi's rear-view mirror, through the rain, the red light district is reflected. 'All the animals come out at night,' the voice-over continues, 'whores, skunks, pussies, buggers, queens, fairies, dopers, junkies ... sick, venal. Someday a real rain'll come and wash all this scum off the street.' The camera tilts down on the tarmac, propelled at speed, as though boring down into the road which is awash with rain and oil and the reflection of coloured lights. If it isn't rain, it's fire hoses, spraying the city, washing colours into each other, blurring boundaries, fudging focus. Arriving back at the rank Travis downs some pills and gets out of the cab to the accompaniment of his own voice: 'Each time I return the cab to the garage I have to clean the come off the back seat. Some nights I clean off the blood.'

Clearly Travis Bickle, from the beginning, is neurotic about filth, overly anxious about cleanliness, obsessed by various forms of excrescence, substances out of place (that is, pollution): garbage and trash on the sidewalks, come and blood in his taxi, 'animals' who come out at night. And all these excrescences cohere in the image of excrement – later he tells Palantine, the presidential candidate for whom Betsy works, 'This city here is like an open sewer, you know? Whoever becomes the President should just . . . really clean it up, you know what I mean? Sometimes I go out and smell it. I get headaches it's so bad, you know? So I think the President should just clean up the whole mess here, you know? Just flush it down the fuckin' toilet.' Travis's somewhat skewed perspective is emphasised in his first diary entry which signals a contradiction, between the chaos and filth of his own room and his obsession with the filth of New York City. If we assume that dirt and cleanliness are not absolute values, but relative, existing in a dynamic relation (culturally, historically, personally variable) then Travis's attitude here can be seen not as contradictory but as embodying a certain logic. Some anxiety, chaotic disturbance 'at home', is projected out, 'away' onto the city; some repressed fear is transformed into an excessive concern about pollution (later he will clean up his room and his act; he will take action). For Freud the obsession with cleanliness, the compulsion to wash, is one of the most basic manifestations of obsessive neurosis. In *Totem and Taboo* he argues that this neurosis has its origin in the taboo on touch and may be displaced onto a variety of compulsive acts in the form of expiation, penance, defensive measures and purification. He argues that 'the obsessional act is ostensibly a protection against the prohibited act; but actually in our view, it is a repetition of it'.[34] In other words, although washing, for instance, may seem like a protection against the contamination experienced in touching, in fact, in so far as it is compulsive and repetitive, it constitutes a form of enactment (of the very act – touching – which is prohibited but unconsciously desired). Obsessive behaviour defers closure through repetition of the same. The obsessive is caught in a cycle of repression and expiation: Jake La Motta plays out round after round in the boxing ring, Vicky dances, Ethan Edwards wanders between home and away...

Mary Douglas compares the cultural expression of pollution with Freud's account of the way jokes operate: 'The analogy is fair for pollution is like an inverted form of humour. It is not a joke for it does not amuse. But the structure of its symbolism uses comparison and double meaning like the structure of a joke.'[35] Travis Bickle is very taken with two unfunny jokes: 'clean like my conscience' and the reminder to get 'organisised'. If dirt is, as Douglas convincingly argues, matter out of place, in the wrong category, it is an expression of disorganisation. This is what Travis fears most. The signs of pollution exist most threateningly in the boundaries, along the lines of separation, in the interstices between categories (the pavement, for instance, and body orifices). If rubbish is in a rubbish heap it is in its proper place and has no power, but the indeterminacy of the marginal has the potential to evoke the fear associated with anomaly and ambivalence. From this perspective the filthy mess in Travis's room is circumscribed. The almost complete 360-degree pan underscores this: the dirt is contained within his room and therefore is not, to him, mess.

Not simply in its depiction of 'dirt' but in its noirish *mise en scène*, *Taxi Driver* registers the effects of pollution. The body of the film registers, in its *mise en scène*, the unconscious drives that propel it; in particular it enacts the pollution that results from the mixing of two very basic categories, night and day. Travis repeatedly says that he will go anywhere, any time, day or night, it makes no difference. Possessed by insomnia, by a disturbance of basic body rhythms, he is driven to keep moving, looking, restlessly circling.

> *Dance she did, and dance she must, over field and meadow, in rain and in sunshine, by night and by day.* ('The Red Shoes')

Initially Travis's phobia takes the form of a generalised detestation of filth and contamination. But soon he fixes on an objective, to become God's agent, to stand up: 'Here's a man who would not take it any more, a man who stood up against the scum, the cunts, the dogs, the filth, the shit, here is someone who stood up.'[36] Initially he thanks God for the rain, but soon he becomes the rain, the agent of cleansing and purification: 'I am God's lonely man.' His objective becomes even more focused, and dangerously psychotic, when he fixates on a single person – Sport – whom he invests with all the perilous powers of pollution and whom he constructs as a target to be erased, washed away, eliminated (after he abandons Palantine, his first target). He conceives of his murderous mission as an act of pious salvation. The relation between a generalised obsession with filth and the fixation on Sport is mediated by two women onto whom Travis projects his fears and desires concerning the dynamic between filth and cleanliness.

Betsy (Cybill Shepherd) is construed as pure, virginal, untouched. His voice-over anticipates her appearance (just as his desire conjures her up as a phantasm): 'She was wearing a white dress, she appeared like an angel out of this filthy mess.'

> 'All I had to do was wait . . . I used to sit there half asleep with the beer and the darkness, only that music from the movie next door kept jarring me awake. And then I saw her, coming out of the sun' – and then Jane Greer, dressed in white, enters the cafe and walks towards the camera, towards Robert Mitchum, towards us. (Out of the Past)

She floats into frame moving in slow motion through the city crowds; the camera follows her and his voice continues: 'She is alone. They cannot touch her.' At the end of the film she floats, disembodied in his rear-view mirror. Iris (Jodie Foster) is the perfect complement to Betsy in Travis's delusional system – she is the child whore who has been contaminated by her pimp Sport, and whom Travis undertakes to 'save'. The object of fixation generally provokes for the obsessive subject extremely ambivalent feelings (related to the phobia about touching and its origin in sexual touching) – affection and desire may mask feelings of hostility and indeed, in the psychotic, murderous impulses. When Betsy 'fails' him he hurls abuse at her: 'You're in hell and you're going to die in hell. Like the rest of them. You're like the rest of them.' Travis both desires to touch and has construed touching as a prohibited act and this contradiction is played out in relation to the two women. But it is played out primarily in relation to Sport, the women serving more of a mediating function. The ambivalence generates a tension that can possibly be contained by ordinary neurosis or by a delusional system that remains systematic – that is, maintains its own system of categories and boundaries. But the borderline between containment and explosion is extremely tenuous, as a reading of The Searchers implies and as Taxi Driver, in crossing the line, will act out in a spectacular display of cinematic psychosis. The relation between Travis and Sport, and its intersection between another pairing – Ethan and Scar – will return. For the moment (and as a foreshadowing) I want to look at the way in which the body is interpreted, acted on, deployed as a vehicle for the *acting out* of prohibited impulses.

A Cinema of Bodies: Men and Machines
The first body we see in Taxi Driver is that of the cab. The camera moves with this body, as though propelled by it; lovingly it details this body: the left front bumper, the driver's side window, hood, mirrors, isolated features that take up the entirety of the frame.[37] 'In Taxi Driver the two bodies of interest are De Niro's and the cab's . . . But which body is which?'[38] The invocation of cab as

body alerts us to the process of embodiment that Travis will be involved in, and to a relationship between the two bodies (of man and machine) that will be developed in a fairly complex series of mutations.

> *On the sound track there's loud rock'n'roll: 'Wind me Up'.*
> *A man is working on a bike, in pieces – shining chrome, chains,*
> *leather, oily gears, gleaming shafts and pipes. He begins to*
> *assemble the parts, to put the bike together, this fabrication*
> *intercut with images of wind-up toys and dinky motor cyclists.*
> *He dresses, leather over naked flesh, shiny spurs, belts, buckles*
> *and studs, skin tight blue denim, to Bobbie Vinton's crooning*
> *rendition of 'Blue Velvet'. (Scorpio Rising)*

'I once had a horse,' says Sport, 'she got hit by a car.' The transposition of the Western into a contemporary urban genre implies more than simply a replacement of the horse by the car; it involves the violence of collision. The car, rather curiously it might at first seem, also signals a concern with the body, particularly with the notion of machine-body. So though *The Searchers* prefigures *Taxi Driver* in many ways the concept of the machine-body is new. This new inflection can also be attributed to the different acting modes, or acting presences, of John Wayne and Robert De Niro. 'Like many viewers,' says James Naremore in *Acting in the Cinema*, 'I often have difficulty recalling or even registering the names of the dramatis personae in old Hollywood movies. For me at least, it is usually John Wayne getting on a horse, seldom the Ringo Kid or Ethan Edwards.'[39]

> *And he said to me one day at lunch at Lucy's, 'Look fella, just*
> *one thing I want to tell you. Don't ever touch me. Because you*
> *touch me I'll knock you down. I can't stand to have fellows*
> *touch me.' (Joseph Losey on John Wayne)[40]*

John Wayne acts as himself (which is quite different from saying that he does not act); he has a range of recognisable gestures and a predictable way of moving ('from stylised gesture to feeling'), a way of holding his body in reserve which is in total accord with the measured Fordian unravelling of repression. De Niro, on the other hand, uses his body not only to signify character but as a site of performative action; he conveys, across characters, a sense of acting through the body.

> *When Cassavetes says that characters must not come from a*
> *story or plot, but that the story should be secreted by the*
> *characters, he sums up the requirement of the cinema of bodies:*
> *the character is reduced to his own bodily attitudes, and what*
> *ought to result is the gest, that is, a 'spectacle', a theatricalisa-*
> *tion or dramatisation which is valid for all plots. (Deleuze)[41]*

Travis Bickle (Robert De Niro) secretes the story like pus from a wound.

Taxi Driver details Travis's bodily obsession at the same time as depicting the cab as though it were a body, and delineating a likeness between taxi and driver. Travis's attachment to his cab is reminiscent of forms of attachment engendered by the red shoes and the boxing gloves, but it doesn't function in quite the same way as an object of investment. The figure of the taxi driver mobilises an image of ambivalence: a precarious distinction between inside and outside, taxi and driver, man and machine. This uncertainty about where the body begins and ends echoes *The Red Shoes* and *Raging Bull*, but there isn't the same preoccupation with being possessed by the object. Rather, there is a gradual charting of a defensive process, of a shoring up of the body by turning it into a machine. *Taxi Driver* doesn't assert that the body *is* a machine (or conversely, that the machine *is* a body) but rather it unleashes the metaphor of the body as vehicle for the acting out of prohibited impulses, and explores the psychic and somatic mutations which this entails.

In his training, in his effort to organise, Travis constructs an extra-ordinary or extra-daily body. In the disciplinary regime he adopts, in the enactment of a variety of ritualistic and repetitive gestures, we can see that this process has much in common with processes of performance discussed in Chapter 1. *The Red Shoes* and *Raging Bull*, in their enactment of the struggle to contain, show that the line between the performance arena and the everyday is tenuous even when the body is circumscribed and contained by a sanctioned arena of performance. In *Taxi Driver* confusion between the performance arena and the everyday amounts to ritualised psychosis; the horror here is that the extra-ordinary body is so ordinary.

Getting Organisised

When he is rejected by Betsy, Travis gets sick. In his apartment the camera moves in a continuous slow pan over bunches of flowers returned by her. At first we see beautiful extravagant bouquets but by the end of the shot the camera has revealed wilted, dried and rotting blossoms. The diary speaks: 'The smell of the flowers only made me sicker. My headaches got worse. I think I got stomach cancer. I shouldn't complain though. You're only as healthy . . . you're only as healthy as you feel.' After he encounters the man who tells him what a ·44 Magnum will do to a woman's pussy, Travis starts getting 'organisised' with a vengeance. He starts work on the body. It is as though he is compelled now to clean up his 'sick' body, to bring it into line with his 'clean conscience'. So begins the regimented training and the cleaning and tidying up, the sorting into categories, making sure that there is no dirt or sickness, no matter out of place. Yet the word that so tickles Travis's fancy inscribes a repetition: organisised – isis, a redundancy, something out of place. As his obsession grows, becomes pathological, Travis is doomed to a repetitive stutter, to repeat his own delusional system

The sequence where Travis begins to clean up his 'act' is worth describing in some detail since it traces out his transfiguration, the ritualistic modification of the 'docile' body into a machine body. There are five segments (corresponding to different actions) which make up the 'getting organisised' sequence:

buying the guns, working out, practising in the shooting gallery, watching porn movies, rehearsing the showdown. In the first segment Easy Andy, the gun dealer, lays out his wares on a bed in a motel room and offers a highly entertaining sales rap. During a lull in Andy's patter – only muffled sounds from the street and a loud ticking can be heard – the camera pans in close-up over the guns. Travis touches, picks up, handles, points the various guns and ends up buying the entire arsenal. Cut from this segment to a jarring frontal shot of him, naked from the waist up, doing press-ups. This initiates a series of discontinuous views incorporating abrupt changes of angle and focal length. From above: a long ugly scar cuts across his back.

A kind of scar has been formed in the shape of piety.

Over shots of him lifting weights and doing pull-ups his diary voice narrates: 'I got to get in shape now. Too much sitting has ruined my body. Too much abuse has gone on for too long. From now on fifty push-ups each morning.' The segment ends with a mid-shot of Travis in profile as he stands by a gas cooker, his fist clenched over the flame, the muscles and veins in his arm swollen, protruding (reminiscent of the scene in *Mean Streets* where Charlie holds his hand over a flame). 'Fifty pull-ups.' The camera begins to move in and around him as he unclenches and clenches again his fist. 'There'll be no more pills. No more bad food, no more destroyers of my body. From now on there'll be total organisation. Every muscle must be tight.' The third segment consists of a fast montage of shots showing Travis at the gun range firing round after round of ammunition straight out of the frame, at us. The segment opens with a long shot zooming in, and it ends on a close-up of him firing. In the next (single-shot) segment he is in a film theatre, lounging back in comfort, around him a red sea of seats, and on the soundtrack the moans and phatic utterances of a blue movie. He lifts his finger, takes aim and points in the direction of the screen and then in a continuous movement brings his hand/gun to his face, makes a frame around his eye, then points again. In the last segment in this sequence Travis is shown again in his apartment (which is now clean, neat, sparse, like a military cell, or a monk's), assembling the arsenal on his body and rehearsing his quick draws in front of the mirror. On the soundtrack, just as in the opening segment, there are only muffled street sounds and a loud ticking. Could it be the cab meter ticking over? Or a clockwork device (Travis is well and truly wound up) or an internal time bomb?

The first segment details guns, machines, killing machines; the second details the body and its disciplining; the third puts into practice the material of the first segment (target practice); the fourth puts into practice the material of the second segment: the disciplined extra-ordinary body is alert and prepared, ready to take aim and fire any place, any time, in the ordinary everyday world; the final segment brings together the elements introduced initially – machines and body – presenting the trained body-as-machine. Significantly, the yellow cab is absent from these shots, but its presence is evoked through the ticking and through the method of montage (the taxi meter comes to figure more and more in the film, along with traffic lights, in repeated flashes of montage). The sequence is reminiscent of *Scorpio Rising*, of the bikers dressing themselves and assembling their bikes in preparation for the death drive. Like the bikers the driver is becoming one with his machine; he is a finely tuned driven machine.

Travis's attempt to make his body whole, to impose 'total organisation', can be seen as a way of making the body impregnable, untouchable (untouched by the pain of the flame burning), and water (or fluid) tight. Every muscle must be tight; there can be no softness or liquid oozing, no possibility of pollution. If it is in the interstices between categories that the dangerous signs of pollution are made manifest, and if body orifices and the skin itself (a thin membrane separating inside from outside) are particularly dangerous because they introduce anomaly, then the anomalous must be eradicated, and separations clearly defined. A key to the nature of Travis's anxieties is given early in the film, in a sequence already discussed, where he talks of having to wipe come and blood off the back seat of his taxi. For Travis both are pollutants, definitely matter out of place in his cab, but more than this they seem to represent a besmirching of his own body. They are associated because they both involve a spilling, a rupturing of the division between inside and outside, but also because they coalesce around the sexual. In *Mean Streets* Charlie has a dream that prefigures Travis's anxiety, he dreams he 'comes' blood. The association between 'coming' and the shedding of blood suggests an original guilt about sex so that sex is associated with wounding. In making himself inviolable, in sealing up the cracks, Travis projects his own 'dirt' onto others, and as his obsession becomes psychotic he transforms his own semen into others' blood. This conversion of semen (his own, representing the forbidden desire to touch) into the blood of others (which he spills) corresponds to the transforming of the material fleshy body containing fluids – semen and blood – into a killing machine-body.

> *My Brain is a scar. I want to be a machine. Arms for grabbing legs to walk on, no pain no thoughts.*
> (Heiner Muller)[42]

Foucault discusses regimes of discipline and training that transform the 'docile body' into a machine body. 'A body is docile that may be subjected, used, transformed and improved'[43] and the process of transformation involves an overarching attention to detail, to the construction of the body as a surface, lacking in interiority, machine-like in its functioning. He uses the classic example of a soldier, who, through regimentation and training, not only becomes part of a greater mechanism (the fighting machine), but tunes his body as one. As an ex-Marine Travis is no stranger to such regimes, but there is an added dimension in that his subjugation of the body is self-imposed, the degree of repression involved gestures towards a struggle for containment that isn't entirely successful; Travis almost becomes all surface, but not quite: crossing the surface of his skin there is a scar that indicates not only the assumption of piety, but also an exchange between inside and outside (and home and away) that isn't entirely resolved.

The Terminator *needs to make repairs to his body. The organically grown flesh that conceals the machine is wounded and rotting. Standing in front of the mirror he inserts a scalpel into his eye socket and begins repairs. Through the bloody meat: a gleam of metal. This is the first glimpse of the 'real' machine that lies beneath the skin, but is also coterminous with the surface of the body.*

Thou Shalt Not Touch

The scene in the porn movie house is pivotal. It is within this coterminous terrain – of substance and surface, of machine and body – that the visual trope of finger-as-gun operates. 'A well-disciplined body forms the operational context of the slightest gesture,' writes Foucault.[44] Travis takes aim and points his finger at the screen, a highly stylised gesture enacted with all the deadly efficiency of a 'real' shooting. What is significant here is not the substitution of finger for gun (and/or penis) but the evocation of a continuous surface linking machine and body.[45] In his desperate effort to organise, to redraw the boundary lines, Travis reduces the distinction between machine and body. The ritualistic performance of the gesture, emphasising the looking and taking aim (a continuity too between cinephilia and killing), confirms the deadly coherence of his delusional world. On one level 'pointing the finger' is an act of accusation and projection – it locates the blame somewhere else, on an other body. It is also an act of mimicry, a miming of killing, a performatively phatic act. But for Travis, as his obsessive transforming of the body progresses, the phatic becomes invested with deadly effect. The deadliness of this effect can best be understood in relation to the targeting involved in fixation. We do not see the object that Travis is aiming at, just as we do not see his target in the shooting gallery, and this is because in some important and deadly sense the object is not important. The object exists as a way of focusing a fixation.[46] Travis fixates on Sport and as a target he matters. It matters that he is hit, but someone else could have served the purpose just as easily and that someone is not necessarily an obvious enemy. It could be anyone or anything encountered in the daily round (driving around, picking up passengers, talking to the other cabbies at the Bellmore Café, going to porn movies); and it could be an image on a screen. Just as the object in and of itself is not significant, so, in this delusional system, the distinction between the finger and the gun, between the body and machine, is not significant – the pointed finger is deadly.

But it is not terminal, it is repetitive. This is conveyed in the gesture where Travis, bathed in blood and surrounded by slaughtered corpses, raises a finger to his temple and pulls the imaginary trigger three times. What is signified here is not his desire to kill himself but his belief that he is untouchable and his compulsion to repeat a murderous gesture. Of course he does not kill himself (or anyone else) just by pointing the finger, but this gesture is coterminous with the gesture of aiming and pulling the trigger on a 'real' gun. He will rise to kill again. Travis, like Ethan Edwards, is 'obliged to reproduce the struggle and the taboo resulting from it'. The pointed finger is the perfect admonition of the obsessive: 'Thou shalt not touch'.

So, although Travis is propelled by 'psychic torment where energy erupts corrosively and wildly in proportion to its own constraint',[47] the explosion of violence signals not the end, but a repetition. The ending of the film, then, in which Travis lives and is hailed as a hero and which has provoked perplexity and criticism, is perfectly consistent with a certain demented and terrifying logic. The finger is both 'just a finger' and therefore doesn't kill, and 'absolutely a gun', because the gesture signals both the compulsive repetition of obsession and a continuity between machine and body that means Travis will be resurrected to continue in his deadly dementia.[48]

You Speak Good Comanch, Somebody Teach You?

A man is shaving. He begins to cut himself, and continues shaving and cutting, so that by the end of the film there are great quantities of blood on his face and on the screen. His shaving is performed to the sound of Bunny Berigan playing 'I Can't Get Started'. It ends with the title, 'Viet 67'.

There is an obvious irony here in *The Big Shave*, a six-minute short made by Scorsese in 1967. The man's problem is not that he can't get started, but that he can't stop. Like the US military presence in Vietnam, like Ethan Edwards, like Travis Bickle. But as well as this obvious irony there is a sense of the repetitive gesture that prohibits the obsessive from moving on, a self-immersion in blood.

Both Ethan Edwards and Travis Bickle have returned from war, having fought on the losing or retreating side. For both of them the dividing line between war and peace is a wavering line. Ethan returns from the Civil War still wearing his Confederate coat and carrying his sabre ('Didn't turn it into no ploughshare neither'). Travis is a mixture of urban cowboy and Vietnam vet – he wears rider jeans, cowboy boots, a plaid Western shirt and a worn beige army jacket with a patch reading 'King Kong Company, 1968–70'. When Ethan arrives home in 1868 the war has been over for three years. What has he been doing during this time? Where did he come by the newly minted money he carries? 'You wanted for a crime, Ethan?' the Reverend asks. Travis has been restlessly roaming the city at night, insomniacal.

The Searchers and *Taxi Driver* both map out a milieu where criminality and the law are intricately, if uncomfortably, entwined. This is of course a common feature of the movies, particularly Hollywood. What is peculiar to these two films is the way the vigilante element emerges, slowly, obsessively building, and the way this is developed through the hero's racial and sexual fixations. Ethan Edwards is arrested for shooting a man in the back and taking his money. But shortly after the arrest is made Clayton returns Ethan's gun and appoints him a civilian scout so that he can join the posse setting out, yet again, in pursuit of Scar. The first time Travis approaches Sport he takes Travis for a cop: 'Oh Officer . . . I'm clean, man.' They are standing on the street, Sport in his doorway; next to them, on the pavement, an overflowing rubbish bin.

Travis: I'm not a cop.
Sport: Then why you asking me for action?

Travis: 'Cos she sent me.
Sport: I suppose that ain't a ·38 you got in your sock?
Travis (hitches his jeans over his ankles, patting his boots): I'm clean man.
Sport: You're a real cowboy man, that's nice.

Cowboys and the Law, here, are interchangeable. And in *The Searchers* too. In a landscape covered in snow Ethan shoots in a demented manner at a herd of buffalo: 'They won't feed any Comanche this winter.' Over his gunshots we hear the sound of bugles, heralding the arrival, with their Indian hostages, of the US Cavalry. Shortly after this Martin and Ethan arrive at the Indian camp, which has been utterly decimated, burnt to the ground by the cavalry. The aftermath of massacre.

Cowboys and Indians: another distinction which becomes blurred, though in this instance the categories are not exactly interchangeable. The 'Indian' in both cases becomes, via the 'cowboy's' projection, a locus of pollution. In *The Searchers* the issue of race is foregrounded; the prohibition on touch that propels Ethan Edwards is mediated through an entwining of race and sex.[49] Touch is dangerous because it involves the possibility of contagion and transference; for Ethan the Indian 'other' becomes the locus of pollution, and the white girl is seen to be contaminated by his touch. In *Taxi Driver* the racial issue is more dispersed, but no less germane. In his commentary on the film on laserdisc Scorsese reveals that Sport was originally conceived of as black, and it is worth remembering that the Motion Picture Production Code of 1930 stated that 'miscegenation (sex relationship between the white and black races) is forbidden'.[50] Travis is driven by an abhorrence of all that is other: skunks, whores, pussies, and so on; all that radiates the power of pollution, but there are a number of quite specific assaults on non-whites. There is the black youth Travis shoots in the hold-up in the supermarket; on television there are the black couples dancing on Bandstand whom he aims his gun at; but most of all there is the decisive encounter with the psychotic passenger who talks about taking a ·44 Magnum to his wife's pussy because she is with a 'nigger' (it is after this incident that Travis buys a Magnum, even though, or because, he is told by Easy Andy that 'they use that in Africa to kill elephants').[51]

Though Ethan and Travis are driven by a vehement hatred of Scar and Sport, both films trace out a network of similarities, a kind of cinematic scar tissue that stretches, extends over the continuity of the celluloid surface. Just as the Western hero restlessly roams and circles the vastness of the desert landscape, wandering forever, surfacing eventually in the compressed immensity of New York City. For all his disparagement of the Indians, Ethan has somewhere learnt some language and lore. When they find the grave of a Comanche, Ethan shoots the dead man between the eyes so that he will never enter the spirit land and will have to 'wander forever between the winds'. He is able to identify another name – Noyaky – as indicating the presence of Scar: 'Not so strange when you think about what it means; "Noyaky", round about: man say he going one way, means to go another.' To describe the 'classic' scene, who better than J.R. (played by Harvey Keitel, who will later play the Scar figure in *Taxi Driver*):

J.R.: Oh there was one scene in that movie that was a classic, you know the, the chief of the tribe, his name is Cicatriz, Spanish for Scar you know, he talks English to John Wayne and Wayne says . . . 'Uh . . . You talk good English, somebody teach you?' but real nasty you know, and then when Wayne talks Comanch to – not Comanche but Comanch – to Scar, Scar says 'You talk good Comanch, somebody teach you?' you know, but . . .

Girl: Sounds like a nasty fella.

J.R.: Who?

Girl: Oh the, the man with the sc . . . , the Indian.

J.R.: Cicatriz.

Girl: Yes.

J.R.: Oh he was more nasty than Wayne could ever get, but then again he was a bad guy. There were a lot of nasty Comanches in that picture.

Girl: Nasty picture [they both laugh].

J.R.: Well then again John Wayne could get pretty nasty when he wanted to be.

Cowboys and Indians, good guys and bad guys: a blurring of boundaries. When Travis and Sport, in their first encounter, have made arrangements for the (temporary) exchange of Iris, Sport mimics an act of standard bravado from the cowboy repertoire: drops to a crouch, hands on hips, pulls and fires in a flash both guns. When Travis returns (for the kill) he exhibits an Indian insignia, a Mohawk cut (cut into/onto his body). Sport, who is wearing a bandana and waistcoat, tells him, 'Get back to your fuckin' tribe before you get hurt.'

Like Ethan, Travis conceives of his murderous mission as an act of pious salvation. He becomes obsessed with the idea that Iris has to be saved, and when she is bemused by his concern ('I think I understand. I tried to get into your cab one night. And now you want to come and take me away. Is that it?') he becomes fixated by the 'hold' that Sport has over her. He does not want to touch her, but he cannot abide the thought of Sport touching her. When she tells him 'Hey look, Sport never treated me bad, he didn't beat me up or anything like that once', Travis can only respond with invective: 'He is the lowest kind of person in the world. Somebody's gotta do something to him, he's the scum of the earth. He is the worst ssss–ucking scum I have ever . . . ever seen.' Ethan chokes on the image too: 'He will raise her till she's of an age to, to . . .'

In *The Searchers* Ethan's fantasy (of the sexual touching, of the contamination of the girl by the 'unclean' man) is never shown; we do not see Scar and Debbie together. *Taxi Driver*'s scriptwriter Paul Schrader has commented[52] on the scene where Sport and Iris dance together:

That's a reference to John Ford's *The Searchers*. I feel, and other people feel, that the one thing *The Searchers* lacks – and it is a great film – is a scene between Scar, the Comanche chief, and Natalie Wood, who's lived with him since she was kidnapped as a child. If Ford had had the guts to show that their life together had some meaning, it would have made the ending – when John Wayne 'rescues' her – bitterly sweet.

The withholding of this image in *The Searchers* seems to me acutely strategic: as an 'unspeakable' image, one of a series of such images in the film, its absence bears witness to the phantasmatic aspect of Ethan's revenge mission. In *Taxi Driver* Travis doesn't see what we see of Sport and Iris; in fact it is one of the few scenes from which he is absent, and curiously the effect is not dissimilar to that achieved in *The Searchers*. Whatever Travis's fantasy is, it isn't exactly this. As they turn very slowly in one another's arms the camera also revolves, very close, almost touching. It is a curious moment in the film for on one level it is, like Travis himself, repulsive. We are brought too close to Sport's sleazy manipulation of this twelve-year-old girl. We see him put on the record, his greasy hair, gaudy jewellery and garish coke fingernail, and we hear his guileful murmurings of love. But on another level there is something 'touching' about the scene, a tenderness that survives the set-up. It functions, I feel, to touch us with ambivalence, to immerse us in a dynamic – around touching – that is central to the film.

Certainly I am moved, by the intensity of this moment of tenderness, but by something else too. The sensation of sexual menace that emanates from this image is not easily separated from the desire for (and impossibility of) home as a safe refuge. The oscillation between home and away continues.

Coming to Grips With Ssss—ucking Scum

Travis, like Ethan, is driven by an impulse to rescue – to 'return home' – a girl who does not want to be saved. This pious impulse to save is deviously entwined with revenge; in assuming the role of avenging angel or vigilante Travis acts out, in a displaced way, a complex of prohibited desires. Though these (misrecognised) desires revolve round Iris, and Betsy, the ultimate figure of fixation is Sport.

Misrecognition culminates in the bloody massacre in which Travis kills Sport and several other men, but the massacre (and its devious determinations) is prefigured in a scene which is unexpectedly whimsical. When Iris realises that Travis seriously isn't into sex she agrees to have breakfast with him. In the 'breakfast scene' Iris, like a latterday Holly Golightly – Audrey Hepburn in *Breakfast at Tiffany's* – in her huge green sunglasses, prattles on about star signs and communes ('Not very clean' is Travis's comment), deflecting his accusation that Sport is a killer by asserting, 'He's a Libra.' Travis's interest in her is figured as paternal; he tells her she should be at home, going to school, to which she responds: 'I don't want to go back to my parents. They hate me. Why do you think I split in the first place . . . didn't you ever hear of women's lib?' It's an engaging scene, like the exchange between J.R. and the Girl, but there is an ominously mordant undercurrent, an eddy of perversion when Travis chokes on the word sucking – 'He is the lowest kind of person in the world. Somebody's gotta do something to him, he's the scum of the earth. He is the worst ssss—ucking scum I have ever . . . ever seen.' Inscribed in the paternal is sexual jealousy and abhorrence, and in the abhorrence a perverse desire. The perversion is not in the element of homosexual desire, or desire of the same, but in the way that this is mediated by repression into a particularly violent acting out. *Mean Streets* and *Raging Bull* also elaborate this dynamic of repression and desire, epitomised in La Motta's comment about 'pretty face' Janiro: 'Don't know whether to fuck him or fight him.'

> *If we ask ourselves why the avoidance of touching, contact or contagion should play such a large part in this neurosis [obsessional neurosis] and should become the subject-matter of complicated systems, the answer is that touching and physical contact are the immediate aim of the aggressive as well as the loving object-cathexes. Eros desires contact because it strives to make the ego and the loved object one, to abolish all spatial barriers between them. But destructiveness, too, which (before the invention of long-range weapons) could only take effect at close quarters, must presuppose physical contact, a coming to grips.* (Freud)[53]

Sport is the figure onto whom Travis projects all the desires and fears that he disavows, and so Sport himself has to be disavowed, wiped out, erased. Like Scar, Sport has what the hero lacks, not just the girl, but perceived sexual power. In a lethally castrating gesture, Travis, like Ethan, can take his place and take possession of his woman. *Taxi Driver*, however, makes much more of the hero's unconscious desire, or brings it closer to the consciousness of the film, for the 'other' (rendered as a curious inversion of the same). When Travis takes his money out Sport throws his hands up and stops him: 'Hey, don't take out no money here. You wanna fuck me? You're not gonna fuck me, you're gonna fuck her, give her the money.' The later film also makes more of the anxiety about the body, about the fear of contagion (and concomitant desire for the prohibited exchange, touching of surfaces and fluids), about the boundaries between inside and out, night and day, blood and come. Travis translates 'come' into 'blood'. When he says 'suck on this' (sticking his gun in Sport's stomach and firing) he implies: suck me and I will come (blood). Rather than wine, it is semen he turns into blood. At the same time as he touches and comes Travis enacts a disavowal: 'I have no body fluids, excreta, the blood is yours.' In making himself inviolable, sealing up the cracks, he projects his own 'dirt' onto others, transforms his own come into others' blood, opening up the body, bringing what is inside out, wounding.

Taxi Driver refigures the relationship between Ethan Edwards and Scar in terms that foreground the strong vigilante element (which runs through the Western and into more contemporary genres) and brings out the psychopathic tendencies within the vigilante impulse.

> *What is in question is fear of an infectious example, of the temptation to imitate, that is, of the contagious character of taboo. If one person succeeds in gratifying the repressed desire, the same desire is bound to be kindled in all the other members of the community. In order to keep the temptation down, the envied transgressor must be deprived of the fruit of his enterprise; and the punishment will not infrequently give those who carry it out an opportunity of committing the same outrage under colour of an act of expiation.*

> This is indeed one of the foundations of the human penal system
> and it is based, no doubt correctly, on the assumption that the
> prohibited impulses are present alike in the criminal and in the
> avenging community. In this psycho-analysis is no more than
> confirming the habitual pronouncement of the pious: we are all
> miserable sinners. (Freud)[54]

'*Taxi Driver* was another vigilante film,' writes Joan Mellen:[55]

> The ostensible justification of [Travis's] sick behaviour is his desire to res-
> cue a twelve-year-old whore from her pimp, permitting director Martin
> Scorsese and screen writer Paul Schrader to wallow in one more neo-fascist
> depiction of the poor and disadvantaged as vermin . . . If we know what is
> good for us, argues one vigilante film after another, we will place our trust,
> and our very selves, in the hands of the angry avenger, the authoritarian,
> ever-violent male.

She is very concerned to distance herself from this 'sick behaviour', to assert a
critically healthy position. Yet it seems to me that something other than neofas-
cist wallowing is going on. Scorsese, learning from Ford, manages a brilliant
manoeuvre: he renders Travis Bickle as psychopath, weaving a complex imagery
of glittering putrescence, invoking a delusional world structured according to a
dynamic of filth and purity, sickness and health; he exhibits this, and yet he immerses us within it. The film beguiles, coaxing our own prohibited impulses into action, invoking our viewing presence as both criminal and avenging community.[56]

Delayed Reflection

> It's as if the process of film-making becomes an accessory to the crime
> and makes us all feel guilty. (Scorsese)[57]

Us all: not just the film-maker, but the spectator too. In *Taxi Driver*, as in
Michael Powell's *Peeping Tom* (1960), looking and killing are closely connected. When he's not driving his taxi, looking in his rear-view mirror, Travis
watches movies (like us), or prepares for killing, or kills. For him, however,
'going to the movies' means going to porn theatres. Pornography *is* the movies; he is not aware of film theatres beyond 42nd Street (so when he asks Betsy
out on a date he takes her as a matter of course to a porn movie and is sur-
prised to be given the brush-off). So perhaps it is only the look at pornography
that is associated with killing, not 'normal' viewing. But then *Taxi Driver* itself
has often been described as something akin to porn and *Peeping Tom* was received in 1960 as 'crude sensational exploitation' and described with all the
vituperative righteousness of a Travis Bickle: 'The only really satisfactory way
to dispose of *Peeping Tom* would be to shovel it up and flush it swiftly down
the nearest sewer.'[58]

I remember it [Peeping Tom] opening in 1962 . . . in . . . a neighbourhood
where you really had to be armed to see the film . . . Being a New Yorker,
I didn't risk it . . . . . . When I moved to California in 1970 . . . I saw it for
the first time, complete and in color. The next time I saw it was in 1973,
on the day that John Ford died. (Scorsese)[59]

When they find the grave of a Comanche Ethan shoots the dead man between
the eyes so that he will never enter the spirit land and will have to 'wander
forever between the winds'. This action inscribes his own fate: the restless
searching is posited on a fundamental misrecognition or blindness. In *Taxi
Driver* this zombie-like wandering continues as Travis drives all over New
York City, by day and by night, looking.

*She wanders all over New York City, on foot and by taxi, looking, secretly
watching him, spying, following him by night and by day. From porno
shops and live sex shows to motels to the Fulton Fish Market, Yankee
Stadium, the Staten Island Ferry and the Jersey Shore. Watching and
listening. (Bette Gordon, Variety)*

Taxi Driver is not primarily about spectatorship, about the cinema, in the way
that it can be said of *Peeping Tom* that it 'sets out with astonishing candor and
clarity a psychosexual theory of cinematic spectatorship'.[60] Nor does it exactly
correspond to Kaja Silverman's description of *Peeping Tom* as giving new
emphasis to the concept of reflexivity: 'Not only does it foreground the work-
ings of the apparatus, and the place given there to voyeurism and sadism, but
its remarkable structure suggests that dominant cinema is indeed a cinema
with a delayed reflection.'[61] But since so much is made in the film of the activity
of looking, of the place of pornography, of connections between the gaze and
acts of violence, I want for a moment to look back, cast an eye in the rear-view
mirror as it were, to see how some of the issues touched upon in the chapter
connect with the question of spectatorship.

*Oh wait a minute, was that the picture where Jeffrey Hunter is supposed to
be trading Indian rugs and he winds up trading for an Indian bride, and he
doesn't know what to do with her?*

When at last she remembers *The Searchers* it is by recalling an odd detail, a
comic interlude seemingly inessential to the central drama. They remember
differently, J.R. and the Girl, but if attention is paid to who remembers what,
and how, we might infer that she recognises something to which J.R. is blind.
The incident of the Indian bride involves not only an exchange of women (an
exchange between men, where women, or more specifically Indian women,
are equivalent to blankets) but is also produced out of linguistic and auditory
misrecognition or mishearing. The mistake arises because Martin does not
speak the language of the Indian people with whom he is trading, so somehow
there is a confusion between 'woman' and 'blanket'. Once the misunderstand-
ing becomes apparent it cannot be easily put right; on the contrary, it is man-
ifestly a mistake that can only be further confounded. The woman is called

'Look', or rather she acquires the name when listening to Martin, in an incomprehensible language trying to explain that he doesn't want a wife, that it's all a mistake. Trying to make her see he repeats himself: 'Look! . . . look!' She thinks he is giving her a name, and so she echoes and returns to him (and to Ethan, who has been complicit with the initial mistake) the sound of his voice, 'Look!' Look is (matter) out of place; he doesn't know what to do with her and nor does the film, so she disappears fast enough, killed by the cavalry. But she persists as a reminder of the untouchable other, the white male prohibition: Look, but don't touch! Martin looks and sees something, but Ethan, fixated on the original unspeakable sight, cannot hear or see. Look, at best a shadowy troubling presence, fades fast, but she does not fade entirely. As a shadow of remembrance she persists, in the interstices between films, a reminder that cinematic sight is sounded, touched.

So perhaps it is not by chance that it is this episode that the Girl recalls. J.R. cannot heed the memory. Travis will look, relentlessly, but he inherits Ethan's perniciously intractable memory; what he sees is not what 'Look' invokes. *Taxi Driver* nevertheless reminds us of this Look, circles round it, as does *Peeping Tom*. And *Variety* (Bette Gordon, 1983) heeds the memory, recalling the earlier films, replaying differently, seeing – perhaps – something else. Christine traverses the city, looking, secretly watching; from porno shops to Yankee Stadium to the fish markets she follows. She gets a job as a ticket-seller at a porno movie theatre called Variety and becomes fascinated by one of the customers, who may be involved in some Mafia-like enterprise. But equally he may not be. Her fantasy life becomes progressively more elaborate and variable, her desires intersecting with the porn that surrounds her. She looks like a man (looks), but what does she see?

'What do you want to see? *The Unseen?*' (Christine, selling tickets).

Mark, in *Peeping Tom*, works as a focus-puller in the film industry but also takes pictures for a porn magazine. He is very attached to his camera, carries it with him always and is visibly distressed if separated from it. He kills his female victims while filming them and forcing them to 'see' their own fear. A sharpened stiletto, attached to the tripod leg, shoots out to pierce the victim in the throat while a mirror, mounted on the camera, reflects back at her an image of her face in the moment of death. But we do not know this until the end of the film. What we do know is that Mark, as well as projecting and watching these (silent) murderous images, projects and watches the silent black-and-white documentary film that his father had taken of him as a child. A psychologist studying the effects of fear on the nervous system, the father used Mark as his prime exhibit, subjecting him to a variety of torturous experiments so that he could film the results. We see some of this film, and we see the film that Mark has shot of the women he kills, and we also see his victims through the camera (in the cross-hairs of the lens, like looking through a gun). But we do not see the camera with its extensions – mirror and sharpened stiletto – until he kills himself by duplicating his 'normal' procedures, except that this time he is both film-maker and victim. In order to achieve this he has to separate momentarily from his camera, only to be ultimately reunited or impaled.

In *Peeping Tom* the camera is an extension of Mark's body; as Travis becomes a machine-body so Mark is figured as a camera-body. If Travis's arsenal of weapons and his murderous violence are a way of touching by not-touching, of 'coming to grips' through the use of long-range weapons, Mark's camera is a kind of close-range weapon. By incorporating the murder weapon in the camera as a spike he ensures a tangible connection to the victim, a material through-line between his eye and her throat. Between Travis's machine-body and Mark's camera-body there is a certain continuity, which can be traced out through the motif of the (camera) eye and the mirror. In *Taxi Driver* it is the rear-view mirror that features and frames all mirror images, that introduces the idea of projection.

Before we see Travis we see his eyes, in close-up, washed by the reflection of city lights, bathed in a red filter, framed by the rear-view mirror. At home he performs, and talks, in front of the mirror. While driving he is constantly looking in his rear-view mirror, not just at traffic but to gain an illicit perspective on passengers in the back seat (in that place where blood and come are spilled). The camera is characteristically situated behind his head, the rear-view mirror cutting out his eyes or sometimes just one eye, isolating his gaze, providing a frame within the frame. When he buys a ticket at the porno theatre we see the projectionist (who doubles as ticket-taker) keeping an eye on the movie by watching the rear-view mirror attached to the projector. Via this mirror Travis is aligned with the projectionist, specifically with the projectionist of pornography. The emphasis here falls on the activity of projection. The pornographic exists not in images *per se* but in modes of engagement. Of course it is not by chance that Travis patronises porn palaces exclusively, but the violence he unleashes is not necessarily derived directly from what he sees, nor indeed is it to be exhaustively explained in terms of scopophilia. Projection is about imagining as much as it is about looking, and Travis's imagination represents a particularly psychotic inflection of the pornographic. The film spectator (not just the porn-goer) also projects – that is to say, film viewing involves the projection of phantasmatic scenarios onto the screen. The mirror doesn't just reflect; it is a surface that registers projection. This applies to the mirror on Mark's camera, the mirror that Christine dresses up for in her porn outfits, and the mirror in Travis's apartment. But it is epitomised in the rear-view mirror: an image is thrown over one's shoulder, it seems to come from elsewhere, yet onto the screen the viewer projects a phantasmatic scenario.

A key scene in this respect is the encounter with the passenger played by Scorsese himself, a 'glitteringly morbid role'.[62] He instructs Travis to park by the kerb and leave the meter ticking; he just wants to sit and look – at a lighted window on the seventh floor where the silhouette of a woman can be seen. 'Do you see the woman in the window?' he asks.[63] Edgy, paranoid, sinister, he delivers a long monologue which elicits Travis's attention as listener and witness, but refuses him a voice. Constantly asking questions, the passenger repeatedly says, 'Don't answer.' The sequence is composed mainly of frontal shots of Travis, of the passenger, or of both of them, combined with shots over Travis's shoulder in which he can be seen adjusting and looking into his rear-view mirror. His gaze only slides away, following directions, in order to crane up to the lighted window. The man is insistent that Travis should 'see' what a ·44 Magnum pistol can do: 'Now did you ever see what it could do to a woman's pussy? That you should see, that you should see what a ·44 Magnum's gonna do to a woman's pussy you should see.' What is it that Travis sees in his rear-view mirror? Is he simply keeping an eye on his passenger or is he in fact seeing what the man describes? He is seeing in his driving mirror a projection, a phantasmatic scenario projected over his shoulder onto the screen before his eyes. The sound effects are integral to the production and registering of the image. The narrating voice complements the sounds of porn, the phatic moans and groans and yes-yes-yeses and more-more-mores that we hear in the porn movie episodes – it is the story element that here incites the look – 'You should see.' When Travis, not long after this, 'fingers' the screen in the porn theatre (the image unseen by us) he points a ·44 Magnum and he 'sees' what it can do.

> *You make the move. You make the move. It's your move . . .Try it, you . . .*
> *You talkin' to me? Well, who the hell else are you talkin' to? . . . You talkin'*
> *to me? Well, I'm the only one here. Who the fuck do you think you're*
> *talkin' to?*

He interpellates you (and me): it's your move. If we are moved (through a rippling series of identifications) we also activate motion; projection is never motionless.

Taxi Driver delineates a particular kind of pornographic imagination and the circumstances of projection that invoke violence. In so doing it develops a meditation on the violence of projection. Projection, it seems to me, is not intrinsically violent and neither is the film-making process; but it does incorporate a dangerous potential and it is in perturbation of this potential that *Taxi Driver* enlists us as 'accessories to the crime'. It is not because we are positioned, in a neo-fascist cinematic manoeuvre, to share Travis's point of view.

Taxi Driver journeys over a precarious terrain where sexuality and violence intermesh. It is not, I think, primarily or exclusively about the female image and its violent suppression by the cinematic apparatus. The obsession (and there is a compulsive obsession enacted and not merely depicted by the film) is with inconceivable sexuality perversely imagined as masculinity incarnate. The feminine, however, is not absent. Travis does not use his ·44 Magnum to enact the fantastic story told by the passenger; he does not use the gun on women. But this is not to say that what he sees when he uses it is not the image of a woman's vagina blown apart (the unspeakable image that Ethan Edwards will not let Martin see). Equally, though, he might see another unseen: the 'nigger' – sucking, exploding. The point is that, in a displaced way, the image projected in the rear-view mirror during this encounter persists, is inscribed in the view of Betsy – drifting, disembodied, blonde hair floating like a halo, in the driving mirror at the end of the film. This is a lethally violent pornographic image, epitomising the violence of projection and deadly affectivity of fantasy. It tells a story of the perversion of touch.

But there are other stories. Stories of the entwining of sight, sound, and touch.

> *Other story . . . other story . . . other . . . other story . . . story stories . . .*
> *smooth . . . smooth stories . . . smooth skin smooth sss . . .*
> *smooth black slip . . . against her skin . . .*

Christine's boyfriend is telling her, while they sit in the car eating Chinese take-away, about the investigative story he is doing on union corruption in the fish markets. 'But that's a whole other story,' he says. 'Other story,' says Christine, as though dreaming, following a train of word associations, 'other story . . .' As she begins to 'picture' her fantasy the words flow more fluently. The boy-friend listens in silence and then interrupts violently, outraged by her voicing. Later, when she narrates another fantastic scenario he ignores her, is mute.

Take Me to Your Cinema

> *Don't be a silly boy, there's nothing to be afraid of.*
> *Goodnight Daddy. Hold my hand.* (Peeping Tom)

'All this filming is not healthy': this is the line that people usually remember, but the person who speaks these words to Mark (the blind woman, Mrs Stephens) is alerted to his activities by the sound and sensations of projection. 'Every night you switch on that machine. What are these films you can't wait to look at? What's the film you're looking at now?' By 'filming' she means the whole film-making process, incorporating screening and spectatorship. 'I feel at home here. I visit this room every night. The blind always live in the rooms they live under.' She knows, not because she touches in place of looking, but because of what she hears living in the room under Mark's cinema. She is able to fill the space, to make it tactile, through hearing. It is not the soundtrack of the films that she hears (both his documentary and his father's are silent), but the repetitive, ritualistic bodily enactments. She senses the camera-body. 'Take me to your cinema,' she says. He projects the footage of one of his murder victims, capturing both himself and Mrs Stephens in the projected beam of light. She, however, extricates herself from the image and from the 'cinema' more successfully than Esther Blodgett (who will become a star and pay a price). This is where she says, 'All this filming is not healthy.' She tells Mark to get help, and as she leaves she touches his face, feeling his image. 'Taking my picture?' he asks. 'It's a long time since anyone did that' – thus summoning a memory of the dead father who filmed his son obsessively.

A stab of recognition, an iconic ghosting over the image, registered as an intimation of horror.

The father's method of scientific torture is epitomised in the scene where he shines a flashlight on the child Mark, in bed terrified by a lizard, let loose in order to provoke a reaction of fear. Mark as an adult is compelled to repeat what Carol Clover calls the 'assaultive gaze', but he also enacts the 'reactive gaze',[64] identifying with his own childlike position when projecting his father's documentaries, and identifying with the image of his murder victims when he projects his own film. We are also given the perspectives of the two women in the house – Mrs Stephens and her daughter Helen, with whom Mark develops an intense friendship or precariously platonic romance. Helen is the one wom-an who escapes Mark's murderous mirror, and Kaja Silverman sees her as 'possessed by the desire to understand the ways in which male subjectivity has

67

been organised. She continues going to the cinema, because she knows the symptoms she is looking for are there, and in the darkened theatre she never removes her eyes from the images.'[65] I tend to think that the reason Helen escapes is, as Linda Williams points out, 'simply a result of her status as a non-sexual "good girl"', in other words, she is a generically predictable element of the horror film.[66] Laleen Jayamanne shifts the focus somewhat by contrasting the two modes of spectatorship represented by the mother and daughter, modes that are linked to their voices (tone, pitch, timbre).[67] Like her I find the daughter's epistemophilia unappealing in its prodding insistence (she prods physically as well as figuratively). Helen's voice is the voice of the child always asking questions, wanting to know more, wanting to find out the ending. She is lethally naive. 'It's just a film isn't it?' she beseeches or declares at the end. 'No. I killed her.' It is true that up until this point she has tried to placate Mark, to mother and calm him, but her efforts are reminiscent of the Wizard's (Peter Boyle) response to Travis when the latter asks for help: 'Relax Killer, you're gonna be alright.'

In contrast, Mrs Stephens knows what she's in for when she says 'Take me to your cinema,' for she herself has projected into the space a scenario. She is no stranger to pain and fear, or knowledge imaginatively derived. 'Touch in this film functions as a way of knowing as varied as sight, which includes to look, to stare, to gaze, to glance, and much else.'[68] *Peeping Tom* does not invoke the maternal as a privileged site of touch, nor does it counterpose looking and touching. Rather, it elaborates the imbrication of touch with sight and sound in the cinematic experience. Touch is, as Jayamanne suggests, a form of cognition. Just as the misrecognition that drives Ethan Edwards is fundamentally bound up with touch, manifested in his ambivalent embrace of Debbie, so Mrs Stephen's cognition is anchored in the sense of touch, and we in turn are touched by the sounds and images we encounter in her cinema.

At the climax of the film Mark switches on a bank of audiotapes, sounds recorded by his father. Screams of fear fill the space of the cinema we inhabit. He triggers a timer which sets off a series of flash bulbs to explode at split-second intervals as he runs towards the camera, his image catapulting into the mirror, his body hurtling towards the tripod spoke. The reel on the projector which has been showing his film runs out and we see the blank screen and then darkness and over the darkness the last words of the film, a child's voice: 'Hold my hand.'

A startling affect: exploding flash bulbs, sounds like gunshots, flashes of light, the anticipation of flesh tearing. Just as in some of the fight sequences of *Raging Bull* I want to look away, I want to hold your hand. At the time I don't know exactly what I am doing or seeing, though there is a stirring of memory, an acute sensation of the imminence of death. On reflection I see more clearly: that the film exists only in the play of light and sound, exists only by virtue of the projector beam and a separate soundtrack. Projection is immaterial, and yet . . . And yet I feel the splintering of glass, the flashes . . .

> *There's nothing to be afraid of.*
> *Let's go home, Debbie.*
> *One day there'll be a knock at the door . . .*

Chapter 4

Cracking Up

*I could hear him out of the corner of my ear during takes, saying
'Oh God, that's awful.' He had to turn away to not look at the take,
because he'd be laughing.* (Griffin Dunne)[1]

Imagine a film that begins like this: there is a man who can't get a grip on things.
He opens the door to his analyst's office and steps onto a shiny, highly polished
floor. He slips, slides and slithers in all directions, desperately trying to regain his
footing. All he wants to do is reach the couch, lie back and tell his story. But his
body rebels – conspiring with a hostile and unstable environment, it propels him
into a chaotic trajectory. This sequence lasts about five slapstick minutes, during
which time the chaos escalates dramatically so that by the time he reaches the
couch we can hardly tell whether it is he or the furniture that careens, crashes,
disintegrates. By the end of the film this walking catastrophe, propelled by an
overwhelming death drive, is finally cured. But only in a manner of speaking: his
symptoms do not disappear; they are simply transferred from one body to another, from him to his analyst. In the end it is the analyst who appears as an embodiment of suicidal parapraxis.

In the end: what becomes of the viewer, the surrogate analyst, the some-
times-patient? Is it possible that we too, like Jerry Lewis, might be vicariously
cured, made whole, blessed with perfect co-ordination? Or is it just the beginning of a long process of contagion, of cracking up? Clearly *Cracking Up*
(a.k.a. *Smörgasbord*, Jerry Lewis, 1983) enacts a gleefully sadistic fantasy of
transference. The transference involved in analysis is conceived of as a slippery
affair, and in the spectacle of the patient who slips, slides and crashes we are
witness to a spectacular literalisation of the sliding signifier. However, we are
not there merely to witness: we are also implicated, lured into identification
and interpretation. Retrospectively we can see that this sliding signifier serves
to initiate a chain of hermeneutic delusion, from which we cannot escape unscathed. One way of interpreting the film is to say that it is precisely about the
perilous nature of interpretation; it warns us against the analytic impulse to fix
– that is, to mend and to cure – the sliding signifier (for to do so entails a risk

of ending up like Jerry's shrink). And yet . . . the slippery slope entices, the ruby slippers tantalise, luring us into the perverse pleasures of the maze.

Home and Away
Q: What is it that the patient most desires?
A: The analyst's ear.

All he wants to do is tell his story and go home. But over and over again his story falls on deaf ears, and his attempts to go home are repeatedly thwarted. Paul Hackett spends the whole of *After Hours* desperately trying to regain his footing and only succeeding in slithering further and further into a life-threatening situation. He makes a spectacle of himself, and it's hilarious to watch. Excruciatingly discomforting too.

'I want to go home' – this is all that Dorothy wants. And when she finally gets there she delivers the immortal line: 'There's no place like home.'

> *Anybody who has swallowed the scriptwriters' notion that this is a film about the superiority of 'home' over 'away' . . . would do well to listen to the yearning in Judy Garland's voice as her face tilts up towards the skies. What she expresses here, what she embodies with the purity of an archetype, is the human dream of leaving.* (Salman Rushdie)[2]

If we enter *Blue Velvet* through the ear (there is a zoom in to the interior via the ear near the beginning of the film) we might note that it is a dead and detached ear, and therefore a deaf ear. If we assume that as soon as the patient begins to speak he makes a demand of the analyst, insists on interpretation, it is equally true that he cannot hear what is said (that is to say, he resists unwelcome interpretation) and also is suspicious of the analyst, convinced that she turns a deaf ear to his speech. The intensity of this suspicion may be transferred into a desire to literalise the deaf ear of the analyst – that is to say, to cut it off, to turn it into a dead ear, and return it to sender.

It was just Mum and me waiting at home for the world to end. I was seven, it was during the war and Dad was away fighting. We were Plymouth Brethren see, so there were no movies on Saturday arvos, no liquorice sticks, no frills. Anyway, one day there was big news – Dad was coming home on leave, but just for the weekend and there wasn't time for him to get back home. So Mum and me went on a train all the way to Sydney. The boat was late, and there we were, stuck waiting on a Saturday afternoon in Sin City. My mum must have taken leave of her senses, cos she said, 'Seeing as it's such a special occasion we're going to have a treat. But it's our secret. Don't ever tell your father, or else . . .' And the next thing I knew we were in a picture palace trying to look as though we were just passing through. Look, you have to remember I'd been taught that the movies were evil. And here we were in the jaws of hell. And I knew we'd be punished, God would see us looking and snap his fingers and we'd go blind and the world would end. Or even worse I thought he'd punish me by not letting Dad come home. I'd never see him again. I was scared shitless and spent the whole movie

trying not to look at the screen. Ended up under the seat. But I heard everything,
and could picture it all – in vivid gory detail.[3]

After Hours and *Blue Velvet* are perversely slippery texts. They engage the viewer in a perverse scenario of interpretation and transference, and in both cases the 'perversion' can be deciphered by following the traces left by another film, *The Wizard of Oz*. The slipperiness, we might say, derives from the ruby slippers, those lethally magic totemic objects which, by night and by day and down through the years, keep dancing, tracing an uncanny ghostly trail through various cinematic landscapes.

All three films have a circular structure: they take their protagonists away from home on a fantastic journey which eventually ends where it began – at home. Dorothy leaves Kansas to go on a dream journey to the Land of Oz. Her return home coincides with waking up from the dream. *Blue Velvet* begins and ends with the frame of 'home' as small-town suburbia, where the flowers have the same technicolor intensity as the flowers of Dorothy's dream world. Home here 'frames' the hero's journey (into a vividly depicted world of ostentatiously perverse characters and scenarios), initiated by a zoom into the interior of an ear. At the end there is a zoom out – back to 'normality'. *After Hours* opens with Paul Hackett at work in a shiny streamlined New York office. The gates close after him as he leaves work – and so begins his nocturnal journey into the infernal and nightmarishly alien world of downtown SoHo. At the end he arrives back at work (structurally homologous with home) just as the gates are opening the next morning.[4]

In these films the relation between home and away, the dream-of-leaving and the wish-to-return, is structured in terms of fantasy – a fantasy which is more overt in *The Wizard of Oz* than in either *After Hours* or *Blue Velvet*, where, although the distinction between what is real and what is imagined becomes blurred and the journey becomes nightmarish, it is not clearly marked as a discrete fantasy. *Blue Velvet*, however, offers more possibilities for designating the journey as dream: at the end of the film Jeffrey wakes up. It is this particular (fantastical) articulation of the home-and-away dynamic that serves to locate a strain of perversity running, sometimes merely as an undercurrent, through and across the journeys, running, like a 'lazy line', through and across the dramatic scenarios of interpretation in which we are engaged. To put it another way, it is not in the content of the dreams that perversity is to be located, but in the nature of the engagement elicited, and the forms of transference that take place. Now, if there is an errant strain that weaves a path of perversity connecting these texts, it is equally the case that it changes colour, that it shows up in a different hue in the different films. Borrowing a formulation from *The Wizard of Oz*, we might say that perversity is by its nature a horse of a different colour.[5] And the films, we'll find, are variegated.

Unaccountably We Remain

Laugh, laugh; laugh, laugh; this misery is just . . . too much for me . . .
Can't go on . . . Everything I had is gone. ('Stormy Weather')[6]

After Hours is excruciating to watch, painful even, and yet there is a driving compulsion to keep watching, and indeed to keep laughing, more and more hysterically. Our laughter registers pleasure but a pleasure that is decidedly perverse. I find myself in oscillation, literally shaking, rocked erratically between a compulsive desire to keep watching and an acute imperative to avert the gaze.

> *The anxiety of the movie struck all of us as hilariously funny. We always thought it was a nightmare, and it was so scary that it was funny. The expression on Marty's face when we'd watch Paul Hackett go through something was like, 'Oh no! Oh, my God, oh!' I could hear him out of the corner of my ear during takes, saying 'Oh God, that's awful.' He had to turn away to not look at the take, because he'd be laughing. And you'd see the silhouette of his back, jumping up and down from trying to hold in his laughter. 'Oh boy, oh God, what are we gonna do, oh God, this is awful, this is the worst!' And he would keep laughing.* (Griffin Dunne)[7]

This anecdote echoes so many other tales Scorsese tells about watching – and not watching – movies: 'I recently looked again at the Val Lewton films when they came out on video, including *Isle of the Dead*. I remember I saw it by myself when I was about eleven, and I ran out of the theatre before the finish because it scared me to death!'[8] And of *Duel in the Sun*: 'I couldn't watch the end, it was all so frightening . . .'[9] Best of all I like the story he tells of being taken by his Aunt Mary to a double bill of *Bambi* and *Out of the Past*. All he can remember of *Out of the Past* is plaguing his aunt by continually asking, 'When is *Bambi* coming on?' She kept saying, 'Shut up. This is good, I'll kill you!'[10] All this looking-away or looking-under-duress circles round what seems to be the quintessential perverse pleasure of cinematic viewing, where we choose (no longer compelled by the parental voice) to watch even though it is painful or discomforting. For it is also pleasurable. What was once, in the past, unwatchable or unendurable becomes an image that fixates, from which we cannot tear ourselves away. Or perhaps it is not temporal, but simultaneous: we turn away doubled up with laughter even while we gaze unflinchingly, overwhelmed by horror.

> When I saw *Vertigo* I was scared. I don't know why. I loved that I was scared, I loved the picture. (Scorsese)[11]

In his marvellous little essay 'The Imp of the Perverse', Edgar Allen Poe suggests vertigo as the prototype of all perversions. 'We stand upon the brink of a precipice,' he writes. 'We peer into the abyss; we grow sick and dizzy. Our first impulse is to shrink from the danger. Unaccountably we remain.' Poe then goes on to describe in spine-tingling detail how we gradually come to actively desire the sensation of falling, of 'rushing annihilation', even though we know where it leads: death. We perpetrate perverse acts, he says, 'because we feel we should not'.[12] This account of peering into the abyss corresponds very closely to my experience of watching *After Hours*; but the sensational aspect of vertigo (we desire the vertiginous sensation, not just of falling, but of spatial and bodily dislocation) is at odds with the way in which cinematic perversion has predominantly been theorised. Film viewing has indeed been conceived of as intrinsically perverse but with the stress on a specific sense, the sense of sight. Within this framework spectatorship represents a variant of scopophilia, the desire to look, and is manifested primarily in fetishism and voyeurism: 'a relaxed, socially acceptable practice of the perversion', as Metz puts it.[13] He also speaks of spectator-fish, 'taking in everything with their eyes, nothing with their bodies: the institution of the cinema requires a silent, motionless spectator, a vacant spectator, constantly in a sub-motor and hyper-perceptive state . . . a self filtered out into pure vision'.[14] While I hesitate to turn a blind eye to such a fishy affair, I find myself turning to the vertigo analogy as most suggestive for thinking about how senses other than sight are mobilised when watching films, and how somatic responses are psychically mediated. Poe describes how we stand upon the precipice, peer into the abyss, grow sick and dizzy and yet unaccountably we remain, indeed are drawn in by something like a thought except that it is palpable; it chills and lures us 'with the fierceness of the delight of its horror'.[15]

The Fierceness of the Delight of its Horror

This realm of the palpable is usually mapped in terms of the horror film, and, while a kind of perverse sensationalism is here most pronounced, I don't think that the horror genre has a monopoly on the 'palpable lure'. On the other hand it does open, precisely because of the excessively palpable, a way into thinking about what's going on when we 'feel funny' in the cinema; and some inspired discussions of the horror genre (particularly by Carol Clover and Phil Brophy[16]) touch a more general cinematic nerve, triggering shock effects that ripple through a range of genres, through a chimerically changing cinematic screamscape.

Attention to the sensational serves to highlight a range of curious conjunctions in contemporary horror genres, particularly a tendency to shift registers abruptly (for instance 'between something like "real" horror on one hand and a camp, self-parodying horror on the other')[17] and a tendency to combine, simultaneously or in quick succession, apparently incompatible responses. Humour, horror and pleasure are brought together under the sign of what Clover refers to as a 'self-ironising relation to taboo'.[18] Brophy encapsulates it thus: 'The contemporary Horror film in general plays with the contradiction that it is only a movie; but nonetheless a movie that can work upon its audience with immediate results.'[19] What rises to the surface of these critical accounts is a contemporary mode of cinematic pleasure that imbues a razor-sharp knowingness with voluptuous somatic surrender.

> What remains unspoken in, for instance, Hitchcock's *Vertigo*, is explicit here [in *Peeping Tom*]. It's as if the process of film-making becomes an accessory to the crime. (Scorsese)[20]

Poe's perversity doesn't have much currency these days,[21] and vertigo does not feature strongly in psychoanalytic theory. But if the perversions generally involve action and are marked by a certain degree of self-consciousness (that is to say, desire, though it might emerge circuitously, is not repressed: we *actively* desire and enact, one way or another, that desire), then Poe anticipates some Freudian inflections. The imp lures us to act, or to enact the sensation of falling. Following in the tracks of, but also deviating somewhat from, the classical psychoanalytic accounts are approches that understand perverse scenarios as delusions that harness the body's capacity for action and excitement in order to ward off threatened annihilation, to prevent the death of the self. 'Death or delusion' is André Green's phrase.[22]

The pervert acts, and risks. To risk is to libidinise anxiety and to gain control through action. Perverse constructions hold out the promise of overturning pain, passivity and ruin. The mechanism of such a reversal entails an imaginary switch of significations from negative to positive: where there was pain, now pleasure will be. Perverse constructions conceived of in this way can be seen as imaginative attempts to regulate and control a dangerous terrain of ambivalence, manifested in a series of precarious oppositions – between distance and closeness, touching and being out of touch, detachment and intimacy, separation and integrity, abstraction and embodiment, home and away.

The cinematic 'perversions' of voyeurism and fetishism (roughly corresponding to sadistic and masochistic inflections of the scopic drive) have been in terms of distance. Part of the pleasure of the cinematic experience has been located in the scenario of looking-without-touching and seeing-without-being-seen (and sometimes the looking is seen as a substitution for touching, as an act of compensation). Christian Metz posits the cinematic signifier as primarily perceptual and argues that the perceptual (visual and auditory) drives have a stronger relationship with the absence of their object than the other drives, so that distance is part of their very definition: the 'distance of the look, distance of listening'.[23]

I didn't understand what my tonsils had to do with my eyes either.

In my experience, the cinematic signifier is never a matter of 'pure vision' or perception. It is impure, a sliding signifier, slithering or crashing through sensory barriers, about (and in the midst of) which I often have a funny feeling. What all the looking-away or looking-under-duress stories convey is the multifariously *sensational* quality of the film experience. It is not simply sight that is mobilised when 'watching' a film, but a variety of senses, so that even when not-watching the screen, we are hearing and seeing (out of the corner of eye and ear). And when watching, we project onto the screen alien sensations, imported images, memories from elsewhere, which might arise through conscious association or which might soar up, out of the past, involuntarily.

Do I Have to Die for It?

I was very much engaged by the game, the trap, the maze. The whole idea of
    what he [Griffin Dunne] says at the end, 'All I wanted to do was to go out
        with a girl and have a nice time. Do I have to die for it?' The answer is:
                YES!' (roaring with laughter). (Scorsese)[24]

In fact Paul Hackett doesn't die; he returns 'home'. But by the end of the film it is clear that 'there is no longer any such place as *home*',[25] no return to safety. Dream and reality are equally unsettling. As Paul's evening progresses so his anxiety and suspicion increase and so the nightmarish aspects of the journey become more pronounced. Our uncertainty also escalates: is this really happening or are we being inveigled into complicity with a paranoid vision?

The trajectory of *After Hours*, in this respect, foreshadows *GoodFellas*. We watch Henry, dogged by the repeated return of the repressed corpse (like the body that wouldn't die in *Blood Simple*), become more and more frenzied and suspicious and coked out. His final day of freedom, the day before he's busted, is a *tour de force* of cinematic frenzy, as he rushes wildly hither and thither, trying to do a thousand things, including fetching his kid brother from hospital, shifting drugs and guns, making the sauce for the family dinner, keeping out of the way of the helicopter that he's convinced is trailing his every move. Obsessively, he repeats, 'My plan was . . . this was my plan . . .' But already his plans are careering out of control, his world is closing in, his desire to 'go anywhere' is materialising in a consciousness that's all over the place. The paranoia feels tangible; it feels as though we are enmeshed in an elaborate psychic and cinematic structure that is likely to collapse, or blow up, in our faces at any moment.

Initially Paul is motivated by the 'human dream of leaving'. All he wants to do is leave home for the evening and meet a nice girl. Sitting alone in a café reading Henry Miller's *Tropic of Cancer* he meets Marcy (Rosanna Arqette), who gives him the phone number of a friend who makes plaster-of-Paris bagels-and-cream-cheese paperweights. He goes home, calls the number and is invited by Marcy to come over to the loft she shares with the sculptress, Kiki (Linda Fiorentino), in SoHo. When he arrives Marcy is not there but Kiki throws the keys down to him. From Paul's point of view we experience the keys plummeting down, hurtling towards us like a hand grenade. From now on Paul will be plagued by much troublesome business involving doors and windows and locks.

> *The tornado, swooping down on Dorothy's home, creates*
> *the second genuinely mythic image of* The Wizard of Oz;
> *the archetypal myth, one might say, of moving house.*
> *In this, the transitional sequence of the movie, when the unreal*
> *reality of Kansas gives way to the realistic surreality of the*
> *world of wizardry, there is, as befits a threshold moment, much*
> *business involving windows and doors.* (Salman Rushdie)[26]

When the work gates close on Paul his troubles with keys and doors and windows (he witnesses two 'shocking' scenes through two 'rear windows') are just beginning. Repeatedly women invite him home and offer to help him, only to withdraw their offers or to turn on him vindictively (Marcy does so by committing suicide). He is threatened by burns, traps, suffocation, lynching, forceable head shaving. His 'dream of leaving', like Dorothy's, soon turns into its opposite, a desperate desire to get home. When at last an opportunity presents itself Paul has first to perform a task involving a detour and an exchange of keys. He meets a friendly bartender, Tom (John Heard), who is willing to lend him money for a fare home; in exchange for the favour he agrees to check Tom's apartment to make sure his burglar alarm has been switched on, since there have been a number of robberies in the neighbourhood. He takes Tom's keys, leaving his own as security. At the apartment he is mistaken for the thief by a suspicious group of male residents. Dogged by repetition and a series of ominous coincidences (such as Marcy turning out to be Tom's girlfriend), he is unable to retrieve his keys and becomes the target of a vigilante lynch mob made up of revengeful women and hysterical gays.

In the end he escapes and fortuitously finds himself back where he started. But to declare this a happy ending is rather like saying that Jerry Lewis is cured by the end of *Cracking Up*, when the catastrophic symptoms have merely been transferred. Paul is eventually 'saved' from the vigilante mob by another sculptress who encases him in plaster of Paris, whereupon he is stolen by the real thieves who mistake him for a work of art. He falls out of their van right outside his office in the early morning. The plaster disintegrates around him, he picks himself up, the gates open. The film ends as it begins: with Mozart's Symphony in D Major and Paul 'at home' in the office. The rigorously classical symmetry, whereby the opening rhymes so elegantly with the closing, would once have indicated closure and resolution. But no longer (no longer after *The Searchers*, we might say) can this classical structure serve as an effective means of containment; it can only gesture towards the tenuous and contingent nature of resolution. Indeed, the very rigour of the structure suggests a rhetorical dimension; it serves to signify closure and resolution (the return home) as precisely fantasy, as a structure of hyperbole. The return (after the film's obsessive patterning of malevolent coincidence) consolidates the tyranny of repetition, leaves us whirling (confirmed in the swooping, careening camera) in a continuous cycle of fateful recurrence.[27]

Actually, I exaggerate slightly. We are not exactly consigned to that notoriously Manichean Washing Machine in the Sky. But we do not escape entirely unscathed – just as the residue of the nightmare is transferred to Paul's body in the form of flaky plaster dust, so his 'symptoms' of paranoia and anxiety are transferred to us.

The anxiety of the movie struck all of us . . .

If the spectacle of the disintegrating sculpture evokes anxiety about dissolution and disintegration then the ending might be thought of as a delusive structure warding off such anxieties. The return home is not so much wish fulfilment (as would seem to be more the case in *The Wizard of Oz*) as a perverse fantasy which entails an imaginary switch of identifications from negative to positive. In so far as the perversions are marked by a degree of self-consciousness, and correlative acting out, we might think of this perverse fantasy as a knowing delusion (rather than, for instance, the abandonment of catharsis). By turning death (the logic of utter paranoia) into delusion we survive, through perversity. In these terms the film implicates us in an imaginative attempt to regulate and control a series of precarious oppositions, between, for instance, detachment and involution, abstraction and embodiment, distance and proximity. For Paul, the protagonist, this is manifested in a peculiarly unknowing *modus operandi*; for us it is manifested as a terrain of ambivalence around interpretation and transference.[28]

. . . struck all of us as hilariously funny.

In the transference of paranoia and anxiety something else is generated: the delirium of laughter. *After Hours* achieves a transposition of affect through combining comedy and some of the *affective* characteristics of horror and suspense. It is partly because of the comedic inflection, the ostentatious generation of a surplus of pleasure (registered in the irruption of laughter), that the equally pronounced engagement with unpleasure – paranoia and anxiety – is rendered potentially perverse. There is, however, an element of undecidability about the humour in *After Hours*, though it is a difficulty not unique to this film; indeed, it pertains to a range of contemporary texts where laughter is imbricated with knowingness and horror. In these texts (*Blue Velvet* presents itself as another obvious and much discussed instance) laughter is entwined with knowingness and recognition.[29] While it is the case that all comedy plays on a tension between the familiar and the unexpected, these texts invoke a particular kind of knowing viewer and elicit a mode of laughter consequent on that knowingness. *After Hours* and *Blue Velvet* display a certain knowingness about both their subject matter (stagings of psychoanalytic scenarios) and their cinematic location (a self-ironising allusiveness, a playfulness around genre, a leaning towards the cinematically parodic). The issue has to do with the presentation of a self-conscious discourse, and a mode of address which invokes a knowing viewer. The viewer who is addressed is knowing on two counts at least: about the cinema and about psychoanalysis. Whether viewers truly know or not is immaterial; the important point here is the invocation of an audience in the know, an in-audience. From this point of view we would say that much of the pleasure and humour comes from engagement with 'the game, the trap, the maze', as opposed to identification with characters or psychic investment in the emotional propulsion of plot.

> *Q:* I got the feeling you weren't particularly engaged by *After Hours*.
> Is that fair?
> *A:* Not necessarily by the characters, but I was very much engaged by
> the game . . . [30]

Paul is not a well-rounded psychological character. Although he is trapped in a quasi-Freudian farce he is a bundle of symptoms rather than a 'personality', more akin to the characters of screwball comedy than psychological drama. Griffin Dunne's performance is brilliantly geared to reaction, timing, rhythm, rather than to the nuances of interiority. There is still an impulse to identification, but it is of a different order: it has to do with identifying tropes, allusions, self-reflexive patterns. It is sometimes argued that the laughter in these cases is 'cool' – superior and distanced. Though this may be the case I would argue that it isn't necessarily so. A distancing from character identification does not necessarily entail a form of detached and 'safe' laughter. To some extent these films are about interpretation, and the laughter – an oscillation between delusion and death – often indicates the perilous nature of the enterprise. These films stage interpretation itself as a drama enacted on the borderline of detachment and investment. There is a logic of separation operative in the kind of engagement elicited; but it does not exclude somatic surrender. Knowing, in these films, generates a funny feeling.

A Key Exchange Problem: The Oblivious Transfer

From now on Paul will be plagued with much troublesome business involving doors and windows and locks. First there is the exchange with Kiki. The keys are hurled at Paul, like a weapon. Then there is the key exchange with Tom. Then there is the image of the death's head, a latent image which lurks in this city of night, materialising in tattoos, ashtrays, belt buckles, key chains.

Analysis can only be produced out of some kind of identification and transference. So, even in these sorts of post-modern texts, transference takes place, but a mode of transference characterised, at least initially, by a logic of detachment. The kind of post-modern procedures of exchange by which signifiers circulate and new knowledge is produced might be characterised by the notion of the 'Oblivious Transfer'. This is a procedure designed to guarantee the security of secret messages, the correct transfer of funds, protocols for sending certified mail and signing contracts at a distance. It falls within the domain of public-key cryptography, and is dealt with as part of the key-exchange problem.

> *The transfer is somewhat like a simple game played with a locked box requiring two different keys. A sender transfers the locked box to a recipient, who finds one key that partially unlocks the box. The sender has both keys and, without seeing what the recipient has done, must now pass on one of the two keys. Depending on which key is sent, the recipient will either succeed or fail in opening the box. Although the sender's choice controls the outcome, the sender never knows which choice to make to guarantee a certain result.*[31]

The 'keys', of course, are mathematically generated and the 'game' hinges on an abstraction – the difficulty of factoring large numbers. 'Any mathematical operation that enables such a scheme to work must act like a trap that's much easier to fall into than to escape.'[32] Although each party knows the 'rules' and has access to keys there is no lock, as such, but rather an abstraction, a void, a nothingness.[33]

> *The key in her hand turns into a knife; a flashed image, almost subliminal, haunting.*
> (Maya Deren, *Meshes of the Afternoon*)

Hearsay: Stop Making Sense

The key to *Blue Velvet* is the ear. It provides an opening; it unlocks the box although there is no lock, as such, but rather an abstraction, a void, a nothingness. *Blue Velvet* opens with a series of vignettes, scenes of Lumberton life which include firemen waving for the camera, a close-up of a pointed gun on television, and a man in the garden seized by a heart attack. This is Jeffrey's father, and it is after visiting him in hospital that Jeffrey finds the severed ear, and begins his investigation. There is a zoom in to the ear accompanied by a muffled roaring on the soundtrack; at the end of the film there is a zoom out from another ear – Jeffrey's own, and we find ourselves once again in his parents' garden, the family fully intact. Jeffrey's investigation brings him into contact on the one hand with the town's detective and the detective's daughter, Sandy, and on the other hand with a variety of dubious characters, including Dorothy Valance (Isabella Rossellini), who wears a blue velvet dressing gown and red stilettos and is connected in a sado-masochistic way with the violently aggressive psychopath, Frank (Dennis Hopper). Dorothy's husband and child (Don and Donny) are being held captive by Frank, who has cut off Don's ear.

Where the journey in *The Wizard of Oz* is clearly located as a dream, in *Blue Velvet*, although the device of entering and leaving the ear is used, the relationship between reality and fantasy is far less clearly delineated. This is also true of *After Hours*, but the dialectic of distance and closeness is worked out and through quite differently. Rather than complicating the relation between home and away *Blue Velvet* effects a conflation. It is concerned with an elaboration of two homilies. First, beneath the banal appearance of American small-town life there is a seething world of fascinating perversions (that is, like Dorothy, you don't have to leave home to have fun); and, second, perverse actions and images are no more or less meaningful than homely images. Lynch's remake of *The Wizard of Oz* is ultimately dedicated to the demonstration that there is no difference between home and away and fantasy and reality, to a flattening out of difference rather than to an exploration of zones of indeterminacy. Ironically, despite its extravagant depiction of perversity, *Blue Velvet* neutralises the ambivalence that injects *The Wizard of Oz* with a strain of perverse energy. This neutralisation is tied in with a discourse around the very question of meaning, of interpretation, of making sense.

Blue Velvet is a noisy text. The noisiness is there not only in the sounds of the jungle (albeit it a miniaturised, David-Attenborough-type jungle where insect sounds are amplified[34] and the lion's roar is miniaturised) but in the concatenation of quotation, allusion, mimicry, ultimately condensed in the sound-image of lip-synching (a sound-image at once a composite and a separation/detachment). This is most striking in Dean Stockwell/Ben's rendition of 'In Dreams', but it occurs with a somewhat different inflection every time Dorothy opens her mouth and we hear the distinctive voice of 'her' (Isabella Rossellini's) mother (Ingrid Bergman). An aural screen memory which returns to us the voice of the mother, a voice which is, however, separated out, detached from the visual signifier. The ear serves to transmit a series of detached images, fragments of meaning, soundbites, figures of speech rendered as quotation, allusion, imitation, mimicry. These fragments are accorded, within the film, the same status as rumour and gossip, *hear-say* (a sound-image at once a composite and a separation/detachment). Interpretation is presented (diegetically in Jeffrey's detective quest, but with ramifications for the viewer's interpretive engagement with the film) as on a par with idle speculation; it is meaning derived from overhearing or listening in. The camera, as it zooms slowly into the interior of the ear, 'revealing' an enigmatic sound of roaring, is literally listening in. Sandy, who initially gives Jeffrey some 'bits and pieces', thus enabling him to begin the investigation, says, 'I hear things.' She overhears things because her room is over her father's office, or orifice. Jeffrey avoids hearing things, by flushing the toilet (flushing away the evidence of his own bodily presence) at the very moment when Sandy toots the horn.

The first 'performance' of the 'candy coated clown they call the sandman' ('In Dreams') consists of Ben miming in accompaniment to the 'original' song, on tape, emanating from a tacky ghetto blaster. He holds what appears to be a mike but is in fact a torch illuminating his heavily made-up face. Frank silently mouths the words. Later, in the 'lipstick' scene, Frank speaks the words belatedly, as though echoing the song. He also, in this scene, quotes 'Love Letters from my Heart'. 'Blue Velvet' itself is, of course, a quotation, both of an earlier era (and the romantic nostalgia of Bobby Vinton's version) and of Anger's appropriation in *Scorpio Rising*. This predilection for quotation and pastiche and the way it is manifested in hear-say and allusion tends to repeat (obsessively, or anxiously, it could be argued) the knowledge that there is no difference between the thing and the name, the source and the quotation itself, the real and its parody, the copy and the original. And hence no scope for hermeneutic endeavour. The problem, which exists as a potential trap, is that while disavowing difference it nevertheless invites a form of hermeneutic identification; in order to make its point it relies on the viewer identifying the original, the source.

The viewer is enticed, to listen and interpret. She is a listening viewer, and hear-say is simultaneously all-important and meaningless, signifying nothing. But how does *Blue Velvet* lay its lure? The film is self-consciously littered with 'psychoanalytic tropes' and cinematic allusions, enactments almost encased in quotation marks.[35] The temptation, of course, is for the viewer-analyst to frenetically identify the quotations, to get caught up in hermeneutic delirium and in the process to miss the joke (the about-turn that says 'it's just a joke, this is only a quotation, nothing but pastiche'); or to anxiously and repeatedly assert the joke so that the analysis itself becomes a running gag. Either way we fall into the trap. To borrow a phrase from Shoshana Felman: 'Entering into the game, we ourselves become fair game for the very "joke" of meaning'[36] (a trap that's much easier to fall into than to escape).

The film presents us with psychoanalytic scenarios but refuses to take these too seriously. For instance, we might say that *Blue Velvet* relentlessly gestures towards Freudian theory by alluding to the relation between a range of perversions and the existence of infantile sexuality. But as soon as we make this interpretation the tables are turned on us: the film declares the theory, and indeed its own procedures for making sense, a joke, as knowingly epitomised in Frank's coyly demonic refrain 'Baby Wants to Fuck'.[37]

His films exemplify Demme/Byrne's slogan: Stop Making Sense.
*So, for you to turn a deaf ear to what he's saying is to accede to his
demand to be seen at face value.*
(Letter from a friend)

The gist of my argument must now be emerging – that perversion in *Blue Velvet* is to be located not simply on the level of depiction, but on the level of textual practice. Perversion here has to do with the simultaneous eliciting of, and desire to gag, interpretation. The notion of interpretation entails a conception of the analyst, who is here invoked as a textual presence, as the mother 'presumed to know'. Symptoms of perversion are, in a sadistic scenario of wish-fulfilment, transferred onto her body. The film enacts a sadistic infantile fantasy in which revenge is effected against the one presumed to know (the analyst or film viewer/reader presumptuous enough to offer an interpretation) through the transference of symptoms from one body to another.

If we enter *Blue Velvet* through the ear we might note that it is a dead and detached ear, and therefore a deaf ear. If, in the analytic situation, we assume that as soon as the patient begins to speak he/she makes a demand of the analyst, insists on interpretation, it is equally true that he/she cannot always hear what is said (turns a deaf ear) and also is suspicious that the analyst turns a deaf ear to his/her speech. The intensity of this suspicion may be transferred into a desire to literalise the deaf ear of the analyst – that is, to cut it off, to turn it into a dead ear, and return it to sender. *Blue Velvet* is exhibitionist, going to great lengths to secure attention, to ensure that mother is listening. But she who listens also interprets, and the film anticipates this potentially threatening activity by alternately demeaning and deafening.

The Oblivious Transfer evokes another image of exchange, another conceit. The Immaculate Conception involves an exchange which emphasises distance, detachment, the bypassing of erotogenic zones (or, one might argue, the eroticising of some other zone of exchange). The Annunciation is sometimes figured as a shaft of light or stream of words issuing from the Angel and entering the Virgin's ear.[38] Thus, she becomes pregnant with meaning; thus the word is made flesh. The analyst, receiving (hearing) the words of the patient, is presumed to know. But she returns these words to the subject, makes the words into flesh. The transference and detachment or separation essential to the cure is materialised in *Blue Velvet* as the severed ear, the word made flesh. There is a form of reversal happening here: the ear, as an organ of incorporation, can also be repudiated, expelled like faeces from the body and returned to sender. Thus the severed and rotting flesh found by or given to the would-be analyst/detective.

The Oblivious Transfer serves as a metaphor for a mode of analysis and transference characterised at least initially by a logic of separation and detachment. It pertains to *After Hours* and *Blue Velvet*, both of which elaborate a self-conscious discourse and mode of address that invokes a knowing audience. But if *After Hours* poses interpretation itself as perilous, as a drama enacted on the borderline of detachment and investment, *Blue Velvet* is more retentive in its regulation of distance. Its tabloid depiction of perversions may well represent a delusive structure warding off anxiety (made manifest in the ear-exchange fantasy); but rather than implicating the viewer in a running gag – an extended ravelling of knowledge, humour, and horror – it enacts a desire to reduce engagement, to stop making sense; in short: to gag. So although I feel funny in *Blue Velvet,* I tend to gag on the humour. In *After Hours* I feel funny laughing at what isn't necessarily funny, but the anxiety grows and the more it grows, the more I laugh.

If *After Hours* plays with fire ('Is that all there is to a fire?' asks Peggy Lee's voice on the jukebox when Paul returns to Club Berlin in the early, deserted hours of the morning), if it lures you in even though you know there is a danger of getting your fingers burnt, *Blue Velvet* is inflected differently: 'Hands off!' it declares and consolidates the declaration with an 'Ears off!' warning. An intimation of these issues – of cutting and burning tissue – is filtered through a fairy tale that oscillates between monochrome and garish Technicolor. *The Wizard of Oz* performs, perhaps, a retrospective intimation.

Negative Magic

The Wizard of Oz is not concerned with a depiction of perverse practices, even in a covert form, but its enduring popularity (evidenced not just in video rentals but also in the variety of appropriations) must be partly attributable to the magical dimension of its fairy-tale structure, and to its inflection of sexual identity as fundamentally precarious. Fairy tales, particularly those of a Grimm persuasion, are of course seldom benign; far from assuming that childhood is 'innocent' and devoid of sexual desire, they posit infancy as a vaudevillian stage where repressions, psychoses and perversions are previewed in an endless series of luridly amateurish acts. The beneficent fantasy of *The Wizard of Oz*, the dream as wish fulfilment (resolving tensions between leaving and staying, anxieties about home and away, about the threshold between infancy and adulthood), comes very close to the enactment of a perverse structure – of turning negative to positive: where there was pain now pleasure will be. Where negative and positive refer to a wish-fulfilment structure, the pain–pleasure dynamic moves us into the realm of perversity. But where is the pain in *The Wizard of Oz*? Well, there is the clearly articulated pain of bodies without organs, 'men' without brains and hearts, but the pain that motivates the journey to the Wizard is Dorothy's homesickness. The red shoes become crucial as magical objects which finally enable a resolution (they enable Dorothy to go home); but narratively, and prior to acquiring this beneficent function, they represent pain, danger, the 'unhomely'. A transformation is effected. Not only a transformation, however; there is also a transference, and it is this that is crucial in delineating a rudimentary structure of perversion.

'And that's all that's left of the Wicked Witch': her ruby slippers and striped socks sticking out from under the house which has plummeted from the sky crushing her in its fall. Then, in a puff of acrid orange smoke the other Wicked Witch (of the West) materialises, threatening revenge. 'Aren't you forgetting the ruby slippers?' the simpering Glinda sweetly enquires. She waves her wand, and the slippers disappear off the Wicked Witch's feet, which curl up and shrink. The camera pans and we see the slippers on Dorothy's feet. Cut into a close-up: homely gingham skirt, childish blue socks and brilliantly scarlet shimmering sexy shoes. 'There they are and there they'll stay,' says Glinda. But this is not altogether reassuring and Glinda doesn't at this stage seem to know everything there is to know about good and evil. She offers a guess – 'Their magic must be very powerful or she wouldn't want them so badly' – and a warning: 'Never let those ruby slippers off your feet.' Dorothy has suddenly, without asking, acquired something powerful, magical and inescapable: female sexuality.

> On the River of No Return Marilyn wears denims and long boots and a man's shirt, but she carries her red shoes with her. Those ruby stilletos in which she used to sway as she sang her torch songs in seedy saloons.

Significantly the shoes are transferred from the body of the Wicked Witch to the body of the girl-child; in order for them to appear as part of Dorothy's body (they cannot be taken off) something or someone has to disappear. So there is an implication of negative magic attached to the shoes, and an aura of loss, disappearance, castration.[39] The slippers are deeply ambivalent; they are figured as desirable, their possession implies power, yet their transference brings about contagion. Has Dorothy been magically blessed or irredeemably polluted? And what about us? Do we really want to be in her shoes? The film from now on has its work cut out: not merely to turn negative into positive but to negotiate the transformation of pain into pleasure. Yet a simple transformation is not possible. The transfer produces an inmingling of the two: in pain there will be pleasure. Powell and Pressburger's The Red Shoes carries this to its logical extreme, pursuing the deadly intimation of perversity in dancing beyond the pleasure principle.

> She was very much frightened, and tried to throw off her
> red shoes, but could not unclasp them.
> She hastily tore off her stockings; but the shoes she could
> not get rid of.
> They had, it seemed, grown on to her feet. Dance she did,
> and dance she must, over field and meadow, in rain
> and in sunshine, by night and by day.

The Wizard of Oz stops short. It transforms the shoes from an uncertainty into their own solution. What is a threat inscribed on the body (the threat of loss, bleeding, castration, detachment and separation) becomes a solution to all that is threatening, the key to recovery, making whole, and going home. In the final showdown with the Wicked Witch of the West Dorothy says she will exchange the slippers for Toto, who is being held hostage,[40] but when the witch tries to take them from Dorothy's feet she burns her fingers. Too late she remembers: 'They will never come off as long as you're alive.' She is not, however, deterred: 'But that's not what's worrying me; it's how to do it. These things must be done delicately, or you'll hurt the spell.' The threat that the red shoes have implicitly embodied is now made explicit. Death or delusion. In the nick of time we, and Dorothy, are saved from death. The Wicked Witch is 'liquidated', her green fingers reaching out for the red shoes are engulfed in yellow flames as she involuntarily goes up in smoke and melts down to nothing. In the place of death there is delusion. Anxieties of dissolution and disintegration are transformed into the delusion – or a perverse scenario warding off threatened annihilation – that it is possible to go home. It is only after the Wicked Witch has been destroyed (after two transfers: first, the slippers are transferred from one body to another; second, touching produces a transfer of heat, the shoes are too hot to handle, but with the burning of the witch the heat is taken out of the shoes) that the magic residing in the shoes is revealed as good magic, and the shoes themselves are revealed as the key to getting home.

I can hear the river calling 'no return, no return.'

Yet, as Salman Rushdie in discussing how Dorothy is 'unhoused' points out, 'we understand that the real secret of the ruby slippers is not that "there's no place like home," but rather that there is no longer any such place as home'.[41] The magic of the slippers is not entirely good magic either – their agency in transferring Dorothy from the land of Oz back home to Kansas is what Freud calls 'negative magic'. It is a technique for undoing what has been done or, in literal translation from the German, a making unhappened.[42] In other words, they provide a means by which to libidinise anxiety and to gain control through action (to ward off sexuality and adulthood).

And in the end, what becomes of us? Is it possible that we too, like Dorothy, might find our way home? Or is it just the beginning of a long process of contagion, of cracking up? And what does it mean anyway, in the cinema, to find one's way home? Dorothy might return to Kansas but we might well be doomed to repeat the experience of this film, over and over again, hanging on to those transitional objects incarnate – the ruby slippers – and heading into the desert like Marlene Dietrich at the end of *Morocco*, or slipping and sliding like Jerry Lewis's analyst, the unfortunate recipient of his catastrophic symptoms. If the question of 'What makes a man to wander?' persists, unresolved, so there exists 'a foreign legion of women too' who traipse through cinematic deserts, always leaving home, and heading for home, and never getting there.[43] The 'unhappening' effected by the ruby slippers signifies wish fulfilment but it doesn't actually cancel out the journey, or erase our exposure to a world of entrancing seduction as well as lowering threat. Perhaps *The Wizard of Oz* persists not because of its homilies but because of its hovering on the edge of perversion, its enlivening oscillation between points of identification, its sliding signifiers in the realm of colour and gender. Just as the 'horse of a different colour' magically transmogrifies through purple, orange and gold, so the instability of identity will be played out across a range of cinematic landscapes. Dorothy mutates, and as viewers we are tantalised; even as we sit in the darkness of the cinema, looking the other way, we oscillate between Dorothy's desires and the Wicked Witch's, between a hands-off (and feet- or ears-off) impulse and the risk of getting our fingers burnt.

A Kind of Scar Has Been Formed
Marcy tells Paul about her wedding night and about her husband who was a movie freak, obsessed in fact by one movie: 'You've seen the film haven't

you? Whenever he . . . you know . . . when he came he'd yell out "Surrender Dorothy!" that's all. "Surrender Dorothy!" Pretty creepy. He just couldn't stop.'

> Kiki induces Paul to give her a massage.
> Just make it hurt and you're on the right track.
> You have a great body.
> Yes. Not a lotta scars.
> It's true. Never occurred to me.
> I mean some women I know are covered with them head to toe. Not me.
> Scars?
> Mmm. Horrible, ugly scars.

This elicits from Paul a story about how as a kid he went into hospital to have his tonsils out and after the operation there was not enough room in paediatrics and so he was put in the burns ward:

> Before they wheeled me in this nurse gave me this blindfold to put on and she told me never to take it off. If I did they'd have to do the operation all over again [laughs]. I didn't understand what my tonsils had to do with my eyes either . . . but anyway . . . that night, at least I think it was night, I reached up to untie the blindfold . . . I saw . . .

At this point in the story Kiki, who has fallen back against his cheek, begins snoring. Paul, prying in Marcy's bag whilst she is showering (in preparation for a wild night ahead: 'I feel like I'm going to let loose or something!') finds a tube of burn ointment, which she, however, claims is skin moisturiser. On the bed she pulls her gown down to hide what looks – in a flashed exposure – like burn wounds. Later he finds a large volume by her bed entitled *Reconstruction and Rehabilitation of the Burned Patient*. As he flips through it there is a speedy montage of almost subliminal images, flesh, wounds, bleeding, and a disembodied wailing on the soundtrack. His face is shown grimacing and shuddering: 'Oh, ooh, ah!'

And did you know that Margaret Hamilton's hand was badly burned during the filming of the scene in which the Witch writes SURRENDER DOROTHY in the sky over the Emerald City, and that her stunt double, Betty Danko, was even more badly burned during the reshoot of this scene?[44]

You Freud, Me Jane?
In the Hitchcock film *Marnie,* the heroine, a compulsive thief, is caught in the act by a man who saves her from the law by marrying her. Then he tries to help her, by interpreting or beginning to analyse her problem. She turns on him, and asks: 'You Freud, me Jane?' She recognises that there is a thin line between the Law of the Jungle and the Law that is instituted in the Name-of-the-Father, between the jungle and the domain in which reason reigns and in which interpretation and analysis take place. She also articulates something that the film

dramatises: the complicit relationship between detective and criminal, between analyst and patient, between film and viewer.

> *Sandy*: I don't know if you're a detective or a pervert.
> *Jeffrey*: That's for me to know and you to find out.

There is no detective in *After Hours*. But there is a great deal of paranoia; and paranoia is closely entwined with detection and interpretation. The paranoiac suffers from 'delusions of reference': everything means something, every utterance and image refers to something else, the world is full of signs, of coded messages. When Freud says, in a throwaway remark, that 'paranoiac delusion is a caricature of a philosophical system',[45] I take him to mean that paranoia is something like a perversion of rational thought, a parody of the (philosophical) interpretative method. If this is the case then does the converse also hold true: that rational interpretation is potentially paranoid? If the pervert wards off death through the construction and enactment of perverse structures, does the analyst ward off death (the dissolution of meaning) through the construction and enactment of structures of analytic delusion? And, in the encounter between viewer and film, who is the detective and who the criminal? Who the patient and who the analyst? Who is Jane and who (or where) are Freud and Tarzan?

Paranoiacs Don't Laugh

> *His eyes slide to the left and the camera shifts slightly to capture the*
> *object of his gaze: a graffiti drawing of a shark about to close its fanged*
> *jaws over an erect penis.*

Paul is in the Terminal Bar for the first time, standing in front of the mirror in the bathroom (the first in a series: no less than five times in the movie do we catch glimpses of him washing, glimpses that serve no narrative purpose but which indicate a compulsion to repeat, an obsession with cleanliness that is otherwise never made a moment of).[46] He averts his eyes from the graffiti, turning back to look momentarily in the mirror, conjuring up a memory of Francis Bacon's 1976 painting, 'Figure at a Wash Basin': 'huddled over the oval of the wash basin, with its hands clutched to the spigots, the Figure of a body makes an intense and motionless effort to escape through the drain'.[47] Cut to the interior of the bar, the camera moving over emptiness till it comes to settle on Julie (Teri Garr), the waitress, in the background. We laugh, Paul doesn't. He walks into the jaws of fate. He can't afford humour: paranoiacs don't laugh.[48] We laugh. Of course, it could be that our laughter is nervous (and gender no doubt has something to do with our 'sense' of humour here), but it is also the kind of laughter elicited by the cartoon-like quality of the graffiti, by the recognition of a Tashlinesque form of condensation. It dispenses with the narrative and vividly imagines the 'idea' of that epic blockbuster *Jaws*, the lurking presence of a vagina dentata. Here, the toilet graffiti declares itself (to us) not so much as a representation but as a declamatory sign: hey, watch out, castration anxiety let loose! We laugh at this sign of Paul's anxiety, at the way in which his imagination keeps producing evidence to feed his paranoia; for to him the graffiti appears as a personal address, a sign that confirms his sense of persecution, his helpless engulfment in the jaws of fate.

> *Through a rear window: a woman shoots a man several times at point blank range, then tosses the gun away. Paul Hackett (hiding on a fire escape ladder) witnesses this scene. 'I'll probably be blamed for that,' he mutters.*

After Hours depicts paranoia in action and to some degree involves us in the mechanisms of a paranoid fantasy – but only to a certain degree.[49] If paranoiacs don't laugh then our laughter serves to confirm the fact that we are not paranoid. Although often put in Paul's place and given his point of view, we are also distanced by all the signs that the movie offers of his delusion. Narratively, this double movement is achieved through the device of locating Paul as an ordinary nice guy who ventures out of his neighbourhood and encounters a hostile and malevolent world. Paul just wants to meet a nice girl (and get laid) but, although he meets a series of women (strangers) who seem initially to hold out the offer of 'something like love', they in fact show him nothing of the kind and indeed their actions seem like hatred.

> *The meaning of their delusion of reference is that they expect from all strangers something like love. But these people show them nothing of the kind; they laugh to themselves, flourish their sticks, even spit on the ground as they go by . . . and considering, too, the fundamental kinship of the concepts of 'stranger' and 'enemy', the paranoiac is not so far wrong in regarding this indifference as hate, in contrast to his claim for love.*[50]

The fact that this happens over and over again, along with other repetitions and coincidences, alerts us to the fact that perhaps the film is 'acting out' Paul's paranoia. From this perspective we would say that of course the girls do not come up with the goods because basically Paul doesn't want to get laid (in fact this is his greatest fear); and the enmity that he perceives (from the gay men as well as the women) is, as in classic paranoia (and in the films of Jerry Lewis, particularly the sardonically entitled *The Ladies' Man*), merely a reflection of his own hostile impulses.

In thus identifying the parameters of the fantasy, in delineating patterns of repetition, the critic can perhaps momentarily feel at home in the domain where reason reigns; she can even derive pleasure from the 'game, the trap, the maze'. But this very enterprise, this compulsive reading of signs, could well indicate delusions of reference, a strain of paranoia intrinsic to the analytic or interpretive project itself – where no detail is indifferent, everything means something, everything refers to something else and all details are interconnected.

Talking of patterns, did you notice the ubiquitous patterning of black-
and-white squares that turns up everywhere, a harbinger of incipiently
malevolent meaning (on the cushions in Kiki's loft, on the walls of the
Club Berlin, on Julie's bedspread) and which no one comments on,
around which there is a palpable conspiracy of silence?

If the graffiti-as-sign functions differently for the viewer and for Paul there might nevertheless be, in the process of interpretation, a transference. For Paul looking involves a kind of contagion. In the case of the graffiti it is as though he has been touched by the power of the image, is subsumed by its meaning and compelled by fate to act out its import. The image will return to threaten him, embodied in the illuminated rat traps (and the trapped mouse) that surround Julie's bed like a shrine. His response to the murder he witnesses is very funny, both because it is hyperbolically paranoid and very likely accurate. He feels contaminated by witnessing the murder, almost by default 'an accessory to the crime'. Clearly, *After Hours* sets in motion a circuit of impulses, a chain of affective images that generates guilt by association, and the viewer is hooked up and woven into this circuit. To disavow paranoia, then, would be like crying wolf. However, our paranoia, although it might involve analytic delusion, is not tied in the same way as Paul's to a sense of persecution. It feels funny (unlike Paul's experience) and, while this sensation partly reflects the instigation of a knowing delusion, it also reflects an uneasiness or discomfort that is more free-floating, more like anxiety.

Something Is Let Loose

The anxiety of the movie struck all of us as hilariously funny. We always
thought it was a nightmare, and it was so scary that it was funny.

Paul Hackett is an anxious man, no doubt about it, but when Griffin Dunne speaks of the anxiety of the movie he indicates that it is not just with a character that the anxiety is to be located, but rather that the film itself generates anxiety. And humour. The scariness seems somehow entwined with this combination of anxiety and humour, rather than to be the sort of fear associated with suspense. The sense of paranoia that is also generated (or perhaps tapped?) by the movie seems similarly to be tied in with the anxiety.

Anxiety, like vertigo, is an affective state. In the first place, it is something that is felt, and that is experienced as unpleasurable. Definite physical sensations accompany anxiety, ranging from an almost indefinable restlessness to breathing disturbances, sweating, palpitations, and so on. Such a description, however, doesn't distinguish anxiety from other unpleasurable feelings, such as fear. What seems to give a specificity to anxiety (*Angst*) is that it has 'an unmistakable relation to expectation: it is anxiety about something. It has a quality of indefiniteness and lack of object',[51] it is free-floating. Something is let loose. (I feel like . . . I feel like . . . I'm gonna let loose!)

Once it acquires an object it becomes fear (*Furcht*). So anxiety is about something, but it is round about rather than attached to some objective correlative (we might suppose that it surfaces more in narratives of circularity and repetition than in those narratives in which the linear and the hermeneutic objective prevail. Generically speaking we might expect it to surface more in the musical, say, than in the detective film.[52] Anxiety is a response to danger, but to a dangerous situation that is not clearly defined or focused, and it is marked particularly by helplessness. This sequence – anxiety, danger, helplessness – indicates an original response to a traumatic situation. Later on, the same response (anxiety) is produced in anticipation of dangerous situations. The neurotic not only anticipates but in a sense produces these situations. He/she who experienced the trauma passively now repeats it actively in a weakened version in the hope of gaining control and determining the outcome: 'Anxiety is therefore, on the one hand, an expectation of a trauma, and, on the other, a repetition of it in a mitigated form' (Freud).[53] The original trauma may be a number of things, but for Freud, of course, it is associated with the anxiety of castration and is a reaction to loss and separation. In such cases, Freud argues, 'What the ego regards as the danger and responds to with an anxiety-signal, is that the super-ego should be angry with it or punish it or cease to love it.' This manifests itself as 'the fear of death (or fear for life) which is a fear of the super-ego projected onto the powers of destiny'.[54] Anxiety and paranoia dovetail here: the indefiniteness and the sense of helplessness encountered in anxiety produce a feeling of being at the mercy of invisible forces; and the sense of everything conspiring against one in paranoia produces a conviction that fate or destiny is masterminding such a state of affairs.

If it is true that *After Hours* most effectively generates an excess of free-floating anxiety (and if it is more than a matter of depiction, if the spectator is infused with this atmosphere) a few perplexing questions arise. I suspect that *After Hours*, in generating free-floating anxiety, simultaneously provides mechanisms for the viewer to convert this anxiety into humour by way of a procedure that is essentially perverse. But where exactly does the humour come from? How is laughter possible, and what is the connection between anxiety and humour? It is easier to grasp the relation between paranoia and laughter (because a mechanism that meshes exaggeration with a logic *ad absurdum* is common to both), but the links between anxiety and humour are more obtuse. The nature of the connection might, however, best be understood by introducing another mediating term: the uncanny.

Paul Hackett is, let's say it again, an anxious man, and also a very straight guy. He is not an obsessive near-psychopath like Jake La Motta or Travis Bickle. He is a naif (like the Dorothy from Kansas), not a pervert, which also means that he fails to convert – to libidinise – his anxiety. Much of his anxiety is channelled into paranoia (his indefinite fears are objectified), but much of it is still free-floating. Much of our anxiety is libidinised, mediated and converted by the uncanny into a pleasurable bodily response: laughter. Laughter is here a form of action, a way of acting on troubling matter, gaining control through interpretation. The pervert acts and risks; to risk is to libidinise anxiety and to gain control through action. It is also a registering of the uncanny as a return of the same and an exploration of this uncanny dimension in a pleasurable engagement with the game, the trap, the maze. Something ripples through the viewing body, comes out in phatic explosions: giggles, guffaws, shudders. The physicality of the laughter, or the 'insubstantial materiality of laughter', as Samuel Weber has put it,[55] indicates that sense and the senses – like distance and closeness – are mixed up here: 'Making sense' is mixed up with 'feeling funny'.

Conversion might happen, but still anxiety circulates, escapes (even in the guffaws and giggles) and returns. This is uncanny: the way it returns, the way laughter does not provide enough relief, does not exhaust the supply but seems, paradoxically, to generate more of the same. The hilarity provoked by *After Hours* has still to do with an indefinable – or indefinite – air of unease. This is where it differs from *Blue Velvet*. In Lynch's film the characters within the diegesis do libidinise their anxiety: Jeffrey, the straight guy, the would-be detective, exhausts his anxiety (and imagination) in the construction of perverse scenarios. The viewer's situation is somewhat different: although the film is driven by an anxiety about interpretation, rather than letting loose this anxiety, it ultimately absorbs it through a relentless depiction of the perverse, through a fixing of potentially sliding signifiers (or, to put it another way, through a fixation on the signifier). *After Hours* lets loose anxiety, performs it as an affect, as a kind of acting out, whereas *Blue Velvet* puts on an act and closes the curtains.

They're Both Dead!

> *Huh – is that coincidence? No!*
> *Because the same girl I came downtown to see was dead too.*
> *That's because they're the same person. They're both dead!*

Having checked Tom's apartment, and having revisited the loft where he discovers Marcy has died from an overdose of sleeping pills, Paul returns to the Terminal Bar to retrieve his keys only to find it locked up with a note on the door: 'back in 2 minutes'. Julie, the waitress, rescues him from the pouring rain by taking him to her apartment across the road, where she proceeds to terrorise him with her bizarre behaviour. He flees as soon as he hears Tom opening up, but under duress promises to return in a few minutes. Tom is sympathetic to his dilemma: 'So take off. What's she gonna do? Kill herself?' As Paul starts to reply – 'You're right. Just give me my keys. I'm gonna go home' – the phone rings. Tom answers it: 'My girlfriend . . . sleeping pills . . . It's my fault . . . Marcy, Marcy, Marcy, Marcy!' When Paul tries to tell the story later the uncanny repetition of events presents itself as a macabre doubling: 'They're both dead!' The bodies multiply, return to haunt, reproach and victimise him.

> *A fleeing man, convinced that he is a murderer, lifts up one trap-door after another and each time sees what he takes to be the ghost of his victim rising up out of it. He calls out in despair, 'But I've only killed one man. Why this ghastly multiplication?' We know what went before this scene and do not share his error, so what must be uncanny to him has an irresistibly comic effect on us.[56]*

Paul Hackett is in the grip of terror. It is not, however, fear of a monster or killer that plagues him; rather, his anxiety and paranoia are exacerbated by a series of uncanny repetitions and recurrences of the same (he keeps returning involuntarily to the same place, the same people keep turning up to persecute him, each time he meets a new woman the situation turns out to be uncannily familiar). We, however, find the situation irresistibly comic. In asking what distinguishes the uncanny from mere coincidence Freud stresses this aspect of involuntary repetition: 'It is only this factor of involuntary repetition which surrounds what would otherwise be innocent enough with an uncanny atmosphere, and forces upon us the idea of something fateful and inescapable when otherwise we should have spoken only of "chance".'[57] The uncanny (*unheimlich*, which translates as unhomely) at first appears to be novel, but is actually a return of the same, a revisiting of childhood fears, an index of the compulsion to repeat (the desire to go home, to recapture the *heimlich*). We all at some time or another experience a sense of the uncanny, but obsessional neurotics are particularly susceptible to uncanny recurrences.

On one level it seems accurate enough to say that the film exhibits Paul's susceptibility to the uncanny and thereby provides us with irresistibly comic relief. However, I would argue that this isn't simply a straightforward matter of the film giving us a privileged perspective on Paul's 'misfortunes'. Rather, it is to be understood in terms of fairly complicated procedures of conversion. In *After Hours* the uncanny is both the source of anxiety and the means of conversion (in this sense not unlike Dorothy's ruby slippers which become the solution to the problem they pose).[58] The film generates a sense of acute uneasiness which is hard to identify because, precisely, it is not tied to identification. It is not to be located exclusively in Paul's consciousness, but neither can it be explained through pointing to devices such as alienation or estrangement, say. It has to do with the circumstances (not with the particularity of place or person), with the very patterning itself of coincidences, the structuring of returns and repetitions. This tends to provoke anticipation of a situation of danger, which is 'a recognised, remembered, expected situation of helplessness'.[59] It arouses in us a sense of traumatic resonance, a sense of being at the mercy of invisible undefined forces.

Caught in the uncanny, however, we are also caught up in a maze that provides a great deal of pleasure. By its very nature the uncanny involves a compulsion to repeat, and the film itself exhibits an almost obsessional attention to detail and precision in charting the returns of places and people – lofts, bars, coffee-houses, apartments – on each occasion playing wickedly with a tension between the *unheimlich* and the *heimlich*. The returns, the doublings, the recurrences are narrativised as running gags, extended double entendres and the critical 'slow burn'.

> The 'slow burn', that comic moment based on someone's smoldering and understated, rather than explosive, reaction to some indignity they are suffering. (Dana Polan)[60]

Top and Bottom: *The Disorderly Orderly* (Frank Tashlin, 1964)

Narrativisation is crucial here, for it is in the threading together of incidents, the accumulation of detail that both the comedy and the knowingness are generated. We are drawn into a game (which could however also be a trap) of identification, lured to identify the signs of repetition, signs of Paul's delusion. The uncanny itself provides an object for focusing the vagueness of our anxiety, and thus alleviates the symptoms somewhat; or more than alleviates: actually transforms the negative into pleasure. There is a sense, however, of being on a roller-coaster and even in the midst of hilarity a nervousness, an anxiety, not just for Paul, but that the intricate elaboration of the structure might collapse, that the sculptural perfection of the process might crack, that this world so full of signs and coded messages might be bared as a structure of analytic delusion, revealing nothing but a void.

> *Jerry Lewis gets so carried away by orderly zeal when taping up a patient that he turns him into a sculpture (or mummy); he is totally encased, though we do see his eyes moving behind slits in the face. The 'patient' is tipped over and starts rolling down a hill, crashing and careening and eventually disintegrating in a heap, revealing – nothing. Shards of plaster are strewn all around, but there is no person inside.*

We half expect this to happen at the end of *After Hours*. In so far as the film might be thought of as a delusive structure warding off anxieties of dissolution and disintegration then Paul's presence at the end is certainly ghosted by the absence of the *Disorderly Orderly*'s phantasmatic patient. Paul's return home is decidedly uncanny, about this there is no doubt, but about our laughter – is it knowing or hollow?

Repetition Is Death, Franky

'Repetition is death, Franky,' the hero tells his beloved dead cat as he starts to encase him in plaster in Roger Corman's *A Bucket of Blood*. Walter Paisley (Dick Miller, who turns up again as an ominously recurring waiter in *After Hours*) is a nerdish busboy at a beatnik coffee-house where poets and would-be philosophers declaim and artists exhibit their art and themselves. He buys some plaster with the befuddled intention of becoming a sculptor, but is distracted from the task by the yowling of his cat, which has got into the lining of the walls and can't escape. Walter takes a carving knife to the timber cladding in order to free Franky but instead impales him. Clutching the beast, which has instantly succumbed to rigor mortis, he has an inspiration: covering the corpse and knife in plaster he produces an instant art work, a sculpture (heralded as the 'Return of Realism') which brings him immediate fame and admiration. In order to retain this glory he has to repeat the process – and so he embarks on a series of murders (progressing quickly to human victims) to secure a supply of corpses as the basis for his sculptural practice. In the end, when his game is up, he's discovered hanging from the ceiling. One of his pursuers supplies the last word: 'I suppose he would have called it "Hanging Man".'

Tancred unwittingly kills his beloved Clorinda in a duel while she is disguised in the armour of an enemy knight. After her burial he makes his way into a strange magic forest which strikes the Crusaders' army with terror. He slashes with his sword at a tall tree; but blood streams from the cut and the voice of Clorinda, whose soul is imprisoned in the tree, is heard complaining that he has wounded his beloved once again.[61]

Pursued by a lynch mob led by Gail the Mr Softee Girl (Catherine O'Hara), Paul Hackett stumbles into a studio in the cellar of the Club Berlin. He clutches, as though at a lifeline, at a rope hanging from the ceiling. But this is Paul Hackett and the rope is not a lifeline – it's attached to a bucket of wet plaster, which he manages to tip all over himself. June (Verna Bloom), the woman whose studio this is (she and Paul were the only people to turn up to a Conceptual Art party at the club), saves the situation when she realises that this is the perfect camouflage; she proceeds to transform him into a papier-mâché sculpture, working methodically away as the zealous mob prowls around her ('Do you all sense the pressure here?!' Gail portentously enthuses). Eventually they leave and June completes her sculpture. Paul wants out, but is told that it isn't safe yet. Although his voice is muffled we can hear and feel the panic rising: 'Let me out! let me out!' She pastes a strip of paper over his mouth and leaves. In extreme, discomfiting, close-up we see his eyes moving behind slits: he is imprisoned and utterly helpless.

The narrator of Poe's 'The Black Cat' is a humane and docile man who falls under the sway of alcohol and becomes moody and violent. His malice is indiscriminate, but he refrains from maltreating his beloved black cat, a gigantic creature called Pluto. One day, however, he unaccountably turns on the hapless beast and gouges one of its eyes out. At first he is seized by horror and remorse but soon his feelings change to irritation and malice:

> And then came, as if to my final and irrevocable overthrow, the spirit of PERVERSENESS . . . It was this unfathomable longing of the soul to vex itself, to offer violence to its own nature, to do wrong for the wrong's sake only, that urged me to continue and finally to consummate the injury.[62]

He slips a noose about its neck and hangs it from a tree. That night his house is destroyed by fire, all the walls collapsing except one: 'I approached and saw, as if graven in bas relief upon the white surface, the figure of a gigantic cat. The impression was given with an accuracy truly marvelous. There was a rope about the animal's neck.' Although at first he thinks it is an apparition he eventually deduces that someone must have cut the cat from the tree and thrown it through the window to wake and warn him of the fire. 'The falling of other walls had compressed the victim of my cruelty into the substance of the freshly-spread plaster; the lime of which, with the flames, and the ammonia from the carcass, had then accomplished the portraiture as I saw it.' Filled again with something like remorse, he looks around for another cat to take his beloved's place. One night a cat bearing a remarkable resemblance to the original pet follows him home. Although initially fond of it, his affection soon turns to disgust and annoyance and then to the 'bitterness of hatred'. One day he takes an axe to the beast but is intercepted by his wife. Infuriated by her interference, he sinks the axe into her head. A question arises: What to do with the body? Finally he hits upon the idea of walling her up in the cellar. This done, he proceeds to look for the cat, but it is nowhere to be found. After a number of days the police come and search the house; three or four times they search the cellar and at last are about to leave, thoroughly satisfied, when the narrator is somehow compelled to draw attention to the skilfulness of his crime. He starts bragging about how well constructed the house is, how solid the walls are, and as he speaks he taps with his cane on that very portion where the body is concealed. He is answered by a voice from within: a hideous inhuman yowling. 'I had walled the monster up within the tomb.'

This, however, is not the end of the story. Nor is it the beginning; it is but one episode in a series of repetitions, coincidences and elements that recur in various configurations. When Paul first goes downtown to see Marcy (who isn't there when he arrives) he finds Kiki, in black leather miniskirt and black bra working away on a life-size papier-mâché sculpture which reminds him, he says, of Munch's 'The Shriek'. Kiki corrects him in a bored and laconic manner: 'The Scream'. Leaving the loft some time later he notices, incidentally, a $20 bill stuck on the statue and although nothing is said both he and we are reminded of the bill that was so cruelly whisked out of his grasp and into the night on his mad taxi ride downtown. Kiki initiates him into an utterly alien

After Hours (Martin Scorsese, 1985)

art world by getting him to take over her work (dipping the pieces of newspaper and layering them on the sculpture) so that she can have a rest. Then she demands a massage, and the exchange about scars and burns takes place. Later on that night, just after he has been accused of being a thief, he surprises Neil and Pepe (Cheech and Chong), the real neighbourhood thieves, loading Kiki's television and the sculpture into their van. He shouts and gives chase, causing them to drop the TV and drive off in haste; the statue falls out onto the pavement. He heaves it onto his shoulders and returns it to Kiki, only to find out that the objects had been legitimately bought and sold. Yet later, when the momentum and paranoia has escalated even further, he returns again to Kiki's loft while she is at the Club Berlin and 'helps himself' to the $20 bill. He hails a cab. At last, the journey home is conceivable; but it turns out to be the same manic driver whom he failed to pay on his trip downtown. The guy grabs the money and careers off into the night, leaving Paul stranded.

Stranded, and bleeding. As Paul is trying to get into the cab the person getting out inadvertently opens the door on him, causing an injury. She insists on taking him home so that she can bandage his bleeding arm. As she is about to do so she notices a scrap of newspaper (from the papier-mâché) stuck to his flesh. She reads out an item that bears an uncanny (and prophetic?) resemblance to Paul's situation: 'A man was torn limb from limb by an irate mob last night in the fashionable SoHo area of Manhattan. Police are having difficulty identifying the man because no form of ID was found on his shredded clothing and his entire face was pummelled completely beyond recognition.' She tries to tear it off but it is stuck like adhesive to his body. 'Stop touching me! Stop touching me!' he shrieks. Her response is to propose burning it off, which provokes another screaming fit – 'Lady no lady no lady no!' He manages to escape Gail but further misadventures await him. In the middle of the deserted street in the dead of night he falls to his knees and screams to the heavens: 'What do you want from me? What have I done? I'm just a word processor for Christ's sake!'

> A cry, at first muffled and broken, like the sobbing of a child, and then quickly swelling into a long, loud, and continuous scream, utterly anomalous and inhuman, a howl, a wailing shriek, half of horror and half of triumph, such as might have arisen only out of hell, conjointly from the throats of the damned in their agony and of the demons that exult in the damnation. ('The Black Cat')

In extreme, discomfiting, close-up we see his eyes moving behind slits: he is imprisoned and utterly helpless. Sounds of sliding and scraping are heard. Cut to a mid-shot with Paul/the sculpture in the foreground; in the background the cover is slid off a manhole and Neil and Pepe descend into the cellar/basement. They are checking the place out when suddenly one of them is transfixed by some object off camera. 'My sculpture!' Cut to a point-of-view shot which zooms in fast. They load what they think is the sculpture they bought from Kiki into the van.[63] As the van hurtles round a corner the back door flies open and the sculpture crashes onto the road. We hold our breath, but, as it disintegrates, Paul emerges out of the debris. He has by chance been deposited right outside his office.

As a Feral Bluestocking . . .

> 'I'll fuck anything that moves!' Zoom in on Frank's face, his demonic
> laughter swells into a long, loud, and continuous scream that continues
> over the next shot, merging with the shriek of tyres, 'a wailing shriek, half
> of horror and half of triumph, such as might have arisen only out of hell'.
> The camera bears down, moving at high speed over the bright yellow lines
> of the road. (Blue Velvet)

> Just follow the yellow brick road! Just follow the yellow brick road!
> (The Wizard of Oz)

> The camera bears down, moving at high speed over the bright yellow lines
> of the road. There is an explosion, flashing red lights, a cyclist crashes in the
> race. On the soundtrack: 'Wipe Out.' (Scorpio Rising)

Entering the jungles of Lumberton, I feel conspicuously exposed as a bluestocking, or perhaps a plain jane. Surrounded by the sounds of falling trees
and roaring insects and screaming men I claim my right, as a feral bluestocking, to a form of 'wild analysis', what Ferenczi described as a kind of 'compulsive analysing'.[64] To isolate a dream or a dream-fragment from its context, he
argued, is merely 'seeking to enjoy a gossamer omnipotence'. Gossamer omnipotence seems to me a quite appropriate demeanour to adopt in the face of
Blue Velvet, a text which is littered with part-objects and fragments, and self-
consciously so. My interpretation, then, is based upon free association around
the part-elements of the formations of the film text, privileging what seems to
me part-object *par excellence* – the ear. The fragments, allusions, quotations,
function like part-objects (an example of such a fragment is when Dorothy on
the telephone utters a name that comes from out of the blue, so to speak, and
hovers there, provocatively inconsequential: 'Is that Madeleine?' she asks;
Madeleine, the heroine of *Vertigo*); and like foreign bodies they are subject to
repudiation, to be internally excluded, excreted. In a Kleinian drama of intro-
jection this implies expelling dangerous substances (excrements) out of the self
and into the mother.[65] 'He put his disease in me.' Dorothy repeats this, 'He put
his disease in me.' This alerts us not simply to a dynamic being played out
between the dramatis personae of the film but to a dynamic involving the analyst. What is being manifested here is an infantile sadistic desire, on the part of
the film or film-maker, to contaminate the analyst/mother by implanting foreign bodies, or transferring symptoms (disease).

Lip, Slip, Slap: The Slippery Slide of Sadism

> And like a pair of polished shoes, it had just the rightworld-
> weariness and erotic sheen.
> (William Gass)[66]

Blue Velvet slips and shines and slides. Rather than literalising a sliding signifier, however (on the contrary, its literalising tendency is much more inert), or
deploying slapstick, it smears the surface with a slippery substance, lipstick. It
is not the substitution – of lips for slaps – that is significant, but the metonymy:
kissing and hitting, seduction and sadism. There are two scenes that I will take
as exemplary of the kind of exchange that the text initiates with the interpreting subject. These are the lipstick scene between Frank the psychotic and Jeffrey the would-be detective, and the SM gagging scene featuring Dorothy and
Frank. Although my interest lies primarily with the drama of interpretation I
am not arguing that the characters exist allegorically, or that they stand in a
one-to-one relationship to the players in an extra-diegetic drama; rather, I
wish to signal a concern with the dynamic of exchange and a relative uninter-
est in identifying who's who.

The 'lipstick scene' takes place at night in a stretch of barren land on the
outskirts of Lumberton. A girl dances on the top of a car, 'In Dreams' plays on
the transistor, Frank smears his mouth with ruby lipstick, and then aggressive-
ly kisses Jeffrey, on the lips, all over his face. He then uses a scrap of blue velvet
to rub off the lipstick that has been transferred to Jeffrey, and proceeds to
punch him repeatedly in the face. In this scenario the analyst-ingénue is seduced, lured into the complicity of exchange and interpretation. But the kiss,
emblematic of this exchange, materialises as an act of violence – not only an
act of contamination, but also a slap on the smacker. To offer an interpretation
of *Blue Velvet*, to open your lips (to speak, to be kissed) is to invite abuse, to
have your lips forcibly closed, to submit to an act of scarlet desecration.

The red lips are clearly homologous with the red shoes that Dorothy Valance wears (even when she wears little else) just as the ruby slippers are echoed
in Judy Garland's precociously voluptuous scarlet lips.

> *On the river Marilyn wears denims and long boots and a man's shirt, but
> she carries her red shoes with her. Those ruby stiletto slippers in which she
> used to sway as she sang her torch songs in seedy saloons. Shoes red and
> succulent as painted lips, lips that glide and twirl and dawdle, opening just
> enough to murmur . . .*

Before turning to the SM gagging scene, there is a question. What is the meaning of 'Blue Velvet'? Predictably, given the *modus operandi* of the film it is both
everything and nothing: it is purely immaterial, a song, a series of sounds; and
it is nothing but a piece of material. These conceptions are not actually incompatible. The point is that 'blue velvet' is not an object *per se*; it is a materiali-
sation of blue fantasies which may be manifested in a variety of part-objects.
One of its manifestations is the film itself, proffered as a gift to the viewer/
analyst, but also as a gagging device, to gag interpretation. The potpourri
primal scene, featuring Frank and Dorothy and voyeuristically witnessed by
Jeffrey, is characterised by an excessive acting-out of sado-masochistic tropes.
Despite the fact that a certain degree of distance or separation is instituted,
between fictional protagonists, and between viewer and screen, a connection
or identification is also maintained. The piece of blue velvet that runs between
Frank and Dorothy, that they grip between their teeth, binds them together in

a bondage ritual. It is effectively a double bind and a running gag: it invites interpretation (to be identified – as umbilical cord, fetish object or whatever) and gags criticism (or interpretation). The sadistic force of this gagging device is more forcefully driven home when we see the strip of blue velvet gagging the corpse of Don, the dead father. The Name of the Father, The Don, is not insignificant in *Blue Velvet*, but it also functions in a routine manner (the garden scene at the opening, which includes the father having a heart attack and the hose spurting, represents a fantasy of being able to piss further, of out-pissing papa).[67] It is in the body of the Mother, battered black and blue (the naked apparition that rises out of suburban darkness, prompting Jeffrey's friend to ask, 'Is that your mother?'), that the fantasy of revenge materialises; or, to put this slightly differently, the one presumed to know materialises as a perversion of the maternal function.

There is a texture for torture. (Carolee Schneeman)[68]

Velvet is characterised by its texture and it is tempting to argue that 'blue velvet' functions in the film as a textural potential, that it plays upon the 'feel' of velvet to affect the feelings of the viewer. The allusion to *Scorpio Rising* might seem at first to endorse such a view. The pertinence of this underground classic to a film-maker like Lynch is immediately apparent in its reputation for outrageous decadence and blasphemy, its magpie-like appropriations, its revelling in kinky sex, drugs, rock 'n' roll and the occult; but most of all in the fact that it is now, despite having once been banned from museums, considered a minor masterpiece of American art cinema. *Scorpio* is driven by music and at its centre Bobby Vinton's rendition of 'Blue Velvet' is cut to naked male bodies in narcissistic display, dressing in torn blue denim, leather and heavy metal. Anger's quotation of the song, 'Bluer than velvet was the night, softer than satin was the light', is camply ironic, though not parodic for it carries an affective charge in its radical reformulation of the torch song's romantic filtering of sex. It uses velvet to evoke texture, but this evocation exists in contrasts: pale flesh and dark leather, jarring colours, cutting rhythms. It does not show, does not depict velvet. It is about display, masquerade, pleasure and the death drive; but the signifiers slide, the viewer is whipped from here to there; although very vivid, it is not literal.[69] *Blue Velvet* literalises. Similarly it literalises and banalises the SM. When Dorothy says 'Hit me', Jeffrey slugs her across the jaw. Thus too the film responds to the viewer's perversity – 'I like to be scared' – by showing as much kinkiness in as arty a way as possible. 'And like a pair of polished shoes, it had just the right world-weariness and erotic sheen.'

The Sound of My Own Breathing
It is in the very substitution and conflation – a banal instance indeed – of ear and air that the sinister underside of hearsay makes itself felt. The fresh air of Lumberton materialises as a part-object supreme, a very fresh ear. It is at once a material object, severed and hairy and bloody, and nothing but thin air. Like the imaginary locked box of the Oblivious Transfer. There is another instance in which this substitution can be traced. In *On Being Blue*, William Gass[70]

describes a recurring fantasy scene revolving around his neighbour's wife. He watches her through the window as she stands at the sink washing salad. Eventually he realises he is not in the scene:

> Suppose, as I had wished a moment ago, I were inaudible. I should find, very quickly, how much I need to hear the sound of my own breathing. To hear the scene, but not myself: how odd . . . how horrible . . . how whimsical . . . how unnerving. Now I understand what a difference any kind of distance makes.

In *Blue Velvet* distance is dramatised, but we are not entirely excluded; indeed, the film labours to put us in the picture, aurally. The sound of our own breathing materialises on the soundtrack as the consummate pervert Frank labours to breathe. Not fresh air, we assume, but some unnameable and unknowable substitute.

The Mohawk Conversion, Or How Wax Casts Were Made of Wounds
Paul Hackett, soaked by the rain, sits on Julie's couch like a drenched rat, desultorily twirling a giant pair of opaque plastic lips between his hands.

> *Lips that glide and twirl and dawdle, opening just enough to murmur or to scream.*

As he sits and twirls, Julie waxes lyrical about her day-to-day existence. She takes offence at his sarcastic 'gee whiz' response to her story of life in a Xerox shop, and as her offence escalates into hysteria – 'Hey what is that? Gee Whiz? I mean you humouring me? I don't have to take that kind of shit you know, I mean what is it with people today' – Paul freezes in terror and the lips are suspended in mid-air. So here he is, this guy who just wants to meet a nice girl, do some kissing, get laid, here he is holding in his hands an embodiment of his desire. Or, holding in his hands an abstraction of his anxiety. The embodiment and the abstraction actually coalesce in this image, in these lips which are literally blown out of proportion, which represent a hollow promise or a hollow threat depending on how you look at it. And how you look at it is all-important for what you feel.

This image epitomises a process that recurs in the film, a process that works on at least two levels: first, as a process of psychic conversion within the diegesis, to do with Paul's story; and, second, as an uncanny device enabling a perverse conversion for the viewer. What we see here is Paul touching, and therefore presumably in touch with his feelings. His desire, which is also his greatest fear, is in a sense literalised, but the very process of concretisation is also a way of distancing and disembodying. Paul repeatedly anticipates a dangerous and dreaded situation by producing a literal projection in close-up, by conjuring and 'making safe' the dread. Thus he attempts to regulate and control a dangerous terrain of ambivalence, manifested in a series of precarious oppositions, between detachment and involution, abstraction and embodiment, distance and proximity.

Kiki's talk of scars (a response to his remark about her 'nice body') anticipates Paul's story of his tonsils experience when the nurse told him that if he
took the blindfold off they'd have to do the operation all over again.

I reached up to untie the blindfold . . . I saw . . .

Of course we never find out what he saw, but, in a sense, *After Hours*
repeatedly enacts this process of anticipation. Latent images of cutting and
burning materialise in vividly sensational flashes of lacerated and scorched
tissue. Sensation and imagination are superimposed. 'If something is to stay
in the memory,' says Nietzsche, 'it must be burned in.'[71] When Paul and
Marcy are on the bed we catch a glimpse of burn wounds on her thigh
(before she quickly pulls her dressing gown down) and later, when he discovers that she is dead, Paul gingerly lifts the black sheet that covers her
naked body. In place of the wounds we see a tattoo – of a death's head, a
grinning skull in top hat. The series of substitutions here suggests a potentially endless chain in which a fear of death, projected onto fate, materialises as an image cut into flesh (just as the macabre newspaper prophecy
inscribed on his body elicits a threat of burning) or, most terrifyingly, as the
ultimate paradox, a lifeless embodiment, a corpse. In his desperate attempts
to evade the threat of being cut (or having it cut off) or being burnt, Paul is
constantly reopening old wounds, repeating the operation.

> *In the 19th century, wax casts were made of wounds and then
> placed in glass jars, sometimes simulating the appearance of a
> real object floating in liquid.*
> (Gregory Whitehead)[72]

Anxiety is both free-floating and bottled up; danger is both imagined and real.
Paul's fear in the Club Berlin, on the night of 'Mohawk day', for instance,
seems reasonable enough. He is initially refused entrance to the club by a
hugely sinister bouncer (who quotes a line from Welles's *The Trial*, a
Kafkaesque film about a man who is accused of a crime without being informed of what it is) because he does not have a Mohawk cut. Eventually he is
allowed in but is forced to submit to an impromptu razor treatment and loses
a clump of hair before managing to break free. Running away through dark
deserted streets he screams incoherently:

Cut . . . cut . . . dreadful . . . cut . . .bald . . . barbaric.

The threat of scalping is made manifest in the Mohawk 'cut' just as Paul's terror and his conviction that he's being persecuted, as expressed in his shrieking,
is perversely validated when he becomes 'The Scream', a sculptural imitation
of the Munch painting (though Neil and Pepe take him for a George Segal
artefact, 'sometimes simulating the appearance of a real object'). The common
nightmare of not being able to run for cover, of being immobilised and
silenced, materialises with uncanny resonance in the sculpture scenario, just as

the imprint of Poe's cat persists. Paul's fear (and desire to not be touched) is abstracted and embodied; the sculpture performs in the same way as the lips and the Mohawk head and the bottled floating wound. The 'scalp', like blue velvet in the film of that name (though affectively different), materialises here as a particularly cinematic part-object or metonymic trope: the Mohawk stands for, paradoxically embodies, an abstract threat – of cutting. The threat materialises most vividly and is most economically 'made safe' in the Western genre where, through a process of abstraction and displacement, it is embodied by the Other, the Indian, the Mohawk.

Travis Bickle incarnates this heritage, and turns up again like a malevolent ghost in the Club Berlin, screwing the screwball comedy a notch tighter, imbuing the laughter with a razor-sharp knowingness.

> *Get back to your fuckin' tribe before you get hurt. (Taxi Driver)*

To Do the Operation All Over Again

Paul doesn't laugh. The way he sees the plastic lips, the sculpture, the Mohawk cut, the death's head tattoo, is not the same as the way we do. His pain becomes our pleasure.

> *'Oh boy, oh God, what are we gonna do, oh God, this is awful, this is the worst!' And he would keep laughing.*

The image of Paul's eyes, the only sign of life, moving nervously in the slits of the mummy's face is almost like a caricature of Metz's 'spectator-fish': they who 'take in everything with their eyes, nothing with their bodies'. But rather than taking in, he has himself been taken in, ingested; it is as though the shark, rather than biting off a titbit, has swallowed the whole story. But already this distinction between distance and closeness, as regards the senses, emerges as dubious. If in *Blue Velvet* the kiss, emblematic of the exchange involved in interpretation, materialises explicitly as an act of violence and contamination, the (plastic) lips in *After Hours* function somewhat differently, evoking a more incipient threat, a more ambivalent promise. The film articulates Paul's looking as absolutely to do with bodily sensation, but his attempts to abstract and distance are translated, for us, into somatic immediacy. It is as though the shudders that pass through him, when flipping through the burns book, for instance, or when he witnesses the murder, are channelled through a circuit of exchange and are registered in our bodies as giggles, titters, chuckles and guffaws. Paul's mode of conversion is neurotic and fails to afford him pleasure (it is a holding operation); on the contrary, he involuntarily repeats himself, is haunted by the return of the same. We are witness to this uncanny process. We know, on some unconscious somatic level, through the rhythm of repetitions that the film has set going, that if we keep watching it will be necessary 'to do the operation all over again'. And we keep watching, in anticipation. We laugh. We enact a perverse conversion, but if our laughter affords voluptuous somatic surrender the simultaneous knowingness is razor-sharp and

102

double-edged, and hence the tinge of horror. For there is also the possibility that we too have been taken in, that we have swallowed the story whole, and that it will turn, like a knife, in our stomachs.

An Uncanny McGuffin, a Palpable Lure

Paul is enticed downtown by a curiously palpable lure: a plaster-of-Paris bagel-and-cream-cheese paperweight. When he meets Marcy in the coffee shop she offers him not her own phone number but that of a sculptress from whom he can buy one of these alluring objects. His face is a study in bemusement, but he misses no more than a beat before expressing appropriately 'cool' interest (appropriate to this SoHo coffee bar where the waiter practises dance movements while attending to customers). As soon as he gets home he calls the number, speaks to Marcy and heads to SoHo to see her. He seems very keen to make out but she is evasive and keeps deferring any sexual encounter. When she does eventually kiss him she does so with serious intent; he becomes totally inert. After a long pause he makes a conversational gambit: 'How about that joint?' He takes a few puffs and becomes, in an instant, hyperbolically aggressive and paranoid. 'Cough up!' he demands (cough up, that is, a bagel-and-cream-cheese paperweight), 'because as we sit here chatting there are important papers flying rampant around my apartment because I don't have anything to hold them down with!' She runs from the room crying, giving him the opportunity to escape. Later (after he has discovered Marcy's overdosed body), when Julie declares that he should be 'commended and rewarded' for returning to her as promised, his anguished face reflects anticipation of some unspeakable sufferance. The camera cranes from Julie's face down her body and outstretched arm to her open palm on which the 'prize' is displayed, and then the movement is reversed, the camera returning to her face. 'Do you know what this is?' There is a frightful snapping sound off screen: cut to a wriggling mouse that has just been caught in one of the traps around Julie's bed. 'This', she says, 'is a plaster-of-Paris bagel-and-cream-cheese paperweight.'

The suspense and 'revelation' of the object in this scene are treated somewhat parodically. As a device the improbably recurring paperweight functions rather like the jaws graffiti, as an index of Paul's paranoia and panic. It might also seem to function as a Hitchcockian McGuffin, an object which sets the story in motion but which in itself means nothing, and as such is a pure device for luring both characters and viewers and generating suspense. While it does function thus this is not its only function; it is densely overdetermined and for such a stolidly indigestible object amazingly mobile in its ramifications. *After Hours* displays the plaster-of-Paris bagel-and-cream-cheese paperweight as a McGuffin, but as an Uncanny McGuffin, hands it to us on the palm of its hand as it were, as concrete evidence of Paul's disturbed perspective; but at the same time its very improbability (not only is its recurrence improbable but its very existence) lures us into a milieu where reality and nightmare coexist, where an excess of free-floating anxiety is generated and converted, but not entirely contained, by the deictic tendency. Between anticipation and suspense: parody.

> *Deixis is . . . the primary means whereby language gears itself to the speaker and receiver (through the personal pronouns 'I' and 'you') and to the time and place of the action (through the adverbs 'here' and 'now', etc.), as well as to the supposed physical environment at large and the objects that fill it (through the demonstratives 'this' and 'that', etc.).* (Keir Elam)[73]

The question of deixis has been important to performance studies and semiotic approaches to literary texts, but has not been given much attention in film studies.[74] Perhaps this is because the term 'deictics' designates a linguistic category, a group of words which Jakobson called 'shifters'.[75] In the dramatic text or script these words can be seen to create dramatic presence, to engender spatial relations – between actors, and between actors and audience. But if we think of deixis in terms of a dynamic of exchange, if we foreground the I-you and this-that pairings, we can see that its pertinence to film might be located on a rhetorical level. The point would be not to delineate a taxonomy of shots but to indicate a modality of address, a particular way in which the authorial voice summons the viewer via a demonstrative inflection.

The graffiti declares itself (to us) not so much as a representation but as a declamatory sign – hey, watch out, castration anxiety let loose! We laugh at this sign of Paul's anxiety, at the way in which his imagination keeps producing evidence to feed his paranoia; for to him the graffiti appears as a personal address, a sign that confirms his sense of persecution, his helpless engulfment in the jaws of fate.

The deictic tendency, as it is manifested in *After Hours*, invokes a knowing viewer. It has to do with the exhibition of paranoia that sometimes seems close to parody, or to caricature, or suspense. Paul's predilection for projecting his dilemma (or his sense of victimisation) onto the powers of destiny is frequently displayed through through combinations of camera movement, angles, cutting and sound effects. These rhetorical manoeuvres tend to carry the charge of suspense without the affect. That is, they are usually not convincingly motivated, or entirely plausible, though the force of convention elicits engagement, and often the irrationality of the perspective is revealed in hindsight. During the shot or the sequence we are somehow caught up in Paul Hackett's expectations, but a split second later we are hurtled away, at a distance where we can see the irrationality and see it originating with him. But our laughter is delayed for a split second, and in that delayed reaction our anxiety is stretched out, and strands escape, float free. And even while we are distanced from the paranoid perspective, we are drawn into the game of expectation.[76] The filmic language is not entirely or exclusively parodic.

> The angles themselves are parodies: the angles, the cuts, and the Fritz Lang-type shots, the Hitchcock parodies.
> (Scorsese)[77]

The first (steadicam) shot of *After Hours* is extraordinary: speedy, vertiginous, it traverses in a flash a huge space. At breakneck pace we are propelled through an expansive open-plan office, rushing precipitously at a quarry: Griffin Dunne. Pascal Bonitzer lucidly identifies the dynamic at work here:

> There is always an 'ecce homo' in the cinema of Scorsese. Few film-makers know how to give a sense of this deictic power, this value of the index of fate, to their camera. Straightaway, the terror is there, even though nothing has happened, though it seems nothing can possibly happen. The character, Paul, is marked immediately, designated, made the victim in advance.[78]

Malevolent Vitality

Parody elicits our cinephiliac laughter, partly because the hyperbole inscribed primarily in camera movements seems to demonstrate Paul's delusional perspective: he attributes ominous and suspenseful properties to the most innocent of objects and events.

> *Cinematic techniques are employed to give a malevolent vitality to inanimate objects.* (Maya Deren)[79]

In particular, telephones and keys are invested with menacing intent. But it is not only objects that acquire an ominous aura; cinematic techniques are themselves invested with malevolent vitality. When Paul first phones Marcy from his apartment, and she says 'Come on over', there is a cut from him to a clock showing the time as 11.30, back to an extreme close-up and very slow movement over his face and the phone piece. The trope signifies suspense and foreboding and at this stage we are not really sure how to respond, but as the film progresses the hyperbole (or the gap between the formal signification and what is actually going on) becomes more apparent. In Marcy's apartment the phone rings twice and on each occasion a sense of suspense and menace is signified (though not necessarily generated). On the first occasion Paul is alone in the room and looks at the ringing phone with fear and horror; the camera circles him, following his hand as he reaches out very slowly to pick up the receiver, as though in expectation of some dreadful news. On the second occasion both he and Marcy look at it in terror, it keeps ringing, we hold our breath (or rather we recognise the device which is so often used to make us hold our breath).

> *The phone keeps ringing. We can't bear the suspense, find ourselves willing Grace Kelly to pick up the phone even though we know that as soon as she does, she will be murdered. (Dial M for Murder)*

In the course of this nightmarish night Paul goes 'home' with various characters simply so that he can use the phone (in order to get back to his 'real' home), but his desires are invariably and horribly thwarted. The recurring phone shots often incorporate an abrasive alternation between extreme angles, focal lengths, and static framing and rapid zooming. When he meets Gail she invites him up to her apartment so that she can bandage his arm. 'Do you have a phone?' he asks. Cut from mid-shot in the street to a close-up in the apartment, combined with a flash zoom onto the telephone – almost immediately his hand is propelled into the frame to seize the receiver. He gets a number from the operator and tries calling it, but Gail, in the guise of helping, repeats the number in various configurations until he is thoroughly confused and his attempt sabotaged ('I'm just trying to entertain you,' she says). A little later, on a deserted street, he approaches a man hesitantly cruising who warns him that there are certain things he won't do. 'Will you help me? Take me home?' Paul asks. In the apartment Paul cuts short his host's nervous confession – that actually this is his first time with a man – by asking to use the phone. Again there is a flash zoom into close-up on the phone, as though buzzing the revelation of a talismanic object. The object, however, turns out to be a medium of betrayal: he phones the cops to tell them 'I'm being persecuted . . . I have every reason to believe my life is in serious danger', and they hang up on him. 'Hello, hello, hello, hello' – he speaks into thin air, directing his words to someone who has turned a deaf ear. 'Oh wow, oh wow, oh wow! I don't believe this!' he wails, punitively thumping his head on the phone.

> *Hello, hello, hello, hello. The camera circles Grace Kelly as she speaks into the phone to someone who has turned a deaf ear. As the camera circles it reveals the murderer standing behind her.*

The deictic character of the zoom is echoed elsewhere, for instance when Marcy feels like she is going to let loose. She is in the doorway and Paul is watching her from across the bedroom: 'I feel like something incredible's really going to happen here. I feel soooooo excited! I don't know why, I feel it.' She laughs hysterically, and there is a sudden zoom into her face as she delivers a flamboyantly histrionic wink. For Paul this implicit invitation is redolent with menace, menace which materialises in the ominous ringing of the phone as Marcy disappears into the bathroom. The malevolent vitality of this zoom (and its exhibitionism as a rhetorical device, its placement within a series of rhetorical repetitions) begins to insinuate a response to Sarris's dilemma: 'I couldn't figure out what Paul was looking at and why, and what the fragmented objects and people he was looking at had to do with his character.'[80] Paul's tendency to get things out of proportion (or to lose perspective) is reiterated in the instances of alternation between extreme angles and focal lengths. For instance the $20 bill is filmed in slow motion from a low angle as it twirls into the air, sucked out of his grasp and into a vortex, and is then pictured from a high angle as it descends into the gutter. When Paul is checking Tom's apartment an extreme high angle, showing him in the bathroom, flushing the toilet, which overflows and floods the room, is followed by a big close-up of his face. The exchange of keys with Kiki, which has already been described, is reprised when Paul returns to the apartment, this time bearing the statue that he thinks has been stolen. We see Paul in extreme high angle from Kiki's point of view as she looks out of the window, followed by his view of her, gagged and bound and gripping the keys between her teeth. It turns out that Paul has not only mistaken a (probably) legitimate transaction for theft but has also misrecognised a (probably) consensual and fairly innocuous SM scene for assault.

In the middle of the deserted street in the dead of night he falls to his knees and screams to the heavens: 'What do you want from me? What have I done? I'm just a word processor for Christ's sake!'

This is filmed from an extreme high angle, so that our view corresponds to that of the persecuting God, and is accompanied by dramatic drum rolls. It rhymes with the scene in the Club Berlin where Scorsese himself plays a manic overseer, standing on a platform and swinging searchlights over the crowded floor. The atmosphere, thick with sensory overload, and heightened effects – of sound in particular – conjures up a hyperreal and sinister milieu. The club is filled with punk simulacrums of Travis Bickle whilst on the soundtrack the Bad Brains perform 'Pay to Cum', a melody intermittently pierced by the buzz of the razor reaching a chainsaw fortissimo. On other occasions the diegetic motivation of sound effects is even more tenuous. In Marcy's apartment Paul's growing sense of unease (and ours) is nurtured by the 'noise' of an occasional whispering that seems spatially indeterminate, permeating the walls, filling the room, though it is impossible to make out what is being said. This 'noise' is frequently accompanied by a loud percussive ticking, the source of which is not located.

On the soundtrack, just as in the opening segment, there are only muffled street sounds and a loud ticking. Could it be the cab meter ticking over? Or a clockwork device (Travis is well and truly wound up) or an internal time bomb?

To some degree we share Paul's panic in the Club Berlin as he is hunted down, pinioned and forced to submit to a head shave. But our panic is partially deflected into humour as the self-referential joke of Scorsese as persecutory figure of illumination (director, critic, malevolent vitality incarnate) is intensified by the gleefully macabre reference to *Taxi Driver*. But only partially deflected, since Scorsese's self-inscription here alludes to the scene of the father in *Peeping Tom* shining a torch over the face of his young son – the future murderer – in a scene where he is tormenting him in order to provoke, measure and record his fear.

Hey Mom It's Me!

To say that 'Paul goes home with various characters simply so that he can use the phone' is not inaccurate, but it is less true perhaps than the afterthought, the phrase in parenthesis: he goes home with strangers (in order to get back to his 'real' home).

Fleeing from the vigilante mob – the night filled with whistles, flashing lights, running footsteps – Paul ducks into the lobby of an apartment block and randomly presses the buzzers, frantically shouting out garbled names into the intercom. 'Hey Mrs . . ., Hey Mrs . . . I went to school with your son!' And then, in desperation: 'Hey Mom it's me!'

Let's go over it again: Kiki lets him into the loft and then falls asleep and starts snoring just as his story of the burns ward is hotting up. Later she invites him to Club Berlin but once there doesn't acknowledge him or respond to his cries for help. Marcy suicides on him. Julie, or 'Miss Beehive 1965' as she is dubbed, rescues him and is at first solicitous, if somewhat anachronistic. She puts on Joni Mitchell's 'Chelsea Morning' to soothe his soul (in place of the Monkees) and urges him to 'talk to me . . . Just let go, tell me your problems. Tell me your problems.' But when he does: 'Paul, lighten up! What is this, gloom and doom week, and oh goosey goosey!' At the point where relations are becoming very strained she asks him if he likes her hairdo. 'Why don't you touch it?' Betwixt Scylla and Charybdis he gingerly reaches out, then, at the very moment when he is about to touch the beehive, there is an almighty bang, crash and smash. As he flees, we hear her voice behind closed doors: 'Well you're going to be sorry for this 'cos I'm going to get you!' Gail's offer appears initially to be genuine enough – 'Why don't you come with me and I'll get you a bandage' – but while the night is yet young she inexplicably changes her tune: 'You're dead pal!' (Not so inexplicable, however, when we realise that she has caught sight of Julie's sketch of him which has been reproduced as a 'Wanted' poster. Paul's ostentatious boredom when Julie told him about how she could get free photocopies returns to haunt him. Her job is turned to good use as his image is multiplied and plastered all over SoHo – repetition with a vengeance.) The gay guy takes him home to his apartment but when Paul asks if he can just sleep on the couch he says, 'Why don't you just go home?' Finally June seems to offer a safe refuge. As the vigilante mob is battering the door of the Club Berlin and as Peggy Lee sings 'I'm not ready for that final moment', she leads him downstairs to her studio, where she cradles him in her arms, stroking his hair. She encases him in plaster and as her final touch pastes a strip of paper over his mouth. 'No, you aren't safe yet,' she murmurs.

> *In the operating theatre the camera is situated with the patient, looking up into the face of Jerry Lewis, the would-be doctor. From the soundtrack are emitted the most excruciating, blood-curdling shrieks of agony. All we can see of the patient are his feet, which jerk wildly in paroxysms of pain. Lewis's face mirrors these paroxysms as he flinches, cowers, shudders, the face registering every nuance of excruciation. A point beyond endurance is soon reached, and he turns and flees, screeching, as he disappears down the corridor: 'Ma! Ma!'*

In *Disorderly Orderly* Jerry Lewis plays a would-be doctor who, because he over-identifies with the patient or body-in-pain, becomes a hospital orderly. The other's symptoms are involuntarily manifested in his body. This process of transferred somatisation transforms him from sympathetic witness to violent exhibitionist, from operative (he who performs operations) to aggressive victim.

Could it be that some stray thread traces a lazy line through these texts, connecting Paul's compulsion to look, Jerry Lewis's aversion of the gaze, and the way in which, at threshold moments, they both call out for mother?

> *In* The Curse of Frankenstein, *there are two utterly horrible, vividly remembered moments, one from Frankenstein's point of view, the other from the monster's. First, there is the moment when the creature unravels its*

bandages and reveals a ravaged monstrous face; and, second, when he kills the maid the camera moves into a close up as increasing terror registers on her face.[81]

The nurse tells Paul that if he takes the blindfold off they'll have to do the operation all over again. Despite this interdiction, 'I reached up to untie the blindfold . . . I saw . . .' Of course we never find out what he saw, but every time he flees from a threatening situation we might surmise a repetition of the anticipated horror, of a dangerous situation which is 'a recognised, remembered, expected situation of helplessness'. Unbandaging or untying (the blindfold) does not literally reveal a ravaged face, lacerated flesh or a burn wound, but these images are all evoked by the expression of anxiety and horror so central to this comedic character called Hackett. And there is an uncanny sense in which the same image returns, recurs across periods and genres, and returns obsessively within this particular text. The situation which is repeated over and over again in *After Hours* is this: a strange woman seems to offer something like love, and then turns on him threateningly so that he has to defend himself against assault – 'Stop touching me!' – and is forced to flee. His perception of enmity, however, is articulated by the film as a possible reflection of his own hostile impulses. He flees like Jerry Lewis from the potential sight of the imagined operation or wound. This wound, via an elaborate metonymic chain – fanged jaws, burn scars, death's head, bagel, steel mousetrap, beehive, plastic lips – is associated with woman. There is the idea of woman as wound (or rather female lips, genitalia as wound), and woman as wounding, as potentially lethal. (These ideas are condensed in the beehive. It is not here a question of revelation, but of what will be unleashed if and when Paul touches. The almighty crashing which erupts on the point of touching is both an intimation of disaster and a pretext that saves him from the fatal sting of swarming bees.) In other words, woman is associated with fatality. And, each time, the strange woman is uncannily familiar, indicating the female lips/wound as curiously *unheimlich*.

The Story of These Scars

Freud, argues Samuel Weber, thinks that he has solved the curiosity of the repetition compulsion, when in fact he is simply acting it out.[82] In all the tales he tells Freud finds nothing but the same, and fails to recognise or reflect upon certain elements that recur in his descriptions. Weber rather cunningly insinuates a parallel between Freud himself and the hero of his final tale in *Beyond the Pleasure Principle*: Tancred, who, if you remember, unwittingly killed his beloved twice over.

> *The Schicksalszug [trait of destiny] that Freud asserts it represents is not simply the recurrence of destiny, but a recurrent fatality linked to the female: she either eliminates the male or is eliminated by him. But nothing is more difficult to do away with than this persistent female: you kill her once and her soul returns, 'imprisoned in a tree'; you 'slash with [your] sword at [the] tall tree' and a voice returns to accuse you. The activity of*

> *the subject, in this final story, consists indeed of a repetition,*
> *but what he repeats, actively, is the narcissistic wound*
> *that never heals without leaving scars.*
> *Freud tells the stories of these scars, but instead of reading*
> *these stories as the signal of something else he sees them*
> *as more of the same.*

Tancred, Freud, Paul Hackett. Enticing though it is to contemplate such a wryly metonymic chain, perhaps the underlying analogy is strained: Paul Hackett doesn't of course go around killing women (any more than Freud does). On the contrary, it is they who are out to get him. Weber's point, however, is that woman is relentlessly aligned, in the imagination, with fatality. 'They're all trying to kill me. I mean I just wanted to leave, you know, my apartment, maybe meet a nice girl and now I've got to die for it!' This relentless repetition, in *After Hours*, serves to continuously reopen an old wound, and so to intensify the scarring, a scarring which is reminiscent of, though not identical to, the scar that is formed in the shape of piety. Different, they are nevertheless coterminous, these scars, like trails crisscrossing on a terrain of ambivalence, a landscape mapped by a peculiarly masculine narcissism.

Paul's ambivalence towards women (or more generally towards a sexuality not bound by narcissism) is crystallised in his attitude towards the original love object, the mother. A psychic dynamic revolving round the maternal which is savagely foregrounded in *King of Comedy* is here, in *After Hours*, manifested as more of a shadow play, its dramatic impetus ghosting the text. Paul is never situated within a familial scenario but in his hour of need he invokes the Maternal and appeals to Her for recognition: 'Hey Mom it's me!' But his request (for love) falls on deaf ears, his attempt to get back to his 'real' home is thwarted and he is returned to the night, to the mercy of a cruel fate, consigned to a cycle of merciless repetition. Each encounter with a strange woman resonates with an uncanny echo precisely because it incorporates a return of the familiar, of the imagined maternal. But Paul's ambivalence does not manifest itself as does Travis's in psychotic behaviour; in fact the entwining of the uncanny with anxiety in *After Hours* indicates a somewhat different inflection. Paul's fascination with wounds (and lips and keys) suggests an inmingling of fear and desire that relates not only to the other, but conjures his own bodily presence. Extrapolating from the notion of negative magic, we can see in Paul's fear and desire (of transference, the transfer of wounds and scars and red shoes) what might be conceived of as a form of 'negative sympathy'.

Tania Modleski argues that Hitchcock is characterised by a thoroughgoing ambivalence about femininity and her concern is to show how, in his films, masculine identity is bound up with feminine identity. Of *Vertigo* she writes:

> It is as if he were continually confronted with the fact that woman's uncanny otherness has some relation to himself, that he resembles her in ways intolerable to contemplate – intolerable because this resemblance throws into question his own fullness of being.[83]

110

Sarah Kofman puts it this way:

> Men's fascination with [the] eternal feminine is nothing but fascination
> with their own double, and the feeling of uncanniness, *Unheimlichkeit*,
> that men experience is the same as what one feels in the face of any double,
> any ghost, in the face of the abrupt reappearance of what one thought had
> been overcome or lost forever.[84]

These words poetically capture the spirit of *Vertigo*, the way in which woman
keeps uncannily returning, keeps reminding man of what he in turn keeps trying to overcome, to master.

Stop Touching Me!

'Hey Mom it's me!' rhymes inversely with another shrieking protest: 'Stop
touching me!' Paul's ambivalence is epitomised in his screaming, and it could
perhaps be argued that this screaming materialises in the textual 'voice' of
After Hours itself as a kind of misogynistic hysteria. Certainly the film skates
over the thin edge of the wedge, but I tend to think that the textual voice is
inflected more towards the deictic than the hysterical. Although the film toys
with an association between woman and fatality it doesn't present us with
women as literally lethal or female sexuality as intrinsically dangerous, as do
films like *Fatal Attraction* or indeed *Jaws*, where the vagina dentata is a literally lethal presence,[85] but rather provides the possibility that they are being
conjured up in this way by Paul's paranoid imagination. In fact the ambivalence is not just about women; it expresses a more generalised anxiety concerning sexuality and gender. Paul 'makes safe' the threat of sexuality posed by
the gay man by desexualising, by positioning him as, yet again, a figure who
will save and protect: 'Will you help me? Take me home?' (It is surely not in-
cidental that the man has no name: for Paul he represents the unspeakable, or
that which cannot speak its name.) This tactic of 'making safe' is a recurring
defensive manoeuvre which, perversely, operates as a fail-safe mechanism for
eliciting further treachery and betrayal. So when he shrieks, 'Hey Mom it's
me!' he is appealing to the very figure from whom he flees. This double movement – which we might think of as running on the spot – is epitomised in *The
Ladies' Man* when Lewis, on discovering that the pet pussy called Baby is
actually a tiger, runs screaming for Ma. Paul's ambivalence is epitomised in his
screaming: between 'Hey Mom it's me!' and 'Stop touching me!' a long, loud,
and continuous scream.

> *. . . utterly anomalous and inhuman – a howl – a wailing shriek, half of*
> *horror and half of triumph, such as might have arisen only out of hell,*
> *conjointly from the throats of the damned in their agony and of the demons*
> *that exult in the damnation.* ('The Black Cat')

Sight (a demand – for recognition) and touch (a refusal – of contact) are connected, then, by a long, loud, and continuous scream. Not simply a matter of
sound, this scream serves as a conduit, and as an imaging of a certain desire, a

111

desire to do with orality. It is also, in so far as Paul becomes the scream, at once an embodiment and an abstraction.

> And the scream, Bacon's scream, is the operation through which the entirety of the body escapes through the mouth. (G. Deleuze)[86]

Paul might be horrified by the expectation of an encounter with female lips, but this incipient horror is at least in part to do with a fear about (his own) orality. Instead of kissing, Paul opens his mouth and talks, tries to tell his story, but is continuously being ignored or silenced. Storytelling (and *After Hours* is very much about the telling of tales) is here a way of deferring sexuality (situating Paul much more within the domain of *The Wizard of Oz* and aligning him more closely with Dorothy than with Don Juan, who tells stories in order to seduce, or, to put it slightly differently, who seduces by discoursing).[87] It might not seem that Paul wants to be silenced, but there is a horrible logic to the denouement whereby June, the most obviously maternal figure, seals his lips by pasting a strip of paper over his mouth, thus completing the process of mummification (and inverting the trope of taking off the bandages, lifting the blindfold). It is a process that has been underway since Paul went downtown and encountered Kiki, dressed in black leather, working on a sculpture reminiscent of 'The Scream'; it is a repetition that is epitomised by the 'Hey Mom it's me!' episode. All the women (and the gay man and the police) turn a deaf ear to Paul's stories, but here the maternal presence is conjured up as supremely absent. If she is a deaf ear, we might also infer that she is, as in *Blue Velvet*, a detached and severed ear. The connections between touch and sight and taste (the taste for words, for lips, for licking wounds . . .) implicate both protagonist and viewer.

The Analyst's Ear

> *What is it that the patient most desires?*
> *The analyst's ear.*

As soon as Paul begins to speak he makes a demand of the mother/lover/analyst, insists on interpretation, but it is equally true that he cannot hear what is said (that is, resists unwelcome interpretation) and also is suspicious of her, convinced that she turns a deaf ear to his speech. Both *After Hours* and *Blue Velvet* evidence a disturbance around the mother, but *After Hours* is less aligned with its depictions, more humorous in the way it engages the viewer in the perilous enterprise of interpretation. Paul slips and slides between his imaginative projections of the mother as Good and Bad. *Blue Velvet* very directly appropriates the personifications of *The Wizard of Oz*: Sandy materialises as the Good Witch and Dorothy Valance as the Bad Witch. But *After Hours* eschews personification; the mother, in her various guises, is more ghostly, more of an abstract presence. She is more clearly articulated as the fantasised projection of a rather anxious but also familiarly 'normal' masculine imagining. This issue of the 'normal' is important. Although *Blue Velvet* is wedded to the notion that there is no difference between the normal and the perverse it also revels in articulating a contrast between the banal and the aberrant, and between male and female (Hopper's wired performance, in its difference from the other performances, signifies aberration; and the masochistic maternal provides the springboard for deviance). *After Hours* is more acutely cutting about 'normal' masculinity.

Even so, you might say, even if the film is more of an exposé than an instantiation, there isn't much fun for women, as either viewers or filmic protagonists, in an endless exposure of regressive masculine narcissism, of tremulous misogyny. Yet there is a lot of fun to be derived from the female performances in *After Hours*, from the enactments of charged and borderline loonyness, suggesting that performance itself – and gender as an acting out rather than a fixity of attributes – has a privileged place in the film. There is an energy that animates the performances just beyond a point of naturalism, a self-ironising allusiveness that nevertheless retains an unnerving degree of undecidability. A rippling perturbation is produced in the shifts in register, sometimes almost imperceptible and at other times alarmingly pronounced (particularly in the performances of Rosanna Arquette, Teri Garr[88] and Catherine O'Hara), in the fraying of charm and solicitation, the eruptions of hysteria and violence. 'She was loony tunes. She was just out to lunch, Marcy,' says Rosanna Arquette, with relish.[89] I am reminded of the early Keitel performances, in *Who's that Knocking at My Door?* and *Alice Doesn't Live Here Anymore*, of De Niro as Johnny Boy in *Mean Streets*, of Joe Pesci in *GoodFellas*. The edginess of these characters keeps us on edge, undecided, strung out in expectation. Though the characters in *After Hours* don't actually duplicate the signs of masculine instability (outbursts of very visceral violence) a certain continuity can be discerned spanning the different films – a performance dynamic which, while it has a great deal to do with gender, is not definitively aligned with male or female. The performances – as opposed to characters *per se* – are instrumental in moving us, through a range of positions; they are a transformative element. Of course, it might be said that there is something quite perverse in the pleasure we – any of us, but particularly female viewers – take in these female performances. And yes, I think this is true, but the conversions involved (the imbrications of humour and horror, pleasure and aggressivity) make for a potentially transformative textual space.

In the encounter between viewer and film the question of 'Who is Jane?' and 'Who (or where) are Freud and Tarzan?' elicits a range of mobile responses. Turning a romantic comedy like *It Happened One Night* into a horror film, and turning a horror film like *Night of the Living Dead* into a comedy, *After Hours* exacerbates both anxiety and the pleasures of the maze. It also, particularly in this intersection of horror and comedy, meshes questions of genre with those of gender.

In the cinema we are, like Paul, silenced. Or perhaps it is the case that we choose to be in the dark, to be (relatively) quiet, to participate in the storytelling through indirect means. Even though *After Hours* is often excruciating there is a driving compulsion to keep watching, and indeed to keep laughing. Perhaps part of this perversity is to do with the fact that the self-dramatisation that Paul is engaged in engages us. A very basic primal taboo around touch is played out cinematically through a discourse around storytelling and sensory desires. The film returns our touch to us; it voices, and converts, our horror. If Bacon's scream is the operation through which the entirety of the body escapes through the mouth, perhaps the cinema is sometimes, as in the instance of *After Hours*, the medium, the celluloid mouth, through which our bodily intimation of horror escapes, is returned to us, converted into laughter.

Is That All There Is to a Fire?

Films are ephemeral, incendiary; they burn up before our very eyes. Think of Hollis Frampton's *Nostalgia*, where a series of still images burn up on a hot plate, in the process of burning turning into a continuous moving image; or think of the end of *Two Lane Black Top*, where it looks as if the celluloid has caught fire in the projector.[90] Remember films like *Ju Dou* and *House of Wax*, where conflagrations effect a transubstantiation of matter, and where, long after the images have faded from the screen, flames remain imprinted on the retina. Any love affair with the cinema burns briefly, a fleeting and fiery romance. But where flames consume, they also generate stories: *A Chinese Ghost Story II* begins by replaying some scenes, and recapping the narrative of the first film, before artificial red flames leap onto the screen and eat up the image, accompanied by an announcement: 'And so the story continues.'

> *Someone tells me: this kind of love is not viable. But how can you*
> *evaluate viability? Why is the viable a Good Thing?*
> *Why is it better to last than to burn?*[91]

At the end, in Club Berlin, Peggy Lee's voice sings: 'Is that all there is a to a fire?' Listen to the intonation, as this phrase recurs throughout the song, and see if you can decide where the emphasis falls. To me it is one of those songs that shifts like quicksand (an impression created in part, I think, by the indeterminacy of a voice fluctuating between speech and song). Yet despite this it keeps drawing one back; over the years it returns, as a reminder. Listening, you know there is a danger of getting your hands burnt, but also a possibility of surviving, of emerging from the cinema intact. So much depends on how you hear and see that 'all': is it 'all' or 'nothing'?

Chapter 5

Remember, Remember: It's Not Blood, It's Red (Frame-Work)

> *I started with the prologue, and I was reading, and there was a*
> *prologue all the time and at the end of the prologue the book was finished.*
> (Raul Ruiz)[1]

The lights in the theatre dim. Out of the darkness images appear, images as red and as hot as the desert. Or piercingly cool images: the ice blue of eyes that cut through the night. Or the blue of a gingham frock, or of bruised flesh. I am at the cinema again – to see a new release on opening night, or perhaps it is an old movie never seen before, or perhaps I am here for the fifth night in a row. Always this experience of a new beginning is intriguing, the anticipation of

Alice Doesn't Live Here Anymore (Martin Scorsese, 1974)

strangeness tantalises; and yet there is a strong sense of familiarity, almost of *déjà vu,* as it begins all over again. As it begins all over again I find myself transported, entranced by these images, utterly absorbed.

In the Beginning: A Flashback
In the beginning a deep red sunset saturates the sky. The redness of this sunset, in *Alice Doesn't Live Here Anymore,* suffuses the entire studio set, pervading the whole of the opening sequence. It is a vaguely archaic rural scene, dirt road edged by a wooden fence. In the distance a small figure appears walking towards the camera. In pink letters a title is superimposed over the red: 'Monterey, California. Alice, a young girl'. This red is absorbent: characters, story, myself. All are absorbed.

> Goddam script opened, said, 'Flashback, 1948. Monterey, California.'
> The dialogue's exactly the same as it was in the script. Here's a little
> girl and the farm and the whole thing.
> And I say, 'How am I going to do this?' The production guys at Warner's
> said, 'Well, you know, you could shoot it in black-and-white.' I said,
> 'Yeah, that'd work. Everybody would know it was a flashback.'
> They said, 'you could shoot it with a fog filter.' I said, 'That'll work
> too. It's a flashback.' They said, 'You could put up a title and then
> you shoot it straight.'
> I said, 'That'd work, too, but there's got to be another way.' (Scorsese)[2]

An oxymoronic ambition this: to open a film with a flashback. Doubly so, when the ambition is fuelled by a desire to find 'another way', to invent a flashback that is not immediately recognisable (as a flashback). If we think of the flashback as a kind of closed circuit that leads from a narrative present to a narrative past, and back again to the same point in the present, then clearly the opening of *Alice Doesn't Live Here Anymore* would have to strain to be conceived of as a flashback. When there is no present from which to flash back (that is, before the 'now' of the story has been established), how can an opening possibly be read as a narrative event existing prior to any event we have yet witnessed? Scorsese appears to solve the problem (or find a way of articulating the dilemma, which is really a dilemma about the nature of beginnings and the operation of memory in inaugural moments) by filming the opening in red and calling it a prologue. He does not, however, when discussing the film, replace flashback with prologue but tends to use the terms interchangeably.

> I like the red prologue. I had a chance to use a Hollywood set.
> I mean, how else are you going to do a flashback?
> How do you want to do a flashback?
> That's the whole point. (Scorsese)[3]

Prologues actually come *before* (before the text begins) whereas flashbacks are referential – they refer us to what has gone *before* (before the story begins). But a distinction cannot be sustained merely, or only, in terms of the temporal; differences between story and text, questions of address, also enter the picture. The prologue here, just as in the case of a quotation that precedes a work of fiction, or a vignette in the theatre, has a commentative and framing function. It reflects upon the rest of the film; it offers us a lens through which to view. Although it may have a temporal location, it also stands in a relation of simultaneity to the story, as in the quotation from Talleyrand which prefaces *Before the Revolution*: 'Those who have not lived the years before the revolution cannot realise the sweetness of life.' The 'red prologue' to *Alice Doesn't Live Here Anymore* is undoubtedly coloured by the past. We know this as we watch it, not just retrospectively. And this is partly because it seems very contemporary in its mode of address: its evocation of the past is achieved through a vocative stance. Its stylisation, its 'colouring' of our point of view foregrounds the fictional dimension of narration. The red prologue is at once a provocation and a resolution: a resolution to the problem of temporal order and address, and a provocation to remember.

> *From the centre of a black screen redness seeps. The image opens out: a desert landscape washed by the luridly setting sun, blood red. A man's voice, portentous, speaks over the music: 'Deep amongst the lonely sun-baked hills of Texas a great weather-beaten rock still stands. The Comanches called it Squaw's Head Rock. Time cannot change its impressive face nor dim the legend of the wild young lovers who found heaven and hell in the shadows of the rock. . .'*

The Red Prologue

'But there's got to be another way.' If the character is really hung up
on movies a lot, I felt then that she would sort of remember – half
fantasy and half remembrance – if it's 1948,
then the flashback would look like it was shot as a movie in 1948.
Which means that all the exterior scenes are really indoors.
That's what I tried to do.
I got a little crazy with the site and the redness and all that stuff.
(Scorsese)[4]

1. A deep red sunset saturates the sky. It is a rural scene, dirt road edged by a wooden fence. In the distance a small figure appears walking towards the camera. In pink letters a title is superimposed: Monterey, California. Alice, a young girl.
2. Long-shot of a man outside a barn scattering corn to chickens. In the foreground is the wooden fence from the first shot. The camera moves to the right and begins moving in on the scene.
3. A large wooden house in the distance. The windows are brightly lit and two figures are silhouetted. On the left the wheel of a ploughshare intrudes into the frame and on the right the bonnet of a 1940s station wagon. The camera moves in towards the house.

4. The dusty road again, edged by a wooden fence. In the distance Alice, about ten years old, walks towards the camera. Alice Faye's voice and the musical accompaniment fades out, and the young Alice's voice fades in, speaking, 'I can sing better...' She starts to sing, 'You'll never know just how much I care.'

5. In medium-close-up we see Alice, holding her doll, wearing her hair in pigtails and dressed like Dorothy in *The Wizard of Oz*. 'I can sing better than Alice Faye, I swear to Christ I can,' she tells her doll. A voice off calls, 'Ally!'

6. In long shot the back porch of the house is shown, where a woman stands shouting, over the sound of barking dogs, 'Ally!' The camera pans right and begins moving in. In a normal speaking voice she says, 'Alice Graham, you get in this house before I beat the living daylights out of you. Do you hear?'

7. Alice, framed as in shot 5. 'You wait and see,' she says, pouting, 'and if anyone doesn't like it they can blow it out their ass.'

8. A longer shot of Alice, walking along the road, by the fence. The camera moves from left to right with her as the barn, and then the house, comes into view. Swinging her doll she sings, 'If there is some other way to prove that I love you I swear I don't know how. You'll never know if you don't know now.' The camera cranes up and out and suddenly the square image contracts; it is as though it is sucked into the blackness of the rectangular film frame. In a simultaneous rushing in and out the image disappears. The end of the song echoes, becoming a loud concatenation, a reiteration of Now! Now! Now! Now! Now! which culminates in an auditory explosion becoming the loud rock music of Mott the Hoople ('All the Way from Memphis'). The sound transition is accompanied by a cut, an aerial travelling shot of desert and suburbia, rendered in 'normal' (if somewhat sun-bleached) colour, over which is superimposed a title: 'Sirocco, New Mexico. Alice 27 Years Later.'

Before the Beginning

Duel in the Sun, it is true, opens in the red desert with a sort of prologue and a voice announcing the story of 'the wild young lovers', Pearl Chavez and Lewt McCandles (Jennifer Jones and Gregory Peck). But is this really the opening? It is preceded by a credit sequence, which although it may not carry any narrative weight might well imbue the prologue with a certain lurid vibrancy, a sensational affectivity that propels the film: black lettering is scrolled over a painted flat of a red and yellow sky, in centre screen a piercing white sun. The title of the film itself stands out in scarlet: red against red. The title sequence ends with a fade to black.

And, come to think of it, something comes before the beginning of *Alice Doesn't Live Here Anymore* as well. First, the contemporary black-and-white Warners logo appears on a red background: sharp lines, clear colours. Then, the old Warners logo in the shape of a shield set against a blue sky and rippling white clouds. This image is almost square, framed in the old aspect ratio of 1:1.33, and inset, masked by black. This frame-within-a-frame format is maintained throughout the following credit sequence and the red prologue-flashback. As the shield logo fades into the background the blue sky dissolves to blue satin, fallen in folds, over which the credits are superimposed in red, as a woman's voice (Alice Faye) sings 'You'll never know how much I love you' (from the song 'Where or When?').[5] As the credits end there is a dissolve from the blue satin to the redness of Monterey.

> *Gregory Peck tears the locket from Jennifer Jones's neck and flings it into*
> *the pool, a cool oasis in the desert. The icy water shimmers: sapphire*
> *blue dissolving to the redness of fiercely leaping flames.*

So, not only is there some confusion over the status of the opening – is it a flashback? or a prologue? or even 'half-fantasy'? – but also an uncertainty about where in fact the film begins. We can add to this confusion and uncertainty the possibility that Scorsese's bottom line, in dealing with this strange opening, is simply 'What the hell!':

> I had fun with the fog. You know, you've got fog machines, use a fog ma-
> chine. See what happens. Got a crane; use a crane. It's fun. Also I figured it's
> a very strange opening for a picture, so what the hell.[6]

Perhaps he's just having fun, and critical anxiety about where and when is inappropriately pedantic. And yet I am provoked by the indeterminacy of *Alice*'s inauguration; something darts in and around this red prologue, a flit-tering bait, a red herring perhaps. I have a suspicion that already I'm being led astray, enticed into speculation, apparently about the nature of beginnings, but in fact lured by a pretext (or by a chimerically luminous prologue), a pre-text for indulging in wild goose flights of fancy, in following alchemical mem-ory traces as they flash across the screen, across and through acoustic space, across and through and just under my skin. But it may turn out that in the cinema (elsewhere too, but especially here) memory is particularly and acutely mobilised in opening moments – not simply after the event, but also In the Beginning. It is around these connections that this chapter will circle, turning on cinematic inflections of memory, on the cinema's status as a form of narra-tive fiction that is bound by technology and industry, on cinema as a zone where techniques of memory and histories of technology, as well as public and personal memory, are intricately bound up together. Cinematic inceptions are most interesting for the way in which they structure the new and the old, call upon memory/familiarity and anticipation/novelty.

Beginnings are interesting as framing devices. As are techniques of memory. How some of these techniques may be related to histories of technology will be explored by focusing on technologies and contexts of reception (technologies sometimes referred to as delivery systems), and by foregrounding questions about screen size and aspect ratio, and the phenomenon of colour. Inevitably, as soon as you activate a framing device the framed begins to escape. But in its errantry it in turn frames. Hence the herring which escapes the prologue, stained nevertheless by its redness.

So Much Depends

Fiction (in general) is characterised by a more allusive and affective mode of elaboration than is generally the case with more documentary and discursive genres. Narrative, on the other hand, tends towards finality. This tension between two divergent tendencies – evocation and statement, dispersal and containment, the indirect and the directed – repeats itself in a number of guises across the length and breadth of every narrative, but is particularly concentrated and dramatised In The Beginning. As William Carlos Williams put it:

so much depends
upon

a red wheel
barrow

glazed with rain
water

beside the white
chickens[7]

In the Beginning anything is possible. But as soon as more than one word is written or spoken, as soon as images appear out of the mists of time, as soon as 'things' are delineated, so the possibilities begin to narrow. Every story proceeds from and continues stories that have gone before. 'Once upon a time' marks its kinship with other tales, and yet every story has, very early in the telling, to stake out its difference, to inscribe its originality by casting the beginning as the origin of all that is to follow. 'Once upon a time there was a little girl who wore a gingham frock and pigtails and lived in Monterey' marks this story as different from that one, the one that begins 'Once upon a time there was a little girl who wore a gingham frock and pigtails and lived in Kansas.' The process of naming, then, marks a difference (this story is different from other stories) but simultaneously it reduces difference (the choice of place-names no longer exists; she – who has been chosen as heroine even though a lion or a cyborg or a taxi-driving psychopath could have filled the role – is fixed in Monterey). Out of the original darkness a voice: 'I shall never forget the weekend Laura died. A silver sun burned through the sky like a huge magnifying glass', or 'In early April 1974 Ignacio Vega, a literature teacher, had to learn the names of 15,000 anti-junta resisters. It took him only one week', or 'You don't make up for your sins in church, you do it in the streets. You do it at home. The rest is bullshit and you know it.' Or just the sound of crying in the dark. We listen and imagine, luminous sensations emanate from the voice, in the darkness we project; and then the screen lights up and almost immediately we are absorbed by the celluloid image.

If so much depends on the beginning of a narrative, so the first few minutes of a fiction feature film are crucial. A lot has to be concentrated into the opening of a movie. The play of repetition and difference has to be inaugurated with economy, and the viewer's attention must be caught, she needs to be lulled by the assurance of familiarity and startled by the unexpected, lured by the promise of something new. To achieve all this poses particular difficulties for the film as fiction, as narrative; the circumstances in which films are produced and screened impose certain restrictions, and also have generated a range of specifically cinematic conventions. People often arrive late to screenings (they are not prevented from entering as is often the case in theatre), are settling in, sharing popcorn, finishing conversations, so that there is a general air of distraction which militates against the divulging of any important diegetic information. But there is yet another hindrance to fictional absorption. All fiction requires forgetting – forgetting that it is a fiction – yet the cinema also requires that we remember, through the convention of the credit sequence, the industrial and commercial dimension of fictional production.

> *The film opens in black-and-white. A man (Tom Ewell) stands in the centre of a square frame. He clicks his fingers and the sides of the frame draw back, transforming the space into a CinemaScope screen. He announces that the film is in 'gorgeous life-like colour by Deluxe' and when nothing happens he repeats the announcement, looking pointedly upward. The set is instantly flooded with colour. (The Girl Can't Help It)*

If all fiction requires forgetting (that it is fiction) it also provokes the 'reader' to remember, partly to remember the details of the story but also to activate memorial associations. This screen memory might seem to be inactivated during all the distractions of the opening; and, because the credits themselves are so ostentatiously to do with information, we tend to think of the surrounding elements as constituting 'noise'. Like noise, though, they filter through, permeate our consciousness and perhaps orient our ways of being attentive, summoning an art of memory that engages in flashing, in superimpositions (maybe a layering, maybe a screening out), in fragmentary liaisons. This aspect or potential of the cinematic, of the celluloid image, blurs the edges of concepts such as definition, definiteness, definitive, and opens a space between the viewer and the indexical sign where anything (almost) is possible. To speak of the closing down of possibilities I mean only to suggest a tendency, not an absolute. It is also true to say that as a particular story unfolds so it potentially opens out into a multiplicity of tales. What I want to draw attention to is a kind of twilight zone where cinematic fiction is enacted, a zone of indeterminacy. It is when we are absorbed into this zone that magic happens. An aspect of the cinematic image (both celluloid and fictionally immaterial) that can be activated at any time is intensified in the opening moments or minutes of a film.[8]

> *On certain occasions the unexpected association of an image we are shown with another which we recall makes us take a conceptual leap across a zone where images are linked in an impermanent way. At which point the images are organised so as to produce fantasies. Fantasy is not the bridge between the hidden images and the ones we are shown. Nor is it what permits the rescue of other images which form a temporary bridge. The stimulation is mutual: images come to fill a zone formerly occupied by fantasy. (Raul Ruiz)[9]*

Twilight Zones

'How do you want to do a flashback?' This question, hovering over the opening of *Alice Doesn't Live Here Anymore*, suggests more than an anxiety to avoid, in the name of originality, the obviousness of all the clichés of flashback presentation; it suggests a desire to find a way that at once attracts the viewer into the fictional world and also, in the beginning, evokes a twilight zone where images are not entirely consumed by a carnivorous narrative but escape in phantasmatic configurations.

For the flashback, in all its permutations, is not as straightforward as might be implied in the metaphor of a closed circuit. What the flashback, any flashback, opens onto is *discrepancy* – between here and there, and now and then, and between various speaking (or enunciating) positions. The flashback signals not just the past, but also the generative work of memory and fantasy; and in this process it also incorporates a potential to focus the question of fictional address. Flashbacks are generally framed (hence the closed circuit analogy where the present frames the past) but they equally serve to frame, to turn the tables on the 'master' discourse, to turn things inside out, as is so perfectly epitomised in a film like *Out of the Past*. Clearly we aren't being asked, in the red prologue, to recall an event that has occurred in earlier story time, but there is a sense in which we are being teased, nudged into remembering. And there is a fairly strong sense that we are being interpellated – not directly, but through the hyperbole of cinematic language. Maureen Turim discusses the way in which the flashback has entered contemporary language, as in the common phrase 'I just flashed on . . .'. She writes:

> This colloquial use of the term indicates how movies as popular culture begin to affect the way people think about their own experience. Cinematic renderings of storytelling and memory processes may have borrowed from literature and sought to reproduce human memory mimetically, but ironically, the cinematic presentation of the flashback affects not only how modern literature is organised and how plays are staged, but perhaps also how audiences remember and how we describe those memories.[10]

The red prologue 'flashes' the past, incites us to flash. For each individual the sensory overload of this opening will reverberate differently, but there are also more public resonances, allusions to a shared past, to a sphere where images circulate in the popular imaginary, to The Movies. The past that is being evoked here is a movie past, and in a way it makes the opening very much a 'movie beginning' (just as the film has a 'movie ending').[11]

The excess of red flashes back to *Duel in the Sun* and *Gone with the Wind*, forward to *Mean Streets*, *GoodFellas*, *Cape Fear*. In the background Tara burns, the redness of flames spreading through the whole image. In the foreground Scarlett O'Hara weeps and rages and swears she'll be back. 'You wait and see,' she says, pouting, 'and if anyone doesn't like it they can blow it out their ass.' They return at night, the goodfellas, to dig the body up: like grave diggers in a horror movie they are silhouetted against a raging red sky.

122

> *Then the gleam of a conflagration takes on a sinister character and the colour of red becomes thematic red.* (S. M. Eisenstein)[12]

It is not so much a semantic equivalence that conjures up particular scenes and movies, but rather a kind of 'thematic red', a peculiarly cinematic lushness that hovers between the evanescent grandeur of high passion and studio artifice laid on thick. It also represents a somewhat anachronistic 'look' associated with a period that has passed. A sense of the past, then, and an intensity. The evocation of Dorothy in *The Wizard of Oz* evokes both childhood and fantasy, where there is a kind of inversion or reframing, so that the 1939 black-and-white scenario which connotes home and reality (as distinct from the Technicolored rendition of Oz) is re-imagined through a red filter, and in the process somewhat fantasised. The line between fantasy and memory wavers. The very process of recall, and this applies to many flashbacks which are subjectivised or attached to a particular character's consciousness, tends to confer retroactively on the past episode a meaning that in its own time it did not have.[13] When we reach the transition to the movie's present and the subtitle 'Sirocco, New Mexico. Alice 27 Years Later', we can read the 'red prologue' retroactively, either as a flashback to Alice's childhood, or as the origin, the founding event and 'key' to the story that is to follow. Or we can see it less definitively (and the rendering of the sequence I think encourages this), as somewhere between memory and fantasy. The Monterey of the red prologue is not so much a real place, what we see does not so much constitute a real event, as it is a sensory sign, a charged moment that pervades the present. There is an event that can be seen as inaugural, as having diegetic consequences – the child Alice's determination to be a singing star motivates her escape and gets this quasi-road-movie going, and the grown-up Alice spends the whole movie trying to get home to Monterey just as Dorothy spends the whole movie trying to get home to Kansas; but here 'home' is figured both as a locus of nostalgia (and thus is metonymic of the past in general) and an impossibility. It is impossible to return and yet the past pervades the present, in fact is conjured up by the present. It is also impossible for us to return to the past that is Hollywood, to recover that lost object, and yet it can be conjured into being as a public memory in a zone somewhere between memory and fantasy. Hence the contemporary feel to the Scorsese flashback-prologue. At the end of the movie Monterey is literally figured as a sign: a billboard against the sky, advertising a gas station.

Border Crossing: Courtly Love, Ketchup and L'Amour fou or A Wild Goose Chase

A letter arrives from someone I don't know. All letters are welcome in this wilderness. I have fled the city for a month to write in peace, and indeed there are few distractions here on the edge of the rain forest. I write, and ride through these forests on a speedy pony which gallops up mountainous tracks impervious to the flocks of black cockatoos which swoop overhead darkening the sky and thunderously cackling. Back at my desk I yearn for distraction, for city life and for the large screen. The letter says:

> I screened *Mouchette* for a seminar on Bresson. Immediately following this, the first reel of *Lancelot du Lac* was thrown onto the wall of the auditorium. The first shot, of a knight decapitated and the intense, excessive surge of blood issuing from this scene (after the cool, smooth surface of the previous film) provoked an affective spectacle within the audience. As the titles do not appear until the end of the slaying montage, some became rather vocal in their comparisons with Monty Python's thematic version. These opening shots were subsequently re-screened, to be met with subdued tongues and transfixed eyes, as the graphic cinematographic violence bled into iridescent crimson heralding text.[14]

Her letter is fortuitously timed; although she writes to tell me about the red hotness of *Lancelot* I am now writing about something else and am struck by this account of a Beginning. It is a long time since I saw the film but my memory of the opening is of the clanking of armour and of knights on horseback moving slowly through a forest. I remember nothing of the decapitation, though I do recall an ominous sensation that pervaded the screening, an incipient nausea despite the beauty. Later, back in Sydney, I borrow the print and discover that she has misremembered and so have I, but differently. The decapitation is not the very first shot. But it has the impact of a first shot, all the intensity of an inaugural moment, precisely I think because it is unheralded: the film begins without announcement, without any form of framing, and indeed it does feel as though the reels have been put on in the wrong order. It opens close to the action; there is the sound of clanging swords, an awkward duelling. You can feel – in the sounds (and the colours: browns and greens and metallic grey) of the movement, the weight of the armour and swords – a palpable heaviness. Swords fall to the ground; the camera follows a hand as it picks up a sword and slashes, slicing a head off a torso heavily encased in armour. Blood spurts out of the decapitated figure, which falls forward, towards the camera, blood streaming, staining the screen. The carnage continues and is at once shocking (so shocking that I have totally suppressed it) and uncannily reminiscent of Monty Python in its hysterical literalism.

This graphic cinematographic violence bleeds into iridescent crimson text appearing over a black background with the outline or reflection of a silver chalice centre screen: 'After marvelous adventures . . .'. The prologue goes on to talk of the search for the Holy Grail, the disappearance of Percival, and the return of the knights. Then white script announces: 'The film begins with the knights, their ranks decimated . . .'. The prologue, in short, is a decimation.

This opening reminds us that beginnings are always to some extent arbitrary, only retrospectively invested with significance; and yet they are made to bear an inevitable textual burden. So much depends on the red surge of blood. In dismantling a well-known legend Bresson documents a slaughter and situates this event as one in a series that is the war; the characters are subordinate to a momentum (called fate). It is shocking not because of its singularity, not as a founding moment, but because it is a repetition. Nonetheless, and despite the fact that the film begins *in medias res,* the opening surge of blood (even if we repress its memory) stains the story irremediably. The desire of Lancelot and Guinevere, a desire which exceeds the constraints of courtly love, which transgresses all boundaries of sociality, is, despite the austerity of its depiction, written in blood.

Duel in the Sun is very different, it would seem. It announces and frames its story; it even gives away the ending (in which the lovers, after shooting one another in the desert, die in each other's arms). It will tell 'the legend of the wild young lovers who found heaven and hell in the shadows of the rock. For when the sun is low and the cold wind blows across the desert there are those of Indian blood who still speak of Pearl Chavez, the half-breed girl from down along the border, and of the laughing outlaw with whom she there kept a final rendezvous, never to be seen again. And this is what the legend says: a flower known nowhere else grows from out of the desperate crags where Pearl vanished, Pearl who was herself a wild flower sprung from the hard clay, quick to bloom and early to die.' This is what I have designated the prologue, but for other readers the prologue begins with the first dramatic scene.[15] As the voice-over comes to an end so the desert rose dissolves to bright yellow movement – a low-angle shot of Pearl in a yellow blouse dancing to flamenco music. In this prologue Pearl's father kills her mother and is in turn executed. It is this event that initiates Pearl's journey to the MacCandles ranch, in accordance with her father's wish that she should be looked after by his first love, the good and pure (unlike Pearl's mother) May Belle (Lillian Gish).

The voice of the father invariably takes me by surprise, colours my experience of the film. The first time I saw *Duel in the Sun* I was totally taken aback when Herbert Marshall (Pearl's father) spoke, overwhelmed by an involuntary sensation of sorrow. Even now I am transported back to childhood, to a hot Sunday afternoon listening with my mother to a recording of *The Snow Goose.* Herbert Marshall's voice takes us far away, far from the farm in Africa, to somewhere inconsolable.

> *Long before the snow goose had come dropping out of a crimsoned*
> *eastern sky to circle the lighthouse in a last farewell, Fritha, from the*
> *ancient powers of the blood that was in her, knew that Rhayader*
> *would not return.*

The beginning of *Duel* (credit sequence, prologue with voice-over, prologue of Pearl's 'origins') seems overly explanatory, compulsive in its framing, the obverse of *Lancelot.* Yet it is not just in the words of the voice-over that the meaning resides. Colour, timbre of voice (both the narrator's and the dead father's) and the heightened *mise en scène* all set the scene. The memory of *Duel* surfaces in another country almost a decade later, in another strange example of naive cinema. *Jedda* opens with written text explaining that the film was cast with real Aborigines and asserting: 'The story of Jedda is founded on fact.' The titles, almost as lurid as those of *Duel,* are superimposed over a series of primitive painted landscapes. And then a prologue – a portentous male voice narrates over a series of aerial shots of the Australian outback (and welling melodramatic music accompanied by a weird chorus of unearthly

Jedda (Charles Chauvel, 1955)

voices): 'This is part of the oldest land in the world, the Northern Territory of Australia. It is my land. And the land of Jedda, the girl I loved. My name is Joe. I'm the half-caste son of an Afghan teamster and an Australian Aboriginal woman. I was reared by a white woman and her husband.' Then, over the red desert, over Uluru (Ayers Rock) and Katajuta (the Olgas), the heart of the matter: 'Mountains of Mystery, red tombs in Australia's dead heart which hold the secret of Aborigines' dreamtime, the burial place of the old totem men. A native race so old that their laws and religion stretch to a past beyond our thinking.'

The story of *Jedda* begins with a white woman on a remote cattle station who has just lost her baby. At the same time an Aboriginal woman dies in childbirth on a cattle drive nearby. It is sunset and we hear the sound of a baby crying but do not see it. The next day drovers bring the baby Jedda to the homestead. As they approach we hear the sound of Aboriginal women keening; the white baby is being buried. Jedda is taken in and brought up by the white woman. The real melodrama erupts some years later when a black man, Marbuk, from another skin group, abducts Jedda, breaking a taboo twice over as she is forbidden him according to kinship rules, and also she is living a white life. A wild chase follows across the wilds of northern Queensland, ending as they struggle on the edge of a cliff, falling together to their death. The camera tilts up to the sky where a single white goose flies, soon joined by a whole flock. 'Was it our right', the narrator's voice over asks, 'to expect that Jedda, one of a race so mystic and so removed, should be of us in one short life time? The Pintjaris whisper that the soul of Jedda now flies the lonely plains and mountain crags with the wild geese. And that she is happy with the great mother of the world in the dreaming time of tomorrow.' The story fades out to the accompaniment of the curiously anomalous and disembodied heavenly choir.

Jedda and *Duel* also present legends, but from a differently inflected extreme: their openings are prologues that frame the action and provide commentary, and yet from the very first pre-diegetic moments – of colour, of titles, of crudely painted 'flats' – we are immersed in a dilation of naturalistic codes. The 'half-caste' issue frames both *Jedda* and *Duel*, and will be inscribed as a problem of place, of the crossing of borders and transgression of boundaries, racial, sexual and generic. The mixing of melodrama and the Western produces a particular 'feel' registered chromatically. *Duel in the Sun* has been described as 'a ketchup prairie bathed in *amour fou*',[16] and *Cahiers du cinéma* referred to 'the truly prodigious hideousness of the colour' in *Jedda*.[17] Yet both these films generate a story in excess of the commentary, generate passions which remain somehow inexplicable. What is interesting about these two films is that they dramatise the dilemma of so many narratives (both how to get going and how, subsequently, to deal with the repercussions of opening gambits); they don't opt for the self-reflexive comedy of *The Girl Can't Help It* or the perverse naturalism of the *Lancelot* legend, but through overstatement, through elaborate overture, they indicate a textual passion which exceeds the narrative. Other films try to diminish address, to heighten fiction. *Duel* and *Jedda* exaggerate address and thereby heighten the actual process of fictionality.

You Bet I Won't Forget

A pre-credit sequence: the screen is black; in the darkness crying can be heard. A title comes up: '1917'. A man's voice: 'Want to see it again little girl? It shouldn't frighten you.'

It's a 'pig'-in-the-box that is causing these tears, and a little blonde girl, Jane, who is crying. We next see her on stage as a precocious child star performing 'I've Written a Letter to Daddy.' In the wings her mother watches with her sister, Blanche. The mother tells Blanche that she hopes that one day when she is famous she'll be kinder to her sister and father than they were to her. She asks Blanche to remember this. 'I won't forget. You bet I won't forget,' swears Blanche. Cut to black, with a title: '1935'.

The credits are superimposed over the next sequence: a montage of shots depicting a car being driven towards a gate (we are positioned in the driver's seat), foot on the pedal, crash, a smashed doll, devastation. Cut to a bright sunny day, a car driving along a leafy suburban street, bright music, with the title: 'Yesterday'. The neighbours are watching an old movie starring Blanche (who we soon discover is now confined to a wheelchair) on television. The film on television is interrupted by a dog-food ad, and the film proper gets under way.

The opening (the pre-credit sequence) of *Whatever Happened to Baby Jane?* uncannily prefigures the prologue/flashback of *Alice Doesn't Live Here*

Anymore, not in look but undoubtedly in other ways. Both are uncertainly situated as either flashback or prologue or origin (as in founding story event), sharing a first scene that 'flashes forward' into the future ('Alice, 27 years later'). And equally they vacillate between memory and fantasy. Both revolve around precocious child singing stars (or would-be child stars) and inscribe a particular moment with memorial potency. The difference is that in *Baby Jane* the memory is attached to a motif of revenge and the Aldrich film unfolds as a macabre instance of contemporary gothic in which the two sisters, both ghoulishly living in their respective pasts, systematically and slowly torture one another. Alice, on the other hand, never quite makes it as a star, but she remains transfixed by the memory (or perhaps it is truer to say that the force of the opening transfers the memory to us) of performance and impersonation, to 'be' better than Alice Faye, to 'be' a star.[18] Though Alice is not deluded in the same demonic way and so not rendered grotesque (and since she is played by a method actress and not by a melodrama queen) both films conjure a relationship between the past and the present that is lived as disjunctive; Alice is still trying to outdo Alice Faye in an era when Alice Faye *et al.* only exist on television reruns (when Alice is trying to score singing jobs, her bored son, a fan of Matt the Hoople, watches Betty Grable in *Coney Island* sing 'Cuddle Up a Little Closer Lovely Mine').

In the very beginning of *Whatever Happened to Baby Jane?* there is an intimation of torture, an echo of *Peeping Tom* as the sinister intimation of 'There's nothing to be afraid of' is echoed in 'Want to see it again little girl? It shouldn't frighten you.' *Peeping Tom* and *Baby Jane* are like the underside of all childhood tales: entwined in the reassuring tones of 'You'll never know how much I love you' there is: the horror, the horror. This subterranean current remains mostly underground in *Alice Doesn't Live Here Anymore*; though it surfaces occasionally it is more strongly present in other Scorsese films.[19] *Alice* foreshadows later Scorsese, colours the future in its rendition of the past.

Taking the Credit

> *In* The Patsy, *a lengthy pre-credit sequence (the first event of the story and narrative) culminates with Jerry Lewis, the klutzy waiter who is about to be made into a star, walking backwards and falling out through a window.*

Credits detract from the fictional integrity of a work by drawing attention to its constructedness;[20] hence the various devices to separate them from the fiction by presenting them discretely at either the beginning or the end. Nowadays it seems that the dominant convention is to signal the production context and main players at the beginning, with most of the credits at the end (often incorporating a repetition of the opening credits). Conventions have changed over time and credit sequences have rarely been entirely self-contained. Although it might seem straightforward to determine where credits begin and end, the difficulty of locating where the film 'proper' starts can be seen if you try to ascertain the difference between a pre-credit sequence, a diegetic credit sequence (where credits are superimposed over moving images, a slice of narrative action) and an autonomous non-diegetic segment (where titles are superimposed over a background that is frequently though not invariably fixed and abstract). In very early cinema, the studio logo frequently appeared in each shot, not scripturally superimposed as one might expect, but actually appearing on an element of the *mise en scène* – painted on a table, for instance.[21] A contemporary variant of this can be found in *Gremlins 2: The New Batch*, where, amidst a Bacchanalian orgy of ingenious destruction, one of the Gremlins tattoos himself – and we only catch a fleeting glimpse of this – with the Warner Bros. logo. In a slightly hyperbolic sense, these examples indicate the instability of the integration (or separation) of credits from the body of the text.

> There is a cut to the outside, to Jerry falling from the top floor of a
> multistorey building. With the cut the credit sequence commences. The
> credits are superimposed over the outside of the building, each shot
> descending a level and accompanied by a cut-out Jerry Lewis frozen in a
> variety of falling postures. As the credits conclude, Jerry reaches ground
> level, falls onto a diving board and is flipped back up and through the
> window from which he had disappeared. The film resumes with
> scarcely a hitch.

The formulation and presentation of the credits sequence – a peculiarly cinematic phenomenon (or telecinematic, but it is from the cinema that television inherits its credit conventions) – expresses a conjunction of fiction, commerce and industry. At least by 1897, it seems, the Edison company added a title with the firm's name and a copyright statement. Janet Staiger noted: 'Company titles and trademark decorations became more elaborate, particularly when illegal duplication of prints threatened profits.'[22] In 1911 Edison included a brief credit list of the cast, and a year later the story writer's name was added. The credits gradually became more elaborate and complicated as film production became a capital-intensive industry. Credits became a way of inscribing a structure based on an intricate hierarchical division of labour and a competitive terrain of technological innovation. From the beginning, technological developments have introduced new types of labour, and the ensuing demarcation disputes can be traced in crediting procedures. In part these disputes merely reflect processes of standardisation and differentiation, but they also register tensions between labour and creativity. For most film workers credits are there for the industry's rather than the public's recognition, which is why the bulk of the credits can appear at the end of the film. But this kind of generalisation is precarious – questions about authorship and control, technology and fiction are there from the outset. A history of legal battles around copyright and patents, around intellectual and industrial property relations, traces not only crediting procedures in general, but each individual film and its evolution as both art and entertainment.

An ostentatious display is made of that evolution in the opening of Tashlin's *The Girl Can't Help It*, which initially absorbs the credits into the fiction

– or, to put it differently, the fiction is immediately located within a technological-industrial context (the transition to colour and CinemaScope).[23] A delightfully trenchant visual gag, playing on the cinema's material existence and magical impermanence, links these issues to questions of labour and creativity. The appearance of the wide screen and colour lags behind the announcement or accreditation, provoking the host figure to click his fingers and raise his eyes to the heavens. 'Sometimes you wonder who's minding the store,' he remarks, confidentially, to the audience – an allusion to either God as the original creator, or the director as God, or the industrial machinery which grinds on, less than efficiently we note, ignoring human desires (and the title of the film Tashlin would make with Jerry Lewis some seven years later). If the director is God, then His presence and intentionality, as the parodic overture to *The Girl Can't Help It* seems to imply, is totally subverted by the contingencies of technology and the vagaries of exhibition. Yet the reflexiveness of the opening does inscribe an authorial position of sorts. If the framework incorporates a signature-effect, then it in turn serves to provide a kind of a frame.[24]

At the London Film Festival, where an American-dubbed version of Salò *was shown to British Film Institute members only, this audience of 'specialists' and 'cinephiles' hissed the most innovative shot in the film, the inclusion of a bibliography in the credit sequence. This made* Salò *into the first major commercial film to acknowledge publicly that it is not merely 'based on' or 'inspired by' a novel, but that films themselves are no more than textual fragments embedded in a far wider set of discourses.*[25]

Credits are governed by conventions which, though they serve to ensure recognition, are equally dedicated to misrecognition. However, the very existence of the credit sequence as a part of (or, ambivalently, apart from) the film's fictional body reminds us that cinema is always, as it were, 'in-production' in a space between commerce, industry and fiction. The opening scenes of both *Alice* and *The Girl Can't Help It* deploy a mode of address which ostentatiously alludes to technology and change, that is to say, to the cinematic past which provides the necessary conditions for these particular films to be possible. Histories of technology, though they might appear to contain and situate the past, are nevertheless in their turn (we might say: in their *significance*) mediated by techniques of memory.

The story ends with Jerry again walking backwards and disappearing over a balcony. As his girlfriend weeps inconsolably he reappears, walking along outside the window of this high-rise office. 'It's a movie set!' he explains, and dismantles the balcony to show the hidden platform. He invites her for lunch and shouts (towards the audience), 'Crew, that's one hour for lunch!' As they turn, the camera swings and follows them through a crowded studio set, with closing credits over the image.

Elephants in Space
Do you remember the old 'squarish' (3:4 ratio) format and the way it was displaced by the coming of widescreen and its association with colour? And do

you remember how spectacular and exciting these innovations were? I remember, vividly, even though the first films I ever saw were (already) in colour and widescreen. But perhaps I should say the first films I saw in the cinema. At home, on the farm, there was an 8mm camera and projector so we saw home movies, millions of Warner Bros. and Disney cartoons and silent shorts, Chaplin, Keaton, the Three Stooges, but mostly Laurel and Hardy. In those days 'flicks' came in tiny boxes and were silent, and we all talked loudly over the sound of the projector, except for the time when the films from our trip to Gorongoza, a game reserve in Mozambique, came back. The images, like those of other home movie footage, were familiar and yet there was something uncanny about them. The exotic quality of the wildlife seemed exaggerated, the events depicted seemed fictionalised, as though we were witness to an adventure that had happened to other people. The year was 1957. I am able to fix the date not because the films remain, or any other documents, but through a curious chain of associations.

About ten years ago, researching a film on epitaphs and public memorabilia, I was directed to the Gold Coast in Queensland, to a small statue of a dog standing outside a mock-Tudor restaurant in the heart of flamboyantly tacky surfdom: 'MATEY – Friend to thousands of tourists and residents of Surfers Paradise for 12 years showed no distinction to class, colour or creed. This memorial was erected by residents and visitors to Surfers Paradise in 1957, the year man sacrificed a dog in space to help make safe the pathway to the stars.'

Suddenly I saw an elephant, huge, Kodak-coloured, moving almost at the speed of light. I remembered: 'Sputnik!' The year 1957, home movies, the Russians, space and elephants. When the lights were switched off and we saw elephants *en masse* on the living-room wall, swaying serenely and slowly flapping their ears, we yelled out in sheer delight, 'Sputnik! Sputnik!' Although the elephants my father had captured on film were benign they represented very immediately for us the rogue who had charged. One moment he was part of a herd, the next he was thundering towards us, blackening the world with his fury. At the last minute he veered off, intimidated, we later decided, by the sight of our tiny car suddenly propelled through the bush like a Russian sputnik. Invocation of the word 'Sputnik' – a word very much in the news – had turned our terror into humour and our ignominious retreat into an exotic trajectory into the future. Somehow the association between sputniks and the movies hit me with force that day in Surfers Paradise. I could recall very clearly an elephant, framed full square, flapping its ears and then, in a flash, charging straight at us, out of the frame. A sense of intense *déjà vu* provoked me to write home to Zimbabwe, to find out what happened to that 8mm footage. It was put in storage, the reply came, had moulded and been thrown away. But the metaphor remains, or rather some transient connection between cinema and metaphor: the cinema is shot through by metaphor, like a sputnik through the stars.

I made no connection then between real movies and the experience of watching flicks on the wall on Saturday nights. The first real movie I remember was *Lili* (1952), projected against the sky at the drive-in, an unbelievably enormous image suspended in space. For years after, Leslie Caron remained the latent image of cinema itself, materialising in a totally other dimension, quintessentially ethereal (and square). One of the first films I saw in a proper cinema – it wasn't the very first, but it was my first experience (or so I remember) of a conjunction of immensity and the theatrical, my first taste of how sensational cinematic narrative can be – was *Around the World in Eighty Days*. For weeks afterwards my cousin and I would try to reconstruct and re-enact the story, to recapture the excitement and fear, returning again and again to the moment of flames lapping the edge of the screen, to what for us was the pivotal, and most enigmatic, scene: the burning of the Indian widow on her husband's pyre.

Around the World in Eighty Days was made in 1956 in Todd-AO, and lasted 3 hours and 30 minutes. It was the beginning of the blockbuster era; in the same year King Vidor's *War and Peace* (VistaVision; 3 hours 28 minutes) and Cecil B. DeMille's remake of his own *The Ten Commandments* (VistaVision; 3 hours 39 minutes) were released (and, incidentally, *The Searchers* and *The Girl Can't Help It*, both in widescreen). *Around the World in Eighty Days* would probably have arrived in Rhodesia a year later, in 1957, the year of the sputnik.

In the cinema we are absorbed by 360-degree sound, by patterns of colour and movement; but we are also absorbed by various histories, histories of technology, for instance, which are mediated both by very localised enactments of popular memory and by global events which often seem to have little immediate connection with practices of spectatorship, like dogs in space, the cold war, tourism in Africa. Idiosyncratic memory and official history always shadow and colour one another in complex and discontinuous ways. When we talk of technology in the cinema, we tend to think of 'hardware' – cameras, lenses, film stock, sound-recording devices, and so on, all of which are conceived in terms of mechanics, physics, chemistry and, increasingly, electronics. But implicated in the very process of cinema – that is, in the transformation of hardware into images – are techniques of memory, ways of experiencing and remembering that may well be peculiarly modern, characteristic of the age of cinema, inscribed within the cinematic imaginary. Against this, it might of course be argued that the cinema can more accurately be identified as an art of forgetfulness, that it is the quintessential form of escapism. From such a perspective it might be pointed out that my memory of the Gorongoza event is a movie memory; the film image becomes a surrogate for reality (moreover, the memory itself is incorrect: what I remembered, in that moment of *déjà vu* in Surfers Paradise, was an image of an elephant charging straight at us, out of the frame; but in reconstructing the events I recall that the moment of charging, not surprisingly, was not recorded on film). Like Alice, I stand accused: 'Alice's past is a movie past, a surrogate for real experience in a three-by-four screen ratio.'[26] But 'movie memories' are not necessarily false or divorced from real experience. I would argue that a work of memory is taking place through the cinematic medium, and through the years, historically, not just in the moment of viewing which is the 'originary moment', but in the layerings of images over the years and the way in which the movie image comes to function as a kind of mnemonic device, an aid to memory. The cinematic imaginary can also yield a recovery, a reshaping of memories that have disappeared, been submerged. Memory is imaged and experienced via cinema. The process of recall involves an in-mixing of voluntary and involuntary memory. Charged moments, when one is seized by an overwhelming, almost physical sensation of reminiscence, are filtered over time through other memories, other histories.

Images appear like confessions. (Chris Marker, *La Jetée*)

A startling memory, though attached to a charged image, may turn out in the end not to be about elephants at all. Imagine a superimposition, a conflation of two apparently incompatible technological frames: 8mm technology, which, because of miniaturisation and economy, enabled home-movie-making and domestic reception; and the technology of widescreen cinema, which emphasised hugeness and theatricality. I suspect that the widescreen spectacle of *Around the World in Eighty Days* has been superimposed in my memory over the elephants on the living room wall, and that this composite film comes somehow to constitute the imagery of my childhood, or at least a certain genre of fiction, shaped not just by the cinema but by the phantasms of colonialism and the cold war. The connections between *Around the World* and my father's Gorongoza footage is not purely fortuitous. They are both versions of the travelogue, inflections of a genre that conjures up as exotic and untamed those zones that have in fact been colonised, but 'imperfectly' so. The imperfections are frequently transferred to animals and women. The Gorongoza footage also echoes a Hollywood genre epitomised by the Tarzan movies (which were, however, all shot in a studio). The more recent Hollywood films in the Tarzan lineage, such as *King Solomon's Mines*, have used Zimbabwe as a location, taking advantage of the superb climate and scenery. The Zimbabwean film culture[27] that is beginning to develop now is vividly contemporary and not interested in 'safari films' or magnificent scenery:

> I, and most of my acquaintances, have never visited Victoria Falls, Great Zimbabwe, Lake Kariba, Lake Kyle, Chimanimani, Vumba, and a host of other places. We would never ever dream of doing so – I hope the Tourist Board is reading this and will take appropriate disciplinary measures. (Dambudzo Marechera).[28]

When these memories started appearing and jostling I made a trip to the video store and borrowed *Around the World*. It was rather dispiriting to watch it so reduced (by time and by the television monitor) and Sarris's description of it – in the course of discussing *The Searchers* – as a 'camp curiosity' seemed remarkably apt. I was chagrined to see that flames do not lap the edge of the screen, and interested to note that *suttee* or 'widow sacrifice' is referred to by the ancient men in the London club as 'wretched murder'. Phineas Fogg is reluctant to intervene on behalf of the Indian widow, but when he is told that she had been educated in Britain he changes his mind. 'That decides it!' he declares, taking off in his balloon for India. A phrase from elsewhere (from a reading of Gayatri Spivak, I suspect) reverberates around this image: White men are saving brown women from brown men.

133

I Remember Vividly . . .

What can it possibly mean to say 'I remember vividly' (the old square format and the way it was displaced by the coming of widescreen and colour) when my only point of comparison would have been the drive-in image and the home-movie frame? Moreover, it would seem that it is not difference (between small and large, square and elongated) that I have been describing, but conflation (superimposing a Todd-AO format over the square frame on the living-room wall). My intention, however, is not to gloss over the history of technological change but rather to stress that those changes are sometimes registered less in a chronologically sequential manner and more as a series of differences played discontinuously across space, a series of points temporarily relating to one another. These mobile points in space can be contextualised, realised concretely, by place (and modes of reception, spectatorship). So, in my early history, silent cinema is associated with the domestic, and sound with the theatre and the drive-in; silent comedy and home movies form a sort of homogeneous genre, differentiated from musicals and blockbusters, characterised more by their bigness and less by their shape, and Westerns are quintessentially television.

Other modes of distinction come to overlie these early experiences. For we also absorb various versions of official, and often teleological history, myths and legends of cinema such as the series of 'firsts': *The Jazz Singer* (Alan Crosland, 1927) as the first sound film, *Becky Sharp* (Rouben Mamoulian, 1935) as the first colour film, and so on, so that we come to remember these films though we have never actually seen them. We also inherit screen memories: just as in a more oral culture stories are passed down and appropriated as memories, so conceptions and memories of cinema are passed down, through generations.

The Dynamic Square: Reshaping the Screen

Alice Doesn't Live Here Anymore is announced by a frame within a frame. What is Scorsese doing when he incorporates the old Warner Bros. logo in a square frame within the more familiar wide screen to which we are now accustomed? Does the framing indicate an exercise in nostalgia, a homage to archaic technology and old-fashioned techniques of showing and seeing? Or is it a rhetorical device signalling to us that the frame of reference is above all the process of referencing itself, that self-consciousness and self-reflexivity are to set the scene, to put in process a staging of cinematic *mise en abîme* (a receding, Chinese-boxes-like perspective)?

From a certain vantage point, the 'square' frame is archaic, but from another it is probably the most familiar and ubiquitous screen today, as embodied by the television set. The 'normal' cinema screen, nowadays, is comparatively wide (1.85:1 in America and 1.66:1 in Europe), compared, that is, with television, but also with the 'old' cinema format. In existence from 1889, this old format (1.33:1) was standardised by the Academy of Motion Picture Arts and Sciences in 1932 and lasted in Hollywood (as always, with variations) into the 50s. But the 'academy ratio' is still with us in the form not only of the television screen but also of 16mm productions and standard 8mm home movies (in fact these are 1.37:1, but they are still considered to be academy ratio). Various forms of widescreen cinema had also been in sporadic existence from the early days, but in the early 1950s there was a veritable flurry as dozens of new and different ratios were introduced with great fanfare, including Cinerama, CinemaScope, VistaVision, Todd-AO. Eventually a new standard evolved – less wide than CinemaScope (which had an aspect ratio of either 2.55:1 or 2.35:1), but wider than the old format.

The process of widescreen standardisation proceeded in tandem with a process of differentiation. The new formats were introduced as a way of defending (ironically, as it has turned out) and differentiating the cinema from its new competitor: television. It is often argued that there is a lag between technological possibilities and ideological requirements, so that so-called 'inventions' often occur many years after the necessary scientific knowledge has been in existence. In this respect widescreen, like colour and 'motion' pictures, is exemplary. CinemaScope was yet another military spin-off, emanating from tank gun-sighting periscopes. 'It was an optics professor, Henri Chrétien, whose work during the First World War perfecting navy artillery telemetry laid the foundations for what would become CinemaScope thirty-six years later,' writes Paul Virilio.[29] Indeed the 'invention' was deployed to fight a war, though one which is usually posed as primarily economic rather than ideological or aesthetic. Television was introduced in black-and-white on a screen with more or less the same aspect ratio as the cinema screen, but much smaller. The film industry's response to the popularity of television was to exaggerate difference, to make the big still bigger and to stretch the image to incommensurable proportions in order to insure that television could not appropriate cinematic space. Hence the new, large cinema formats and the rapid conversion to colour between 1952 and 1955, the era of the blockbuster – expensively produced spectacles filmed and exhibited on wide-film formats and in multitrack stereophonic sound. The space opened up by the wide screen was imagistic, but also economic. It was hailed by the industry as a technological innovation that would revolutionise and rehabilitate an ailing industry.

> I do not desire to be exaggeratedly symbolic, or rude, or to compare the creeping rectangles of these proposed shapes to the creeping mentality of the film reduced thereto by the weight upon it of the commercial pressure of dollars, pounds, francs, or marks.

This was written in 1930 by Sergei Eisenstein. It is from an essay called 'The Dynamic Square', a response to a meeting he had attended organised by the Academy of Motion Picture Arts and Sciences to discuss new screen dimensions suggested by the wide films that had recently been introduced.[30] Twenty-three years before what legend claims as the first widescreen films, Eisenstein sounds a warning note that prefigures Belton's analysis (made some thirty years after their advent): 'By a strange coincidence, American currency is almost exactly the same shape as CinemaScope.' Nowadays, Belton argues: 'The shape of money has become the shape of the television screen.'[31] Eisenstein's essay is wickedly wily: at first it appears that he is defending the 'square' frame against widescreen, but soon his parodic tone seeps through the veneer of reason. Although he is rhetorically acerbic in attacking economistic motivations,

135

he does not simply brandish aesthetic arguments as a counterforce. He points out that many of these arguments are essentially nostalgic in that they call upon precedents established in the other arts or in some appeal to 'nature' (for example: a nostalgia for infinite horizons, fields, plains, deserts.)

> *Like a fish in the biggest aquarium,*
> *the cowboy is most at ease on the wide screen. (André Bazin)[32]*

Regarding invocations of the golden section in painting, Eisenstein says, 'And why the hell should we drag behind us in these days of triumph the melancholy memory of the unfulfilled desire of the static rectangle striving to become dynamic?'[33] His polemic is against an ontology of the cinema; he is not interested in any so-called technological innovation that merely reproduces static modes of perception, but rather urges a welcoming of widescreen for its 'constructive possibilities'. It is useful now to recall this rather eccentric and marvellously pertinent little essay. What is significant is the way Eisenstein draws attention to the question of framing as a question of 'dynamic perception'. I am interested in the dynamics of screen aspect ratio.[34] My focus, however, is on the nature of transitions (from one format to another) and differences (of format, but manifested often in exhibition practices).

> *When Cinemascope arrived many cinemas 'widened' screens*
> *by cropping the picture, thus giving the desired impression.*
> *So, when old films were shown with projectors masked for*
> *scope, the top of the image, where the most expressive part,*
> *the human face, tends to be, was lost. Halfway through*
> Wuthering Heights *I bitterly complained. Came the reply,*
> *'You're not supposed to see the faces, it's a dark film.'[35]*

The issue of screen ratio serves to vividly highlight a process – industrial, aesthetic and ideological – which was inaugurated in the 50s and still continues today. It concerns a reframing of the cinematic experience and revolves round shifting relations between film and television. In positing aspect ratio as a relational issue (rather than dwelling upon the advent of widescreen formats as a privileged moment in the history of technological innovation), I want to explore its manifestation as a (shifting) series (of differences). On one level it provides a heuristic device, as a most economical index of industrial change; on another but related level, it opens the way to a discussion of spectating practices, focuses on ways the 'optical unconscious' is framed, ways in which the exhibition context shapes what we see and how we remember.[36]

A Television Screen That's Bigger Than the Whole House: Film and Television
The process by which the widescreen format becomes normalised coincides with the passing of the Hollywood studio system (actually it is, of course, no

coincidence, but for the moment it is useful to hold the two processes in tandem). Although some of the widescreen spectacles proved to be short-term money-spinners, in the long term the industry did not recover, and it is sometimes argued that the small screen was responsible for the decline in cinema attendance and in effect destroyed the film industry. However, the film industry did not of course simply collapse. Rather, it had to accommodate to a changing situation and this meant diversification and realignment of interests, of patterns of ownership and control. The advent of widescreen cinema (and the coming of television), we might say, inaugurated a long period of complex organisational reconfiguration, as well as fundamental changes in the way people view, receive, consume and remember movies. Post-war perception has been shaped by a profound entanglement of film and television.[37]

It is often thought that Hollywood, already weakened by the anti-trust legislation which forced the studios to divest themselves of their exhibition outlets, passively submitted to the television onslaught. In fact, as more recent research shows, the industry did attempt to acquire television broadcast licences very early but were thwarted by anti-trust legislation.[38] Nevertheless, the film studios began forming subsidiaries for television production and various shifting alliances between Hollywood and television soon developed.

> We were one of the first families on our block to get a
> television set in 1948.
> I recall I was playing in the backyard and my cousin Peter rushed
> out shouting, 'Come and see a television screen that's bigger
> than the whole house!'
> Of course it was only a sixteen-inch RCA Victor. (Scorsese).[39]

An idea of Hollywood's intervention in the world of television can be measured by the transition from predominantly live broadcast to filmed material: during the early 50s, nearly all prime-time programming emanated from New York and was broadcast live. By the late 50s, nearly all prime-time programming emanated from Hollywood on film. In 1955, Hollywood produced close to 20 per cent of the prime-time programmes and close to 40 per cent of the average television station's daily schedule. Hollywood, in other words, produced ten times as much film for television as it did for theatrical motion picture exhibition.[40] The studio system was changing fast, and if we take 'studio' to designate not only the company structures which constituted Hollywood, but also a representational practice, then we can see that the aspect of film was being substantially transformed: 'By mid-1959, 23 different TV programs were in production at the Warner studio, but no feature films (most theatrical releases were shot on location).'[41]

> *And though television has realised Léon Gaumont's dream to*
> *bring the spectacles of the whole world into the most wretchedly*
> *poor of bedrooms, it has done so by reducing the shepherd's*
> *gigantic sky to Tom Thumb's size. (Jean-Luc Godard).*[42]

Hollywood's formation of subsidiaries for television production was indicative of a trend towards diversification into every aspect of television as well as allied leisure-time activities. During the 60s and 70s motion picture companies were either taken over by huge corporations, or absorbed into expanding entertainment conglomerates, or became conglomerates through diversification. The same period saw changing exhibition practices – not only the transformation of conventional theatres and the building of large multiplexes in suburban shopping centres but also extensive showing of motion pictures on television. The 80s witnessed the development of technologies providing new outlets for feature films and an opening up of non-theatrical markets. The VCR and cable television did not, as anticipated, kill the movie theatre; in fact ancillary markets increased interest in the movies and since the 80s the theatrical exhibition market in America and other countries still dominated by Hollywood has increasingly strengthened.

> *We will come through television to cinema again.* (Alexander Kluge)[43]

The exhibition of films on television and the marketing of films on video, though they might involve a particular reframing of the cinematic by what we may refer to as tele-perception, have also been instrumental in stimulating and restructuring patterns of motion picture production – that is, in independent production of movies for the big screen (or, more accurately, movies in the first instance for the big screen).[44] For instance, in 1989 HBO, the largest pay cable service in America, was already the 'largest financier of motion pictures in the world'.[45] The libraries of old films turned out to be gold for the companies, a continuing source of revenue (from television rentals) which could be ploughed back, one way or another, into production. Since the studios, however, no longer exist in their old form the old studio film has disappeared in the wake of these processes of reframing. But it has resurfaced in a curious way.

I have alluded to the industrial and technological transitions that Hollywood has undergone, particularly in relation to television, in order to set in place some of the elements for elaborating the notion of frame-work, for discussing spectating practices. 'Hollywood' in this discussion will reverberate in a number of ways. On the most straightforward level it refers to the studio system, and the period of classical film production. On another level it exists as an index of desire, an inscription of memory. *This* Hollywood is not divorced from the first one; indeed, it is a history of transitions and transformations, changes in aspect, that is alluded to. But this italicised Hollywood is phantasmatic, and it exists in an era where the tele-imagination has a privileged shaping function. Hollywood isn't then swallowed whole by the advent of television, but it is reconfigured (and the wide screen is to some extent regurgitated). What does disappear, to resurface as a memory, reshaped by tele-perception, is the studio picture.

Frame-Work

> *Alice Doesn't Live Here Anymore* was the first time in my movie
> career that I was able to build a proper set. It was also the last picture

to be shot in the old Columbia sound-stages on Gower Street. We even had the set decorator from *Citizen Kane,* Darrell Silvera. Russell Metty shot the tests for me. He happened to be on the set. In the opening sequence, showing Alice as a little girl, we tried for a combination of *Duel in the Sun* and *Gone with the Wind* in the William Cameron Menzies style of *Invaders from Mars* . . . He painted a red sunset that went 180 degrees around the entire stage, and we made up this little girl to look like Dorothy in the *Wizard of Oz.* (Scorsese)[46]

The square frame for Scorsese is like the crystallisation of a process: the passing of the studio system.[47] It is the concept of the studio that is to be evoked, that is the strength of the reference. It is not nostalgia for the square frame in and of itself, but rather what is evoked by the substance of the frame: the Warners Bros. logo is a metonym for Hollywood itself, for the heyday of the studio system. The square frame is therefore like a mnemonic device. Ironically, what is a *new* experience for Scorsese (for the first time he gets to work on one of the old sound stages, to paint a studio set, to use a crane, and a fog filter, and so on) is associated with a kind of death. *Alice* is the last film shot on the old Columbia sound stages before they are turned into tennis courts. The death of the studio system is not mourned or summoned as a 'melancholy memory'; on the contrary it is resurrected in a spirit of histrionic delight, and yet various histories do shadow the square frame – or perhaps it would be more accurate to say that histories are evoked, memories provoked, in the space between the two frames: the cinema screen now and the inset, a cinema screen then.

> There is such a thing, that is, as 'frame-work' (like dreamwork).
> The frame works. (Jacques Derrida)[48]

We might think of the prologue (and here I include the credit sequence) as a part, and a small part at that, of the film, and the square frame as part of the whole image or cinema screen. But there is a way in which this very process (or work) of framing turns inside out so that the 'contained' image or object comments on or 'frames' the frame that contains it. That is to say, the thing contained reflects back on the frame, so that relations between inside and outside are unsettled, displaced by an enfolding.

The Good, the Bad and the Missing
Fairly early in the history of television the major studios began selling off film libraries to the television networks, but rights and royalties negotiations restricted these films to pre-1948.[49] In 1960 the guilds and studios reached an agreement which paved the way for the release of more recent films, including widescreen productions. In 1961 the first of this new package of post-1948 features, Twentieth Century Fox's *How to Marry a Millionaire* (1953), was aired on NBC's *Saturday Night at the Movies. Millionaire* ushered in not only the era of the prime-time network feature film but also that of the

panned-and-scanned film.[50] There was always the possibility of preserving the original aspect ratio and broadcasting in a 'letterbox' format, but television chose to crop and reframe during a shot or to edit from one side of the CinemaScope frame to the other, prompting Belton to comment: '*The Good, the Bad and the Ugly* suddenly became the Good, the Bad, and the Missing.' As William Lafferty points out:

> It is ironic that Twentieth Century-Fox, which pioneered wide-screen films with CinemaScope as a means to lure audiences away from television and back to movies, also pioneered the process by which audiences could see those films on television – and won an Oscar from a grateful industry for each.[51]

The film industry responded to television's reshaping by what might be described as a form of self-regulation: in 1962 the 'safe action area' was inaugurated. This was the portion of the picture area inside the camera aperture borders within which all significant action should take place for 'safe' or full reproduction on the television screen. Camera manufacturers began to produce viewfinders which indicated this area with a dotted line, a frame within a frame.

> I've been obsessed with 'Scope for years and would love to shoot everything in 'Scope, but I realise that when it's shown on TV the power of the picture will be completely lost. (Scorsese)[52]

When *Alice Doesn't Live Here Anymore* is shown on television something very alarming happens, something which could be interpreted, in the light of an account of television's propensity to ingest and corrupt cinema, as bitterly prophetic. A reshaping occurs: we see a square within a square instead of a square within a rectangle. Difference is effectively obliterated. The 'squareness' of the interior frame, of the prologue, is barely noticeable when it is located within a screen that has the same aspect ratio (1.37:1, whereas in the cinema it would be 1.85:1). The enframing effect persists (and in fact the *mise en abîme* process is emphasised) but it might be less tenable to speak of the relationship between the two frames as being between 'the cinema screen now and the inset: a cinema screen then'. In fact 'the frame of reference' is often taken to be television itself, since this is what the square frame connotes for most people, and particularly for young film students, say, who might come to *Alice Doesn't Live Here Anymore* without much experience of seeing 'old' films in a film theatre (but certainly with an experience of television as 'the place' where old films are resurrected).

In such a situation, and if so much depends upon the opening moments of a film, what effect does television's reshaping have upon the film's significance? Would someone whose primary frame of reference is television, who has no memory or much knowledge of the transition to widescreen and colour, no memory of the arrival of television and the passing of the studio system, be in a position to read the prologue, to apprehend the play between past and present that is enacted in the (original) enframing?

> *The problem of fitting the ninety-six-minute* Jailhouse Rock
> *(1957) into a 78-minute afternoon movie block [was solved]*
> *by cutting all of Elvis's musical numbers.*[53]

To ask how a film makes sense when subjected to television's literal reshaping is to draw attention to the more general and systematic propensity of television to reduce and mutilate the cinematic text. Films shown on commercial television are censored, cut to fit into allotted time slots, and interrupted by advertisements; films on video are shrunk, trimmed and flattened. It would seem, on the face of it, that the television era, with its associated technologies, has ushered in an unparalleled assault on the originality of the movies.[54] But it is worth remembering that Hollywood itself has never been squeamish about cutting up and redistributing the cinematic body. Silent movies were easily modified and different versions were routinely distributed to different markets within America. But it was in export prints that variations were most noticeable: not only were scenes excised and rearranged, but subtitles were substantially modified for different countries. Moreover, foreign exhibitors often cut movies to fit into a given time slot. The coming of sound made post-production alterations more difficult, but not impossible. Titles and dubbing have always been deployed 'creatively' for Hollywood's export market.[55] The more recent phenomenon of 're-releases' and 'the director's cut' can be seen, in the light of such a history, as another marketing strategy rather than an impulse towards restoration and preservation of originality. Television and related electronic modes of reproduction do not simply introduce a breach and violation, but in a sense continue a tradition inaugurated with photographic technologies of reproduction. In the case of film (as Walter Benjamin has pointed out) there is no original, only a negative.

This is not to say that watching a film or video on television and watching it in a movie theatre is, since nothing is original, much the same sort of thing. Nor is to propose that the square-within-the-square in *Alice*'s prologue epitomises, as certain post-modern views might have it, a fall from history into the endless procession of simulacra. Every viewing situation is traced by specific histories of technology as well as by the political and cultural inflections of exhibition and the variety of personal memories brought to bear on the film. I would merely stress a couple of things: first, it has always been the case that a diversity of exhibition and reception modes have coexisted, influencing how and what we remember, how we make sense of both individual films and cinematic histories; and, second, although there are certain continuities, there are are also historical differences, differences in perception, we might say, but these are not tied in a deterministic way to particular technologies. What does seem new, and it is related to the advent of new 'delivery' technologies, is that cinema and television, as signifying practices, are today intertwined in complex ways, and experienced as intertwined rather than imagined and remembered separately.

It is of course conceivable that someone whose primary frame of reference is television would indeed read the enframing of *Alice Doesn't Live Here*

141

Anymore as a play between past and present but in such a way that film and television are temporally inverted. The film spawned a television series, *Alice*, for Warner Television, and for those brought up on television it might well seem that the film, seen later on video, occurred as a by-product of the television show. The film–television relation here anticipates that enacted by the current crop of films based on classic television series, such as *The Munsters*, *The Fugitive* and *The Flintstones*. For a generation which might have been born about the time that *Alice Doesn't Live Here Anymore* was made, television, as 'the place' where old films are resurrected, is the locus through which a filmic past, a cinematic nostalgia, is mediated. And the cinema becomes a way of re-enchanting an outmoded television past, of reanimating a kind of collective, inherited, memory of television.

> There was one programme in the fifties called 'Million Dollar Movie',
> which would show the same films twice on weekday evenings, at 7.30
> and 9.30, and three times on Saturday and Sunday . . . I remember
> seeing Powell and Pressburger's *The Tales of Hoffmann* on this
> programme; it was in black and white, cut and interrupted by com-
> mercials (it wasn't until 1965 that I saw it in colour). But I was
> mesmerised by the music, the camera movements and the theatricality
> of the gestures by these actors who were mostly dancers. There's a lot
> that can be said against *The Tales of Hoffmann*, yet I've always said
> that those repeated viewings on television taught me about the
> relation of camera to music. (Scorsese)[56]

Take a film like *Blade Runner*. The opening night of its re-release in Sydney was an exciting cinematic occasion, rather like an old-fashioned gala opening, I imagine. The crowd (retro-fashioned, however, rather than gala glitzy) was dense and voluble, the air bristling with expectation. I had not seen the movie on a big wide screen since my first viewing in Hong Kong, and there was a sense of *déjà vu* about this event, experienced as a re-enactment of some 'mel-ancholy desire' for wide crowded spaces. Many people in the audience would never have seen it in a theatre at all; they would have known the film only as a small-square phenomenon. Because it initially bombed at the box office in 1982 it was pulled from theatrical release and immediately saturated on tele-vision and video release (with additional footage added for the video version) as part of a new marketing device, 'rapid pullback strategy' (posited on the co-ordination of different Warner Bros. subsidiaries).[57] Much has been written about *Blade Runner* as a post-modern film but a good deal of this rests on a textual analysis;[58] in fact, a case could be made about its mutation in terms of exhibition, the impossibility of assigning with any certainty an originary ver-sion or a 'correct' memory. I have to admit that my pleasure in this new version involved a revelling in the immensity of the wide screen, a degree of jubilation at having the 'correct' proportions restored. But listening in on conversations before and after the screening clearly revealed that there were many people there who knew the film (in one of its versions anyway) extremely well, pre-sumably through playing the video over and over again, through pausing and slowing and freezing, and memorising the imagistic scenario. The audience generally seemed elated by the large wide screen, but not necessarily as a corrective, rather as a sort of mapping of a film's history, and through that of various personal histories.

> *While I had a personal history as an individual, had it not been for cinema, I wouldn't have known that I had a history of my own. It was the only way, and I owe it to the cinema.* (Godard)[59]

Many feature films now actually address themselves to changed viewing circumstances, a fact of which many critical studies are fully cognisant.[60] Take the case of *Gremlins 2: The New Batch*, where the 'Gremlins Take Over the Projection Booth' sequence was replaced by a 'Gremlins in the VCR' sequence for Warner Home Video cassette release. This post-production sequence features frenzied channel switching and the startling presence of gremlins in a range of genres: Westerns, news reports, cartoons, biblical epics, climaxing in a shoot-out between John Wayne and gremlin rustlers. 'I don't need varmints on my ranch and you folks don't need 'em in your TV sets,' says the Duke, 'Start that movie up again.'[61]

Although contemporary readings of *Alice Doesn't Live Here Anymore*, or at least of the opening, may understand the significance of the square frame in a new and idiosyncratic way (from an old perspective) they nevertheless arise out of a history of technological change that is implied in the opening. In positing the relation between two aspect ratios as representing the past and the present, two movie times, I have also traced the ghostly presence of television

Hud (Martin Ritt, 1962)

as the (repressed) term of transition. The foregrounding of this term does involve irony, but it seems to me quite amenable to being mapped onto the discourse of enframing that opens *Alice*.

> *You'll never know how much I love you*
> *If you don't know now*
> *now*
> Now! Now! Now! Now! Now! Now! Now! Now!

There are enough elements in the credit sequence – the blue satin fallen in folds, the old Warner Bros. logo, the generic nature of the credits, and so on – to suggest an evocation of the past. If this past appears to be framed by television, and if the television screen appears in its turn to be framed by the cinematic, then there is still a relation between past and present but a kind of inversion, a turning inside out or perversion of part–whole relations. If the present is experienced as the Age of Television (and this experience might register primarily in the optical unconscious, be manifested in a generalised aspect or outlook) then the allusion is less to films made in the studio system and more to films made under the aegis of (though not necessarily for) television or contemporaneity. We would then be led to expect not a re-creation of the past but an imaginative projection from now – in other words, a very contemporary outlook or aspect on the past. It is as though the past is articulated in the present tense. If *Alice* 'looks like it was shot as a movie in 1948' the emphasis falls on 'looks like'; it certainly doesn't look as though it is a 1948 movie. It's 'half fantasy, half remembrance'; it's like a television-age fantasy of a 1948 movie. There is a sense of *déjà vu* as though we have been here before, but 'where or when?' As the strident 'Now! Now! Now!' drowns out the 'now' of the old love song, as the rich red screen contracts to a tiny square, fantasy and remembrance intersect

The Splendour of Colours . . . Carnivorous, Devouring, Absorbent

Do you remember the pink Cadillac in *Hud*? It has never faded in my memory or in the various prints and formats I've seen over the years. It is a desolate film, its desolation etched in the black-and-white stock that Ritt chose, anachronistically, in 1964. The film enacts, through the agency of Paul Newman, a curiously morbid rendering of masculine sexuality which is somehow energised by an anomalous but highly charged correlative: a pink Cadillac. Of course, it is only as a virtual image that it is pink; in actuality it appears in monochrome. But it exists.

> *It's pink. It's a pink leopard.*
> (Scorsese, on finally catching up with Visconti's *The Leopard*
> and discovering how badly the colour had deteriorated)[62]

The persistence of the pink Cadillac suggests to me a peculiarly cinematic process of engagement and memory. Certainly I don't tell this story in order to illustrate the power of human imagination over an impoverished phenomenality of the image. On the contrary, the memory of that pink is imbued by the framing context: it is a cinematic memory, it is Technicolor pink. Paradoxically, it is perhaps because of its black-and-white incarnation that it persists where other memories and images fade (and I wonder if this virtual image didn't persist for Scorsese too, to such an extent that he made it actual in *GoodFellas,* in the car with the VIP numberplate, containing the murdered bodies of husband and wife). I am sure that the dispiriting sensation I experienced on watching *Around the World in Eighty Days* was not entirely to do with the reduction from a large widescreen format to a small square format. It also has to do, as indicated, with larger historical and cultural contexts, with a reframing of perception that is not exhaustively technological. But also I think that it must have to do with the loss of colour on the video (not only would it have been electronically copied from a print that had probably already faded, but it would no doubt have been copied and played many times over, leading to massive degeneration of the image, and in addition to all this there would be the mediation of the television monitor). I think that long ago burning flames did lap the edge of the frame. They do so no longer for a variety of reasons, in a zone where techniques of memory and histories of technology intermesh.

> *The image on the screen in the sudden darkness was of a woman seated in the sunshine, cutting up a fish. It was inexpressibly beautiful. When on second viewing the image came round, it was disappointing, as the colours in a fish you have just caught and thrown into the bottom of the boat swiftly fade before your eyes.*[63]

At the beginning of the red prologue pink script is superimposed over the red: Monterey, California. Alice, a young girl. That combination of red and pink is unusual, lusciously synthetic, emanating trouble. It recurs in *Written on the Wind,* where it is associated with Kyle Hadley/Robert Stack and his sister, Marylee/Dorothy Malone, the bad ones. Stack attempts to impress and seduce the upright Lauren Bacall by taking her to a sumptuously vulgar hotel ('Nice little boarding house you have here,' remarks Rock Hudson); he escorts her, in her muted tasteful suit, down a lengthy pink corridor and into a suite where a gigantic vase of long-stemmed crimson roses is ranged against the pink background, next to a window featuring a rear-projection view of the ocean. Later, and in association with Malone, the colours vie in a more lethal configuration. After she has provoked a fight in a far less salubrious hotel, Marylee, in a hot pink dress, lounges against her flaming red sports car, taunting Rock. And while her father is plummetting to his death she dances alone, an erotically demented dervish, flashing pink and red. These colours, in their juxtaposition, produce a garish effect, it is true, but they also generate a surplus attraction: it is as though the red absorbs the pink into its orbit just as we are lured into the passionate fatality of the drama surrounding the 'bad' characters, so much more luminous than the matt tones of Bacall and Hudson's picture. Sirk has talked about *échec,* failure, the dead end, no way out,[64] and this trajectory, this exploration of what is at stake in sexual and economic power, is traced through a melodramatic register where timbre, colour, gesture resonate more strongly than character and plot, where from a conventional state of things an unlimited virtual world is derived.

This notion of 'an unlimited virtual world' is taken from Deleuze and his interesting exposition of colour in the cinema. He delineates three forms of the colour-image: what he calls 'surface-colour', 'atmospheric colour', and 'movement-colour', and argues that they perhaps originate in the musical comedy and 'its capacity for extracting an unlimited virtual world from a conventional state of things'. Of the three forms he suggests that only the movement-colour seems to belong to the cinema, the others deriving from painting. Nevertheless, movement-colour is defined by a characteristic which it shares with painting though it gives a different range and function: [65]

> This is the *absorbent* characteristic. Godard's formula, '*It's not blood, it's red*' is *the* formula of colourism. In opposition to a simply coloured image, the colour-image does not refer to a particular object, but absorbs all that it can: it is the power which seizes all that happens within its range, or the quality common to completely different objects. There is a symbolism of colours, but it does not consist in a correspondence between a colour and an affect (green and hope . . .). Colour is on the contrary the affect itself, that is, the virtual conjunction of all the objects which it picks up. Thus Ollier is led to say that Agnès Varda's films, notably *Le Bonheur*, 'absorb', and absorb not only the spectator, but the characters themselves, and the situations, in complex movements affected by the complementary colours.

Deleuze goes on to discuss Minnelli who, particularly in his musicals, 'made absorption the properly cinematographic power of this new dimension of the image'. He writes: 'If states of things become movement of the world, and if characters become the figure of a dance, this is inseparable from the splendour of colours, and from their almost carnivorous, devouring, destructive, absorbent function (like the bright yellow caravan of *The Long, Long Trailer*).'[66]

> *As the voice-over comes to an end so the desert rose dissolves to bright yellow movement: a low angle shot of Pearl in a yellow blouse dancing to flamenco music.*

The yellow of that movement is carnivorous; the dissolve from red and pink to yellow is devouring, destructive, absorbent, like the yellow of the moving sports car that whips through the pre-credit sequence of *Written on the Wind*, or the primary yellow of Dick Tracy's trench coat. *Duel in the Sun* also, and like *Jedda*, charts a motif of failure through a melodramatic register, and in each case the frame-work of the beginning presents colours according to a particularly absorbent function. But cinematic colour is transparent; even while it is absorbent we can see through it. We see through colour: as it absorbs the frame – the framing narrative voice, say, or the titles, that delineate the legend – so it transforms the frame from a rectangle or square to a luminous substance, a transparent screen. In the beginning there is colour and a screening of memories.

Look at That Sunset . . . It's Like the Daytime Didn't Want to End

In the beginning a deep red sunset saturates the sky. This red is absorbent: characters, story, myself – all are absorbed.

> Look at that sunset Howard . . . It's like the daytime didn't
> want to end . . . like it was gonnna put up a big scrap
> and maybe set the world on fire to keep the night time from creepin' on.
> (Rosalind Russell in *Picnic* by Joshua Logan, 1956, from the prologue to
> *Night Cries: A Rural Tragedy*, Tracey Moffat, 1990).

There are times in *Night Cries* when the set is flooded with a red transparent light, but the sky is mostly a deep iridescent blue, a painted sky reminiscent of Albert Namatjira's paintings.[67] The setting is an outback station, a desolate desert-like terrain where the ground is red and there is a continuity between the floor of the house and the outdoors, a single vast shiny surface, as though the ground has absorbed and now reflects the 'big scrap' of the night sky. *Night Cries* fights to keep the night at bay, to 'keep the night time from creepin' on', and yet it invades every moment and every spatial dimension of this film shot entirely in a studio. It looks as though it was shot in a studio and it feels like the night, a hot red night when out of the past sounds and memories and colour sensations invade our space, literally, the theatre where we watch, but also the theatre that is memory ('memory is not an instrument for exploring the past, but its theatre,' Benjamin reminds us).[68] It is a testament to the 'theatricality of the cinema' where Now! Now! Now! Now! Now! overlays the past and disinters history (memory 'is the medium of past experience, as the ground is the medium in which dead cities lie interred', continues Benjamin).

The prologue appears in white script over a black background. Out of the darkness sounds emerge, are amplified in their eeriness, sounds that are evocative but not immediately recognisable or nameable – a train perhaps, a grinding and scraping that evokes abrasive metallic textures, a distant semi-human crying which snakes its way through the *mise en scène*. There is no dialogue in this film (though words are spoken, in the singing of the Aboriginal country and western singer, Jimmy Little);[69] in contrast to films like *Duel in the Sun* and *Jedda*, it is austerely minimalist, desisting from explanation or the oneiric overtones of a framing legend, yet in the way in which sound plays over the movement-image it is similarly charged.

This drama, however, although it revolves around two figures, is not a story of doomed lovers. The figures are a senile dying white woman and her 'daughter', an Aboriginal woman. You can feel the heat, the weight of the wheelchair, the grating squeak of the wire-screen door, the tedium of empty time and years of accumulated resentment that oppress the daughter (played not by an actress but with marvellous perspicacity by Marcia Langton, a well-known activist and anthropologist). She pushes the wheelchair, waits for her mother outside the dunny, bites venomously into an apple, reads a tourist brochure. Outside, in the

Night Cries (Tracey Moffat, 1990)

distance, she cracks a whip over and over again, an act of idle ferocity, while inside in the foreground her mother lies in a blue haze behind a mosquito net, flinching each time the whip is lashed. The sound of the whip, an aural-tactile close-up, cuts through a wave of demonic laughter which simultaneously breaks over the image. We assume that this laughter issues from the daughter, but there is a slight echo effect, a rippling of voices as though of children giggling raucously. In close-up the young woman washes her mother's feet – old, gnarled, and fragile feet – and together they hum 'Onward Christian Soldiers'. Every so often memory-images, vividly recalled details, are cut into the present.

> *One detail, many details, are memories. Each of them, when it emerges in a shadowy setting, is relative to an ensemble which lacks it. Each memory shines like a metonymy in relation to this whole. From a picture there remains only the delicious wound of this deep blue.* (Michel de Certeau)[70]

One detail, many details: a small girl by the sea-shore playing with other Aboriginal children, laughing; a young white woman framed with her back to the camera, looking out to sea; the little girl tangled in seaweed, alone and panicking; an empty inanimate seascape, marking the mother's absence, her disappearance from the frame and the world; desperate childish sobbing which we see but don't hear; mother and child in a golden glow, the little girl wrapped in a blanket, cradled and secure.

In the present, in the blueness of night, the two women are lying, side by side, on the railway platform. The daughter, her body heaving with silent sobs,

148

covers the dead mother's face with a handkerchief, and curls up next to her in a foetal position. An uncanny sound emanates from her body: the terrible unrequitable crying of a baby.

White men are saving brown women from brown men.

It was when I looked at *Night Cries* again that this phrase resurfaced and this time attached itself to a voice. The voice I hear is Gayatri Chakravorty Spivak's and suddenly it comes back to me: in discussing various discourses around widow sacrifice, specifically the British image of themselves as representing the good society after they abolished suttee in 1929, she borrowed and reworked a phrase from Freud: 'A child is being beaten.' The sonic manifestation of this fantasy – the sound of a baby crying, and also of adult women keening – reverberates as a memory in *Night Cries*, a memory from an earlier Australian film, *Jedda*. Jedda, the black baby whose cries are heard near the beginning of the film, is adopted and brought up by the white woman whose own baby has died, but despite an apparently successful process of assimilation Jedda, as a young woman, is drawn back to her origins. Joe, the half-caste narrator, and a group of white men track and follow Marbuk, the abductor, in an attempt to save Jedda. They are not as successful as Phineas Fogg and Passepartout in *Around the World in Eighty Days* in saving this brown woman from a brown man, but despite the diegetic thrust of the film it nevertheless performs a fantastical projection that is profoundly ideological. *Jedda*'s formulation of race relations in terms of a maternal melodrama of adoption serves to elide the barbaric practice by which Aboriginal children were until quite recently frequently removed coercively from their mothers and often fostered out in a programme of forced assimilation. *Night Cries*, made by an Aboriginal woman in 1990, remembers *Jedda*, but is also haunted by the history of Aboriginal people in Australia.

In focusing an aspect of this history on a relation between two women Moffat bypasses the white masculine fantasy of saving brown women from brown men (remember *The Searchers*: there too an economy of salvation), but she also deflects lurking fantasies of a straightforward political narrative. Her method, in this highly coloured landscape, is more allusive, associative, visceral. It is hard to read this film, where there is so little denotative grounding, but through the colours and sounds you can sense something bloodcurdling, an extraordinary mixture of the perverse and the tender, which permeates this relationship born out of historical contingency. The film exists in a twilight zone 'where images are linked in an impermanent way' and 'organised so as to produce fantasies'.

Night Cries, despite the fact that it is shot entirely in a studio and has a studio look, does not refer in quite the same way as *Alice Doesn't Live Here Anymore* to the studio era, or to a particular genre, or range of Hollywood genres. But the prologue does alert us to the cinematic as a frame, it alludes to 'big pictures', not to the privileging of psychological or mimetic principles that may pertain to these pictures, but to the *memory* of a certain expressive intensity, a melodramatic impulse manifested, for instance, 'through the splendour of colours, and . . . their almost carnivorous, devouring, destructive, absorbent function'.

> *When you drive in Paris at night, what do you see? Red, green,*
> *yellow lights. I wanted to show these elements but without*
> *necessarily placing them as they are in reality. Rather, as they*
> *remain in the memory: splashes of red and green, flashes of*
> *yellow passing by. I wanted to recreate a sensation through*
> *the elements that constitute it.* (Godard)

The Wild Goose Comes Home To Roost

I find a published version of the paper I heard Gayatri Spivak deliver about ten years ago. It is called 'Can the Subaltern Speak?' and in it she writes:

> I am not suggesting that 'White men are saving brown women from brown men' is a sentence indicating a collective fantasy symptomatic of a collective itinerary of sadomasochistic repression in a collective imperialist enterprise. There is a satisfying symmetry in such an allegory, but I would rather invite the reader to consider it a problem in 'wild psychoanalysis' than a clinching solution. Just as Freud's insistence on making the woman the scapegoat in 'A child is being beaten' and elsewhere discloses his political interests, however imperfectly, so my insistence on imperialist subject-production as the occasion for this sentence discloses my politics.[71]

I find a book from childhood: *The Snow Goose*. On the inside cover my mother has written in pencil the details of Herbert Marshall's recording of this book accompanied by a note: 'keep off 45 speed'. A technology which is now almost redundant was for her new and rather mysterious; for me it is now a conduit, a mediation of memory, just like the Technicolor sunset. Colour and voice cohere in that moment when 'the snow goose had come dropping out of a crimsoned eastern sky'.

It's Not Blood, It's Red

> *We so often forget . . . that when a colour film is seen pro-*
> *jected, the colour is not in the Bazinian sense a direct indexical*
> *registration of colour in the natural world; it is dye; what you see*
> *is dyed. Obviously it is an iconic approximation; there is, in fact,*
> *no direct indexical link between the colour of the natural world*
> *and the colour of the projected colour film. A whole technology*
> *of dyeing has intervened.*[72]

In the beginning there was colour, which is to say that colour films appeared as early as 1896 and the first patent was awarded in 1897. The early technologies included hand-tinting and painting and stencilling, but with increasing mechanisation and standardisation tinting and toning processes, involving dyes, were developed. For a long time, however, colour appeared only sporadically and imperfectly. Early camera and projection processes proved clumsy and inaccurate and the coming of sound complicated matters enormously. But all this changed with the development in 1932, by the Technicolor Corporation headed by Herbert Kalmus, of a three-colour process. This process included a beam-splitting camera housing three black-and-white negative rolls of film sensitive to blue, green and red. Dudley Andrew writes:

> The rolls became colour matrices which were then submitted to the famous imbibition method of dying pure, complementary colours on a virgin colour stock, guided by information permanently etched on the three black and white records. Perfect control as well as perfect consistency in the laboratory were thus possible, for the colour records were all in black and white and technicians could adjust the various colours for brightness, hue and saturation until all the requirements were satisfied.[73]

Technicolor almost immediately cornered the market, partly through the unparalleled quality and reliability of the product, and partly through the method by which Kalmus controlled and marketed it.[74] The first films to appear in Technicolor were cartoons. Kalmus offered Walt Disney the exclusive rights to its three-colour process from 1932 to 1935 and the shorts *Flowers and Trees* and *The Three Little Pigs* won Academy Awards (the first Disney feature was *Snow White and the Seven Dwarfs*, 1937). The first feature, *Becky Sharp*, was produced by Pioneer Films in 1935 but was not a great commercial success and Pioneer Films sold their contract with Technicolor (to produce eight features in full colour) to Selznick International. 'It was three extremely successful color features in three successive years by Selznick – *A Star is Born* (1937), *The Adventures of Tom Sawyer* (1938), and *Gone with the Wind* (1939) – that clearly established the economic viability of three-color Technicolor.'[75] Even so, it was to be some time before colour became established as a norm.

While it may well be the case that the first three-colour films were animations, the link between Technicolor and cartoons is not purely historical; it also functions rhetorically. The association, which recurs in many popular discourses, is suggestive of the way in which colour has been both conceived and exploited in the cinema. Although the Technicolor camera was bulky – 'we used to call it "The Enchanted Cottage"', said Michael Powell[76] – and required a great deal of light, the stock was considered ideal for studio use, as opposed to Agfa, for instance, which was considered 'more natural' with its comparatively 'muted edges'. The colour was consistent and brilliant, yielding matchless saturation and pure blocks of colour. 'But even Technicolor', as Dudley Andrew notes, 'was aware that its advantage in the "strength" of its colour must be kept in check or else it would risk having that colour assume an animated cartoon tone.'[77] 'Cartoon', used adjectively, is almost synonymous with 'Hollywood' as a pejorative ascription. The French attitude towards Technicolor, for instance, was bound up with their view of Hollywood as vulgar and garish. From their perspective, as Andrew puts it, 'Technicolor had (and promoted) a Hollywood notion of colour: purer than reality, needing strong artificial light, aggressive, almost whorish.' But the French view is not entirely foreign: in the pre-war era, colour generally was associated primarily with fantasy and extravaganza and confined to particular genres (between 1921 and 1930 the bulk of colour films were musicals).[78] Ed Buscombe points out that colour was resisted in Hollywood on the grounds of its unreality. Where it did occur – in cartoons, for instance – it was often used self-reflexively and in order to celebrate technology and cinematic stylisation.[79] Indeed, at different times, and for different purposes, colour has been invoked as an index of fantasy and as an index of reality or realism (the latter argument comes more to the fore in the 60s and after, when Hollywood fully converted to colour in the wake of television's adopting colour).[80]

> *In a* Loony Tunes *cartoon two huge animated creatures are chasing a tiny bird through the landscape when suddenly colour disappears from the image and the music grinds to a halt. They scratch their heads, retrace their steps till they find a sign, saying 'Technicolor ends Here'. On one side of the sign – that is on one half of the screen – there is colour; and on the other, black and white.*

Technicolor did not sell their Tri-Pak cameras (or processing equipment), but leased them out along with a camera operator and an extensive team of personnel who 'advised' on every aspect of colour co-ordination from make-up through to questions of art direction and set design. The chief and best-known of the colour consultants was Natalie Kalmus. 'She and her fellow "advisors" enforced a consistent set of aesthetic values that favoured the harmonious use of complementary colours.'[81] The monopolisation by Technicolor, and the extent of control exerted over the studios and every production, presents itself as a perfect example of standardisation, and indeed almost every study of colour in Hollywood cinema seizes on this exegetical gem and also casts Natalie Kalmus as prime villain. Sometimes she features as the Evil Avatar of Realism, and sometimes as the Dragon of Unification, perniciously codifying according to the tenets of Hollywood artifice.[82] Steve Neale, for instance, invokes Julia Kristeva, quoting her pronouncement that colour 'achieves the momentary dialectic of law, the laying down of One Meaning so that it might at once be pulverised, multiplied into plural meanings. Color is the shattering of unity.'[83] He goes on to argue that

> It is this aspect of colour that Hollywood, Technicolor, Natalie Kalmus sought to control. These were the effects that required organisation. The capacity of colour to produce a 'pulverisation' of meaning, a multiplicity of meanings was marked, recognised and contained through the construction of colour systems, the matching of colour to dramatic mood, on the one hand, and to the referential exigencies of landscape, decor and so on, on the other. . . . Colour ought only to bear the 'significance necessary.' No more, no less.'[84]

This approach, it seems to me, overstates its case. If Natalie Kalmus's favourite film was indeed *The Red Shoes*, as mentioned by Peter Wollen almost as an aside, tossed away in a stray footnote,[85] then it seems to me she and her advisors might have had a lot more appreciation of the affective power of colour than they are usually credited with. Of course the story might be apocryphal, but it is already attached to those red shoes which dance their way through night and day, crossing a variety of cinematic landscapes and leaving scarlet traces in the least fanciful, most black-and-white of texts. While I won't go so far as to posit Hollywood (against Neale and Kristeva) as a site of fantasy incarnate, of polymorphous colour perversity, I do want to argue against the critical reduction of colour, against its invariable subordination to the invincible mastery of narrative and realism. I want to reclaim the association with cartoons, to remember the overwhelming sensation of large-screen colour, and in particular the memorableness of early Technicolor films. Even though I saw them a lot later than their introduction, nevertheless the colour saturation, and the sheer splendour of movement-colour, particularly in the works of someone like Minnelli, as Deleuze points out, contributes to their memorability and to the evocation of cinema as somewhere that is sensuously rich in its fictionality. When Dorothy opens the door to Oz, the sheer wonder of the spectacle, the over-abundance of primary colours, heralds a totally absorbing world of once upon a time, a world rich in fictional promise.[86]

Notes on the Passage of Time

In a remarkable series of films made since 1975, the experimental film-makers Arthur and Corinne Cantrill have explored the properties, and variables, of cinematic colour. What hit me as an absolute revelation when I first saw these films was the relation between colour and temporality, between magic and technology, a relation that is also alluded to in *Before the Revolution*. This black-and-white film has one colour sequence, set in the camera obscura. Lina, inside, in black-and-white, watches as Fabrizio cavorts in colour in the piazza. Fabrizio comments about the camera obscura: 'It is magic, but true!' He would like 'nothing to move . . . and us in the picture motionless'. But Lina knows that everything passes: 'You'll remember as if I were dead.' A curious thing happens in this short sequence: the seasons change. The colours in the piazza turn autumnal, but there are no longer any figures in the landscape.

The Cantrills' *Three Colour Separation Studies* were made by filming each subject three times on black-and-white negative, using red, green and blue filters consecutively. The three strips of black-and-white negative were then printed onto one strip of Eastman colour print stock (7381), superimposing them in three passes through the printer, using red, green and blue printer lights. In lengthy static shots, movement registers when the three strips (shot at different times) are superimposed as a perturbation, an abstract rainbow-like colour flickering. This is most stunning in *Notes on the Passage of Time*, which curiously echoes *Before the Revolution*: the same scene – a shed with the sea in the background and pedestrians, cyclists, occasional traffic in the foreground – is shot during the progression of a winter and then a summer day. The stationary objects are opaque and retain a permanent and saturated quality, while the moving objects are transparent and ephemeral, flitting like ghosts through the frame.

> To really stop Columbia from redoing things, I suggested the idea of
> draining the colour out of that scene. I had wanted to do that
> originally, because I wanted to do an experiment in draining colours
> out of the shots like John Huston did with *Moby Dick.*
> But it was also a way of making it appear that I was doing something
> to tone things down in the scene.
> When I finally saw the scene with Julia, we started laughing – the
> toning down of the color made it look even worse!
> (Scorsese on the massacre scene in *Taxi Driver*)[87]

In the early 50s colour began to change. The fading process began. In the late
40s, an anti-trust suit was brought against Technicolor, forcing the company
to make key patents available to competitors. A few years later, Eastman
Kodak introduced a new colour method: three dye-sensitive layers were combined on one roll. This meant that there was no need for special cameras, and
prints could be struck on conventional black-and-white printing machines.
Like black and white, but unlike Technicolor, Eastmancolor was a photochemical printing and processing method; the colours were less stable and not
as bright as those produced by the imbibition process, where the three different colour dyes were applied directly to the film base. But with this new multi-
layer film colours could be obtained more quickly and easily and
economically. As a result Eastman soon displaced Technicolor in holding the
monopoly for colour; Technicolor was forced into co-operating, into processing Eastman stock, and gradually into moving away from the old methods,
and closing down its 'imbibition' plants. The Hollywood plant went in 1975,
the London and Rome plants in 1978 (and, rather curiously, in 1977 one
opened in Beijing).

Even after the introduction of Technicolor's three-colour process only a
minority of films were made in colour.[88] There was an increase, in conjunction
with new widescreen formats and stereophonic sound, in the mid-50s, and in
the face of television the industry promoted colour as a superior feature of the
movies.[89] Once television started buying up and leasing their pre-1948 film
libraries, the film industry reverted, on the whole, to black-and-white production, seeing colour as an area of viable economisation. The eventual impetus
for the whole industry to convert to colour came from television: the major
shift to network colour which began in 1965 was followed by Hollywood's
conversion. This was partly a matter of straightforward competition, but it
was also that Hollywood now conceived of television as a prime exhibitor of
its product. After 1961, once the studios started selling their post-1948 films
to television, to show more contemporary black-and-white motion pictures
on television would no doubt have seemed old-fashioned, identifying Hollywood with the past.

Most historians record the invention of Eastmancolor as a revolutionary
innovation, in terms of technology as well as economics; and most archi-
vists, film buffs and collectors cite it as one of film history's darkest hours.
Eastmancolor, in fact, was bought at a great cost, for auto-destruction and

impermanence were built into this easy and 'economic' new invention.[90] The basic problem with the Eastmancolor 'multi-layer' film was its lack of stability, giving rise over a short time to changes in colour balance. If, for instance, blue and green fade, the result will be an overall effect of magenta or pink (Visconti's 'pink leopard'). Prints of old Technicolor films are of course subject to the ills that befall all nitrate material, but the three-strip Technicolor system itself was a stable one, and although the colours will not last for ever they are not subject to rapid fading and severe distortion.

I have witnessed the deterioration and sometimes the destruction of most films I have seen. With the introduction of Eastman Kodak colour film in 1950, any hope for colour stability vanished. All films made in the Eastman colour process are about to deteriorate beyond repair. Some have already done so. Methods of restoration are so costly that if a film is not considered important it is left to die. (Scorsese)[91]

In 1980, Scorsese spearheaded a campaign to draw attention to the problem of fading colour and to questions of restoration. He describes a *Raging Bull* pre-production meeting with United Artists:

I told them that the colour stock fades. I went into the whole business, that I was very upset about the Eastman color stocks fading, the prints fading in five years, the negatives fading in twelve years – things like that. I said, 'I just don't want it. I want it to be something very special.'[92]

He used the release of *Raging Bull* to draw attention to the issues, and followed the film's theatrical opening with an illustrated lecture on the problem of colour fading. The Scorsese campaign was well organised and waged on several fronts; it incorporated the suggestion that film-makers should insist contractually on the latest and best methods of preservation at the time a film is made, and included the lobbying of Eastman Kodak 'to find a solution to the problem . . . to assume a major role on the research and development of a stable colour film stock'. Since the launch of the campaign, Eastman Kodak have developed and released a stock considerably less prone to fading, and new methods of restoration (involving computer technologies, laser scanning, and the like) are being developed.

This new focus on restoration and reissue has provoked considerable debate about origins and authenticity, with many fierce adherents of IB Tech (buff talk for the Technicolor imbibition process) refusing to contemplate any prints other than those struck from a pure IB Tech original. In 'Technicolor and the True Believer', Scott MacQueen provides a lucidly informative and somewhat sardonic corrective to such enthusiasms. Technicolor means different things to different people, he points out. 'For some, it is a system of photography or a printing process. For others, it is a trade name, a marketing gimmick. For others still, Technicolor means Maria Montez.'[93] His chronicling of the various stages involved in producing a print and his charting of historical developments serve as a reminder that there are always a range of technologies involved in the emergence and duration of colour. It is not purely and simply Eastmancolor that is the villain. Bad lab work and cheap business practices contribute to poor colour transfers and impermanence, but other factors also intervene, such as codes of cinematography and predominant notions, or memories (themselves so often manufactured and subject to a range of variables), of what constitutes 'old Technicolor'. Moreover, the 'look of Technicolor' itself is not entirely stable, varying over the years due to changes in dye formula and printing practices, and 'Imbibition prints of the same subject frequently differed from each other. In *The 5000 Fingers of Dr T*, does little Bart hide from the fruity Dr Terwilliker in a big blue urn, as it appears in some IB prints, or is the urn purple, as rendered in other IB copies?' Two laserdiscs have been issued of *The Wizard of Oz*, one from Criterion (from an Eastman interpositive) and one from MGM/UA (from an IB print, vintage unknown). 'Each has virtues and problems not found in the other' and, while both portray Kansas in sepia, neither has attempted to fix the transition to colour 'to recreate the 1939 prints'. MacQueen claims that since the 80s Eastman colour prints made of three-strip Technicolor subjects 'not only match but surpass IB printing' and this because it is now possible to excavate information that was always in the negatives but lost owing to the nature of the imbibition process.

Jodi Brooks noted:

> Cinema and television have come to operate as an ever-expanding terrain of discarded wish images, where one's own memories and history of viewing are entangled with generational memories. Cinema (and as we move into the third television generation, we must include television here also) is often intricately connected with a sort of mythical childhood, both the mythical childhood of film and television and the mythical childhood of a generation. Cinema perhaps has a privileged place in this regard, or at least a particular idea of cinema, the idea of 'Hollywood' as lost object.[94]

Déjà Vu: Where or When? Or The Most Photographed Barn in America

The red prologue features a vaguely archaic and familiar rural scene. In the distance a small figure appears walking towards the camera along a dirt road edged by a wooden fence. A man scatters corn to chickens outside a barn. The acousmatic voice of Alice Faye fades away, but the song 'Where or When?' remains, embodied by the young Alice. Or, retrospectively we might say: by the 'now' Alice in her aspiration towards a future which she conceives of as encompassing all the promise of the past.

> *I liked the idea of 'Where or When?' because it has to do with a sort of déjà vu, which is what the movie is about really, being in the same place before, only with new people, making the same mistakes.*[95]

The girl is uncannily familiar, at once like and unlike Dorothy in *The Wizard*, and the house is reminiscent of other movie houses (*East of Eden*, *Tobacco Road*...), and the redness evokes other manifestations of redness (*Gone with the Wind, Duel in the Sun, Lancelot du Lac* . . .). Even the barn, though anonymous and unspecific, is oddly familiar. It is like a quotation that has been cut adrift from its context, an actual image that summons an array of virtual images, reminding me of 'the most photographed barn in America'.

In Don DeLillo's novel, *White Noise*, Murray, who is destined to teach a course in the cinema of car crashes, arrives at a small parochial college and asks the narrator about 'a tourist attraction known as the most photographed barn in America'. They drive into the country, passing many signs announcing 'The Most Photographed Barn in America', they watch tourists taking photographs on an elevated mound, they look at the man in the booth selling postcards and slides of the barn taken from the elevated spot, and Murray muses:

> What was the barn like before it was photographed? . . . What did it look like, how was it different from other barns, how was it similar to other barns? We can't answer these questions because we've read the signs, seen the people snapping the pictures. We can't get outside the aura. We're here, we're now. He seemed immensely pleased by this.[96]

The barn is one in a series of barns for which there is no original. Just like the spectacular red sunsets in which each one figures as just 'another postmodern sunset, rich in romantic imagery', ushered in by the 'airborne toxic event'. This mysterious and lethal phenomenon conjoins spectacular Turneresque beauty with the toxicity of industrial waste, and one of its by-products is *déjà vu*.

> *That's no sunset. It's a nuclear war.*

Déjà vu, the uncanny, the sense of having been there before, literally means 'already seen', but what is yielded to consciousness in *déjà vu* is precisely a troubling sensation of incompleteness; what we 'see' in our mind's eye is an incomplete scene. The 'where' and 'when', the markers that would locate the scene historically, are missing. *Déjà vu* implies a work of memory, but simultaneously a failure of memory.

> *What do you see? Red, green, yellow lights. I wanted to show these elements but without necessarily placing them as they are in reality. Rather, as they remain in the memory, splashes of red and green, flashes of yellow passing by. I wanted to recreate a sensation through the elements that constitute it.* (Godard)

Fragments, moments, severed intensities, detached parts: the whole film, the entirety of the image, the technologically given, always seems to be missing or a blur. And yet it is this history of the cinema, as a curiously indefinite presence, that throws into relief the fragments, the part objects, the flashed images. And it is from cinema as a whole, a sensational imaginary, that these fragments are 'chosen', conjured into being by the 'mobility of memory', in De Certeau's phrase. He also says: 'Like those birds that lay their

157

eggs only in other species' nests, memory produces in a place that does not belong to it.'[97] Memory, in other words, is not simply about repetition; it also implies a process of excavation and invention. This invention, however, is never purely arbitrary. Place – a cinema in a particular town, in a country that is not-any-old-country, situated in a specific cultural and personal context (that is, mapped by a time and context of reception) – provides a stage for the acting out of memory. Cinema is not so much an instrument for exploring the past as its theatre.

Theatres of Memory: Picture Palaces

There is a Renaissance memory technique that takes the theatre as its architectural form, but the theatre here does not exactly imply a building consisting of a stage and an auditorium. Rather, the stage is evoked as a dynamic space, and the idea of memory as a staging is foregrounded.

> *Memory is not an instrument for exploring the past but its theatre.*
> *It is the medium of past experience, as the ground is the medium*
> *in which dead cities lie interred.* (Walter Benjamin)[98]

Let me return for a moment to those initial questions revolving around the status of the opening as prologue or flashback or dream. I have been absorbed by the red prologue and in turn have used it as a theatre of memory. I have used it not as a way into a reading of *Alice Doesn't Live Here Anymore*, but as a pretext, and I use the term advisedly, to suggest a relation between the work of memory and the logic of textual production. Rather than locating the opening in terms of character, of attaching it to a diegetic consciousness, I have been interested in the way it enacts, almost magically, the problematic of cinematic openings, in how it condenses and opens out the logical impossibility of cinema, opens out a textual space.

> *If you take two images and link them by superimposition, a*
> *simple enough device, you – the spectator – are actually in two*
> *places at once: a logical impossibility.* (Raul Ruiz)[99]

My desire has been to occupy the place of 'she' who 'would sort of remember – half fantasy, half remembrance'. The Red Prologue is like a Dream of Cinema, and a Cinema Dreaming, existing in the public domain, touching personal nerves. The *déjà vu* provoked by the Red Prologue has led me astray, through a process of remembering, and forgetting. To remember, for instance, the gleaming conflagration of *Gone With the Wind*, to preserve and cherish it, I must also forget what exactly it is that is gone. It is, of course, as the the opening titles tell us in tones reeking of melancholia, 'the Old South, a Civilisation'. To watch *Lancelot*, I have to remember that 'it's not blood, it's red'. I have to remind myself that the blood, like *l'amour fou*, is only ketchup; and, moreover, as celluloid, it is dyed. Actually it does no good at all to point to the technological preconditions of cinematic blood. On the contrary, the disturbing liminal associations, the sensation of *déjà vu*, is precisely implicated in the technological being of cinema. Light passing through celluloid shines in the the dark, exposing, in momentary flashes, memories deeply interred, like ruined cities, in the unconscious.

And if some things are recalled and others actively forgotten in the viewing situation, there is also a marked propensity to remember wrongly. Films exist in the realm of popular culture, and while they constitute a form of public memory it is nevertheless intriguing that the memories people have of individual movies and scenes are often wildly discrepant. This is partly because of differing personal histories, but also has to do with the circumstances of reception. Memory operates differently through film and video (and theatrical and domestic contexts). It is much harder to remember films you see on video than ones you see in the cinema, for instance. Often I borrow on video a film seen a few years ago on television and it's almost as though I'm seeing something never seen before. With a video of a film seen in the theatre it is very different, more like recall or *déjà vu* or sometimes even the shock of discrepancy: I experience a kind of nostalgia for something that never was.

Raoul Ruiz tells of how, when he returned to Chile after being in exile, he experienced a kind of saudade, *a nostalgia for something that never was. Fabrizio, somewhat differently, in a historical climate before the revolution, experiences a nostalgia for the present.*

Or I am taken aback by the gap between 'my' version of the film and what is 'really' there, by a failure of memory that is characterised not by forgetting (though clearly this is involved) but by invention. The invented, or projected, image, however, exists very strongly as a memory. These kinds of failures of memory or misrememberings are often tied up with intense memory sensations: you remember vividly, intensely, but you get it wrong. Memory, however, gets hold of something in this experience. We might say that 'memory produces in a place that does not belong to it'.

There are many arguments that differentiate between the viewing experiences of film and television (often based rather crudely, and ironically, on Benjamin's distinctions between contemplation and distraction) and there are some critics who argue that television and home viewing have fundamentally changed the theatrical experience.[100] While I do believe that different sorts of memory processes are brought into play by the domestic and theatrical context, this is merely to say that technology is always contextualised. The history of technological innovation and change is not merely a matter of supersession and replacement; rather, different framings coexist. The VCR and the way it is used provide an interesting riposte to positions that ally new viewing technologies with distraction and fragmentation. Just as there are institutional and technological supports for the processes of memory – libraries, archives, CD-ROMs – so, in a sense, the VCR is a revolutionary resource for film study (even though it also violates via panning and scanning, among other things).

> *Fire destroyed castles in other Poe films, and since one roaring
> blaze looks as good as another in a long shot, I cut the* Usher
> *sequence into the other films.*
> *It certainly never occurred to me back in 1960 that people
> someday would rent these films on cassettes, watch them at
> home back-to-back, and notice the same flaming rafters
> crashing down in different movies.* (Roger Corman)[101]

Video is useful as an *aide-mémoire,* a notebook, because of its capacity for repetition; but I would argue that it is not merely instrumental: it provides a focus, even a way of cathecting, the compulsion to repeat. It has become significant not only for film studies but more generally for how we know (as well as experience) and remember movies, as was evident at the re-release of *Blade Runner.* We can see the compulsion to repeat manifested perfectly in the infantile habit of watching particular videos or particular scenes over and over again. This very process has an effect on the way we come to experience and remember. The fetishism represented by this activity is quite different from the distraction of 'the glance mentality' which is apparently so characteristic of contemporary culture. Clearly the compulsion to repeat here is not just about remembering; it is also that something always escapes. Memory is about more than just recall.

Looking at *Alice Doesn't Live Here Anymore* now in 1993, twenty years on, I am undoubtedly bringing to bear on it a contemporary sensibility, one shaped moreover by a milieu of cultural studies. And so 'the most photographed barn in America' resonates as do references to the permutation of the aura. I realise there is a way in which the Red Prologue could be seen as a kind of failed nostalgia, therefore kitschily post-modern. Or its allusions and self-reflexivity could be interpreted as a moribund attempt to resuscitate tradition.

Scorsese's genre homages – *Alice Doesn't Live Here Anymore, Taxi Driver,* and *New York, New York* – are certainly much more resonant and complex than Bogdanovich's similar efforts. They are felt variations on the basic themes rather than mechanistic parodies. But the ultimate effect is the same. Neither the cold and egotistical Bogdanovich nor the feverish, introverted Scorsese has been able to make those old genres actually come alive again. There is the smell of decay about them. It's as if they were refrains in a bad dream of the Old Hollywood: endless repetitions and regurgitations from phantoms of the Hollywood Hills. The children seem to have been possessed by the fathers. Maybe Hollywood should be closed down for twenty years, quarantined, or permitted to lie fallow. The weight of tradition oppresses.[102]

I, on the contrary, derive much pleasure from this prologue, and am rather wary of appearing to be like Murray in *White Noise,* the hip cultural critic who is 'immensely pleased' at discovering the aura everywhere – though I suspect my critical pathology is more fetishistically inflected, returning again and again to the scarlet stain, to the scene of the crime. I am intrigued by the way the Red Prologue alludes not just to representation as repetition (the most photographed barn in America) but to repetition as an effect of the fog machine, always reshaped by memory. It sets in process a mapping of knowledges, images, histories and technologies.

You know you've got fog machines; use fog machines. See what happens.

In *White Noise*, the endless simulacra of sunsets are produced by the 'airborne toxic event', a nuclear disaster in which beauty and destruction dissolve into one another. Scorsese's sunset, too, is both beautiful and lethal, like the urban space through which Travis moves, the boxing ring in which Jake La Motta moves in balletic slow motion. It is the cusp between the everyday and the extra-daily. The Red Prologue persists. At the end of the yellow brick road we will find not Kansas but a post-modern sunset, a conjoining of the toxic and beautiful. The red seeps through the Scorsese text; it absorbs from other films and events, traversing the past, filtering into the future, eliciting a memory that is mobile. And alert to danger.

Life Is a Dream: Written on the Wind

> *A king dreams he's king*
> *deluded in his rule*
> *In his borrowed grandeur*
> *written on the wind.*
> (*Life Is a Dream*, Calderón[103])

> *Prologue: the lights in the film theatre dim. Out of the darkness a voice*
> *speaks: 'In early April 1974 a literature teacher, Ignacio Vega, had to*
> *learn the names of 15,000 anti-junta resisters. It took him only a week.'*
> *Colour appears on the screen, a wavering greenness like luminous*
> *chiffon, over which the voice continues: 'He had found a mnemonic.' As*
> *a teenager he had once responded to a bet by learning off by heart the*
> *whole of Calderón's seventeenth-century play* Life Is a Dream.
> *Later he uses the play as a mnemonic device for consigning to memory*
> *the 15,000 names: 'Each line had a militant's name, each metaphor an*
> *address, each stanza an armed operation.' But shortly after this amazing*
> *feat he is caught and has to forget everything. With the loss of memory*
> *the screen goes black, a voice announces 'Ten years have passed.*
> *And our story begins.' (Raul Ruiz,* Life Is a Dream *[La Mémoire des*
> *apparences/La Vie est un songe])*

How can one create a memory for the human animal? How can one impress something upon this partly obtuse, partly flighty mind, attuned only to the passing moment, in such a way that it will stay there? (Nietzsche, *The Genealogy of Morals.*)

The Beginning: our hero has to remember: in order to remember the names he has to use the Calderón text, but in the process of forgetting the names he has also forgotten every word of the play. Groping for a way out of this amnesia, he recalls the cinema of his childhood where the programme would begin at 2.30 every day with Flash Gordon, followed by Zorro, Superman, Batman, Davy Crocket, Jungle Jim. He returns to this theatre where 'Remarkably, the theatre shows the same movie as twenty years ago.' The male narrating voice, over images of a toy train, located in some indeterminate spatial zone, tells us: 'He suddenly remembers the opening of the play, linked with images of a pre-war British thriller.' This male voice is displaced by a marvellously throaty female voice, speaking in French the fabulous opening lines of the play – 'Violent hippogriff, vying with the wind.' Thereafter, he goes to the cinema every day to reconstruct the play, image by image.

Ruiz tells how he made this film after reading Francis Yates's book *The Art of Memory*, which traces the work of 'artificial memory' from its use by orators of antiquity, through Gothic transformations in the Middle Ages, to the occult forms it took in the Renaissance, and finally to its use in the 17th century by the scientific philosophers. 'In the art of memory,' says Ruiz, 'you need a place that you know perfectly, it can be your body, your house, your town with your church. Then you need to put a sign there, particular and unforgettable images. I wanted to make a film about what happened in Chile without using Chilean elements.'[104]

Memory, for Ruiz, is located in the cinema, in the cinephiliac imagination. But this imaginary is not simply 'in' the cinema; rather, the cinema provides the pretext for its staging. Moreover, while this cinema is situated historically, it also serves as an agency of dislocation. There is a peculiar discrepancy between the two 'lost objects', the immense list of names and the Calderón play; and this discrepancy elaborates a highly complex and slippery relation between the real and the realm of dreams, between memory and experience.

> *The next film is* The Iron Mask, *a movie he's seen so many times he recognises the visuals, but feels he understands nothing.* Déjà vu *becomes never seen.*

In this cinema sounds, images, colours are mercurial and nomadic; they migrate from one place to another, never settling, always resonant though in perverse and unexpected ways. On the screen we see fragments of films, evocative of a range of genres utterly familiar and alluringly exotic. Dialogic exchanges take place between characters in logically different spaces, on the screen and in the auditorium, for instance. Sigismundo, the hero of *Life Is a Dream*, shows up not only on the screen, but also in the intradiegetic theatre as a spectator; and the hero also projects his own images, fantasies, sense of history and memory, onto the screen. At one stage he appears in a theatre-cum-futuristic-night-club where people are wearing battery-powered glasses that enable them to see others naked, but without nipples. Clopping hooves migrate from the loudspeakers to the theatre itself, sounds of torture, blood-curdling shrieks and moans emanate from behind the screen, a location whence people are intermittently dragged, struggling. Intimations of violence escape the screening process and infiltrate the spatial texture of 'daily' living. When the hero discovers that a police station is situated here, he realises that the uncanny feeling he is experiencing comes from 'someone being beaten'.

> My father is beating the child
> I am being beaten by my father.
> A child is being beaten.[105]

> White men are saving brown women from brown men.

Images err, stray from the screen, multiply and divide, conjuring up a scenario that is 'logically impossible' yet imaginatively true. The narrator tells us, 'The film images generate others, those of his childhood, familiar objects, toys, story book images.' Images from the screen are reflected back, superimposed over his face; childhood images (castles and toy trains) transform in an almost alchemical process into embodiments of desire. 'He gets stuck at Act Three. The lines, linked with objects, remind him of long forgotten events that evoke forgotten movies suggesting strangers' names, that conjure the face of a woman better forgotten.' His attention is distracted from the film by a woman sitting in the audience. They strike up a conversation in which she tells him about her scars, some of which are hidden. He wants to see them, 'if it's no bother'.

> Men usually hate seeing scars.
> It depends. I have some too.

Across time, over cinematic bodies, the scar is transferred.

I'll Kill You When They Kiss

> One can well believe that the answers and methods for solving this primeval problem were not precisely gentle; perhaps indeed there was nothing more fearful and uncanny in the whole prehistory of man than his mnemotechnics: 'If something is to stay in the memory it must be burned in: only that which never ceases to hurt stays in the memory.'
> (Nietzsche, The Genealogy of Morals)

The ending is continuously deferred, as is the point of full recall, always arriving too early or too late. Remembering and forgetting stalk one another, circling, lying in wait. Our hero asks his childhood friend what he is waiting for, to which his friend, who turns out to be a traitor, responds: 'For the film to end. I'll kill you when they kiss. Love scenes bore me.'

Shots ring out; figures jump over seats, run down the aisles, dodging bullets which fly in all directions. Then, in the light of the projector, surrounded by a halo, our hero's nemesis appears, his face all bloodied.

163

> *Will this bullet ever come?*
> *Wanna read while you wait?*
> *What've you got?*
> *OK Magazine*
> *Too Late*
> *Lenin's State and Revolution*
> *Too Early*
> *Here's the bullet.*

They disappear in billowing mists. And wake, with other recognisable figures from the film, though all are transformed by blood-streaked faces signifying their status as the living dead. 'Look, a real sunset!' someone says, looking off screen. 'That's no sunset. It's a nuclear war.' Where? 'Somewhere in Europe I guess.' Over a backdrop of the ocean the hero and heroine kiss. At last we have the sense of an ending, but remember: the assassin waits until the kiss to fire his bullet. From the kiss there is a cut to a deep red which saturates the screen. The camera pans, the redness takes shape as a sunset, and out of the mists of the fog machine a castle materialises, a phantasmatic childhood landscape, over which the end credits begin to roll. But it could equally be the pretext for another beginning.

The Man Who Left His Will on Film (Nagisa Oshima, 1970)

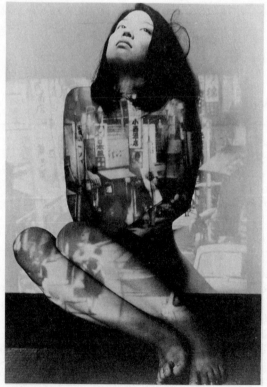

Although we witness the mobilisation of a mnemotechnic, a contemporary practice of the art of memory, Ruiz makes clear in this film that the relation between cinema and memory is not just or even primarily about seeing. In Ignacio's childhood cinema, and by extension in our cinema, there is no exact fit between word and image; memories cannot be excavated as a series of intact entities, each in its proper place. Rather, memory is a process, a kind of textual inscription. So for Ruiz our memory works cinematically, is in a sense structured by the technological possibilities of the cinema. Structured yes, but not constrained or determined by technology. If the night-club scene is vaguely futuristic, it is also curiously anachronistic, suggestive of 3D cinema and of all technological utopianism. The desire for transparency, to see through the world, always incorporates a blind spot, a kind of censoring. As one of the characters says concerning the absence of nipples: 'That's censorship!' Screening always involves a projection of libidinal desire at that point where it intersects with technology and techniques of memory; screening always, as it invokes memory, also institutes forgetfulness and a screening out, be it of nipples or of the edges of the screen via panning and scanning, or of colour fading.

Before the Beginning: A Flashback
The lights in the theatre dim. Out of the darkness images appear, images as red and as hot as the desert. Or piercingly cool images: the ice blue of eyes that cut through the night. Or the blue of a gingham frock, or of bruised flesh. I am entranced by these images, absorbed, wrapped round by them and swept away, by a teasing anticipation, the stirring of memories. In 'The Storyteller', Walter Benjamin discusses the way in which stories are assimilated. Listening to oral storytelling we submit to a state of relaxation, the story is absorbed into our own experience, woven into the fabric of personal memory. This process of assimilation enables the story to be repeated.[106] Elsewhere, Benjamin describes the experience of reading as a child

> Wholly given up to the soft drift of the text that surrounded you as secretly, densely and unceasingly as snowflakes. You entered it with a limitless trust. The peacefulness of the book that enticed you further and further! Its contents did not matter much. For you were reading at the time when you still made up stories in bed. The child seeks his way along half-hidden paths. Reading, he covers his ears. To him the hero's adventures can still be read in the swirling letters like figures and messages in drifting snowflakes. His breath is part of the air of the events narrated, and all the participants breathe with his life. He is unspeakably touched by the deeds, the words that are exchanged, and, when he gets up, is blanched all over by the snow of his reading.

... And when she gets up from her seat in the cinema she is read all over by the evanescent image(s); they move through her still. Benjamin's evocation of the reading experience captures something of the cinemory moment ('cinemory' as a condensation of cinema, memory and story), but rather than the 'snow of his reading' I imagine Technicolor blood that flows in a circuit – through the screen, through the magical space of the theatre, through my body. I am assimilated by the images, as well as absorbing them into my being. Of course the experience might not always be so lullaby-like, so soothing and embracing. It might be piercing. The circuit is sometimes broken, the blood leaks out, messily. I feel, then, besmirched; or over-inscribed, literally read all over, even though in black-and-white, like the woman in Oshima's *The Man Who Left His Will on Film* over whose naked body moving images and hieroglyphs are projected.

This moment, when you get up from your seat in the cinema, is already foreshadowed in the opening. For it is not just the story that we anticipate, but the sensations. Even before the first images, we are remembering. But, no matter how much we remember, this is no safeguard against what we do not know. Your memories will not protect you from what you have never seen before. It might not be an image as such that is alarming. It might be, say, a configuration of colours, and sounds, where colours, at first formless, begin to figure out a menacingly inchoate cinematic substance. Remember the credit sequence of *Cape Fear*, a Saul and Elaine Bass memory, but also an intimation of underwater electricity. An electric shock made manifest.

If it begins like this, what next?

Chapter 6

Creature from the Black Leather Lagoon

Left: *Cape Fear* (Martin Scorsese, 1991)
Right: *Creature from the Black Lagoon* (Jack Arnold, 1954)

> *One must pay dearly for immortality:*
> *one has to die several times while still alive.* (Nietzsche)

Once upon a time there was a cinema built over a swamp. In the swamp there lurked a 'swamp ghost', an avaricious and recalcitrant monster, refusing to die and eternally greedy. In the cinema a never-ending story unfolded. Innocent viewers would be snatched from their seats in the darkness and dragged thrashing through the splintering floorboards, sucked into the gurgling muddy swamp. Later they would themselves mysteriously and menacingly reappear, rising out of the muddy depths, looking for victims. It is a fiction, this cinema built over a swamp, but one inspired by a real film, Tracey Moffat's *Bedevil*. Like *Cape Fear* it begins in the water, and ends in limbo, or rather, just when you think you're safe, it begins all over again.

Love Travis, Part 1

> *One day there'll be a knock at the door and it'll be me,*
> *Love Travis.*

I return to this chapter after a respite – or escape – from its haunting presence. About seven months ago, I went away for the summer to write about *Cape Fear*, but returned to Sydney with an unfinished manuscript and in a state of delayed shock. I put the chapter aside for a while, but could never really get away from it, from the memories it provoked of that awful event, the thing that happened last summer. As I contemplate it now, in all its murky incompleteness, it looks balefully back at me like the *Creature from the Black Lagoon*, and I wonder: will it ever reach a conclusion, be over and done with; will I ever write 'the end'? Let me tell you the story, or at least the beginning, of what it was that happened so alarmingly and suddenly, last summer.

Putrid, Spumy Swamp-Blood

Green water fills the frame, flowing through runnels of sand. This is the opening shot of *Bedevil*. From an extreme close-up the camera moves slowly forward, pulling up to reveal tiny shoots on the edge of a mangrove swamp. In a continuous virtuoso movement it tracks forward, sucking us into the swamp, into a weirdly coloured landscape – purplish browns and sickly umbers merging into what Moffatt herself has called 'a pukey-green, Linda Blair sky'.[1] An Aboriginal boy of about seven sits on a log, dangling his legs in bubbling brown water, feeding lollies into the deep. Suddenly his leg is seized by some invisibly malevolent force, there is a violent threshing around, and he is pulled under. Gone for ever. Or so it seems. But he lives to tell the tale, to tell a ghostly tale of monstrous repetition and eternal recurrence.

> *Just when you think you're safe, that Max Cady/Robert De Niro has drowned, died, disappeared for good, you think* Cape Fear *is about to end; just at that very moment, he surges out of the depths and the horror begins all over again.*[2]

This boy, Rick, and two other Aboriginal kids watch from the mangroves as a timber cinema is constructed like a kit home by a motley collection of white stereotypes and comics from the 50s. There is a blond, squeaky-clean-cut man, the sort who used to feature in advertisements for do-it-yourself home renovation ads, accompanied by his children, a boy and a girl who appear as little clones, wearing the same crisply clean blue-and-white T-shirts, carrying a min-iature version of the grown-up carpentry kit round their waists. The white kids and the black kids exchange looks across the expanse of the swamp. Their expressions are impassive, and yet the exchange, in its timing and cutting, speaks volumes. Later, Rick sneaks into the cinema in the gloom of night; we see him as a tiny figure sitting at the back of a theatre filled with canvas direc-tors' chairs. In close-up, he dangles a knife on the empty seat next to him; there is a sound of canvas stretched, caressed by the blade. And then a rip. Slow at first, but suddenly he plunges the knife, tearing and slashing, upturning the chairs in a *Psycho*-like frenzy. His foot goes through the boards of the cinema floor, and he is caught in an invincible grip. 'Its tongue was all over my feet,' he says, later, as an old man.

> Literally, I have the image of myself always keeping my nose right
> above the water, the waves always getting to me and about to sink me . . .
> (Scorsese)[3]

The cinema theatre, albeit brand-new and squeaky clean, is built over the submerged ruins of other cinemas, other cultures, and is haunted by the past, by cinematic fragments, moments, severed intensities. It provides a stage for the acting out of memory. But if cinema is not so much an instru-ment for exploring the past as its theatre, and if memory, according to Benjamin, 'is the medium of past experience, as the ground is the medium in which dead cities lie interred',[4] we might say that the cinema of this chapter is less solidly grounded; its medium is a watery swamp in which dead men, and brooding vengeful monsters, lie not so much interred as preserved, waiting, in swamp-blood.

> *It starts in the water. In water that is deep and dark. Very low notes*
> *sustained for a very long time, then an arpeggio, then another;*
> *it wells up from the depths, it pushes higher and higher.*
> (Catherine Clément describing the beginning of
> Wagner's Ring Cycle.)[5]

Cape Fear starts in the water, golden water that shimmers prismatically, dis-persing into abstract patternings of blue and green and brown. An eagle is reflected, swooping and hovering in predatory pose. The features of a face swim in and out of focus, barely discernible, seemingly just below the sur-face; but is this face reflected or contained, is it out there beyond the frame or internal, rising up from the depths? A gaping mouth materialises, teeth bared, and the camera seems to pull us in, down into the jaws of Hades. A man's torso is reflected, menacing in its stillness, its truncated immobility. And then the waterscape turns red, a huge drop forms (a drop of blood, or could it be a tear?) at the top of the frame and falls slowly through the liquid texture of screen space, reminiscent of the moment in *The Last Temptation of Christ* where Jesus holds up his heart and drops of blood colour the water until the entire screen is washed in crimson. It starts in the water, and this is where it ends, or fails to end, when he surges out of the putrid, spumy swamp and the horror begins all over again.

> *Why did you live near the swamps so long, until you yourself*
> *have become a frog and a toad? Does not putrid, spumy*
> *swamp-blood flow through your own veins?*
> (Nietzsche, *Thus Spoke Zarathustra*)

In *Opera, or the Undoing of Women*, Catherine Clément invokes the beginning of Wagner's Ring Cycle, where it starts, and will end, in the water. Scorsese's *Cape Fear* is not primarily about the undoing of women (although some women are indeed undone or done in) but it is about remaking and undoing, and it is peculiarly operatic, as signalled in the opening by the way the 'setting' is mobilised, its solidity almost liquidated, by Elmer Bernstein's score. This, though it starts with a dramatic orchestral chord rather than with an arpeggio, certainly 'pushes higher and higher'. After the tutti chord there are a few seconds of woodwind and string tremolo and then the Max motif begins very softly in the background in a bass register. Timpani start softly and build, and the Max motif, heavily scored for brass, swells to a loud and ominous insistence as the credits conclude.[6] The operatic in *Cape Fear* ('operatic' implying an impulse rather than a generic limit) brings together a yearning for the sublime with an invincibly bathetic craving for B-grade Horror.[7] In this conjunction of the operatic and horror certain transmutations occur. For instance, where Clément describes classical opera as a terrain where women are 'endlessly dying and coming back to life to die even better',[8] this cinematically inflected opera gives us men who are endlessly dying and coming back to life, to die even more dreadfully. Scorsese's operatic impulse reprises some aspects of the horror genre, but the import of this is registered not just in the presence of horror motifs but in the very fact of reprisal itself. The impulse to recall, repeat, remake, suggests the deferral of an ending. And this in turn suggests a certain problem around masculinity and obsession, a problem which is paradoxically 'resolved' in rendering the ending – that is, the nodal point of irresolution – hyperbolically operatic.

Scenarios that Simmer
Cape Fear is a remake of the 1962 thriller directed by J. Lee Thompson (henceforth the 1962 version will be referred to as *Cape Fear 1* and the 1992 version as *Cape Fear 2*). It is thus part of a very contemporary Hollywood phenomenon. As a remake it marks a new direction for Scorsese. Or does it?

> *Travis Bickle is a kind of resurrected Ethan Edwards, but he is also a*
> *zombie-like figure who roams the streets by night. And he will not die. At*
> *the end he lives again and will be reborn in other Scorsese characterisations,*
> *most notably as Max Cady in* Cape Fear. *But it is not just characters who*
> *are reincarnated; ideas persist, questions that are not answered, anomalies*
> *that drive by night through a variety of cinematic landscapes.*

A notion of the remake has been operative throughout this book, not in the sense of producing a simulation of some original, but rather in the sense of recasting, or acting out a scenario that simmers, remains on the boil, either within Scorsese's own corpus or within a wider film context. *Cape Fear 2* will be read in relation to *Cape Fear 1*, but both films are thrown into relief by a third film. And as soon as a third term is introduced, the field, or the swamp, ripples outwards in several directions, generating, retrospectively, other ghostly antecedents.

> *Robert Mitchum (in* The Night of the Hunter, *1955), swamped by water which rises to his chest, brandishes a knife in the air and emits a long, low inhuman wail as the children whom he is menacing make their quiet escape; on a small bark, under the stars, they begin drifting down the river.*

It is night, the lighting expressionistic, and every noise on the river magnified, as the Bowden family waits on the houseboat. Robert Mitchum (in *Cape Fear 1*) lurks in the river, like a malevolent amphibian or reptilian presence, just his head appearing above the water line.

Just when we think he's finally dead, Robert De Niro (in *Cape Fear 2*) rises out of the water yowling like an animal. After further struggles he sinks, only to rise again, just his head above the surface of the water, babbling in tongues. Eventually we can hear the words he is chanting: 'Who will come with me? I'm bound for the promised land!'

The Night of the Hunter was the only film directed by the actor Charles Laughton. A dismal flop at the box office, it was the kiss of death for Laughton so far as directing in Hollywood was concerned. As Elsa Lanchester (who was married to Laughton) observed: 'What studio wants to invest in an actor who directs and has an avant-garde failure on his hands?'[9] It was, however, appreciated by some audiences, although more, I suspect, for its affiliation with horror than its avant-garde finesse: it became a great success on television, 'a three-decade-long feature of late-night broadcast bookings'.[10] Shot almost entirely in a studio, and making use of a range of ostentatious (and sometimes anachronistic) devices such as wipes and irises, back-projection and expressionist lighting, it is extraordinarily (for Hollywood in the 1950s) stylised. Set during the 30s, it features a demonic self-styled preacher, Harry Powell (Mitchum), who roams the South searching for widows whom he seduces and then murders. In search of money, he 'hunts' the two children of one of his victims. He knows they have a small fortune (entrusted to them by their father, subsequently hanged for a murder committed during the bank hold-up in which he stole the money) though he does not know where they have hidden it. The children find refuge with an elderly woman, Miss Rachel (Lillian Gish), who has become a surrogate mother to a brood of children made homeless by the Depression. When Powell finds out where they are he tries to terrorise her into giving them up, and a long siege follows – a long dark night, during which Powell squats on a log by the paling fence, and Rachel, the children behind her, sits in her rocking chair on the veranda, rocking, endlessly rocking, nursing a shotgun in her lap. During this vigil Powell sings the hymn which is his menacing theme tune, 'Leaning on the Everlasting Arms', and Miss Rachel joins in:

171

in the dark, a strange acousmatic harmonising. In the morning she shoots and wounds him and he is taken away by the police just before the lynch mob get to him. Powell is a figure of pure evil, given no psychological motivation, and played with histrionic relish by Mitchum. The film has always been paid far less attention in the English-speaking world than in France, where it has been likened to Lautréamont (Labarthe), praised as 'experimental cinema that truly experiments' while simultaneously condemned for the failed direction of the actors (Truffaut), posed as a limit point of cinema of the fantastic (Gérard Lenne), designated 'an island and a stepping stone, an accident and a fatality, obviousness and a challenge' (Robert Benayoun).[11] Almost medieval in its allegorical dimension, it fluctuates between fairy story and horror film.

The 1962 *Cape Fear*, based on a John D. MacDonald pulp novel, *The Executioners*,[12] is much more securely a genre film. Shot in black-and-white it is a scary thriller that harks back to film noir. It begins with Max Cady (Robert Mitchum), who has just been released from prison after eight years, turning up in a small Southern town in search of Sam Bowden (Gregory Peck), whom he blames for his incarceration. Bowden had witnessed Cady's brutal sexual assault of a woman and had subsequently testified against him. Bowden is now a complacently established lawyer and a good family man with the perfect wife and daughter. And Cady is set on revenge. He begins a campaign of terror, harassing and unsettling the family, in the process forcing Sam further and further away from legality. Initially Sam seeks advice and help from the Chief of Police (Martin Balsam) and then from a private detective (Telly Savalas), but the cunning and vicious Cady repeatedly outwits him and eventually he is forced to use his wife and daughter as bait to lure Cady to Cape Fear (in the North Carolinas), where the two men slug it out in the muck and mire of the swamp in a drawn-out but melodramatically effective final sequence. In adapting the novel, the film eliminates Cady's history and refrains from elaborating any psychological motivation. As a result (and as played by Robert Mitchum) his sexual sadism, his obsessive desire for revenge, is rendered as unnervingly evil.

Cape Fear 2 presents itself as something more akin to a reading than a simple remake. It incorporates and refers to *Cape Fear 1* in a variety of ways, evoking and simultaneously reworking the 'original'. Although it is in Panavision and colour, it still effectively exploits generic expectations, evoking film noir atmospherics and all the shock tactics of the thriller. But Scorsese's film, although quite terrifying at points, is ostentatiously filmic. From the beginning it addresses the viewer as cinematically literate. Special effects, back projection, and matting are used in conjunction with expressionistically deployed colour, particularly in the repeated red wash and fade to negative, appearing like X-ray film (is it Max, I wonder, who has this X-ray vision, or is it the viewer who can see 'through' the film, and yet sees only an image of terror?). The wide screen is used in conjunction with a highly kinetic camera; frenzied dollies are often executed in close-up, the cutting disregards conventional matches, angles are baroque and much of the time it feels as though we are being pulled and pushed and rushed through space. Actors from *Cape Fear 1* (including Mitchum, Peck, Martin Balsam) make appearances and strong generic associations are planted through the music, the photography, and the credit sequence. The film uses and rescores the original soundtrack by Bernard Herrmann (who wrote the music for so many Hitchcock films, and for *Taxi Driver*); the credits are designed by Saul and Elaine Bass; Freddie Francis, strongly associated with Hammer Horror, is the cinematographer.

One of the most significant departures from the first version concerns a plot change. Where Bowden originally contributed to Cady's conviction and imprisonment in his capacity as a witness, here he does so as a lawyer. And, to tighten the twist, he was acting not for the prosecution but as Cady's defence. Sam had knowingly buried evidence: a report on Cady's victim, who had suffered 'rape and aggravated sexual battery', establishing that she was promiscuous, which might have 'saved' Cady had it been produced in court. During his fourteen years in gaol, Cady learns to read and becomes a legal expert himself. He uncovers the buried evidence, which he uses to intimidate Sam.[13] In 1992 Cady has educated himself as a 'new man'. Now, when he isn't tormenting the family, Cady spends his spare time reading *Thus Spoke Zarathustra*, and figures himself as a kind of bargain-basement Nietzschean Superman.

The last sequence, in the watery swamps of Cape Fear, 'remakes' the 1962 ending (which was in its turn a radical departure from the novel) by amplification, by drawing the ending out, not slowly, but through a breathless orchestration of movement, cutting, turbulence. Almost like *Götterdämmerung*, but here it ends with the hero and the villain, both monster-creatures by now, threshing around in the mud and mire, or, as Nietzsche would have it, in 'putrid, spumy swamp-blood'.

Ruby Gentry (King Vidor, 1952)

Madame Reptile

This fascination women have for grand opera, what is it about? The operatic makes visceral, and spectacularly public, private griefs and passions. This is partly why we return to the operatic scene, the scene of the crime, not simply to identify with the tragic diva, nor to take the father's place, for as Mimi, one of the heroines of Sally Potter's *Thriller* (a film noir reworking of *La Bohème*), reminds us, 'Would I have wanted to be the hero?'[14] We search for new scenarios, a place where new voicings may emerge, different and less restrictively gendered possibilities than those afforded Jennifer Jones in *Ruby Gentry* (1952), a girl from the wrong side of the tracks, truly a swamp creature, condemned to a tragic denouement in the slippery mud and mire; or Glenn Close in *Fatal Attraction* (1987).

> *She wanted to be Madame Butterfly but she was Madame Reptile: slithering along the floor, with Dan chasing her down the hallway* [15]

The Thing Which Refuses to Sink (While Norman Bates Nervously Watches)

What turns high opera into cinematic horror might have to do with remembering. It might also have to do with the 'acting out' of masculinity. Remember *Raging Bull*, driven by a restless compulsion that derives from the same dynamic that drives both an opera like *Carmen* and the fearful desire that is cathected onto the *femme fatale* of film noir. The operatic has always ghosted the Scorsesian text, as have intimations of horror, and in *Cape Fear*'s registering of a certain cinematic lineage, one that privileges the histrionic, the operatic and horrific are instantiated in a kind of hyperbolic condensation. If the three 'swamp' images reverberate, they do so in a number of ways. First, they are linked by a strain of performativity that can be traced, in terms of acting and characterisation, through the figure of Robert Mitchum to Robert De Niro (De Niro in *Cape Fear 2* 'plays' Mitchum in *Cape Fear 1* who plays Mitchum in *Night of the Hunter*), and, in terms of direction, by a common impulse towards cinematic extravagance, towards a limit point of cinema of the fantastic. By mapping these impulses across the three film texts a notion of histrionic cinema will be explored later in the chapter. Second, what resonates across these images is the dramatisation of a fear of that which returns, of something unkillable, of that 'thing' which refuses to sink.

> *Norman Bates nervously watches the car containing Marion's body submerging in the swamp behind his mother's house. When the car stops sinking for a moment our anxiety, like his, increases dramatically.*

The 'thing' may be characterised in a number of ways and certainly it manifests itself in a variety of guises, but one way of positing it is as the bad-object that has been internalised by a troubled masculinity. However, the 'thing' is not necessarily an object: it may be less concrete (than a plaster-of-Paris cream-cheese bagel, say); it may be a nexus of irresolvable desires and fears that recur, that won't go away, that rise up from the swamp, deferring the ending in particular movies, and fuelling an impulse to resurrection across movies, to reincarnation, to remaking.

174

There is no such thing, these movies seem to say, as the river of no return: dirty washing and monstrous desires will always be washed back. In *The Seven Year Itch*, Marilyn Monroe, who once upon a time could hear the river calling 'no return, no return', confesses to having a soft spot for the *Creature from the Black Lagoon*: 'He was kind of scary looking but he wasn't really all bad. I think he just craved a little affection. You know, a sense of being loved and needed and wanted.' Tom Ewell says, 'What did you want? Him to marry the girl?' There is no room left in the movies here to humanise the monster; there are no illusions that either Max Cady or Preacher Powell are simply craving a little affection, or that being loved and wanted would fix things up. But there is a taboo hinted at in the *Seven Year Itch* exchange that is central to this genre of operatic horror: the taboo of bestiality, or of miscegenation, this time not between Indian and Caucasian as in *The Searchers* (and traced through *Taxi Driver*), but between animal and human.

The young girl in *Cape Fear 2*, Danielle (Juliet Lewis), is in many respects characterised as a kind of Marilyn *ingénue*, but even she is more knowing about horror movies; or perhaps she lives in an era that is more self-consciously knowledgeable. On television she watches a video clip of 'Creature from the Black Leather Lagoon' and also a group called The Bog. Or we could say that this movie self-consciously reads the genre while reworking it. Certainly this is so, but the self-consciousness does not militate against a deadly threat, a taboo that lurks in the heart of the family, in the bedroom, in the television set. Black leather – animal skin – associations that will recur.

So, there are a number of arenas: horror-opera, histrionic performativity, the return of the swamp creature (the correlative of which is an endlessly deferred ending and a tendency towards 'remaking'). *Cape Fear 2* also opens onto another arena where (via the introduction, in the Scorsese/Wesley Strick script, of what has been characterised by many critics as an ethical dimension, but which can also be thought of as upping the stakes) questions of reading and writing are dramatised. What might reading and writing in the cinema look like, and, more pertinently, feel like? This chapter, built over a swamp, pursues a curiosity, explores ways in which 'reading' might be embodied cinematically, and the thrilling dimension of the thriller written and 'sensed' through the body.

There is an energy in the cinematic turbulence of *Cape Fear 2*'s ending, the struggle with finality, that draws me in, despite my scorn and loathing. Zarathustra scorns the swamp and all who live in it, and yet he returns again and again to its vicinity. Max Cady, too, is scornful of the virtuous swamp creatures, complacent in their image of themselves as good, but he ends up, ironically, drowning in a somewhat animated and turbulent version of the eternally returning swamp. Listening to the story over and over again, watching the images in the dark, repeatedly, until they become imprinted on one's retina, this assimilation allows for repetition, it enables a retelling, a possible cinematic writing.

I Don't Know Whether to Look at Him Or Read Him

A naked back rises up into the frame and recedes, a figure doing press-ups. Our first view of De Niro/Cady, recalling the reflection of a man's torso that

The Night of the Hunter (Charles Laughton, 1955)

rises to the surface of the water and then recedes in the credit sequence, also provides an intimation of what is to come. This exercising body is marked, an illustrated legend tattooed on skin: TRUTH on one side of the scales hanging from a wooden cross and JUSTICE on the other. This image summons other images: remember the demonic preacher in *The Night of the Hunter* who has LOVE tattooed across the knuckles of one hand, and HATE across the other; remember the first glimpse we get of Linda Hamilton/Sarah Connor in *Terminator 2*, a muscle-bound and sweaty body exercising in a prison cell; remember *Taxi Driver* – viewed from a high angle, Travis Bickle, naked from the waist up, doing press-ups. His back is slashed by a long, jagged scar.

Max Cady's body is undoubtedly scarred, but this spectacle of scarring, though it bears some relation to the kind of scar that has been formed in the shape of piety, is differently inflected. The scar on Travis's back is the sign of a wound that, although it has closed over, has not been properly sutured, whereas the tattoo is a deliberate form of self-desecration, of bodily modification, and – where it involves writing – a mode of direct address. Travis aspires to a machine body, and hence his efforts to discipline and transform his 'docile body'; he attempts to render his body machine-like in its functioning, lacking in interiority, all surface. But in his case the degree of repression involved gestures towards a struggle for containment that isn't entirely successful; he almost becomes all surface, but not quite – crossing the surface of his skin there is a scar that indicates not only the assumption of piety but also an exchange between inside and outside (and home and away) which isn't entirely resolved. It is perhaps this very lack of resolution that ensures that across time, over

176

cinematic bodies, the scar is transferred. But, although this transfer takes place – Travis resurrects Ethan Edwards and returns like the living dead in the figure of Max Cady – the scarring operates, in terms of textuality, differently. De Niro/Cady certainly assumes the mantle of piety: 'You might say I'm here to save you,' he tells Sam in a lethally sardonic tone, and undoubtedly he is propelled by the same salvation-revenge dynamic that drove Ethan Edwards and Travis Bickle as well as the protagonists of horror and vigilante movies, but in contrast to these figures De Niro's Cady achieves superficiality. And *Cape Fear 2*, in the inscribed spectacle of Max's body (and by extension, the inscribed spectacle of his flashy red sports car, which also addresses the viewer in the form of stickers: 'You're a VIP on Earth. I'm a VIP in Heaven' and 'American by Birth, Southern by the Grace of God'), demonstrates the conceit of embodied writing, not in order to insinuate depth of character, but to invite and elaborate cinematically an idea of embodied reading.

I'd like to pick you up and hold you till you were tattooed on me.
(Specter of the Rose)

Later Max Cady unclothes, baring his flesh. We watch, along with Sam Bowden and the Chief of Police (Robert Mitchum), behind a one-way mirror, as he is stripped and searched. Undressing to the waist, he gradually reveals more and more of a body densely tattooed, verbosely inscribed, thick with citation: 'Vengeance is Mine', 'My Time is at Hand', 'I have put my trust in the Lord God. In Him will I Trust', 'The Lord is the Avenger', 'My Time is not yet Full Come'. The camera traverses this body much as a finger traces over written text in a book, guiding the eye. It pauses between front and back, lingering over a cartoon figure holding a bible in one hand and a gun in the other, and then passes over the shoulder to the back on which the cross and scales are tattooed. Moving around the torso the camera is arrested by forked lightning which springs from the belly; situated over the heart is a sign of a heart, a generically familiar emblem, coloured red, broken and ascribed to 'Loretta'.[16] On the other side of his chest, the final message: 'Time the Avenger'. All quotations are acknowledged, the biblical sources inscribed in smaller print almost like footnotes. 'Gee, I don't know whether to look at him or read him,' declares Mitchum.

'I come not with peace, but with a sword,' says Powell, flicking his knife open near the beginning of The Night of the Hunter. *At the end he threatens Miss Rachel: 'Lord God Jehovah will guide my hand in vengeance.'*

He watches and reads Max Cady. In a sense he watches and reads 'himself', or a reincarnation of the Max Cady he once embodied, now a character 'made flesh' by Robert De Niro. Mitchum/Cady was also taken to the police station and stripped but the camera was less familiar, less probing, and there was no one-way mirror to heighten the effect of voyeurism, and to align – so emphatically – our gaze with the legal purview. He also stripped to the waist and, while facetiously declaring himself 'a co-operative guy', maintained an insolently threatening attitude, not, however, through the medium of an articulate tattooed body, but through keeping his hat on his head and his hands on his hips. The tattoos, then, serve not only to mark the body but to signify a difference, a textual difference between the two *Cape Fears*.

Another, though related, difference is inscribed in the beginnings. The credit sequence of the earlier film consists of a montage of shots showing Mitchum, in safari-type suit and panama hat, walking purposefully through a town. In 1992 it starts, the credit sequence, in water. The film 'proper' begins with Cady in prison, exercising (after a framing element: Danielle's voice, over an image of her face, announcing 'My reminiscence . . .'). In the first *Cape Fear*, the credit sequence inaugurated the first narrative segment: Cady, already released from prison, walks up the steps of the courthouse, sucking on a huge cigar. He brushes past a woman carrying a large pile of precariously balanced books and the top one spills over onto the stairs; as she stoops awkwardly to retrieve it the whole pile topples threateningly. He continues walking, never looking back but fully conscious, the framing tells us, of what he has done. The courthouse scene is eliminated from Scorsese's version, where, instead, the emphasis on the incarcerated and exercising body sets in play a variety of apparently new motifs. Yet Mitchum's inaugural gesture, the casual brutality inscribed in this detail of spilling the books, resonates through the years; a motif is lightly tossed in the air and spills over into the later film, where it revolves with other resonances and a work of condensation begins.

> *I learnt to read during my stretch. First* Spot Goes to the Farm.
> *Then* Run Away Bunny. *Then* Law *books mostly.*

Soon after we have seen him exercising, Cady walks away from the prison, a free man, unburdened by any objects. The guard asks him about his books. 'Already read 'em,' is Max's curt response. He continues walking without looking back, just like Robert Mitchum, except that in 1992 he walks straight towards us like a missile, straight into the camera, while behind him an artificially melodramatic sky boils ominously. Cady appears to have occupied himself with two main activities while in prison: he has learnt to read and to write; he reads law books and he writes in blood (when Leigh tells him he's repulsive he says, 'Guess I'm covered in too many tattoos, huh. But you see there's not a whole lot to do in prison but desecrate your flesh').

> *Of all that is written I love only what a man has written with* ·
> *his blood.* (Zarathustra according to Nietzsche).

Before we see him in the prison cell we see the images and objects that surround Cady: the camera pans down over images tacked to the wall, images that include Stalin and an Oriental figure impaled by swords, down to a shelf of books. He sees words and images as instrumental and his attitude to reading and writing is, above all, functional. He has learnt to read in order to understand the law and this has enabled him to work out that Sam, when supposedly acting as his defence, withheld evidence that would in all probability have saved him from fourteen years in prison. Having found the information he wants from the books, Cady has no further need of them, but he doesn't simply internalise what he has read; he actually takes the law into his own hands, transfers it in the form of aphorisms and slogans, threats and promises, from the books to his body. In this way he turns his body into a functional apparatus, an eloquent instrument of revenge. Similarly, the images in his cell are in a sense retained, imprinted on his flesh. The picture of Stalin and the figure impaled by swords represent two fantasies which, in Cady's person, combine and transmute: a totalitarian will to power (and attendant fantasy of omnipotence) and the fantasy of immortality or survival through suffering and torture. Not exactly the Word-made-Flesh, he nevertheless is a functional personification; in a macabre travesty of the Judaeo-Christian law, he is the Flesh made Wordy: his function is clear, his motives are not hidden, he is there to be read like a book.

> It is a matter of creating a memory for man; and man, who was
> constituted by means of an active faculty of forgetting (oubli), by
> means of a repression of biological memory, must create an other
> memory, one that is collective, a memory of words (paroles) and
> no longer a memory of things, a memory of signs and no longer
> of effects. This organisation, which traces its signs directly on
> the body, constitutes a system of cruelty, a terrible alphabet.
> (Nietzsche, according to Deleuze and Guattari)[17]

Just as Cady's body addresses the diegetic viewer as a reader, so the filmic body that is *Cape Fear 2*, while being particularly exhibitionist (displaying on the surface, up front, its filmic effects), also strongly invokes the viewer as a reader, affected by and engaged in the mystery and decipherment of cinematic signs. That decipherment involves bodily apprehension – Max Cady registers somatically, he gets under your skin, he's creepy, insidious; but he himself is impenetrable and impervious, there is nothing under his skin. Nevertheless, it might be possible to conceive of a subcutaneous structure (pertaining to the phenomenon called Max Cady and to the movie called *Cape Fear*) which is not an accretion of psychological clues but an activity, a weaving of memories and movies and intimations of horror.

Illusion Arts, or the Factitious Coherence of All Obsessions

One matte shot comes early in the film, as Cady is released from prison. The
painting, suggested by a production painting by Henry Bumstead, extends
the foreground of the prison gate (shot at a southern Florida women's
detention facility), and features an ominous boiling sky in the background.
Illusion Arts presented Marty with several different skies and asked
'*Which sky do you want?*' (Freddie Francis)[18]

When Max Cady walks out of prison, walks straight into camera, an ominous
boiling sky in the background, he wills a world into being, an ominous world,

boiling with retribution. Like Rupert Pupkin when he performs a stand-up comedy routine with cardboard cut-outs as celebrities; like Henry King, the gangster, when he crosses the road with his girl on his arm and, in an extraordinarily long and mobile take, weaves his way through the Copacabana Club and is served champagne, which seems somehow to appear miraculously out of thin air; like Newland Archer, when he watches the Countess Olenska cross the room to sit beside him – he wills a world into being.

In each case we witness, and perhaps are implicated in, the enactment of an obsession. All obsessions involve a theatricalisation of desire, an impulse to create a world, to carve up space, to compose the elements of existence according to the measure of desire. Scorsese's cinema frequently makes a connection between fictional protagonists driven by obsessive desires and the cinematic process itself, evoking Leo Bersani's phrase: 'the factitious coherence of all obsessions'.[19] If there are heightened moments when this analogy is dramatised, moments of deictic delirium, then clearly the artificial boiling sky against which Max Cady makes his exit from prison and his entry into the world (and into our space) serves to theatricalise his desire for revenge, just as it serves as a backdrop to his enacted desire for superman status: 'I spent fourteen years in an eight by nine cell surrounded by people who were less than human. My mission in that time was to become more than human.'

> We might say that the act of desiring, in its purest form, involves an undisturbed use of the world as a theater for our fantasies
> (Leo Bersani).[20]

If obsessive behaviour defers closure through repetition of the same, then, when cinematic narrative itself is compelled by an obsessive drive, the ending is deferred, or, alternatively, multiplied. *Cape Fear 2*, for instance, seems to end over and over again and the ending itself becomes another extremely amplified moment of deictic delirium. The relationship, however, between an obsessive protagonist and the narrative that renders that obsession is not straightforward, as can be seen in the cases of *Taxi Driver* and *After Hours*. Of *Cape Fear* we might say that the narrative itself is far less pathological and more self-consciously humorous than its protagonist, Max Cady. Scorsese's *Cape Fear*, although it is often very close to the 1962 version, can be differentiated in the way it articulates both obsession and humour, in the degree to which it is cinematically theatrical and monstrative.

In both versions Max Cady is obsessed with what happened in the past and dedicated to revenge. He arrives in town to confront the man he blames for his imprisonment and proceeds to menace and harass him and his family, including wife, daughter, maid and dog. It is the menace that provides the basis for a thriller, and this is well provided in *Cape Fear 1*, both by Robert Mitchum's acting and J. Lee Thompson's direction. Scorsese operatically inflates this element of menace, although Cady is rendered baroque, and in his superficiality can be conceived as cartoon-like, the way in which he wills a world into being, the way in which he uses the world as a stage for his fantasies, is truly terrifying.

180

Love Travis, Part 2

I arrived on a hot Sunday afternoon. Four weeks stretched in front of me, a whole month away from work in which I could focus, exclusively, on writing. I had sublet my flat and rented this cottage in a small coastal town. It was a tiny house surrounded by other houses, but trees gave the illusion of pastoral peace and the beach was only a few minutes' walk away. On his way to Canberra, J stayed for a while and we opened a bottle of wine in the garden, watching the summer light fade slowly and the escarpment grow huge and dark. He left after dark and I immersed myself in a long, deep bath, soaking in the scent of rosemary from the bush growing outside the bathroom window. Then I went to bed with a good book, content.

As Kay Scarpetta held her breath, listening to those ominous footsteps coming closer, so I started to hear what she heard, sounds outside the window. Just the wind in the trees, but still it was creepy. Snuggling under the bedclothes, I was glad to be indoors. Now, however, I was alert to every imaginable whisper and scratch of leaves against the window-pane, so decided to switch to something more sober and soporific. J had left *In Search of Schrödinger's Cat: Quantum Physics and Reality*, which seemed a suitable guard against fanciful acousmatics. Just as I was falling asleep a scratching sound nudged me wide awake. This is ridiculous, I told myself, heart thumping, you always hear strange sounds in a strange place, it goes with the territory. Most likely it's nothing, and if it's not nothing, then it's probably possums. The heavy breathing and slight hissing noise that was now accompanying the scratching seemed to confirm this. That's what possums sound like. Logically I knew, in fact was absolutely sure, that either I was imagining things or there were indeed possums cavorting just outside the window. So I lay there, listening, hearing, imagining. You know the feeling. Eventually I got so exasperated with myself that I thought, fuck this for a lark, I'll close the window and then at least I'll know everything's safe. So I hopped out of bed, strode across the room as I was (naked), simply in order to close the window so I could go to sleep. I pulled back the curtain, and from out of the darkness a figure loomed up and an arm lunged at . . .

I Shall Wind and Wound Them with My Mockery

Scorsese tells of how when he read the original script for *Cape Fear* he found the family too clichéd and happy. 'And then along comes the bogeyman to scare them. They were like Martians to me. I was rooting for Max to get them.'[21] The family in *Cape Fear 1* does now seem revoltingly antiseptic, as though they had all strayed from a television sitcom into this swampy nightmare location (Polly Bergen and Lori Martin as Peggy and Nancy, the wife and daughter, were in fact television actors). Nevertheless, in the realisation of the original script, Mitchum's menace, along with effectively articulated suspense, recruits the audience on the side of the family. But there is no real sense that Cady infiltrates their world and their values. And this is where Scorsese departs from the original. In his version, Cady is able to infiltrate and contaminate the family precisely because they are open to corruption, they are not the perfect family. This inflection, however, is worked out cinematically, and it is on the cinematic level, rather than through the elaboration of a humanist thematic, that we feel the force of the infiltration. Scorsese's appropriation and development of a particular shot in the first film illustrates the difference.

One of the more surprising moments (because it injects suspense with a flourish) in *Cape Fear 1* occurs when the camera, taking Cady's point of view, rises slowly over a hedge for a look at Bowden's house. In *Cape Fear 2* we see Max (from Leigh's point of view, through the shutters) watching the house, perched casually on the garden wall, fireworks behind him lighting up the sky in a fairytale configuration. She wakes Sam, but when he looks Cady is gone. In Scorsese's version, Max looks, and then gets into the house; neither the family, nor the detective, nor ourselves ever know how (and he does so twice: to kill the dog, and to kill the maid and the detective). Sam, on the edge of hysteria, tells Kersek, the slimy detective he has hired, 'I believe he is able to slip into the house and out undetected. Is he out, I can't tell, he's either out or he's in, I'm not sure.' Kersek's comforting response, 'I can't see through walls', almost drives Sam over the edge: 'Why can't anybody do anything for me?' Kersek proceeds to set a booby trap: pretending that Sam has left town on a business trip, they smuggle him back into the house and Kersek strings all-but-invisible fishing line across the doors and windows. During the night, Sam suddenly wakes, and we see from his point of view an X-ray image of Cady standing in the window frame. Cut to Sam rubbing his eyes as though to rub away the nightmare, followed by another shot of the window frame where Cady still lounges, sucking on his cigar and blowing smoke. As the smoke billows the shot is suffused with colour, albeit murky, noirish colour. Sam again rubs his eyes and this time the reverse cut shows an empty window, no Cady. He wakes Leigh and tells her, 'I just had the weirdest feeling he was in the house.' Indeed, he is in the house, as we soon find out. It is as though his X-ray vision extends to an ability to pass through walls and under the skin. He is a malevolent swamp ghost, his presence cinematically summoned. He invades their house, their world, their fantasies.

But *Cape Fear 2* retains, eccentrically, some distorted echo of the phrase 'I was rooting for Max to get them'. De Niro's Cady has the advantage of eclectic reading and has undoubtedly taken some leaves from *Thus Spoke Zarathustra*. Like Zarathustra he begins each day with a little malice and adopts a sardonic and mocking attitude towards the world. While we may be repulsed and even terrified by Cady, he is also the locus of mirthful irreverent sarcasm, and on occasion we are enticed to take pleasure in his needling of niceness.

> *And there are others who are like cheap clocks that must*
> *be wound: they tick and they want the tick-tock to be called*
> *virtue. Verily, I have my pleasure in these: wherever I find such*
> *clocks, I shall wind and wound them with my mockery, and*
> *they shall whir for me.*
> (Zarathustra according to Nietzsche)

Thus Max speaks often like Zarathustra: he takes great pleasure in winding up his opponents, in mocking their virtue and parodying their pretensions to rationality and goodness, perhaps a bit like Scorsese, who takes great pleasure in flexing the genre, in thrilling us, in making us whirr. But also in making us laugh, and here he differs crucially from his protagonist, who does not allow his victims laughter. Cady despises those who sit in the swamp and say, 'Virtue – that is sitting still in a swamp. We bite no one and avoid those who want to bite; and in all things we hold the opinion that is given to us.' He is similarly scornful of those who are proud of 'their handful of justice', in the name of which they commit gross injustices.

But for all his aspirations Max Cady does not achieve superman status, and this is because he is gripped by that sentiment that Zarathustra most abhors: resentment or rancour, epitomised in the obsession with revenge. Revenge is symptomatic of an obsession with the past, a prodigious and unforgiving memory, an inability to let go.

> *This, indeed this alone, is what revenge is: the will's ill will*
> *against time and its 'it was.'*
> (Zarathustra according to Nietzsche)

Cady's implied criticism of Bowden as one of those who 'when they say, "I am just," it always sounds like "I am just, revenged"' can of course be turned against himself. In *Cape Fear 2* there is a struggle over not just the law but readings of the law, the letter and the spirit. Bowden infers that his action remains faithful to the spirit of the law. But Cady holds to the letter of the law, and puts into practice the knowledge he has acquired through his prison reading. He exercises, outside the court, all the wiliness that we are accustomed to seeing in courtroom dramas in order to lure Sam into further violations, eliciting from him threats and bribes and violent scare tactics. Eventually Max turns the tables by hiring the best criminal lawyer (played in uncharacteristically oily mode by Gregory Peck, perhaps a sly insinuation about the fate of the 'virtuous' lawyer in *Cape Fear 1*, not to mention Atticus Finch in *To Kill a Mockingbird*), who succeeds in taking out a restraining order against Bowden and instituting proceedings for disbarment on the grounds of extreme moral turpitude.

> *So here we are, two lawyers for all practical purposes, talking shop.*

However, even though Cady has read the law books well and is capable of acting (with much malicious pleasure) as though he were a lawyer, his desire for revenge drives him to enact a particular reading of the law, to literally embody the letter of the law as the word of an Avenging God ('The Lord is the Avenger'). His resentment is manifested in a fundamentally reactive mode, and therefore (though Nietzsche might not go this far) phantasmatic mode. It is not simply that in 1992 the question of ethics is introduced into a legal framework, but that questions of desire and fantasy are inserted into the process of reading and writing. Sam's adoption of a position outside the law (despite and while making assertions to the contrary: 'I can't operate outside the law. The law's my business') indicates that he too is implicated in phantasmatic readings and in the same economy of revenge and salvation that determines Cady's trajectory.

> *He enters into any skin, into any affect: he constantly transforms*
> *himself.* (Nietzsche)

Cady is an illustrated man, or a personification, if you like, of revenge, and an instrument of salvation. He is also, through this process of embodiment and instrumentality, depersonalised. He is, as the surface of his body tells us, a bundle of signs rather than a fully realised psychologically deep character. This is not to say that he is easy to read or that his function is straightforward; but his skin, while it might not indicate depth, does alert us to his chameleon qualities, to character itself as an acting out. While *Cape Fear 1* (and the acting out of Robert Mitchum) initiates the idea of Max Cady as malevolently superficial, *Cape Fear 2* elaborates the notion, rendering it operatic/baroque. The De Niro Cady adopts a number of personae – prisoner, saviour, drama teacher, maid, anti-nuclear demonstrator (the story he spins the girl in the bar), becoming-car (clinging underneath the car, on the flight from the city, his body almost merges with the machine), accident victim (the story he spins at the airport). Remember, in *Blade Runner* 'skins' is cop parlance for mutants; so here, although thematically we might say he dons a variety of disguises, it might be more accurate to talk of a variety of skins.

> *As soon as he is made flesh, he withers away. Any appearance*
> *suits him, and none. No sooner has he entered into one than it*
> *turns into a sepulcher, and he abandons it. The only skin he*
> *knows is a dead skin.* (Irigaray)[22]

His strongest characteristic is his ability to adopt the signs of character, to take on a variety of personae, to play a number of parts. While characters in films (or novels, or comics) are always constructed, made up of a bundle of signs, and only come into being through our ascription of an imaginary unity to the person, many fictions work to create an illusion of interiority, to encourage a particular kind of reading which ascribes both psychological interiority to character and a certain exteriority – that is, the illusion that characters have a life of their own outside the fiction (an illusion that is aided in the cinema by the physical embodiment of the character by an actor). But the degree to which such work takes place is variable and often generically derived. Different genres operate different modes of character construction. Most simply, this is to say that they produce different kinds of characters; but, more interestingly, it is to imply that genres elicit various, complexly inflected modes of engagement from viewers. While character always demands an element of invested faith from the reader/viewer, this need not be attached to a notion of interiority. Even genres like horror, where protagonists may be semi-human or certainly monstrous, are able to elicit forms of reading that incorporate belief – not belief in the coherence of character necessarily, but belief in the efficacy of the monster-character.

Indeed belief, fear, desire, a sense of being touched, can well be mobilised more strongly (as we know from fairy tales) by fictional mysteries and generic grotesques than by naturalistically developed characters.

This is because fiction, rather than having no connection with the real, has a relation that is allusive and intricate rather than strictly denotative. *Cape Fear 2*, while exploiting some of the characteristics of schlock-horror, also provides a space for meditation upon the connections between character and belief, superficiality and intricacy, reading and palpability. It deploys characters grounded, as it were, by known actors, and it reprises and refers to other films and filmic characters, and yet it is also flamboyantly superficial – that is, committed to a discourse of density rather than depth.

> *The Terminator needs to make repairs to his body. The organically grown flesh that conceals the machine is wounded and rotting. Standing in front of the mirror he inserts a scalpel into his eye socket and begins repairs. Through the bloody meat: a gleam of metal. This is the first glimpse of the 'real' machine that lies beneath the skin, but is also coterminous with the surface of the body.*

For a transitional film object which, by contrast, clarifies some of these issues we need look no further than *The Last Temptation of Christ*. In a gesture of remarkable literality, Christ (Willem Dafoe) reaches into the bloody enclaves of his body and pulls out his heart as evidence of an interiority, of palpable humanity conjoined with superhuman attributes, of an isomorphism between flesh and spirit. I take it as a somewhat sick joke which functions precisely to test the faith or capacity for belief of the audience – their faith in the cinema, that is, and in filmic characters more than their faith in God. It is also often taken as a homage to films such as Cronenberg's *Videodrome* (and remember the scene in *The Terminator* where Schwarzenegger picks up a punk in one hand and rips his heart out with the other). Christ holds out his heart – 'This is my heart. Take it. God is inside of us. The devil is outside' – to his followers, as a sign. It is above all a demonstration that filmic characters are made up of signs (and a reminder that signs are simultaneously forces), but it is also an indication of the materiality of fiction and the bloody stickiness of semiotics.[23] The drama of *The Last Temptation* revolves round the desire of Christ for a human existence and his fantasy of being a fully realised psychological character. So, even while the film is a kind of metadiscourse on fiction and faith, the efficacy of the drama requires that we invest some faith in the human character of Christ. It is another drama of the irresolution of inside and outside, and represents Scorsese's picking over old wounds.

> I enjoyed making those images of the bleeding heart . . .
> I enjoyed probing the wounds. (Scorsese)[24]

Christ is a transitional figure, like The Terminator, part human part something else. Max Cady, although he shares many functional characteristics with Dafoe's Christ, is more decisively without interiority. The point of comparison is not just to distinguish between two kinds of character, but to indicate ways in which character modality is related to performative modes, where 'performative' is conceived in textual as well as in actorly terms. The tattoos, let's say, do not tell us about what is inside; rather, they tell us that performance will be about other things than character.

He Wears His Skin Like a Glove

Max Cady wears his tattooed skin like a glove. Gloves are most commonly made of animal skin and the wearing of gloves indicates both the closeness of animal and human and the distinction. Tattooing is a form of body modification which signals a remaking of the human body; like the wearing of gloves, it has the capacity to evoke a phantasmic zone of contact.

> *The boxing gloves echoe the red shoes as agents of compulsion, compelling and seducing us to look even while forcing us to look away, to avert our gaze from intolerable mutilation.*

As a glove the tattooed skin resonates with those totemic objects of investment in *Raging Bull* and *The Red Shoes*. These objects, once put on, cannot be taken off, and while this is in a certain way true of tattoos (a lack of reversability is endemic to the process) there is also a difference: the tattoo does not exist as an object independent of the body; it only takes shape and acquires substance in the process of application, in the desecration or reformation of the skin. Max Cady is given to us, from the beginning, as a tattooed body; he wears his skin like a glove, functionally, rather than investing in it in the way that Jake La Motta and Victoria Page do. By extension we as the audience are less likely to invest in the same way. Nevertheless, although the tattooed skin/glove does not operate in quite the same way as a totemic object, this spectacle of the tattooed body does evoke some of the attraction and repulsion elicited by the totemic object. The tattooed body, in this instance, is itself a taboo object, and to possess this body is to be possessed. In *One-Way Street* Walter Benjamin has a section called 'Gloves' which bears upon the nature of this attraction-repulsion:

> In an aversion to animals the predominant feeling is fear of being recognised by them through contact. The horror that stirs deep in man is an obscure awareness that in him something lives so akin to the animal that it might be recognised. All disgust is originally disgust at touching. Even when the feeling is mastered, it is only by a drastic gesture that overleaps its mark: the nauseous is violently engulfed, eaten, while the zone of finest epidermal contact remains taboo. Only in this way is the paradox of the moral demand to be met, exacting simultaneously the overcoming and the subtlest elaboration of man's sense of disgust. He may not deny his bestial relationship with animals, the invocation of which revolts him: he must make himself its master.[25]

The spectacle of the human glove we call Max Cady is threatening precisely because it evokes and theatricalises that threatening zone of contact, the 'finest epidermal contact', between animal and human.

Love Travis, Part 3

From out of the darkness, an arm lunged at me. Through the window it lunged, into the bedroom. My heart stopped, the world stopped. Everything froze. Now, months and months later, the moment is unfrozen, it has become a moving image that I now can contemplate, but only as something akin to a film loop. The scene plays over and over, without variation, and what surprises me is that it is so clichéd, such a classic horror-movie moment, a replay of countless scenes, but in particular that horrifying moment in *Night of the Living Dead* when the hand comes through the boarded-up wall, and you know that home is no refuge. The sensation, however, has never left me: when the hand lunged I felt, I feel, the hairs on my skin lift, between me and 'it' nothing but a zone of finest epidermal contact.

Maybe I'm the Big Bad Wolf

In *The Night of the Hunter* Robert Mitchum plays a lycanthropic role. He is introduced obliquely when Lillian Gish, in the opening of the film, reads from the Bible: 'Beware the false prophets which come to you in sheep's clothing, but inwardly they are ravening wolves.'

> *You're not the drama teacher are you?*
> *Maybe I'm the Big Bad Wolf*

In 1992 Robert De Niro resurfaces as the Wolf (this time in a Little Red Riding Hood scenario) reprising many of the animalistic allusions that reverberate through *The Night of the Hunter* and on through the 1962 *Cape Fear*. I will return to the Big Bad Wolf sequence (when Cady lures Danny, the daughter, into the school theatre by pretending to be her new drama teacher and proceeds to play out a gruesomely suspenseful seduction scene) or perhaps it is more likely that the Wolf will return, of its own accord, to haunt us eternally. But for the moment the sequence will serve, like *The Night of the Hunter*, as a stepping stone.

Under the stars, they begin drifting down the river. On the banks of the great Ohio the evil preacher, on horseback, keeps pace with the small children. He has his shotgun and they are unarmed. The atmosphere is eerie and at the same time curiously lyrical, as though time is suspended in the starlit darkness. As they drift, menaced and yet for the moment protected, we see a number of creatures – a croaking frog, a spider weaving its web, a turtle, some sheep – looming up, hugely, out of the darkness. In the foreground a pair of hares crouch in the reeds, quivering, while in the distance we can see the tiny bark floating on the river. The pursuit of the children is dramatised, rendered almost allegorical, by the invocation of nature: 'The whole of nature takes on the responsibility of the children's movement of flight,' writes Deleuze, 'and the boat where they take refuge seems itself a motionless shelter on a floating island.'[26] This 'dome of stars' sequence, in the way that it simultaneously suspends time and creates suspense, delineates a kind of cinematic bestiary in which the Mitchum character takes pride of place. Nature is conceived of primarily as animalistic, and Powell's predatory presence is, within the terms of such a scenario, supremely non-human or, paradoxically, non-naturalistic.

At some of the film's most intense moments the animal analogy is evoked in a pantomimic way with almost farcical resonance. Poised to turn into a kind of Wolf, Powell, under duress, snarls and growls, howls and squawks; and on several occasions Laughton distorts the sound to give an animalistic effect. After he has murdered Willa (the widow of the bank robber whom Powell marries in order to get the money), played by Shelley Winters, and while pretending to the sanctimonious community that she has run off with another man, Powell harasses the children mercilessly until eventually John, the boy, pretending that he is about to reveal the hiding place, lures Powell into the cellar. Pearl, the little girl, terrified by the ogre's rage when he discovers that John is lying, blurts out the secret. In the chaos that ensues, and within a hair's breadth of their lives, the children manage to escape, shutting Powell in the cellar. As they flee we hear him cry out, a cry at first muffled and broken, like the sobbing of a child.

> *If it can be said to have a model, Mitchum's Powell seems closest to the more libidinous, sadistic characters of Disney or Tex Avery. The scene in the cellar where he learns the secret of the doll is built on the slapstick dramatics of* Tom and Jerry. *At one point in the script he is referred to as the Big Bad Wolf.*[27]

The escape, however, is only transitory. The Preacher soon emerges from his underground incarceration. Like Poe's black cat, he persists, and arrives at

The Night of the Hunter (Charles Laughton, 1955)

the river's edge just as the children are reaching the boat. As they evade his grasp once again and make their quiet escape, he, swamped by water rising to his chest, brandishes a knife in the air and emits a long low inhuman wail.

> *A cry, at first muffled and broken, like the sobbing of a child, and then quickly swelling into a long, loud, and continuous scream, utterly anomalous and inhuman, a howl, a wailing shriek, half of horror and half of triumph, such as might have arisen only out of hell, conjointly from the throats of the damned in their agony and of the demons that exult in the damnation.* (Poe)

As that wail echoes back from out of the SoHo night, as the Hunter roams in that timeless stretch 'after hours' when the world moves, to borrow a phrase from Deleuze, 'motionless at a great pace', we listen like Zarathustra when 'he heard a long, long cry, which the abysses threw to each other and handed on, for none wanted to keep it: so evil did it sound'.

The long river pursuit follows and then Powell arrives at Miss Rachel's and begins his vigil, his long night of malice and menace. As the climax approaches we see a night hawk intercut with a small quivering rabbit. Eventually, after a period of sadistic surveillance, it dives and we hear the sounds, off screen, of the slaughter. As the morning light approaches Rachel shoots Powell, who leaps into the air squawking and shrieking. When the law officers come she tells them, as though referring to an animal, 'I got something trapped in my barn.'

The sustained (albeit often subterranean) animal analogy that infects the fairy-tale atmosphere of *The Night of the Hunter* does more than simply connote that man (and perhaps a specific man) is like an animal. While the notion of animalism partly pertains to character what is interesting is the way that it permeates the filmic discourse on a number of levels; the non-humanist is evoked – through non-naturalistic cinematic means – as profoundly threatening and horrific. Elements of the horror genre then begin to pervade a film that is not primarily or exclusively a horror film through the elaboration of a histrionic world realised through a non-human impulse.

In *Cape Fear* (both versions) the inhuman aspect of Max Cady is measured through a series of beastly acts, in particular through the poisoning of a domestic animal, the family dog. The wilful destruction of this creature, posited as innocent and vulnerable, signals a real threat to the realm of the domestic. In both films it heralds a return to the law of the jungle, but in *Cape Fear 2* this reversion to the animalistic is inflected by a rhetorically charged invocation of horror. While the later film is on the whole much more graphic in its depiction of violence, the death of the dog is described (rather than shown, as in *Cape Fear 1*) in the manner, if not the style exactly, of Greek tragedy. 'Then he started howling. Horrible high-pitched howls. They sounded like he was screaming.' The absence of the image corresponds to the ubiquitous though invisible, and therefore supernatural, presence of Max Cady (this is the first occasion that he gets into the house). In *Fatal Attraction* the vengeful female commits a similar beastly act, by boiling the pet rabbit belonging to her ex-lover's little daughter in a pot on top of the stove, in the heart of the family home. By this act of inhumanity she presages a truly monstrous capacity which indicates a horror-movie ending in which she will not die, but rises again and again – like Max Cady 1 and Max Cady 2 – out of the water. Rather than a swamp she surges out of the bath-tub but it is water equally bloodied and muddied by familial humanity's dirty washing. She, however, like Ruby Gentry, pays a different price.

And then she boils the pet bunny in the family cooking pot, and no one can forgive her.

> *'You bitch,' the woman behind me whispers, a long slow hissing noise.*
> *It moves softly over the backs of the seats like a wave,*
> *connecting up our anger.*[28]

The 1962 *Cape Fear* derives some of its intimations of animality from the novel on which it is based. John D. MacDonald lays on the animal analogy with a trowel, using it primarily as a characterising device: Cady is a brutish, albeit 'shrewd animal'; when he attacks the wife she reports that he 'smelled like some kind of animal too'; and when Sam, after hearing his wife's screams, is stumbling towards the house where Cady has been lured, 'he heard a sound that must have come from a man's throat, but it was utterly unlike any human sound he had ever heard. It was a snarling, roaring sound, full of anger and madness and a bestial frenzy.' J. Lee Thompson's filmed version is far more sparing in its direct references to animality, though there are two significant instances: first, the detective whom Sam hires to protect his family (when normal legal mechanisms prove inadequate) tells him, in a direct quote from the book, that 'A type like that is an animal. So you fight like an animal'; and second, the woman Cady picks up in a bar, whom he will later savagely assault, tells him, 'You're just an animal. Coarse, lustful.'

Where *The Night of the Hunter* invokes animality through analogy and the first *Cape Fear* does so through ascription, De Niro's Max Cady flamboyantly announces his animal nature, warning Lori, the woman he picks up in a bar, 'Now you gotta stay sober. If you ain't sober then you taking your chances. Cos I'm just one hell of an animal.' This line is delivered in an ironic tone, but there is little sense of irony either here or later when, on the houseboat, he threatens Leigh and Danny. 'Take off your clothes. Down on your knees,' he keeps repeating. And then: 'Tonight you're going to learn to be an animal, to live like an animal and to die like one.' Earlier he has told Sam, 'Let's get something straight here. I spent fourteen years in an eight by nine cell surrounded by people who were less than human. My mission in that time was to become more than human. You see Grandaddy used to handle snakes in church. Granny drank strychnine. I guess you could say I had a head start, genetically speaking.' He is driven by a desire to reduce the Bowdens to a state of abjection, to the less-than-human, while at the same time elevating himself to the more-than-human. In more general terms we might say that the film instigates, through the notion of animality, a philosophical rumination on the humanistic. Like most horror films, and indeed like much of Nietzsche, the philosophical dimension is both deadly serious and sardonically gleeful.

> *That day, the Wolf-Man rose from the couch particularly tired.*
> *He knew that Freud had a genius for brushing up against the truth*
> *and passing it by, then filling the void with associations. He knew*
> *that Freud knew nothing about wolves.*[29]

In *Cape Fear 2* the reconstructed, literate, man-made body curiously evokes that which is not-man: the Wolf. 'Wolf' and 'man' come together then in the figure of De Niro/Cady just as the terms are conjoined in a particular variant of the horror genre. The Wolf-Man is particularly at home in horror but he crops up, in various guises, all over the place. He looms large, for instance, in a genre adjacent to horror: psychoanalysis, and there is even a Mills & Boon novel called *The Wolf Man* about a sexy anthropologist in the Antarctic. Under the sign of the Big Bad Wolf (a sign which represents a particular variant of the Wolf-Man and indicates the transition from fairy tale to horror) two signifieds mesh: animality and performance. The wolf is frightening because he is 'ravening' and animalistic; but he is also duplicitous – that is to say, he plays a part, he acts, he pretends to be what he is not: 'Beware the false prophets which come to you in sheep's clothing, but inwardly they are ravening wolves'. And it is through his duplicitous performance that 'manliness' is evoked.

> *My sheep's clothing, kid. I grew it in the city of brotherly love.*
> *Back in the grove of academe, 'the wretched lecher,' they call me.*
> (Robert Mitchum in *Secret Ceremony*)

Animality and acting would seem to be incompatible concepts. Acting implies a human act, an act of signification, a fictional representation made possible by processes of culture, sociality, communication. Acting takes place in the realm of signs. Animality implies behaviour which lies outside the processes of culture, sociality and communication. When the two concepts are yoked certain transmutations occur, extending the discursive, for instance, into realms of horror, into cartoon worlds. In *The Night of the Hunter* and the two *Cape Fears*, in the migration of signs from Mitchum's embodiment to the skin of De Niro, the association of animality with the non-human serves to generate kinds of acting that are non-humanist and a certain register of cinematic performativity that we might call histrionic.

Histrionics

Over-the-top, excessive, theatrical, hammy – these are the connotations commonly evoked, nowadays, by the term 'histrionics'. And in any discussion of the cinema use of the term 'histrionic' automatically invokes acting. In using the term I intend to register something about film that is actorly but also to refer to more than the register of acting. Rather, we might say that in the histrionic a particular relationship exists between the actorly performance and the filmic; the film is conceived within the parameters of a dramaturgy that is

191

not centred on character, but that is nevertheless charged by an intense invest-ment in acting. The cinematic codes tend to be ostentatious and their very amplification owes something to the theatrical imagination; not theatre in terms of staging or even representation, but in terms of an enactment, a fictionality realised through a world that is acted out, in the process of acting up. This suggests the creation and mobilisation of a world that is fraught with surplus value, a world in which objects, scenic terrains, the cinematic land-scape itself, are charged as if by the supernatural, as if possessed.

'Histrionic' as an adjective denotes that which is 'theatrical in character or style, stagy', and, while retaining the term's theatrical derivation, its perti-nence to the realm of acting, I want to extend the term to designate a cinematic modality engaged in acting up. But in order to grasp the nature of this cinemat-ic theatricality it might be useful to look at what the term 'histrionic' signified in the period when cinema came into existence, borrowing many of its conven-tions from the stage. Roberta Pearson looks at the years 1908–13 as constitut-ing a transition in performance style, from the histrionic code to the verisimilar:

> The histrionic code is, in a sense, reflexive, referring always to the theatrical event rather than to the outside world . . . actors in most theatres performed in a self-consciously theatrical fashion, ostentatiously playing a role rather than pretending to be another person. Disdaining to mask technique in the modern fashion, actors proudly displayed their skills, always striving to create a particular effect. Performers, audiences, and critics all knew that a theatrical presentation was an artificial construct meant to bear little resemblance to any off-stage reality. Audiences and critics condemned as inadequate those who did not demonstrably act: the pleasure derived not from participating in an illusion but from witnessing a virtuoso performance.[30]

At the beginning of this period film acting was influenced by theatrical conven-tions, particularly those pertaining to melodrama and pantomime, whereas at the end of the period conventions for the mimesis of everyday life were stronger. As psychological causality became a more significant element in film narrative, the histrionic code was supplanted by what Pearson refers to as the 'verisimilar' code.[31] The verisimilar tended towards neutrality and involved, according to Edgar Morin (in *Les Stars*), a repression of the gestural quality of early acted cin-ema and a progressive domestication of the actor's body.[32] This development in silent cinema serves to illustrate clearly what is generally the case: that more real-istic acting is a result of a dramaturgy centred on psychological notions of char-acter. Occasionally the histrionic element in sound cinema, rather than disappearing or being confined to the realm of acting, is amplified, reverberating across a number of codes. *The Night of the Hunter*, as a theatricalisation of the cinema, seems to me just such a film.[33] Charles Laughton, the director, was best known as an actor: for embodying a particular type of quasi-grotesque: Quasi-modo, Henry VIII, Bligh, Nero, a hanging judge. Joseph Losey commented: 'There was a large element of ham in him of course, as there is in most great ac-tors.' However, his performance mode tended to unsettle the easy caricature of the ugly ogre. Laughton developed a quite distinctive performance idiolect, a repertoire of mannerisms and a studiously resonant, sometimes seductive, voice, all of which have elicited the ascription of ham. But for all his apparent hamminess, and despite the fact that he often appears as a fat and soft man, Laughton is in possession of a very 'decided body': his timing and his gestural precision contribute to an extravagant but affectively charged somatic performance, as can be seen in the drunk scenes of Hobson's Choice, for instance ('At times the film is like a silent comedy, with Laughton's funny walks, drunken antics and comic business underpinned by bassoon rumbles on the soundtrack.')[34] Although Laughton is able to transform himself for different parts, although he develops a repertoire of gestures for each character he plays, there is often more emphasis on the 'playing' than on the character. Jack Ravage captures something of this effect when he speaks of an 'abstraction' of dialogue. In his review of The Night of the Hunter on videotape, he wrote:

> Laughton was a man of words; his whole career was built around his own magnificent, resonant voice, and he worked hard to integrate the power of the spoken word in his film. At the risk of appearing stagy or over-acted, he chose to remain true to the overplayed regional dialect reproduced in his source. This abstraction of dialogue in the script and speaking styles remains consistent with the visual and auditory imagery.[35]

Laughton had originally studied acting in England at RADA and had been influenced by George Robey, to some the greatest music-hall star of his day. So, when he came to Hollywood in the 30s, Laughton brought an acting style that was, although very cinematic, not at all like 'Hollywood acting'. François Regnault, in 'Plaidoyer Pro Niro', an article on Robert De Niro which is also one of the most interesting pieces of writing on cinematic acting, discusses the way in which certain actors like Vittorio Gassman and Olivier appropriate the screen and the camera, transforming the rectangle into a space of play or performance; rather than complaining like some Jeremiahs that the cinema constrains, cuts and distorts them. These actors play to the camera and make it their own. He cites Josef von Sternberg's complaint that during the shooting of I Claudius Laughton systematically moved outside the lines marked out for the shot, to such an extent that cameras had to be set up in each corner in order to catch him: 'Can you believe', asks Regnault, 'that he had so little sense of the cinema, he, the director of The Night of the Hunter?'[36]

Brecht, with whom Laughton worked for two years in the USA (1944–5), described the in many ways most un-Brechtian Laughton in A Short Organum for the Theatre as exemplifying the principle of epic acting: 'This principle, that the actor appears on the stage in a double role, as Laughton and as Galileo; that the showman Laughton does not disappear in the Galileo whom he is showing; from which this way of acting gets its name of epic'.[37] In Building Up a Part: Laughton's Galileo, he describes how, because neither spoke the other's language fluently, they painstakingly went through the play, acting out. 'This system of performance-and-repetition had one immense advantage in that psychological discussions were almost entirely avoided,' and 'We were forced to do what better equipped translators should do too: to translate gests.'[38] Brecht was intrigued by Laughton's capacity to transmute 'physical pleasure' into 'intellectual creativeness';[39] but above all he seemed to admire Laughton for providing what was missing from contemporary theatre: 'what we may call a theatrical conception . . . a question of inventiveness'.[40] In the poem 'Letter to the Actor Charles Laughton' Brecht wrote:

> Again and again I turned actor, demonstrating
> A character's gestures and tone of voice, and you
> Turned writer. Yet neither I nor you
> Stepped outside his profession.[41]

Laughton's screen presence is remarkable for articulating a kind of non-realistic acting rare in Hollywood, for what David Thomson refers to as an 'unbridled rhetorical vitality'.[42] The techniques of exaggeration, of heightened effect achieved through gestural and somatic tropes, which Laughton employed as an actor are registered not just in the acting performances of *The Night of the Hunter* but in the filmic performance. A quasi-allegorical discourse is mobilised and animated by a deliberate and precisely mediated non-naturalism, so that the film sustains a high degree of histrionic intensity while nevertheless being very frightening and at moments lyrically bewitching.

The Night of the Hunter: An Island and a Stepping Stone

The opening credits are superimposed over a painted night sky, an impossibly and magically starry sky, reminiscent of Edmund Dulac's fairy-tale illustrations. The music, initially dramatic and foreboding, gives way to a lyrical lull-aby – 'Dream, Little One, Dream' – sung by a female chorus. As the credits end the starry sky fills the screen, the camera begins to move in as though attracted into the night by the brightest star, and then Lillian Gish's face emerges out of the sky. She begins speaking, almost directly into the camera: 'Now you remember children how I told you last Sunday . . .'. In a lap dissolve her face is replaced by a semicircle of children's faces, looking slightly upwards, beyond the frame; they appear like old-fashioned daguerrotypes, cut out and superimposed against this artificial sky.

> *Illusion Arts presented Marty with several different skies and asked 'Which sky do you want?'* (Freddie Francis)

We are warned by this opening (warned by the ominous opening music) that what is to follow is a dream fable. As it turns out there is no encapsulation of a dream within a film, or a story within a story, but rather the proliferation of a number of stories, fables, aphorisms, and the gradual unfolding of a living nightmare. In *Cape Fear 2* the first words are spoken by the 'little one', the pubescent Danny: 'My reminiscence. I always thought that for such a lovely river the name was mystifying . . . Cape Fear . . . When the only thing to fear on those enchanted summer nights was that the magic would end and that real life would come crashing in.' As the children drift down the river the sense of enchantment is checked by a tangible fear that real life, in the person of the preacher, will come crashing in. Danny has the last word, as well as the first:

194

'We never spoke about what happened. At least not to each other. Fear I suppose. But to remember his name or what he did would mean letting him into our dreams. And me, I hardly dream about him any more. Still, things won't be the way they were before he came, but that's all right because if you hang onto the past you die a little everyday, and for myself I know I'd rather live. The end.' Like *The Night of the Hunter*, *Cape Fear 2* is perhaps a 'bedside film' (*film de chevet*), 'a film, in other words, that one only leaves in the moment of plunging into the realm of dreams, that remains close when a nightmare arises, that one rediscovers in the morning, close by, on emerging from the sinister depths'.[43]

The starry dome that protects the children is also like a mantle of fear, a night-time image that persists during the day, that survives in later films. In *Cape Fear 2* there is an image of the Bowden house at night that might have been lifted from *The Night of the Hunter* and colourised: the sky is a deep velvety blue and enchantingly star-studded. By now we have become used to a range of extraordinary skies, all (except the first one of Max leaving the prison) serving as a backdrop to the Bowden home. When they return from the airport and Sam sneaks into his own house the sky is a boiling, turbulent red, like the sky in *GoodFellas* when the gangsters dig up the body they've earlier buried. The enchanted sky is given to us just after Kersek has reassured the family that even the Holy Ghost won't sneak in – it is as though this image is a histrionic monstration, on the one hand declaring that they are as safe as houses, home and hosed, and on the other presaging an 'unhousing', reminding us that this is not a night of domestic harmony, but the night of the hunter.

Love Travis, Part 4
From out of the darkness a figure loomed up and an arm lunged at me . . . Although in retrospect everything seems, at that moment, to freeze, in fact there was no hesitation, no time to think. A scream ripped through the night as I struck back, at the same time leaping backwards, out of his grip. A moment passed and then he backed off and ran, across the lawn of the neighbouring house, a pale figure, but huge, soon swallowed by the blackness. I kept screaming, both to scare him off and to attract attention, particularly the attention of the cops who were literally situated across the road. No response. Throat raw, I stopped and listened to the echo, a long, loud, and continuous scream, utterly anomalous and inhuman. I threw a few clothes on and dashed to the cop shop, which was empty and locked up. There was an emergency phone, so I called and they said they'd be there immediately. Twenty minutes later, I'm still waiting on the pavement, shivering, exposed, by the bright light over the station, to every Max Cady lurking in the shadows.

Film de Chevet
A similar warning, based on the resonance of an earlier image, is given to us in *The Night of the Hunter* itself. The first sequence of the film (after the prologue, that is, but Miss Rachel's voice serves as a crucial bridge: 'by their

fruit ye shall know them') is of a group of young boys playing by a barn and discovering a dead woman. All we see are her legs awkwardly twisted, one of her stilettos prised loose. Remember the ruby slippers and striped socks sticking out from under the house? The allusion here to *The Wizard of Oz* is remarkably economic: the black-and-white farmyard setting sub-liminally prepares us for a fairy story, for the shock of this image, for an 'unhousing', and a degree of perversity. In *The Night of the Hunter* a trans-ference too will take place, but not of the ruby slippers: here it is money that is transferred from the body of the father into the safekeeping of the children, into a hiding place in the body of the little girl's doll. But here neg-ative magic will be less efficacious. The image of the woman's legs is brutal-ly metonymic, in two senses: it stands for the entirety of the woman's body (which is a dead/murdered body), and it stands for the macabre repetition compulsion that drives Powell himself. Without any explanation this scene cuts to Powell driving along in his open car (against a back-projected coun-tryside) talking to the Lord:

What's it to be, Lord, another widow? Has it been six? Twelve? I disremem-ber. You say the word and I'm on my way. You always send me money to go forth and preach your Word. A widow with a little wad of bills hidden away in the sugar bowl . . . Sometimes I wonder if you understand. Not that you mind the killin's. Your book is full of killin's. But there are things you do hate, Lord: perfume-smellin' things, lacy things, things with curly hair.

This image, heralding the theme of sexual sadism, is to some degree explained by the scene which follows but it is nevertheless a bold monstrative move, not fully integrated into the narrative, a kind of full frontal which throws out to the audience threads of suspicion, provoking feelings of unease. But also it eschews characterisation in the usual sense, veering more towards an intima-tion of pathology that will drive the narrative, rather than planting a motiva-tion to be psychologically realised. The characters too will 'act out' in a manner appropriate to the film's histrionic modality.

The Badman Came Back

The starry sky is pretty, enchanting even, but the light it sheds is artificial. *The Night of the Hunter* is extraordinary for light and shadows: a film noir for children and a funereal fairy tale for adults.

> *Every day I consider something new about light, that incredible thing that can't be described. Of the directors I've worked with, only two have understood it: Orson Welles and Charles Laughton.*
> (Stanley Cortez)[44]

There is one scene involving light and shadow that crystallises *The Night of the Hunter*; it is the scene in which Powell enters the lives of the children. It is bedtime and Pearl asks her brother to tell her a story. 'Once upon a time . . . ,' he begins, and proceeds to tell a tale about a rich king in Africa who had a son and daughter (thus allegorising the family romance they are living out). 'And before long, the bad man came back.' He pauses, as if creating a space for the villain to make his entrance, and at this very moment a huge and menacing shadow appears on the wall behind him, a silhouette of the preacher in his hat. John cannot see the shadow which is behind him, but Pearl points and shrieks, and John crosses to the window to the accompaniment of loud dramatic chords. He looks out of the upper-storey window and we are given a high-angle point-of-view shot of the preacher as a small figure standing outside the house, under a street lamp. He turns away singing 'Leaning, leaning on the everlasting arms', and John remarks, 'It's just a man.'

Retrospectively we can see that the 'monstrous' silhouette was in fact an impossible shot, but nevertheless it retains an affective force, as a projection, linked to the threatening figure of the preacher. This scene has a sense of theatricality in its timing, in its staging of storytelling, in its announcement of 'the bad man', very much in the tradition of puppet theatre (Deleuze notes that Powell is 'dispossessed of his own movement of pursuit in favour of his silhouette as shadow theatre').[45] But the scene is also utterly cinematic. Its emotional impact is achieved though cinematic *mise en scène* and an articulation of light that pertains to cinematic space rather than stage space. The articulation of these elements is not merely pertinent; they actually create a space – a sense of three-dimensional space, and also a space of fiction, of fantasy. To draw attention to Powell's appearance here as a larger-than-life shadow is not to imply that he is a fantasy, or immaterial – he is after all embodied very solidly by Robert Mitchum – but rather, that his affect is phantasmic. We do not have to believe in him as a fully rounded character in order to believe in his lethal aggrandisement and the threat he poses. In short, we might say that although the shadow in this shot is logically impossible it is emotionally credible. Although the shot is monstrative it does not encourage distantiation exactly, but rather asks for a different sort of engagement, an engagement in the fiction, which nevertheless, as in distantiation, requires the mobilisation of a tension between proximity and distance, inside and outside, faith and belief, sensation and knowledge.

> *I find that I am far more affected by Borzage, with his mixture of humour and pathos, than I am by such purveyors of stark drama as Fritz Lang and Josef von Sternberg.* (Laughton)[46]

Customer's Moonlight

Laughton chose his cinematographer carefully. Stanley Cortez had been cinematographer on such films as *The Black Cat*, *The Magnificent Ambersons* and *Shock Corridor*, and he was more than delighted to work on the project: 'It was a field day for me in terms of extreme creativity that Charles appreciated.'[47] Much of his skill shows in the lighting and use of black-and-white, but also in the imaginative disposition of shots – often to do with perspective. During the river flight the children go ashore one night and hide in the hayloft of a barn; as they prepare to go to sleep the sound of the familiar hymn can be

History is Made at Night (Frank Borzage, 1937)

heard and the preacher is seen in the distance, a tiny figure on horseback, silhouetted against the night skyline:

> We built the whole set in perspective, between the hayloft and the fence, which was about 500ft away. The figure moving against the horizon wasn't Mitchum at all. It was a midget on a little pony. The lighting gave the illusion I needed; the feeling of mystery, of strange shadows.[48]

On other occasions a sense of flatness is conveyed by the sets and lighting which contributes to the discourse of superficiality. *Cape Fear 2*, although in Panavision and colour, is very meticulous in retaining the film noir elements of the first *Cape Fear*, but it does so in a histrionic register that owes much to the horror genre. In this respect, it seems as much a remake of *The Night of the Hunter* (and certainly a more attentive and imaginative reworking than the 1991 made-for-television version, directed by David Greene, with Richard Chamberlain dismally cast as the Preacher). Scorsese's choice of Freddie Francis as director of photography is in this respect significant:

> The main thing was Freddie's understanding of the concept of the Gothic atmosphere. . . . He knows the atmosphere that I want for this picture. He knows the lighting – whatever it takes to get that incredible, Gothic thriller

look. He understands the obligatory scene of a young maiden with a candle walking down a long hall towards a door. 'Don't go in that door!' you yell, and she goes in! Every time she goes in! So I say to him, 'This has to look like The Hall,' and he understands that.[49]

Francis directed a large number of horror films in the 60s and 70s for the Hammer and Amicus studios in Britain, and he shot the scary *The Innocents*; but, most significantly, he was camera operator on *The Tales of Hoffmann*, which Scorsese has described as a 'horror operetta' and 'a film of fantasy, and at times macabre fantasy'.[50] Allusions to the genre, and more specifically to Freddie Francis himself, have been woven through Scorsese's work. *GoodFellas*, for instance, includes an obscure number from the soundtrack of *Son of Dracula*, directed by Francis in 1974 (and produced by Ringo Starr). As well as being associated with the horror genre, he has a strong reputation as a black-and-white photographer, which is why Lynch used him on *The Elephant Man*, and Scorsese 'wanted to replicate the stark contrast and murkiness of the black and white photography'.[51] So here we have almost the reverse of the *Raging Bull* situation where the scarlet of the *Red Shoes* seemed to seep through, staining the black-and-white image; here, instead, the black-and-white of horror and film noir 'fogs' the colour image.

In the denouement, when Nolte and De Niro are slugging it out and the boat is breaking up, the lights are killed. 'How', asks Francis rhetorically, 'can I make this absolutely pitch black but so that everybody can see it?' The answer is customer's moonlight: 'It's just enough light so that the customers who pay to see this film can see what's going on. One keeps it shadowless as much as possible, but with just enough exposure to see what's going on.'[52]

A studio river, seen mainly at night, features in both *The Night of the Hunter* and *Cape Fear 2*. The Cape Fear River was created in a 90-foot-long water tank, housed within a sound stage, which was equipped with rocking gimbals for a mock-up of the boat, as well as wind and rain machines. The great white whale, a cinematic ghost of substance, returns: nearly forty years earlier Francis was second unit director on *Moby Dick* (John Huston, 1956), shooting the effects and models. The Ohio River was created in a tank on stage 15 at the Fox Studios and for the eerie underwater scene of the drowned Willa a tank at Republic was used (one that had previously been used for *Wake of the Red Witch*).

Francis was also responsible for introducing Scorsese to the Panatate, a Panavision gadget that permits 360-degree turns, and which can also be used as a 'sea head' to give the feeling of rocking back and forth on a boat: 'Marty gets very involved in these things; he used it in an unusual way, to produce some very dynamic shots, not just to give the sense of pitching and rolling, but to give the story a dynamic twist now and then.'[53] The turbulence which is operatically orchestrated in the denouement permeates the rest of the film, creating a sense of 'malevolent vitality'. The deictic effect of the opening camera movement in *After Hours* is, in *Cape Fear 2*, amplified to create a sustained histrionic address.

They Enact Themselves, They Invent Themselves

> *That life may be good to look at, its play must be well acted; but for that good actors are needed. All the vain are good actors: they act and they want people to enjoy looking at them; all their spirit is behind his will. They enact themselves, they invent themselves; near them I love to look at life: that cures my melancholy. Therefore I spare the vain, for they are the physicians of my melancholy and keep me attached to life as a play.* (Zarathustra according to Nietzsche)

Before he made *The Night of the Hunter*, Laughton looked at all of D. W. Griffith's films at the Museum of Modern Art. Critics generally point to Laughton's rendition of the pastoral landscape as evidence of the Griffith influence, but it seems to me that it is in his eliciting of a kind of acting associated with silent cinema that the real influence is felt. Lillian Gish is clearly cast and deployed as an icon rather than a character; her strong association with a particular cinematic period and genre of performance imbues the film with a decidedly histrionic ambience. As a persona, through the Griffith films particularly, she represents a sentimentalised version of virginal femininity, but in a decidedly melodramatic register.

To speak of Gish as an icon, rather than a character, is not to imply that she does not act; rather, it is to draw attention to the memories that accrue around her screen presence, the kind of plots in which her 'character' was implicated. Certainly she did act, but often in somatic rather than psychological ways. There is a story that Griffith's advice to her as a very young actress was to study small animals and birds and we can see this in her fluttering, in particular in the way she uses her hands, and in one of her most famous scenes: the broom cupboard scene from *Broken Blossoms*. In this scene she is trapped in a narrow and claustrophobic cupboard by her brutal stepfather, who is battering at the door, intent on killing her. In a state of traumatised panic she spins round and round, flailing and fluttering. Trauma, or we might call it a melodramatic plot moment, is registered not through nuanced facial expression, nor through a supernatural engagement with some prop (like Brando's engagement with Eva Marie Saint's glove), but in an excessively somatic gestus. (A possible allusion to this scene occurs in another highly histrionic text, *Whatever Happened to Baby Jane?*, when Joan Crawford, apparently at the mercy of her monstrous sibling, spins grotesquely round and round in her wheelchair, claustrophobically boxed in by the camera angles and movement.)

> *It is expressed . . . by the arm from the elbow to the fingers and depends entirely on rhythm – the gradual quickening of movement up to the pitch desired.* (Lillian Gish)[54]

In explaining how to produce a trauma effect, Gish conveys an allegiance to the gestural and to a non-psychological mimeticism. She deploys a lexicon of gestures, really quite a restricted range, but in varying combination they can produce quite different effects, often very emotionally charged. Her face is not particularly expressive, nor are her famous wide eyes especially nuanced, though they may appear so. This appearance is achieved not through the projection of inner feelings but through lexical combination. She opens her eyes wide to express a range of emotions, from horror through to wonder; the actual import of the facial expression is often determined in combination with the way she uses her hands. In *The Night of the Hunter* Gish's own fluttering is to a large extent stilled, but the emphasis given to gesture, to the affective potential of the hands, for instance, seeps through into the film by her very presence, and the iconic charge persists in the evocation of a melodramatic plot in which, again, the wicked stepfather is in murderous pursuit of innocent infants.

While evoking the iconic associations, Laughton, it seems to me, invokes the 'Gish image' in order to play something close to a macabre joke. She appears as the figure of maternal goodness, but the film is full of substitutions – these are not her 'real' children and she is not 'really' a mother (just as Powell is not 'really' a father, though he takes the place of the real father who was really a criminal). In some ways she is reminiscent of Mother Courage, with all the ambivalences of that figure, evoked particularly strongly in a scene towards the end where she is walking along, the children in her wake, and it is as though she is pulling the horde of children rather than the wagon.[55] But the register of her performance is, of course, more melodramatic. One of the most reproduced images from the film is of the pale, frail and wistful Gish on the rocking chair on her veranda, evoking her rocking of the cradle in *Intolerance*, but here she nurses a shotgun, a vengeful maternal figure, truly the 'steel butterfly', foreshadowing, perhaps, the avenging angel of slasher movies.[56]

There is a tension between the character, Miss Rachel, and the actor Lillian Gish, and perhaps also between the Lillian Gish of the 50s and the Lillian Gish of the early years of the century. She is enacting 'herself', her silent screen persona, but there is also an element of invention, a fictional elaboration that elicits a certain kind of viewing engagement. The histrionic mode of *The Night of the Hunter* involves a putting-into-fiction of the body, a processing of the fictional body. This is not to imply that the body is a fiction (a site of untruth, merely a discursive formation); it is rather to indicate a mode of acting in which the process of the fictional body is pronounced; it is to refer to a certain regime of storytelling, of the fantastic, in which the nexus between character and actor as played out on the body is pivotal. In the cinema there is always a slippage, a misfit, between character and actor: the actor's body is either hidden beneath the character's body – subsumed, that is, by the sovereignty of character – or the character is subsumed by the actor's body.

> *The character reaches us as a bodily effect in the image. He may have been long worked over, defined, constituted in a script, but it is not the order of investigation but the order of exposition that is enounced in a film: first to appear will be the body, the body as an empty mask, and the character will only appear later and bit by bit as effects of this mask, effects in the plural, changing, unstable, never quite achieved, thwarted, incomplete.* (Jean-Louis Comolli)[57]

If there is always a slippage, the audience also always knows that a game is being played; but this knowledge is often boring and routine, particularly where the presence of the body becomes automatic and unadventurous. Comolli argues that the fictional stakes are raised the more we know (that the identity between the body of the actor and that of the character is precarious) and that it is this dynamic of proximity and distance, of complicity and criticism, that produces 'the mechanism of denegation at its regime of highest intensity. The more one knows the more difficult it is to believe and the more it is worth managing to do so.'

An American Cinematographic Bestiary

'All the people in The Night of the Hunter,' writes Marguerite Duras, 'the children, the parents, the murderer, the old woman are perfect prototypes of an American cinematographic bestiary.'[58] She finds the film utterly predictable, a 'standard consumer product', until the point where Mitchum arrives at Miss Rachel's house when all moral judgments are suspended and a 'miracle' takes place, at which point 'It ceases to be the classic fable of fifty years of American cinema.' The bestiary is a telling analogy but, rather than valuing it pejoratively, I would argue that it serves to mobilise an allegorical dimension that is quite eccentric in relation to Hollywood orthodoxy; it institutes, from the very first moments, a tension between character and actor, person and type, fiction and fable, the operatic and quotidian, and in the process elaborates a non-humanist yet highly affective drama. If the 'dome of stars' sequence delineates, as I have argued, a kind of cinematic bestiary, in which the Mitchum character takes pride of place, I think it is possible to conceive of the entire film in these terms. The real mystery of the 'miracle' is, as Duras indicates, the transformation that takes place. But rather than seeing this moment as transforming the entire film (and fifty years of Hollywood cinema) I am interested in how the scene is set up, in how it is that we believe in this fiction, even though we know (that these are figures from a bestiary). In other words, what takes place in the transaction of viewing; what is it that is transformed? How do images, conceived somewhere between fiction and representation, solicit our belief, assault our senses, affect our understanding of the world?

If character reaches us as a bodily effect in the image, what do we make of the Mitchum character, how do we apprehend the spectacle of a histrionic villain played by a matinée idol? How is it that this Wolf-Man (plucked from a standard bestiary), tattooed and supremely superficial, might get under our skin, solicit belief, provoke a dynamic connection between reading and palpability?

The screen persona and acting style that Mitchum had established prior to The Night of the Hunter hardly qualified him as a histrionic performer. If anything, the converse: understated, laconic, nonchalant, a laid-back ladies' man. In casting Mitchum, Laughton (I imagine) read these characteristics as a cluster of signs, as constituting a performance idiolect rather than revealing an actorly essence. In Mitchum's very reserve he must have sensed a 'decided body', a certain vanity in the Nietzschean sense which qualified him as among those who 'enact themselves . . . invent themselves'. In casting Mitchum he seized the opportunity to exploit the slippage that occurs between actor and character, to focus that slippage conceptually as a tension between criminal and star, and, performatively, as the problem (to borrow Comolli's phrase) of 'a body too much'.

The presence of Mitchum's body is never automatic or unadventurous in *The Night of the Hunter*, a film in which the process of the fictional body is pronounced. There are many ways in which our credulity is stretched, in concert with a solicitation of belief, but there are two avenues which strike me as pivotal. A pantomimic imagination and an exploitation of vocal qualities – two impulses that might seem at odds, since pantomime is often conceived of as the art of silence – conjoin to articulate the mechanism of denegation ('at its regime of highest intensity').[59]

> *There's no mystery to acting. But you've got to have the basics.*
> *It's a matter of timing, talent, mimicry.* (Robert Mitchum)[60]

Mimicry: this is one of the characteristics that most writers on Mitchum comment on, and when he delivered the Guardian Lecture at the National Film Theatre in London in 1984, Mitchum reportedly provided 'a series of superbly mimicked portraits of those he had worked with . . . portraits [which] had the same accuracy, economy and flair as the best verse . . . And he even ended up with an uncannily accurate Joan Collins impersonation.'[61] The ability to mimic is a skill closely related to, and sometimes derived from, the art of pantomime. James Naremore discusses *The Night of the Hunter* in the context of the pantomime tradition, and its occasional persistence in talking movies:

> Among these later allusions to pantomime acting, Robert Mitchum's performance in *The Night of the Hunter* (1955) deserves special mention: as Harry Powell, a demented backwoods preacher who might have learned his mannerisms from a vulgarised Delsartean textbook, Mitchum is both comical and terrifying; his honeyed charm and crocodile tears, his booming voice and almost dancerly poses, all these things are a clever fusion of melodrama and expressionism.[62]

The mimetic here operates in a different way from that of method realism: various gestural and somatic tropes function as signs not to express interiority but as visible indices of typage, as clues to a range and register of action. In *The Night of the Hunter* Mitchum exploits elements of his performance idiolect in the service of a pantomimic inflection, a dramatic discourse of superficiality. His familiar 'tics' – the way he curls down his mouth, inflects his eyebrows, tilts his head, clenches the jaw, holds his shoulders – are put into quotation marks, deployed with economy and flair, to suggest a pantomime villain. His performance also alludes to the horror film in, for instance, his adoption of a Frankenstein walk, arms held out in front (in the cellar scene), in his grimaces, and in various animalistic impersonations (the very paradox of impersonating an animal in itself a significantly generative device).

A mystery persists: locating Mitchum's performance within the aegis of the pantomimic does not explain how it is that we might believe in his affective monstrosity. Moreover, given our knowledge of his persona as 'seductive', his pantomimic enactment might easily engender nothing but incongruity and comedy (and failed comedy at that). But Powell is not a silent mimic. He speaks in the familiar and distinctive Mitchum voice, honeyed, drawling, full of mocking self-conscious irony, evoking a vague insolence, and above all an insistently sardonic quality. It is a voice that takes a distance even as it seduces; in many respects it is a narrating voice, a storytelling voice. Some of his most memorable roles – in *Out of the Past* and *Pursued* – remain in the memory precisely as a vocal trace, the distinctive voice-over still resonating, its meaning meandering still these many years later. In these films the voice-over introduces a degree of complexity into the narrative, not just by complicating the authorial position and temporal structure, but by exploiting the tension between proximity and distance, belief and knowledge, through a fraying device. The hermetic status of the fictional world begins to fray at the edges when one of the characters contained within that world starts to comment upon it, and to address the viewer, or reader, or fictional persona out there, beyond the frame. These issues are usually dealt with under the rubric of narrativity, but they may pertain in interesting ways to performance. The narrating voice-over is decidedly cinematic, but it also participates, in the way that it privileges the delivery of a speech, in a theatrical modality. It institutes not so much a separation between body and voice as, within a fictional context, a tension, a fraying of the seamless edge that unites actor and character.

Powell is adept at storytelling, at concocting fictions, at impersonations (his chief duplicities are a pretension to seduce when he is actually propelled by an abhorrence of female sexuality, and a pretension to fatherhood when he is in fact an evil surrogate or stepfather). In this film filled with storytelling, Powell's impersonations are flamboyantly histrionic. His sardonic inflection of the role alerts us to the process of character construction and to the deployment of character as a site for the enactment of phantasmic scenarios. Mitchum, in *The Night of the Hunter*, takes evident delight in storytelling and in impersonation; the film declares its method to be histrionic by showing histrionics in action. The device, however, does not produce distantiation exactly (though clearly for many viewers it elicits a detached critique); rather, the actor's delight in storytelling, in fictionality, in being someone else, can be transferred to an audience as a delight in being taken out of oneself, rather than discovering 'home truths', as it were. The delight in villainy is a special (though not entirely unusual) case, but one in which we can observe this delight in an actor, in a performance, being passed on to an audience, and there transformed, from delight into delighted horror, say. Think for a moment of actors classically adept at histrionic menace, such as Vincent Price and Peter Lorre. But what is it, I still want to know, that makes *The Night of the Hunter* so menacing?

Thou Shalt Not Touch

We never become entirely accustomed to Mitchum-as-Powell, never completely comfortable with his fictional identity; we don't forget, in other words, that this body is being conjured into presence before our very eyes. And perhaps one might think that what follows, axiomatically, is that we are not touched by the drama. Yet it is precisely in the arena of bodily discomfort that a drama about touch is played out, that cinematic tactility is sensationally enacted.

Hands matter in *The Night of the Hunter*. Powell wants to lay hands on the hidden money, though to say this is to skew the emphasis somewhat: it is clear from the beginning that what matters more than the money is the particular pattern, or macabre repetition compulsion, of marriage and murder. In his guise as preacher Powell repeatedly performs a ham routine by entwining his hands inscribed with 'good' and 'evil' and acting out a grand theological struggle. The crassness of this representation is often criticised, but what it alerts us to is that the film is a drama about touch, rather than primarily an allegory of good and evil.

> *A hand fills the frame, a hand on which Love is written.*
> *It takes hold, by the handle, of an open switchblade.*

It is this conjunction of love and laceration that charges the film. Powell seduces Willa by offering love and sexual fulfilment, but on their wedding night he turns on her viciously, making a ferocious display of disgust, and delivering a bellicose lecture on purity. Her murder is depicted mostly in long shot (in their bedroom, an A-frame composition reminiscent of the nave of a church), his stylised movements orchestrated to a waltz tempo on the soundtrack. Poised over her, gripping the knife, he lifts his arm. In close-up she looks up, her throat bared. And then: a vertical wipe to the children sleeping.

> *Look fella, just one thing I want to tell you. Don't ever touch me. Because*
> *you touch me I'll knock you down. I can't stand to have fellows touch me.*
> (John Wayne)

Joseph Losey, who in 1968 was to cast Mitchum in *Secret Ceremony* (a highly histrionic film which is nevertheless absolutely economic), has some interesting speculations on Mitchum, whom he discusses in the context of 'men who wear their cocks on their sleeve', actors who protest their masculinity and their machismo, like John Wayne. He tells a story about when he met Wayne and they were discussing doing a film, and Wayne said, 'Look fella . . .'[63]

Powell finds women literally untouchable. As performed by Mitchum he is like a dormant explosive, his body a threat. 'Touch me and I'll explode' is his somatised message. This is the significance of his decided body; we can sense, even in his slackness, his distance, his acting up and his self-irony, the potential for focused brutality and a murderous modelling of energy. That potential is cinematically realised in the vertical wipe. The cut across the image is metonymic of the slashing knife, and the knife itself takes the place of a caress. What happens between shots is palpable: I feel that wipe; am touched by the slash, by some unwelcome and cutting knowledge.

A bodily knowing rather than specular recognition, a knowledge not about Powell as a character, but about masculinity as a masquerade. Powell's pretences (the pretension to seduction and to paternity) are at once performative and constitutive of a certain masculine identity. In Mitchum's playing a kind of abstraction occurs, or distillation, of a pathology: the pathology is constituted in the very process of performance. Seduction, perhaps, is always duplicitous, a game, and seldom seriously sinful, but in *The Night of the Hunter* the duplicity of seduction is indeed venal. Here, where seduction seems to be motivated by desire, it is in fact impelled by disgust: an apparent attraction turns out to be abhorrence; a seeming impulse to sensuality is manifested as a lacerating and lethal touch. None of this, however, is enigmatic – Mitchum's delineation is hardly well rounded, subtle or deep, and we may not believe in Powell as a character; but we might well be engaged by the drama of the masculine masquerade. While the histrionic method refrains from humanising the pathological, it does more than exhibit – it enacts the masquerade, exploiting a capacity both to seduce and menace, playing upon a tension between proximity and distance, delight and horror.

For many critics *The Night of the Hunter* is a regressive tract. Jacques Goimard describes it as 'a poetic universe of regression' in which the boy 'will never become a man. Undoubtedly, these Americans will always be grown children.' Leo Braudy argues: 'By having the silent-star Gish defeat the 40s and 50s star Mitchum, it seems to reject the world in which Mitchum's personality took shape and to return instead to an Eden of aesthetic innocence.'[64] It's true, as is often pointed out, that Miss Rachel's house is a house without any adult males. But it has less to do with a yearning for the pre-Oedipal and much more to do with the difficulties and dangers of 'normal' heterosexuality. The film inaugurates a family romance, but never resolves it. The father (both the 'true' and 'false' father) remains a criminal and is executed twice over. The fears it mobilises may be manifested in infantile form but they are fears that persist. 'The poetic universe' is not, however, exclusively morbid. A fictional space is opened up, histrionically, for regression and for transformative contemplation, a space not always allowed by naturalistic performance, nor by the exigencies of everyday life. 'Near [vain actors], I love to look at life: that cures my melancholy,' says Nietzsche. If identity is performed, then performances that engage us as performance are more exhilarating, more critically acute, than those that are consummately mimetic. Good actors remind us that action transforms, that the world does not stand still. So, even while I may be cut to the bone by Mitchum's performance, there is a curious sense in which he becomes the physician of my melancholy.

Love Travis, Part 5

I call again. Okay, okay, says the voice at the other end. So then the cop turns up, bored, sceptical, irritated by this run-of-the-mill complaint. He warns me about being more responsible and delivers a lecture on security as we walk around the house and survey the damage done to the window frame. There was a screen on the window so that you could slide the glass open, have some fresh air and still be relatively secure. The noise I had heard was the intruder unscrewing and dismantling the screen. After the lecture he says, 'Well, I'll be off now.' I ask him to stay while I make a phone call to friends in the area. I don't intend to spend the night in this house alone. In a police-issue tone of voice, clearly deployed for reassuring hysterics, he says, 'Don't worry about it, this sort of thing never happens around here.' I insist that he stay while I make arrangements for the night. He looks at his watch, looks at me. His uniform is dark blue, but in this light it looks black. I go to the bedroom to fetch my bag, in which there are phone numbers. But it's not where I left it. It's nowhere. Disappeared. He scribbles a quick description of what was in the bag, looks at his watch again, and says that duty calls. As he walks out into the night he leaves the front door open and calls over his shoulder, 'Don't worry, it won't happen again.'

When and how did he get into the house? When I was waiting at the cop shop? Is that when he took it? Did he watch and wait, anticipating this as a possible scenario? Perhaps it worked before: the solitary woman fleeing to the cop shop, finding it shut up, waiting, easily watched. Or had he already been in the room earlier, when I was in bed, when I'd dozed off? And had he been watching all evening, seen J leave, waited until all the lights were off, except one, the bedroom light?

A Body Too Much

Powell returns. In *Cape Fear 1* Mitchum quotes his own impersonation of evil in *The Night of the Hunter*, and although his Max Cady is less histrionic than Powell and than De Niro's Cady (the film in general is more conventional – shaped, that is, by the conventions of genre and realism) he is similarly rendered as a malevolent force, not through psychological elaboration but through bodily presence. His casual brutality is laced with a thoroughgoing contempt, signalled in his swagger, the way he wears his panama hat, sucks on a cigar, thrusts his chest forward. From Powell he inherits a sexual sadism made manifest in a drama of tactility, in a gestus repeated with variation: before he enters the superior court in the opening scene, to confront Sam Bowden, he crushes a smoldering cigar out in his fist. Later, when he is terrorising the women on the houseboat, he crushes a raw egg in his fist, smears and wipes it over Peggy's chest. And finally, covered in mud and slime, he struggles to destroy Sam with his bare hands. From Powell, too, he inherits a sardonic distance, rendered somewhat more contemporary as in his quip to Bowden – 'Give my love to the family, counselor.' Although he doesn't, in 1962, infiltrate the Bowdens' house (and dreams) in the way he later will, he nevertheless has a habit of materialising almost out of thin air in the most unlikely places. In the most suspenseful sequence of the film he stalks Nancy, the daughter, in her school and his menacing presence is indicated mainly by torso shots so that for much of the time we do not know, for sure, whether it is him or not. This sequence will become the theatre seduction scene in *Cape Fear 2*, apparently quite transformed; but various strands cohere, condensations occur, recur.

When Robert De Niro plays Max Cady there is certainly a body too much, the performative allusions and quotations proliferate. For those who have seen the earlier film there are, on the simplest level, two bodies bearing the same name: Max Cady, Robert Mitchum, Robert De Niro are all names circulating. Also, however, there is Preacher Powell ghosting the text, and the phantasmic bodily presence of Charles Laughton. If *Cape Fear 2* is charged by the theatrical imagination, if it has a particular investment in the actorly, that investment is dispersed

207

beyond the body image of the actors and through the text. If you watch *Cape Fear 2* back-to-back, sequentially, with the other two films, the credit sequence is particularly startling. The torso that is reflected in the water reverberates; the way it stands, the way the hands are held, is very reminiscent of Mitchum. This is probably a trick of the imagination, a mnemonic antic, but it is as though the first Max Cady returns from the depths of the waters, rising up to haunt us again, the shimmering spectre made solid in the inscribed body of De Niro.

Rattling with Discourse and Dice

> *It is my favourite malice and art that my silence has learned not to betray itself through silence. Rattling with discourse and dice, I outwit those who wait solemnly: my will and purpose shall elude all those severe inspectors.* (Zarathustra according to Nietzsche)

Max Cady is loud, like the Hawaiian shirts he wears, retained perhaps, along with a few ebulliently obnoxious characteristics, from Jimmy Doyle's wardrobe in *New York, New York*. His bad taste is an affront to discretion and to the niceties of middle-class values – not just his flashiness but also his literal loudness, his coarse laughter, his wolf-like leering, his fuming and fulminating casuistry. Take the scene in the movie theatre. Cady sits in the front row blowing great gusts of cigar smoke at the screen and laughing raucously, loudly, and continuously. He succeeds in obscuring the picture and drowning out the soundtrack, both for the Bowdens and for us. This is a very irritating, but not unsuccessful, tactic as he manages to draw attention to himself at the same time (in the same act) as throwing up a smokescreen. *Cape Fear* similarly draws attention to its own histrionic tactics. The movie that is affording Cady such pleasure is *Problem Child*, a grotesquely screwball inversion of the family romance. But his pleasure is surely derived as much from his 'winding and wounding' of the Bowden family as from the movie itself. In *Cape Fear 2* much is made of theatricality, with an emphasis not just on performance but also on the context of reception. This encounter between different sorts of viewers – the Cady-viewer and the domestic-unit-viewer – foregrounds and exploits a tension between the domestic and the theatrical. It does so by putting into operation a knowing domestication of theatricality; most entertainment takes place in the Bowden house and particularly the bedroom, via video, walkman and television. The other major theatrical venue, the school theatre where Cady masquerades as drama teacher, also implicates the domestic and familial in the theatrical by its Little Red Riding Hood scenario.

In the theatricalisation of his desire Max Cady rails histrionically against the domestic. One of the most insistent examples of the domestication of acting (that is, making it seem homely, natural, a type of acting that 'speaks for itself') is the so-called Method. And De Niro is often situated as a Method actor. He has indeed turned in some performances which correspond to those Method tropes deployed to evoke (through the presence of a silent or inarticulate hero) a rich interiority. But the loudness of his performance in *Cape Fear 2* suggests something other than interiority. It is much more operatic, but in the sense conveyed by Gertrude Stein: 'There are all these emotions lying around. No reason why we shouldn't use them.'[65]

> With Bob, it happens a lot in costuming, in trying on clothes. We just hang around, we start talking. He feels one thing, and he puts on a shirt or puts on a pair of pants. Those become our character discussions. (Scorsese)[66]

Just as, in trying on Jimmy Doyle's shirts, he enters into another skin and assumes certain characteristics, so he tries out and uses a range of emotions. As he quotes Mitchum so he reanimates some animus rather than character *per se*. In the Steinian approach emotions and feelings are given priority over character, and are to be used, rather than owned. The putative Method actor, on the other hand, arrives at authentic characterisation through owning his or her feelings.

De Niro is not, of course, a modernist in the Steinian sense, but neither is he narrowly Method (or at least his performances range widely, not only in terms of character, but also modality). His history as a performer has incorporated not so much a methodical naturalism as allusions to, and even a kind of homage to, the 'classical' Method. He has quoted Brando twice: in *Raging Bull* he does the 'I coulda been a contender' speech from *On the Waterfront*, and in *The Godfather Part II* he plays the young Vito Corleone – that is to say, the young Brando. This is an extraordinarily interesting performance for the way in which De Niro imbricates a degree of mimicry, and the pleasure afforded by the film is partly derived from the performance, the replaying, the re-enactment; from the sense, also, of newness, of something which escapes the banality of literal repetition. But in order to quote, and for us to recognise the allusions, the 'original' (in this case the Brando performance idiolect, the Method embodied) needs to be distinctive and quotable.[67]

There is a paradox here, embodied by Brando, in that the best Method actor is commonly said to be he who appears not to act, and yet so many assumed or self-professed Method adherents turn in highly mannerist performances. In fact the Method is a mythology – that is to say, the notion of a unified theory producing a distinctive corpus of practitioners is clearly untenable. On the other hand, as a concept it is alive, ubiquitously invoked to summon an aura and sanction a vague though doggedly repetitive notion of authenticity. A rhetoric of naturalism characterises discourses on and about the Method, but is not always easily discernible in the actual practice of so-called Method actors.[68] I want to focus on one aspect of this rhetoric, on the paradox of the method embodied, in order to summon a performative history that precedes and ghosts the text of *Cape Fear 2*.

One of the tropes that emerged in 50s Hollywood was that of silence, articulated as an obsessive thematic of intense feelings trapped inside an inarticulate male persona. The incommunicado attitude of the new rebels was quite different from the kind of stoical studied silence of, say, Bogart.[69] The difficulty with speech, manifested in silence or in truculent muttering, in tortured somatisations and compulsive speech repetitions, began to function as an index of interiority, in a paradigm where interiority was aligned with depth, significance, truth. And in the service of such a thematic, the new stars developed a repertoire of bodily gestures designed to indicate strong feelings, a 'true' and primary interiority, aligned with a newly authentic masculinity. The somatic insistence of this new performative mode marked these acting personae out from the classic Hollywood style of masculinity exemplified by figures like Bogart, Wayne, Cooper. Actors such as Brando and Dean were also instrumental in the development of a new articulation of violence: emotional violence, manifested in 'a virile anger that comes from the heart'.[70] These heroes had 'emerged', to borrow a phrase from Eric Rohmer (describing *Rebel without a Cause*), 'from inauthenticity'.[71]

Now while De Niro, as is well known, adopts some Method modes of preparation – losing weight (*Bloody Mama*), gaining weight (*Raging Bull*), learning to play the saxaphone (*New York, New York*) – and also on occasion adopts the 'signs' of Method masculinity, he also confounds the particular kind of isomorphism that the Method invokes between interior and exterior, and between actor and role. Rather than indicating deep inner feelings and a sensitive soul, his silence, while not exactly Bogartian, certainly gives the impression of being more studied, more of an enactment than in itself a signification. He adopts some of the laconic, sardonic tropes of an earlier Hollywood masculinity, and yet has learnt from the Method boys a rhetoric of the body. Perhaps it is his more catholic and inventive rhetorical ploys that incite an uneasiness, and sometimes hostility, in critics who try to situate him squarely within a Method tradition. Hal Hinson, for instance, is awed by De Niro's capacity to disappear completely into his role, but complains of 'something niggardly and unsatisfying' in his work. 'There's a rigid, unyielding quality in his style as an actor,' he writes, 'an unwillingness to express anything below a character's surface. De Niro discourages empathy and he appears to be uninterested in communicating the inner life of a character in a way that reveals motive.'[72] Virginia Wexman, who writes interestingly on how in recent years the influence of the Method on the creation of male personae has been to some extent reformulated, describes De Niro (along with Dustin Hoffman and Al Pacino) as 'projecting a truculent incommunicativeness that pointedly excludes the audience'.[73]

What these criticisms point to is a certain resistance in De Niro (to the Method isomorphisms) and to a tendency that is more Nietzschean. His performances, like Laughton's, do not console;[74] often his persona is evidenced in a modality 'rattling with discourse and dice' rather than in verbal reticence, and when he is silent or inarticulate there is a sense that he is waiting 'to outwit those who wait solemnly'. He frequently appears, particularly in his films with Scorsese, to relish the very game of performance, to derive and convey a sense of fun in 'making things stylised'.

> *I'll do anything that he wants just to see if it'll work.*
> *It's a lot of fun trying to make something stylised.*
> (De Niro, on working with Scorsese)[75]

Blood Is Not an Abstraction; De Niro Is

One of the high points of *Mean Streets* is Johnny Boy's monologue about the tie, a monologue that simultaneously bears the marks of a certain naturalism (inconsequential raving that feels fairly improvised) and the marks of stylised performance. A very young De Niro plays the incipiently psychotic petty hood Johnny Boy, who is put on the spot to explain why he has not paid his debts. He begins a long and rambling shaggy dog tale about how he was so depressed, about this and that and always being in debt, so he had to buy a tie, and then there was no money to pay his debts. His magnificently loud new tie (I always imagine that he picked it up from Mo/Thelma Ritter, who hawks 'poisonality neckwear' in *Pickup on South Street*) becomes at once the focus and a marvellous distraction. The tie is an aid, but not a super-natural object like Eva Marie Saint's glove; it is more like a visible pretext. There is no music (in a film where music is almost ubiquitous) while he delivers this speech, almost like a stand-up routine. Even while we are aware that he is putting up a smokescreen we are engaged, and delighted, by the performance. We are shown the character Johnny Boy 'trying it on', putting on an act, at the same time as De Niro is showing us that he likes to act, that this is a performance.[76] It is as though he is saying, 'It is my favourite malice and art that my silence has learned not to betray itself through silence.'

> What ought it [acting] to be like, then? 'Witty. Ceremonious. Ritual. Spectator and actor ought not to approach one another but to move apart. Each ought to move away from himself. Otherwise the element of terror necessary to all recognition is lacking.' (Brecht)[77]

Johnny Boy is the first in a line of Scorsesean heroes – Rupert Pupkin in *King of Comedy*, Tommy in *GoodFellas* – who rattle with discourse and dice. By the time this figure reaches its apotheosis in Max Cady the joke has turned very sour. But these figures, in their histrionic dimension, have always served to remind us that the theatricalisation of desire is potentially violent, and that the impulse which tells us 'I like to act', which entertains, may also represent an overreaching will to power and rageful recrimination against a world (or audience) that does not accommodate violent desires. Think of Tommy in that knife-edge moment in *GoodFellas*: he tells jokes, has the diegetic audience (and ourselves, albeit guardedly and uneasily) laughing with him, and then suddenly turns. 'I'm funny, how? I mean, funny like I'm a clown? I amuse you? I make you laugh? I'm here to fucking amuse you? What do you mean funny? Funny, how? How am I funny?' His questions are threats and as he continues the atmosphere thickens. In the flash of a smile humour has turned to violence.

For some critics this impulse goes so over the top in *Cape Fear 2* that De Niro loses all credibility. Hoberman, for instance, says that it is 'a good deal more spectacular than terrifying, and somewhat less than the sum of its parts. Blood is not an abstraction; De Niro is.'[78] Indeed, he is an abstraction, but in the way that Laughton is, and Mitchum in *The Night of the Hunter* and *Cape Fear 1*: not a well-rounded character but a distillation of horror. Jenny Diski argues that 'When De Niro becomes impossibly inhuman we lose the benefits of both the old simplicity and the new complexity . . . in the end it's clear he really resides on Elm Street, and none of us lives there.'[79] To which I can only say: oh yeah?

Love Travis, Part 6

I returned to the house on the coast after spending a few days and nights away, at home, in Sydney, sleeping, changing locks, getting new keys cut. Cut your losses and run, someone said, the house will be haunted. But rationality and bravura reigned. I won't be scared off, I came here to write and that's what I'll do, and after all nothing much happened. I got a fright. But I'm safe, intact. Think about what's happened to other women, what might have happened. For the next six weeks I kept repeating this, and during the day it seemed moderately true. But every night I'd lie awake, listening, to voices whispering, conjuring images, asking: what if?

> *Like Irena in The Cat People 'I wake in the night and the tread of their feet whispers in my brain . . . I have no peace for they are in me . . . in me . . .'*
> *In the house?*

People came to stay, intermittently, bringing company and offerings to keep the demons at bay. J brought me Mio as protection. In Sydney, Mio is a ferocious little watchdog but here she dropped her guard, declared a holiday, wagged her tail at every stranger who came to the door. At night when I imagined a Cady had infiltrated the house I would hear her virtual howling, 'horrible high-pitched howls', and I would dream of walking into the kitchen to see a pot boiling on the stove.

That's Funny . . . You're Not the Drama Teacher, Are You?

All the vain are good actors. Max enacts himself most perfectly, invents himself with the most consummate virtuosity, as the drama teacher. He calls Danny to introduce himself and arrange a meeting. The camera travels in close-up from the cutesy pink phone onto and over Danny's body: she is sitting up in bed in her nightdress – and up to her face. Cut to Max's neat and sterile room, where the camera moves over weights and bars to finally locate Cady, hanging upside down and exercising as he talks. He uses his voice – warm, sympathetic, familiar – to beguile the young girl, adopting the rhetoric of New Age counselling – 'All that negativity, you can use that' – and he deals his winning card by playing her Aretha Franklin's 'Do Right Woman – Do Right Man'. As her face lights up with delight he declares, 'Now you can trust in me 'cos I'm the Do-Right Man.'

> *Children know something they can't tell; they*
> *like Red Riding Hood and the wolf in bed!* (Djuna Barnes)[80]

The next day Danny makes her way down an eerily deserted corridor to the school theatre. On the phone Cady has alerted her to a relocating of the class meeting: 'It's been changed to the theatre. I mean what better place for drama, right?' This is a declaration to us, the audience, rather than to Danielle directly, that he is preparing for another staging of desire. We know that the fantasies that fuel Max are uniformly violent, sexually aberrant and to do with

212

subjugation, and so our expectations are primed for the worst, even more so when we remember *Cape Fear 1* and the suspenseful and ominous sequence in the school.

But De Niro's Cady is cognisant of the real and performs a theatricalisation which entertains the other, which elicits and plays with their desire. The scene which follows is both excruciating and alarmingly fascinating. Danny enters the dimly lit theatre and looks down over the raked seats to the stage in which a set is lit up, a fairy-tale setting, evoking grandmother's small house in the woods. And in the house a figure waits. As she makes her way onto the stage, she becomes a player in a scenario we already know. Cady begins his seduction by offering her a toke on his joint, engages her in discussion about *Look Homeward Angel*, which he designates a *roman à clef* and remarks: 'You can't escape your demons just by leaving home.' The talk turns to Henry Miller and then to adulthood. 'Your parents don't want you to achieve adulthood. That's natural. They know the pitfalls of adulthood', and they 'deflect their anger on to you.' Slowly it dawns on her.

> *Where are you from?*
> *I'm from the Black Forest.*
> *That's funny . . . You're not the drama teacher are you?*
> *Maybe I'm the Big Bad Wolf.*

She is distraught by the thought that he killed the dog, but he convincingly reassures her that he would never do such a thing, would never hurt her, and in fact has come to forgive and save her parents. Then he says, 'Do you mind if I put my arm around you?' His tactic here is very different from that adopted in his approach to Lori, but we have witnessed how this earlier approach culminates in a savage rape and cannibalistic element as he bites a chunk out of her cheek. So when he caresses Danny's face and passes his thumb around her mouth, slips it into her mouth, we hold our breath.

> *She [Little Red Riding Hood] seems intrigued by the situation, attracted and repelled at the same time. The combination of feelings her face and body suggest can best be described as fascination.*[81]

Certainly Juliette Lewis evidences this combination of feelings, but she surely, sucking his thumb, mirrors a possible audience response. I find myself fixated by this scene, at once repulsed and fascinated (fascinated, I think, by my own repulsion). She is at once an infant revelling in orality and an adult, also revelling in the oral but in a scenario where gratification is less clearly located, less simply to do with satisfaction.

Bettelheim, in *The Uses of Enchantment*, argues that the threat of being devoured is the central theme of Little Red Riding Hood, and points out that a sexual meeting between the two has to precede her being 'eaten up'. 'The wolf', he says, 'is the externalisation of the badness the child feels when he goes contrary to the admonitions of his parents and permits himself to tempt,

213

or to be tempted, sexually.' According to Freud, the individual at the cannibal-istic stage wants to destroy the object by devouring it, but also wishes to pre-serve and incorporate it.[82] It is quite possible to read Danny's response within this paradigm – and to gain from this a sense of what infantile desires may be provoked in the viewer. But as well as gratification there is fear: fear of Max Cady (rather than Danny) as the cannibalistic impulse made manifest.

De Sade argues for the right 'to slit the throat and devour the palpitating flesh of the other'.[83] Cannibalism frequently functions as a paradigm of cruel-ty, a synonym for sadism and savagery (for Freud pre-genital sexuality is linked to animality and primitivism). In recent years 'eating the other' has come to figure as a surprisingly insistent taboo motif in mainstream and art cinema, in films as various as *The Silence of the Lambs* (Hannibal Lecter as Cannibal Lecher) and *The Cook, The Thief, His Wife and Her Lover*. Its emer-gence into the mainstream, into the sort of movies that Carol Clover identifies as coming 'awfully close to being slasher movies for yuppies',[84] has often been read cynically as gratuitous and as evidence of increasing sensationalism de-ployed as a compensation for narrative exhaustion. But there are other ways of looking (or not looking) at it. As a cinematic trope cannibalism has a vivid presence and lengthy genealogy in low-budget and B-grade horror movies. Vampirish images of men and women (sometimes lycanthropically inflected and gender-bended) biting into human flesh no doubt stir residual fears and desires associated with the oral phase; but these images also serve a significant sensationalist function: they serve to articulate something about the sensory experience of cinema. The recent phenomenon of cannibalism in the main-stream is an indication of the persistence of a more primitive generic impulse, but above all it is a sign of horror. As such it might be taken as a rhetorical ploy, as an invitation to engage in a reading inflected more towards the functional and the sensational than the psychological. Of course it might be argued that it is rather difficult to avoid a literal interpretation when the force of cannibal-istic images has precisely to do with their explicitness. But it is at this very point that cinematic sensationalism is operative. When Christ, in *The Last Temptation of Christ*, pulls his bloody heart out of his chest and says 'This is is my heart. Take it', he is performing a bad-taste version of the Eucharist which owes much to the horror tradition. Horror, particularly in its cannibal-istic inflections, is about literalising bad taste – not just showing things that are 'off' but inviting the viewer to participate in a tasting experience that might not be entirely wholesome. 'I love you so much I could eat you' has particular resonances when applied to the lover of cinema. The cinema itself is 'my body', given to be consumed; a desire to eat the images, incorporate the cine-matic-made-flesh is to activate the taste buds, to provoke and assimilate mem-ories, to exercise aggression, to activate nausea.

> *And just as attacker and attacked are expressions of the same*
> *self in nightmares, so they are expressions of the same viewer*
> *in horror film. We are both Red Riding Hood and the Wolf,*
> *the force of the experience, in horror, comes from 'knowing'*
> *both sides of the story.*[85]

Another aspect of this sign of horror is as a sign of the inhuman. In those (mainstream) films where people do not actually turn into wolves or reveal themselves as vampires, cannibalism serves to signify something horrific and non-human. Cannibalism, of course, is a human attribute, and indeed we might say that it is only possible to conceive of the inhuman as a modality of the human. But we should be alerted by this cinematic sign to beware of a narrowly humanist interpetation.

I Hacked My Wife into Fifty-Two Pieces

> *As soon as he is made flesh, he withers away. Any appearance*
> *suits him, and none. No sooner has he entered into one than*
> *it turns into a sepulcher, and he abandons it.*
> *The only skin he knows is a dead skin. And anyone who*
> *offers him her body to dwell in suffers the most extreme*
> *violence and survives only a short while.* (Irigaray)[86]

"Cos I'm just one hell of an animal' – this is said sardonically, as though slightly mocking the macho notion that holds animal attraction to be synonymous with male virility, as though, in the spirit of a contemporary reconstructed 'new man' he is putting the phrase 'one hell of an animal' in quotation marks. This sardonic edge is of course generated in the performance, in the inflection of the voice, the tilt of the head, the arching of the eyebrows and the conspiratorial direction of the look.[87] Cady performs thus to seduce Lori, but we the audience might be also seduced in a different way: by De Niro rather than Cady, by an evident enjoyment in the performance, in the different layers of fictionality that are being mobilised. He seduces Lori partly by encouraging her to talk about her sorrows, about Sam, the married man who has stood her up (Lori thinks that this is a chance encounter; we of course know that it isn't), and partly by presenting a duplicitous but potentially attractive 'confessional' version of himself. To her query about what he has done to spend time in prison he says, tongue in cheek again, 'I hacked my wife into fifty-two pieces.' This is a macabre response to her appalling sick joke: 'An unmarried woman meets a guy. He tells her he just got out of prison. "What'd you do?" she asks. "I hacked my wife into fifty-two pieces with a chainsaw." She says, "So, you're single."'

Having made his joke Cady proceeds to tell Lori the 'truth' (although we, again, recognise the fabrication), providing himself with anti-nuclear credentials and an instance of parochial heroism; he explains that on a protest march some macho sheriff got rough with the lady behind him and he (Cady) intervened, and was arrested. The gruesome irony is that the sardonic tone, the sense of quotation, hides the fact that Cady means exactly what he says. When he is seeming to offer himself up on a platter, garnished with self-mockery, he is in fact deadly serious. He is 'an animal' and such behaviour as hacking women up is not foreign to him. The scene in the bar is followed by a disturbingly graphic and extremely violent rape scene, with cannibalistic overtones. This savagery is indeed animalistic but it is

215

also studied, planned as an act of vengeance (against Sam, the woman a means to an end) and in this sense, pertaining to the human, to a particularly violent inflection of masculinity. For some critics, such as Pam Cook and Angela McRobbie, this scene and the way it implicates the audience epitomises the troubling sexual politics of the film. Pam Cook designates *Cape Fear* 'a violent rape movie in which women apparently collude in their own punishment at the hands of a rapist', and she argues that 'Scorsese has produced his most overtly femino-phobic movie'.[88] This scene is indeed repellent and highly disturbing to watch (which also applies to Cady's menacing of the other two women) but it is instructive to compare it to another rape scenario which it calls to mind. The scenes are linked by De Niro's presence, but they seem to me very different, and this difference turns on the question of humanism.

Once Upon a Time in America, for all its apparent toughness, renders a view of masculine violence that is predominantly romantic. The protagonist Noodles rapes twice during the course of the movie, and both acts are vividly rendered. On the second occasion he rapes the woman he has loved since childhood because she has rejected him in favour of becoming an actress. The rape is followed by a scene in which De Niro is situated alone in a vast landscape flooded by elegiac music; he is presented as a figure of desolation, loneliness and abandonment. At the end of the film he meets this woman again and the encounter is played for all the *frissons* of romance. What is repulsive about the way this rape is narrativised and thematised is the extent to which it is unashamedly humanised. The violent assault on the woman is mitigated by a discourse on the human frailty and vulnerability of the male character, and a connection between male virility ('animal' sexuality, that is, and irresistible attractiveness to women) and rape is explained (away) in terms of human or

Once Upon a Time in America (Sergio Leone, 1984)

216

masculine nature. In *Cape Fear* animality serves not to evoke unbridled male virility, but rather (and this is partly conveyed through genre conventions) that zone of 'fine epidermal contact' where something horrific, non-human lurks. Though the animalistic is related to sexuality it is not a question of animal magnetism or irresistible masculine allure; rather, in its violation of sociality and its evidently pathological hatred of the feminine, it is truly horrific, opening onto the inhuman. The rape does not render Max Cady more human, and it is not explained in terms of his sexual nature as a man. Certainly he uses sexual allure and cannily adopts different personae according to the woman he is closing in on; but this is not to say that the women 'collude in their own punishment'. Rather, it seems to me, they are in a similar position to us, as audience, to a male character who can turn on the charm and even make us laugh, only to turn on us in a psychotically violent manner. Like Tommy, for instance, in that knife-edge moment in *GoodFellas*. One moment you're laughing and the next moment you're dead.

Love Travis, Part 7

'Why me?' I raged. 'Why me? All I want is a little time out, to live quietly, to be alone for a while, to be a woman and not afraid of the dark, to write in peace. I never used to be afraid of the dark, of spending time alone, of writing. Now I don't even want to write, can't write. Tell me this: why? What have I done?' And as I ranted I could hear an echo returning on waves of heavy metal: 'I'm just a word processor, for Christ's sake!'

'Well,' H said, 'of course it's happened to you. After all, you did choose to write about Scorsese.' Silenced, I look at her aghast. You asked for it. Is that what she's saying? But no, I imagine not, she too is a writer and, though acerbic, not snide. So I bide my time and ponder this remark.

Give My Love To The Family, Counselor

> The family is the rotten dismal edifice in whose closets and crannies the most ignominious instincts are deposited.
> (Walter Benjamin)[89]

In the snippet we see of *Problem Child*, the movie that provokes Cady to such uncouth mirth, a demented man bursts into the frame, screeching, 'Here's Daddy!' He proceeds to create bedlam by throwing a television out of the window (in our direction), followed by everything else he can lay hands on. 'Bye Junior!' he exclaims gleefully. 'Adios!' This black comedy depicts the family romance run amok. Rather than expressing the child's infantile fantasy that it is adopted, the film seems to tap some desire to disown one's own children. To put this another way, the 'unnatural' child becomes a sign of something awry at the heart of the family, a sign that the nuclear family, in and of itself, is unnatural, even monstrous. *Problem Child*, although a comedy, has its antecedents in a line of movies traced from *The Bad Seed* through *The*

Omen and *The Exorcist*, but the tendency that these films represent is most spectacularly manifested in a thoroughly horrific horror movie. In *Totem and Taboo* Freud has the sons kill the father, but in *Night of the Living Dead* Romero has the girl child turning into one of the living dead and eating her own parents. In these films the 'unnatural' children frequently pose a problem through their precocity and unnatural appetites. But it is a mistake to see these films as in fact being necessarily about children. They are about unnatural relations, adopted children, surrogate parents, mothers and fathers who lose the family plot and commit infanticide (often to no avail since the monster refuses to die and rises up beyond the grave). They are about the family's fear that it is being infiltrated. Even Gregory Peck, the exemplary husband and father from *Cape Fear 1*, turns berserk and kills his 'own' son in *The Omen* (the other histrionically murderous father who figures himself as a Big Bad Wolf is of course Jack Nicholson in *The Shining*). Paternity is often figured as false, and as murderous.

After the Bowdens leave the theatre, driven out by Max, Danny taunts her father: 'You could have punched him', and they scuffle playfully. There is a slight sexual edge to this encounter, a mere *frisson*. As the film progresses the *frissons* recur, but not to any remarkable degree, not beyond any 'normal' family in which there is a pre-pubescent girl and a heterosexual father. But what does happen is that Sam, the figure of the Law, gradually becomes more and more desperate, not to say demented, about asserting his identity, more and more inclined to burst into the screen screeching 'Here's Daddy!' And this is because his place is being taken. Or perhaps it is because paternity is a masquerade.

> *Cause if you're not better than me, then I can have what you have.*
> *And what do I have?*
> *A wife. A daughter.*

Bettelheim proposes that 'the male . . . is split into two opposite forms: the dangerous seducer who, if given in to, turns into the destroyer of the good grandmother and the girl; and the hunter, the responsible, strong, and rescuing father figure'. The hunter is the good father; the wolf masquerades both as father and as lover. In infiltrating the Bowden house Max, in the guise of drama teacher, presents himself as the good father, as a surrogate more congenial than the 'real' father. But he also takes Sam's place as potential lover. Sam's fury when Danny is not respectable enough in her nightdress, and his rage about the theatre incident, both suggest desire and jealousy. Max's presence lifts the lid on the family feelings and exposes the 'most ignominious instincts' in this 'rotten dismal edifice'.

The family romance of *The Night of the Hunter* is echoed in *Cape Fear 2* in the doubling of the father and the criminal, and in the mirroring of Robert Mitchum by Robert De Niro. If in 'Little Red Riding Hood' the father is present in two forms, as the wolf and the hunter, as argued by Bettelheim, then in this movie matrix the Hunter *is* the Wolf. Which is also true of *Secret Ceremony*, where Mitchum again plays (in a histrionic mode that resists naturalistic characterisation) a wicked and incestuous stepfather, who actually declares himself as a sheep in wolf's clothing. The daughter, played by Mia Farrow, is named Cenci, an allusion to Shelley's revenge drama, *The Cenci*. But it is Artaud's reconceptualisation of the play that resonates most strongly in *Secret Ceremony*, accumulating memories in its wake and generating a cinematic turbulence that erupts in the Cape Fear River. Jane Goodall observes that 'Incest is treated in *Les Cenci* as a manifestation of the devouring principle which inhabits the organism of the family in all its members.'[90]

The struggle over paternity is played out as a struggle over keys. As in *After Hours* and *The Wizard of Oz*, there is much business involving windows and doors and keys. The car keys scene is pivotal and replayed very closely from the first version. In *Cape Fear 2* it is followed by the auditory bait: Cady says something that Sam doesn't catch. As a viewer there is also the sense of loss: what he says is audible but you can't actually pick up what he says. Like Sam, we become plagued by this loss, which is actually played out as a slippage between 'laws' and 'loss'. There is a sense that here is the key to the movie and we've lost it. And this is not simply a matter of interpretation: losing keys is hazardous; it means someone else, unknown, can get into your house.

> *A hand takes a key from a purse and drops it. The key falls in slow motion, hits the floor and bounces back and out of screen.*
> (Maya Deren, *Meshes of the Afternoon*)

An unhousing occurs. Max is a consummate agent of relocation, as he says when Sam tries to force him to leave town. 'I have considered relocating somewhere where I'd be appreciated. California, perhaps. I could teach earthquake preparedness . . . But then it hits me: I *love* New Essex, counselor.' The tension between home and away persists; Danny is studying *Look Homeward Angel*, and in the spirit of Thomas Wolfe she is to write her reminiscence about the houseboat (named Moana), a place signifying plenitude, security, home. In the end, of course, it becomes remarkably unhomely: in the end you can't go home (just as the cinema, now, cannot return to the fantasy paradise of Flaherty's *Moana*). The swamp turns into a maelstrom, for Max Cady (like Artaud's Cenci himself, the volatile principle of cruelty incarnate) is associated with extreme atmospheric turbulence.

The Fierceness of the Delight of its Horror

There are those who say everything is fiction, all history is just a matter of storytelling. Not me. I believe in the real, and I don't for a moment imagine that everything is equal and it's all relative. The sensation, for instance, of that hand coming through the window, closing round my throat, is not the same as the sensation I get in the movie theatre watching a horror movie. But the sensations are connected, and movies are not imaginary: they constitute part of my (our?) daily life. The fears and fantasies that were mobilised when I was assaulted by an intruder were, of course, not unconnected with whatever it was that compelled me to write this book. Those connections, however, are not causal, nor can I even identify with certainty what they are. This I know, though: if there is a disjunction between the fun, the thrill and excitement of certain movies (*Cape Fear 2*, say) and the trauma of 'real-life' incidents of intrusion and assault, there is also a phantasmic connection. It is in this tension, between the incommensurate and that which resonates, that sparks may fly and new textual spaces materialise. In the end movies which merely elicit recognition open the way to nothing new; they merely reproduce boring and often nasty social relations. In the end I'd rather a movie that declares 'the fierceness of the delight of its horror'.

And so Scorsese. A lot has not been touched on, but enough is enough and in the end it's time (contingently) to knot the tie (and hope it looks like poisonality neckwear and not as though its been issued by the FBI).[91] This after all is not a book about Scorsese. Or rather, it is round about. It is not exclusively about his movies, precisely because 'his' movies are not hermetic, they are allusive. If there have been many detours and an endless unravelling of threads in this writing it is because of a cinematic body – call it Scorsese – that is never automatic or unadventurous.

Love Travis, Part 8

As soon as I begin to tell what happened, I can hear, ringing in my ears, the cadences of storytelling. And as I try, pedantically, to describe a sequence of moving images in celluloid, it sounds like some tawdry domestic fiction. Writing is not necessarily curative (for the self) or illuminating (for strangers). Mostly I'd rather watch and talk about movies than write about them. But not always. It's true that there are places in the body where words can't reach, where images may touch, and move, more easily. Yet this attempt to put things into words sometimes, without warning, severs me from certainty. And there you are.

Where Will You Spend Eternity? Or *Götterdämerrung*

> *Always in the process of arriving, always in the process of appearing. An advent that happens over and over again. The beginning again of an endlessly aborted beginning. Surging out of the abyss. Rising out of the deepest waves. Suddenly, in a great din of silence and death.* (Irigaray)[92]

When the family is driving off, towards the river, a small amateurish cross by the roadside asks an ominous question: 'Where will you spend eternity?' There's a choice, between good and evil, between hate on the one hand and love on the other, between salvation and damnation, but to refuse these choices one must pay dearly; not only do you have to die several times while still alive, but you cannot reach the end. And you can't go home until 'The End' arrives and the credits start rolling.

Cape Fear 2 takes a long time ending. Max is torched and drowned and still resurfaces. But the ending does not simply function as a narrative denouement. It is an operatic ending; it generates an extraordinary cinematic momentum, catches the spectator up in that cinematic paroxysm, in an affective concatenation of images. Thus, even while we might be cracking up with laughter because the narrative codes have been stretched beyond plausible endurance, we are also shrieking with fear, clutching our neighbour's hands and knees, hanging on to anything that is tactile, hiding our eyes, doubling over to avoid nausea as the roller-coaster plunges down again, and soars into the air.

> *Opera requires a feeling for irreparable tragedy, film for happy endings.* (Alexander Kluge)[93]

There is a happy ending of sorts: the family survives – cleansed, resurrected. But they re-emerge out of, as Nietzsche would have it, 'the sand and slime of our present civilisation', and it is within a paradigm of the monstrous that they return, as a collective swamp creature. And what are we to make of the stigmata, as Sam raises his bleeding hands from the muddy mire? It is perhaps an instantiation of the cinema's capacity for disembodiment and reincarnation, for making things appear and disappear, for touching us in the process. The cinema can wind us up and wound mortally, but also wash away wounds. Traces remain, however, marks written on the body. One day there'll be a knock at the door, a breathing at the window, a rippling on the surface. Memories return, eternally. But is it the same? The same experience, same memory, same movie? Take Fast Eddie Felson. At the end of *The Hustler* he disappears. For twenty-five years he's gone, and then he reappears in *The Color of Money*. Same Eddie Felson. Same Paul Newman. So it seems. The movie ends with him again at the pool table. 'Hey I'm back!' As he shoots – freeze frame. Back from the living dead, as a premonition, here at the end, of another life to come, another movie in the offing.

Chapter 7
Time's Covetousness

> *A ritual is an action distinguished from all others in that it seeks*
> *the realisation of its purpose through the exercise of form . . .*
> *In ritual the form is the meaning. More specifically, the quality of*
> *movement is not merely a decorative factor; it is the meaning itself*
> *of the movement. In this sense, this film is a dance.* (Maya Deren)[1]

In the beginning anything is possible. Out of the darkness images take shape, promises open out like rose blossoms, dark secrets come to light. And as old rooms, musty, shrouded, and empty, are opened up and peopled, as looks are exchanged and glances thrown like daggers, we know: temptation and treachery are just around the corner.

It Invariably Happened As Everything Happened

The credit sequence of *Age of Innocence* (by Saul and Elaine Bass) offers a cascade of lushly blossoming flowers. One after another they explode in time-lapse photography, filling the frame and dissolving, slowly at first and then at an accelerated, delirious pace. Superimposed over this movement is a layer of cursive script, enigmatic but utterly orderly (from an etiquette manual). This layer of calligraphy gives way, almost imperceptibly, to another filter, a 'screening' of the flowers through intricately textured lace. The sequence – almost abstract (as the patterning becomes more insistent, the screen washed by a range of colours) – is cut to the overture to *Faust*, providing a link to the first narrative sequence: a scene at the opera. The transition is cued by a fade to black, and then a huge bunch of yellow flowers fills the screen as Marguerita's voice sings. Over the flowers a title: 'New York City, the 1870s'. A hand enters the frame and as a flower is plucked the camera pulls back to reveal Faust and Marguerita, but not the entire stage. This shot is reframed and held for a short while – we attend to the opera – and then there is an abrupt cut to scarlet and quick pan to a white gardenia in a buttonhole. This is Newland

Archer (Daniel Day-Lewis) standing, as we now see, in front of scarlet drapes. From now on as much attention will be given to audience dynamics as to what's happening on the stage, and we are introduced to most of the main players. The Countess Olenska (Michelle Pfeiffer) is espied through opera glasses – conceived of as a scandalous sight; May Welland (Winona Ryder) is signalled by a close-up of the flowers in her lap, lilies of the valley.

The opera sequence is followed by the ball, story time and narrative time neatly cohering, proceeding in tandem, undeflected by flashbacks or any major temporal ellipse. Nevertheless there is little temporal propriety about the introduction to the ball sequence, a pure example of cinematic magic, a promise of how cinema can transform the world, can conjure matter out of thin air, and stories out of whispers. Our view of the ballroom shows a room of immense proportions, cavernously empty and shrouded in drapes. A dark, empty vista stretches away from us, and in the distance there are doors which open out to a glimpse of sky and trees. Light, filtered through amber-coloured glass in the ceiling, falls in shafts, cutting through the darkness and lifting the dust. As the narrator's voice tells us about the Beauforts and their annual ball – 'It invariably happened as everything happened in those days, the same way' – the patterns and quality of light shift, and slowly, before our very eyes, the room transforms. The huge centrepiece chandelier sheds its cover and begins to glow, dimly at first but growing in intensity; the end doors are blacked out and the amber windows fade to black as the room is flooded with artificial light, revealing furniture and draperies and a gleaming dance floor. And then, as the waltz music begins, figures are faded into the scene. Like ghosts they materialise, and soon the space is volatile, swirling incandescence.

> In this film through an exploitation of cinematic techniques,
> space is itself a dynamic participant in the choreography.
> (Maya Deren).[2]

We have already had a taste of this expansiveness, at the opera – this transforming of space, this capacity of the cinematic imagination to transgress geographic boundaries. The opera sequence, while clearly presenting the theatrical event with all its ritualistic dimensions and 'decided' extra-daily bodies on stage, also and simultaneously transgresses the parameters that distinguish between the daily and the extra-daily. And it does this cinematically, through shots which travel, which reveal the players from beneath the footlights, from high above the stage, via a camera which swoops and glides, and does about-turns to scrutinise the audience from the stage. The choreographing of looks between members of the audience, the overlaying of the operatic voices with whispered gossip, as well as the narrator's voice – all this suggests that the players in this fiction are not confined to the stage. Going to the opera clearly constitutes a ceremonial event for this society, a way of ritualistically defining spatial and social parameters. But as well as the social dimension, the routine of conventions to be observed, we are alerted to the hothouse atmosphere of this world. Sensations, momentary intensities, trajectories of desire that connect people and images, across unimaginable spaces, are rendered cinematically, and burnt into memory.

> *This principle – that the dynamic of movement in film is stronger*
> *than anything else – than any changes of matter . . . I mean*
> *that movement, or energy is more important, or powerful,*
> *than space or matter – that, in fact, it creates matter – seemed*
> *to me to be marvelous, like an illumination.* (Maya Deren)[3]

Here the cinema involves us in the creation of 'other' worlds, the carving up of space, the *mise en scène* of desire. If Scorsese's cinema frequently makes a connection between the cinematic process itself and fictional protagonists driven by obsessive desires, we should of course assume that the magic of these moments, the promise, might eventuate as black magic, via the agency of a wilful protagonist. Yet Newland Archer's desires seem comparatively modest. He doesn't crave power, he isn't driven by an urge to destroy or will to revenge, he isn't gripped by a paranoid vision of New York City. So many negatives to summon Archer up! And yet there is something positive in his make-up, something simple he desires: all he wants is a woman whom he can't have (like Travis, wanting Betsy). *Age of Innocence* is, in this respect, like any old love story. It doesn't end happily, it's true, but this is not what's significant; what matters is that it *never* really ends. Like all obsessives Newland takes his time; he counts time passing. It is a condition of his love that loss and memory are inscribed within the circuit of desire, within the palpability of the present. To be in the grip of an obsessive and transgressive love requires that he construct a world to sustain that obsession, to make it last – an intricately detailed world.

As in *After Hours* and *GoodFelllas* we are in constant fear that the whole intricate structure, the claustrophobic insistence of detail and repetition, might collapse. But we need not fear. Newland Archer, like Fabrizio, is one of those who will always live before the revolution, who will never experience the revolution itself. The paradox is that the 'sweetness of life' to which Talleyrand alludes ('Those who have not lived the years before the revolution cannot realise the sweetness of life') can only be experienced if there is a revolution – that is to say, it is only through the experience of revolution that the sweetness of life after can be realised. At the Communist Fair (it is 1962 and voices in the crowd speculate about the death of Marilyn Monroe, and the Cuban missile crisis) Fabrizio complains about suffering from 'a nostalgia for the present' which he explains thus: 'Even as I experience the present it feels distant. For my sort it's always before the revolution.' The *mise en scène* of *Age of Innocence* does not simply connote a time before the revolution of modernity, nor does it merely register an obsession with period detail (though it is obsessive); on the contrary, it charts the *mise en scène* and theatricalisation of obsessive desire. In fact Newland is not the only character in *Age of Innocence* to will a world into being; the film is thick with narrative thieves and wilful desires (and it is the female characters, or voices – for the narrative voice constitutes the most wily presence – that are most effectively wilful). But there is a stunning moment when cinematic desire and the desire to be a gangster cohere in an aristocratic drawing room, when 'the factitious coherence of desire' is insubstantiated.

> *We might say that the act of desiring, in its purest form,*
> *involves an undisturbed use of the world as a theater for*
> *our fantasies.* (Leo Bersani)[4]

The voice-over says, 'It was not the custom in New York Society for a woman to leave one man and cross the room for another.' The Countess Ellen Olenska moves across the room in a trajectory that erases the vastness of space and simultaneously opens up an aporia. As she glides towards us the camera tracks back, drawing her into our orbit, and then it pans 180 degrees to Newland, moving in on him as his face registers her presence, registers her approach, and we know his world will never be the same again. Then she enters the shot, enters her own point of view, and sits beside him.

> Not only was the camera tracking back with her, it also slowed down
> speed, overcranking, and then as we pan to him we go back to normal
> speed. There's this new device that allows you to do it almost
> imperceptibly [in camera rather than optically], so you get
> the beautiful image with no grain.
> The new Arriflex camera does that. Later we use it when he
> sees her on Boston Common and she's sitting there reading.
> The camera swish-pans, and that swish-pan was done under-cranked,
> and when we landed on her we got back to normal.
> Skip Livesy put sound effects of fluttering wings of a bird over it.
> (Scorsese)[5]

The romance and passion promised by this shot are echoed later, but in a somewhat bitter reversal: another woman crosses the room to Archer, but this time she rises from her seat and comes to stand over Archer (the moment of rising is shot three times, chiselling the impact of this moment into memory). 'I'm afraid you can't do that dear,' says May when Archer makes his bid for freedom, and raises the topic of travel. Winona Ryder, and the smile she wears when making her announcement (that she's pregnant), reminds me of the FBI agent in *GoodFellas* 'wearing a terrifying tie'. The ballroom, also, is echoed (inversely) by a later scene – on the veranda in Boston – where all human presence and vitality is faded out, preserving, in this instance, a precious moment of intimacy. The sweetness of the memory is tinged, however, by the intensity of thwarted desire.

A Hieroglyphic World

Something similar occurs in the carriage scene. She takes his gloved hand in hers. There is a dissolve and in close-up the gesture – the slightness and gravity of the movement – is played again. Through a series of dissolves he takes one of his gloves off and touches a pearl button on her wrist. The buttons are undone. Prising apart the glove's opening he sinks his face into the inside of her wrist. A momentary ceremonial. Remember the rows of white gloves laid out

225

in the ballroom? To me they offer a temptation: to reach out, into the screen, to pick up one of those gloves and blow into it so that it becomes

> a languid boneless hand, a hand without a will, a hand floating in the air like a dead fish with its white stomach uppermost. It was a hand she did not want. It was a hand that could not clench itself. It was a hand which in caressing would in no way be a hand and would not caress; it would lead away.[6]

The glove scene in the carriage is passionate, achingly poignant, but this too – suffocatingly circumscribed, a distillation of all the layerings, the confinements, the rituals necessary to sustain this world and accommodate mildly aberrant desires. The credit sequence, also, is a distillation – voluptuous and encompassing movement in every frame, it nevertheless evokes a sense of repetition which finds its apotheosis in stasis, in the habitual layering, filtering, and screening of every movement in what Wharton referred to as 'a hieroglyphic world'. The roses, though seductive in their promise, are not merely beautiful, not a chocolate-box ornamentation but precisely artificial (hence the inspired decision to deploy the most used and conventional device – time-lapse flower photography – to signify a wasting of time, as flower after flower opens, as round after round is played out in the boxing ring, pirouette after pirouette on the stage). Everything means something in this milieu, every gesture and utterance refers to something else, no detail is indifferent, and all details are circuitously connected. In this world so full of signs and coded messages flowers above all are denaturalised. Marguerite plucks the petals from the daisy, singing 'He loves me, he loves me not'. The flower is put to use, in other words; it is mobilised as a sign. May's lilies of the valley signify, as, of course, do the extravagant bunches of yellow roses Newland Archer sends Ellen (a theatrical sign, inspired by the play that figures in the film, as an annual New York event – Dion Boucicault's *The Shaughraun*).

The flowers, like the red shoes and the boxing gloves, are totemic objects – they signify investment and conversion, and function somewhat differently for the characters within the film and for us. As components of a complex and shifting system of signs their meaning is in their relationship, not in some intrinsic value. So we should be alert to the fact that the meaning of lilies of the valley, for instance, varies over time, and according to place.

It is a mistake to think of this world, as many critics seem to, as being simply about the Victorian era. So much of Scorsese's cinema is about bringing into being imaginative worlds and the rituals necessary to sustaining those worlds. The trick he has is to immerse us so thoroughly that we reach the limits of fantasy (or endurance) and forget that this is an imaginative projection; or feel trapped, threatened by the uncanny return of the same; or get caught up in a running gag that twists and turns. For the illusion is this: that the world is your oyster, that you can go anywhere, do anything – in other words, that this is the only world there is. The scene where Newland and Ellen meet illicitly in the Museum of Modern Art opens on an artefact in a glass case, labelled 'Use Unknown'. An object that once had use value, was in circulation as a sign, is now in a glass case. So the rituals and objects and signs of this Victorian society will fade into obscurity, brought alive again only in a film like *Age of Innocence*, to remind us of our own contemporary passions and prisons. For this is another trick – of reminding – that Scorsese has. All those elaborate meals in *Age of Innocence* remind me of the rituals around food and cooking that the Goodfellas enact in prison. As a silver knife is lifted at a society dinner party an image flies into my head, as fast and clear as its cutting: an image of Pauli slicing garlic with a razor blade, slowly, meticulously, very finely.

Times Change

Why isn't the flower motif resolved at the end of the film?
Well, times change. Sometimes it's beyond resolution, it's been used up,
like a good luck charm that maybe you've used up all the good luck from.
(Scorsese)[7]

At the end of *Age of Innocence* Newland Archer realises that he cannot recapture time past; or perhaps he prefers to live with memory. On the threshold of meeting Ellen Olenska again after many years he experiences an acute episode of *déjà vu*. Looking up at her apartment, he imagines her there and then he sees her again – just as she was that day by the water, in the distance, her back to him (and to the camera), the scene conjured up like a pixellated impressionist painting. It is exactly the same, with one crucial difference: this time she turns around. She turns around in medium-close-up and smiles.

> *The central character of these films moved in a universe which was not governed by the material, geographic laws of here and there as distant places, mutually accessible only by considerable travel. Rather, he moved in a world of imagination in which, as in our day or night dreams, a person is first one place and then another without traveling between. It was a choreography in space.*
> (Maya Deren)[8]

The cut from Ellen back to Newland, who is still looking up at the window, is a jarring cut: the eyelines don't match. She wasn't looking at him after all, but at us. Like Tommy at the end of *GoodFellas*, grinning and firing his gun straight into the audience. And like that moment it is curiously alarming, and exciting. It is as though something new comes alive in the very moment of ending.

It may well be the case that the flower motif is not resolved at the end, and indeed it's true that the film does evoke a painful sense that some things are 'beyond resolution'. Yet the import of the opening is registered in the ending, in terms of what matters, and how. The motif of cinematic promise, of an opening up and coming alive, effected through cinematic magic and imaginative wilfulness, is reprised. But it is in tension with another impulse also set in motion in the opening, in the obsessive repetition and the implosion of circularity. These impulses

227

revolve round questions of time and space, questions to do with a structuring of the social and the phantasmic, with realms of intersection.

> The will cannot will backwards; and that he cannot break time and time's covetousness that is the will's loneliest melancholy.
> (Nietzsche)

Time consumes, establishes habit, turgid resilience, resistance to change. Time seems to be fleeting, ephemeral, abstract, precarious, like the world which the narrator tells us was 'balanced so precariously that its harmony could be shattered by a whisper'. But in fact this world, as we discover, is adamantine in its commitment to self-preservation. *Age of Innocence* revolves round protagonists who are far less rageful about the past, the affront of 'it was'; there is more a sense of 'loneliest melancholy'. Yet the very refusal to end (to resolve the flower motif) suggests a grappling with that affront.

In *The Tales of Hoffmann* there is a wonderful transition between the ending of one tale and the beginning of another. The 'Tale of Olympia' ends with the alarming image of mechanical springs leaping out of Olympia's head, and these become, in a process of abstraction and cinematic instantiation, rippling reflections in the water at the beginning of the next story.

Age of Innocence ends on a city square, serene, emptied of people. It could be the beginning of another movie, and indeed I start imagining the scene coming alive, I start fantasising new scenarios. I don't feel provoked to imagine what happens to the characters, but I do feel in the grip of ideas and sensations raised by the experience of watching this movie. In depicting a world so precariously balanced, so self-enclosed, Scorsese has shattered the certitude of film-making, shown that the way to produce new knowledge is through flying off at tangents, through meticulous spatialisation, through an embodied cinematic practice that flies in the face of time's covetousness.

Notes

Chapter 1

1. Noël Burch, 'A Primitive Mode of Representation?', Thomas Elsaesser (ed.), *Early Cinema: Space–Frame–Narrative*, (London: British Film Institute, 1992), p. 223.
2. 'In a Hale's Tours situation it would seem more effective at the beginnning, in a vaudeville situation billed as a story film of violence its placement at the end would seem more appropriate.' Charles Musser, 'The Travel Genre in 1903-1904: Moving Towards Fictional Narrative', ibid., pp. 129–30.
3. Maurizio Vizno writes, 'It is a funny (what do you mean funny?) shot for an ending, something like an ending for children's comics. It is as if the text itself were now saying to the audience: 'Do not forget how much fun all this was.' '*GoodFellas*', *Film Quarterly*, vol. 44, no. 3, Spring 1991, p. 47.
4. Tom Gunning, 'The Cinema of Attractions: Early Film, its Spectator and the Avant-Garde', in Thomas Elsaesser (ed.), *Early Cinema*, p. 58.
5. The quotations from Friedrich Nietzsche are taken from *The Portable Nietzsche*, ed. and trans. Walter Kaufmann (New York: Penguin Books, 1982).
6. Noël Burch, 'Porter, or Ambivalence', *In and Out of Synch: The Awakening of a Cinedreamer* (Aldershot, England: Scolar Press, 1991 [1980]), p. 148.
7. Scorsese, quoted in Mary Pat Kelly, *Martin Scorsese: A Journey* (London: Secker & Warburg, 1992), p. 39.
8. In an interview during the shooting of *Cape Fear*. See Peter Biskind, 'Slouching Toward Hollywood', Premiere, November 1991, p. 73.
9. David Thompson and Ian Christie (eds), *Scorsese on Scorsese* (London: Faber & Faber, 1989), p. 15. Hereafter, throughout the book, this reference will be abbreviated to SoS.
10. 'Taking over a trope from the avant-garde film-maker Stan Brakhage, who uses it repeatedly and ended his epic *Dog Star Man* this way, Scorsese collapses the sacred moment with a declaration of the ephemerality of the chemistry of colour film. In the film where we would least expect it, a declaration of cinematic specificity marks the end,' writes P. Adams Sitney in 'Cinematic Election and Theological Vanity', *Raritan* vol. 11, no. 2, Fall 1991, p. 59.
11. Talking about *Pierrot le fou* in *Godard on Godard* (London: Secker & Warburg, 1972), p. 234.
12. Mary Pat Kelly, *Martin Scorsese*, p. 252.
13. Tom Gunning, 'The Cinema of Attractions: Early Film, its Spectator and the Avant-Garde', in *Early Cinema*, p. 58.
14. 'Creating Movies with a New Dimension', in VèVè A. Clark, Millicent Hodson and Catrina Neiman, *The Legend of Maya Deren: A Documentary Biography and Collected*

Works,. Vol. 1, Pt 2: *Chambers (1942–1947)* (New York: Anthology Film Archives/Film Culture, 1988), p. 612. Reprinted from Popular Photography December 1946, pp. 130–2, 134.

15. Gilles Deleuze, *Cinema 1: The Movement-Image* (Minneapolis: The University of Minnesota Press, 1986). Deleuze identifies five characteristics of the new image: 'the dispersive situation, the deliberately weak links, the voyage form, the consciousness of clichés, the condemnation of the plot' (p. 210).
16. David Malouf, *Remembering Babylon* (Sydney: Random House, 1993), p. 30.
17. For the notion of embodied knowledge in the context of mimesis, see Michael Taussig, *Mimesis and Alterity: A Particular History of the Senses* (New York: Routledge, 1993).
18. Marilyn Beck, 'The King of Comedy', *New York Daily News*, 2 February 1983, p. 37. For a similar reaction to *Taxi Driver*, see Jack Kroll's review: 'The Catholic Scorsese and the Calvinist Schrader have flubbed their ending. It's meant to slay you with irony, but it's simply incredible when Travis is hailed as a hero after the slaughter.' The review is reprinted in Mary Pat Kelly, *Martin Scorsese: The First Decade* (Pleasantville, NY: Redgrave, 1980), p.187. Peter Boyle, an actor in the film, said, 'I'm one of about three in the world who likes the ending in this film, because I think that without the ending it's a monster film, and I don't think that this is a monster film' (ibid., p. 93).
19. Mary Pat Kelly, *Martin Scorsese: A Journey*, p. 199.
20. Derek Jarman, *Modern Nature* (London: Vintage, 1992), p. 19.
21. Julian Fox, 'New York, New York', *Films and Filming*, vol. 24 no. 1, October 1977, p. 30.
22. And there have always been critics and theorists ready to argue that in progressive films or those that rupture the dominant ideology the constraints of 'the ending' are actually, if perversely, productive. David Bordwell, in the characteristically deflationary mode of *Making Meaning*, points out that 'The contemporary assumption that a film's overall narrative structure will seek to tame its disruptive elements is stock in trade for these early critics. Kracauer and Deming are especially sensitive to the ways in which endings present false resolutions, while Tyler shows his awareness of the arbitrary closure of narrative structure by comparing Hollywood's happy ending to Christian theology and assuming that "all endings are purely conventional, formal, and often, like the charade, of an infantile logic."' See David Bordwell, *Making Meaning*: Inference and Rhetoric in the Interpretation of Cinema (Cambridge, Mass.: Harvard University Press, 1989), p. 98.
23. David Ehrenstein, *The Scorsese Picture: The Art and Life of Martin Scorsese* (New York: Birch Lane Press, 1992), p. 161.
24. Slavoj Zizek (ed.), *Everything You Always Wanted to Know about Lacan (But Were Afraid to Ask Hitchcock)* (London: Verso, 1992), p. 267, note 30.
25. *SoS*, p. 4.
26. Leo Bersani, *A Future for Astyanax: Character and Desire in Literature* (New York: Columbia University Press, 1984), p. 313.

Chapter 2

1. Enzo Ungari, *Bertolucci by Bertolucci* (London: Plexus, 1987), p. 71.
2. Stan Brakhage, 'Metaphors on Vision', in *Film Culture*, no. 30, Autumn 1963.
3. 'Magic is New', in Vè Vè A. Clark, Millicent Hodson and Catrina Neiman, *The Legend of Maya Deren*, p. 310. Reprinted from *Mademoiselle*, January, 1946.
4. Sigmund Freud, *Totem and Taboo* (1912-13), in The Penguin Freud Library (hereafter shortened to PFL) Vol. 13 (Harmondsworth: Penguin, 1990), pp. 8–84.
5. Ibid., p. 80.
6. For a very entertaining (and somewhat caustic) account of the on-set/off-screen clash between the high art of ballet and the low art of celluloid occasioned by this casting, see Michael Powell, *A Life in the Movies: An Autobiography* (London: Heinemann, 1986), p. 656.

7. Eugenio Barba, *Beyond the Floating Islands* (New York: PAJ Publications, 1986) pp. 149–50.

8. Ibid., p. 94.

9. A particular tendency that includes Eisenstein, Meyerhold, Brecht, Barba – all influenced by non-European traditions.

10. Eugenio Barba, *Beyond the Floating Islands*, p. 95.

11. Gilles Deleuze, *Cinema 2: The Time-Image*, (London: The Athlone Press, 1989), p. 191.

12. Ibid., p. 194.

13. Thomas Wiener, 'Martin Scorsese Fights Back', *American Film*, vol. 1, no. 2, 1975, pp. 31–4, 75.

14. *SoS*, p. 80.

15. Scorsese's commentary on *The Tales of Hoffmann*, on Criterion laserdisc, is very illuminating – of his concerns and methods, as well as Powell and Pressburger's.

16. Maya Deren, discussing *Meshes of the Afternoon* in Clark *et al.*, *The Legend of Maya Deren: a Documentary Biography and Collected Works*, Vol 1, Pt 2; *Chambers (1942–1947)* (New York: Anthology Film Archives/Film Culture, 1988), p. 78. Reprinted from *Film Culture*, no. 39, Winter 1965.

17. Sigmund Freud, *Totem and Taboo*, PFL 13, p. 106.

18. 'Investment' is used here in the Freudian sense where it serves as a translation of the German *Besetzung*. A more common English translation is 'cathexis', but I find this term overly technical and wish to retain the sense of everyday usage that pertains to the German.

19. Alain Masson, 'Le Boxeur transfiguré', *Positif*, no. 241, April 1981, p. 49.

20. James Naremore's discussion which dissents from this view is interesting. See James Naremore, *Acting in the Cinema* (Berkeley: University of California Press, 1988), pp. 193–5.

21. Jacques Derrida, *The Truth in Painting* (Chicago: University of Chicago Press, 1987).

22. The extensive glossing of the Van Gogh shoes coheres precariously as a fascinating instance of a critical *mise en abime*. See also Fredric Jameson's essay, 'Postmodernism, or the Cultural Logic of Late Capitalism', *New Left Review*, no. 146, July–August 1984. Jameson compares the Van Gogh shoes, and Heidegger's approach to them, to Andy Warhol's *Diamond Dust Shoes* which he posits as all surface, refusing a depth reading. Shoes of various kinds, and their indeterminate relations with bodies, proliferate in this essay.

23. John Berger, G (London: Penguin, 1972), pp. 190–1.

24. Slavoj Zizek, *Everything You Always Wanted to Know about Lacan (But Were Afraid to Ask Hitchcock)* (London: Verso, 1992), p. 108.

25. See Robin Wood, '*Raging Bull*: the Homosexual Subtext', *Movie*, no. 31–32, Fall 1986, pp. 108–114.

26. For an essay that explores these questions, and is certainly the most interesting piece of critical writing that I know on *Raging Bull* see Pam Cook, 'Masculinity in Crisis?', *Screen*, vol. 23, no. 3–4, September–October 1982, pp. 39–53.

27. As accurately as I can determine. Because of the combination of camera movement focus and cutting, it is hard to tell precisely.

28. There are two very similar shots of Kathleen Byron in *Black Narcissus* – her febrile hysteria transfigured as deadly desire.

29. Maya Deren, discussing her film *Ritual in Transfigured Time*, Clark *et al.*, *The Legend of Maya Deren*, Vol. 1, Pt 2, p. 458. Reprinted from *Dance* Magazine, December 1946.

30. Michael Powell, *A Life in the Movies*, p. 652.

31. Maya Deren, describing the movement of the dancer in her film *A Study in Choreography for Camera* in *The Legend of Maya Deren*, Vol. 1, Pt 2, p. 263. Reprinted from *Film Culture*, no. 39, Winter 1965.

32. Michael Powell, *A Life in the Movies*, p. 653.

33. Programme note for *Meshes of the Afternoon*, in *The Legend of Maya Deren*, p. 628.

34. Annette Michelson, 'On Reading Deren's Notebook', *October*, no. 14, Fall 1980, p. 54.

35. Maya Deren, '*Meditation on Violence*', *Film Culture*, no. 39, Winter 1965, p. 18.

Chapter 3

1. Brian Henderson, '*The Searchers*: An American Dilemma', *Film Quarterly*, vol. 34, Winter 1980–81, pp. 9–23.
2. For the influence of *The Searchers* on the new Hollywood film-makers, see Stuart Byron, '*The Searchers*: Cult Movie of the New Hollywood', *New York Magazine*, 5 March 1979, pp. 45–8.
3. 'In his dealings with Iris, he becomes nothing less than a parody of John Wayne's Ethan Edwards,' writes Robert Phillip Kolker in *A Cinema of Loneliness: Penn, Kubrick, Coppola, Scorsese, Altman* (New York: Oxford University Press, 1980), p. 239. There is of course a thin line between parody and what I have referred to as recasting or resurrection; but to talk in terms of parody here seems to me to underestimate the work of variation that takes place through the process of repetition.
4. *SoS*, p. 4.
5. Joseph McBride and Michael Wilmington, *John Ford* (London: Secker & Warburg, 1974), p. 162.
6. Jean-Luc Godard, *Godard on Godard* (London: Secker & Warburg, 1972), p. 117.
7. McBride and Wilmington, *John Ford*, p. 148.
8. Andrew Sarris, *The John Ford Movie Mystery* (London: Secker & Warburg, 1976), p. 173.
9. In his discussion of memory and perception as duration, Bergson uses the example of a musical tune. Although the notes exist independently and proceed in a succession we experience them as melting into one another; both the past notes and the present notes are simultaneously present in our consciousness. Another way of thinking this is to say that our memory or consciousness of past notes exists along with our consciousness of present notes – thus, even if the notes of a tune succeed each other we experience them as an interpenetration of matter, and states of consciousness, even when successive, permeate one another. See Henri Bergson, *Time and Free Will* [1889] (London: George Allen & Unwin, 1950, p. 100.
10. As Stephen Heath once pointed out, in narrative cinema events take place and their taking place takes time, so that mise en scene is always sequenced and the viewer is always placed. He was concerned then, as so many theorists were, with charting the machinations of narrative as the master code of classic cinema. Discussions of memory-and-time in the cinema seem to have been largely divided between the narrative and experimental spheres. More recently attempts to avoid these categories as definitive are surfacing, in attention to figures like Walter Benjamin who was taken with the idea in Proust of memory images being deposited in limbs. See Stephen Heath, 'Narrative Space', in *Questions of Cinema* (London: Macmillan, 1981), pp. 19-75. See Miriam Hansen's work in this area, particularly her 'Benjamin, Cinema and Experience: "The Blue Flower in the Land of Technology"', *New German Critique*, no. 40, 1987, where she writes, 'Remembrance, in the Proustian as well as Freudian sense, is incompatible with conscious remembering (*Erinnerung*) which tends to historicize, to fixate the image of memory in an already interpreted event (*Erlebnis*); not self-reflection, but an integral "actuality," a "bodily," to some degree absent-minded "presence of mind," is its prerequisite' (p. 200). See also Jodi Brooks, 'Benjamin for Girls: Cinema, Spectatorship, Fascination', Ph.D. thesis, University of New South Wales, forthcoming.
11. Marcel Proust, *Remembrance of Things Past* (New York: Random House, 1981), Vol. 3 p, 905.
12. Gilles Deleuze, *Proust and Signs* (London: Allen Lane, 1972), p. 19.
13. It is often argued that the cinema hall provides an arena for regression to infancy, and specifically that it is conducive to a re-enactment of the primal scene, where the child witnesses, under the cover of dark, a forbidden scene. Whilst acknowledging the womb-like luxury that envelopes the spectator and facilitates regression, my intention – by using the notion of 'sensuous images' – is to err from the account that strait-jackets vision and to suggest that a variety of senses may be activated in the viewer, and a quite different dynamic of time and memory may be operative.

14. Carol Clover, in *Men, Women, and Chainsaws: Gender in the Modern Horror Film* (London: British Film Institute, 1992), discusses a remark by John Carpenter suggesting that horror films are really Westerns, and adds: 'the case could also be made that westerns are really horror "underneath", for the terms of violation and revenge in the western seem often to slide beyond an economic analysis into a psychosexual register. In fact, of course, if the two genres really do stand in the kind of reciprocal relationship that I have suggested, then it must be that both things are true – that each is the other "underneath," that the terms of the one are inherent, if not manifest, in the terms of the other, and that each enables the other to be told' (p. 165).

15. Gilles Deleuze, *Proust and Signs*, p. 56.

16. By recognising 'the little girl in the young woman, the White in the Indian, legitimating his love for Martha and her daughter, accepting his own interior scar.' Jean-Louis Leutrat, *John Ford: La Prisonnière du désert, une tapisserie navajo* (Paris: Editions Adam Biro, 1990), p. 39.

17. Sigmund Freud, *Beyond the Pleasure Principle* (1920), PFL 11, pp. 283–7.

18. Lindsay Anderson in a contemporary review called Ethan 'an unmistakable neurotic' and asked, 'Now what is Ford, of all directors, to do with a hero like this?' See '*The Searchers*', *Sight and Sound*, Summer 1956, pp. 94–5.

19. See Pauline Kael, *Reeling* (Boston: Little, Brown & Co., 1976), p. 286.

20. See Richard Slotkin, *Regeneration through Violence: The Mythology of the American Frontier, 1600–1860* (Middletown, Conn.: Weslyan University Press, 1973). The 'captivity narratives' are discussed by Leutrat, and also by Robert Ray in relation to *Taxi Driver* in *A Certain Tendency of the Hollywood Cinema, 1930–1980* (Princeton, NJ: Princeton University Press, 1985), p. 358–9.

21. On this point McBride and Wilmington have an interesting comment: 'But of all Ford's Western heroes, only Ethan turns his violence against his family – against Debbie, who could just as well be his daughter – and that is what makes him such a profound and disturbing figure . . . Here, as in *Pilgrimage*, Ford has faced up to a contradiction which, as Jim Kitses points out, is also at the basis of Anthony Mann's Westerns: "Mann's vision of the family as a microcosm of humanity is profoundly ambiguous: the highest good, the source of all evil"' (*John Ford*, pp.150–1). In the end though they opt for a reading which, like Leutrat's, emphasises recognition and redemption – 'He has been freed from his memories of Martha by a deeper, tribal memory' (p. 162).

22. Travis writing to his parents. When Pauline Kael in her review of the film, 'Underground Man,' called *Taxi Driver* one of the first truly modern horror movies, this isn't exactly what she meant, but for me this line is a reminder that Ethan persists and that Travis isn't dead, that he will return with more deadly intent than either those old familiar madeleines or Freddy Kruger. It's one of the more chillingly macabre lines of contemporary cinema. See Pauline Kael, 'Underground Man', in Mary Pat Kelly, *Martin Scorsese: The First Decade* (Pleasantville: Redgrave, 1980), pp. 183–6. Reprinted from *The New Yorker*, 9 February 1976.

23. Sigmund Freud, *Totem and Taboo*, PFL 13, p. 80.

24. Ibid., p. 122.

25. Although it is not by mistake that it is a 'white' name by which he is branded (his other name – the Spanish 'Cicatriz' – is also white, not Comanche).

26. Leutrat weaves an interesting analogy between the 'scar' and the 'lazy line' that exists in Navajo rugs, a thread that's askew so that the pattern is just out. No two rugs are the same; every one is singular. This singularity is to be found within the rugs as well: the oblique line runs not between colours or patterns, but within. Similarly, he argues, the scar is a trace of a wound that is within, not between. Thus *The Searchers* is not about a contradiction between colours or races or sexes, but about an interior wound. In his reading, then, Scar and Ethan are one. See *John Ford: La Prisonnière du désert*, pp. 43–7.

27. Bernard Herrmann's score reprised the three-note signature of *Psycho*. As Michael Bliss points out, it recurs in the final credit sequence, 'indicating that although we are presumably in the safe area beyond the film's action, the possibility of unpredictable violence

still exists'. See Michael Bliss, *Martin Scorsese and Michael Cimino* (Metuchen, NJ: The Scarecrow Press, 1985). p. 109. Similarly the 'love theme' is reprised at the end of the massacre, but this time with a sinister variation: 'Benny explained that the reason he did it that way', says Scorsese, 'was to show that this was where Travis' fantasies about women led him. His illusions, his self-perpetuating way of dealing with women had finally brought him to a bloody, violent outburst and Benny's music certainly illuminated that to me.' See Carmie Amato, 'Scorsese on *Taxi Driver* and Herrmann', *Focus on Film*, no. 25, Summer/Autumn, 1976, p. 7.

28. Scenario for *The Eye of Night* (c.1952) which became *The Very Eye of Night* (1959), in *The Legend of Maya Deren*, p. 160. Reprinted from *Film Culture*, no. 39, p. 25.

29. Godard, talking about the colour in *Pierrot le fou*, *Godard on Godard*, p. 234.

30. In his commentary on *The Tales of Hoffmann* on the Criterion laserdisc Scorsese acknowledges this influence. The close-ups of De Niro's eyes were filmed at 36 frames a second and although the slight slow motion is scarcely perceptible, it does produce a sense of disturbing concentration.

31. 'Ethan turns away from us in the final frames of *The Searchers*, but the madness in Travis Bickle's eyes hold us, remorselessly, inescapably, to the very end,' writes David Boyd, in 'Prisoner of the Night', *Film Heritage*, vol. 12 no. 2, Winter 1976–97, pp. 24–30. 'No doubt,' he goes on, 'it says something about the distance between 1956 and 1976 that Scorsese and Schrader are able to make of the darkest of Ford's films something darker and more disturbing still, and that they feel compelled to do so' (p. 30).

32. Carolee Schneeman, 'Kenneth Anger's *Scorpio Rising*', in *Film Culture Reader*, ed. P. Adams Sitney (New York: Praeger, 1970), p. 277.

33. David Morgan, 'Scorsese's Journey into Fear', *The Age*, 10 May 1991, p. 4. Reprinted from *The Washington Post*.

34. Sigmund Freud, *Totem and Taboo*, PFL 13, p. 106.

35. Mary Douglas, *Purity and Danger: An Analysis of Concepts of Pollution and Taboo* (London: Routledge & Kegan Paul, 1978 [1969]), p. 122.

36. He is lying down when this voice-over occurs, his paralysis demonstrated by a high-angle overhead shot which cranes down on his inert body.

37. Michel Cieutat discerns in this sequence the style of Ozu and Bresson, and so infers the influence of Schrader, particularly his 'transcendental' view of cinema, as elaborated in *Transcendental Style in Film: Ozu, Bresson, Dreyer* (Berkeley: University of California Press, 1972). Perhaps this is the case, but I am more interested in the way in which the filming here mimics a common way of fetishising the naked body (usually female, though not always; *Scorpio Rising* is a case where the fetishised bodies are male and machines) and so anticipates Travis's look at porn movies. Cieutat does however make an interesting point about the taxi view: 'Scorsese has invested his film with his now legendary camera movements which endorse the irresistible journeying of the character towards his goal. Taking advantage of the constant movement of the taxi, the camera makes us go through hell in all directions. When outside of the taxi, the camera continues to move in the same way, as in that lateral tracking shot on Travis watching a porn movie, or when he's lying on his bed with insomnia.' See *Martin Scorsese* (Paris: Rivages, 1986), pp. 119–20.

38. Victoria Spence, 'To Die For: Some Meditations on the Body of Robert de Niro and Other Things', unpublished paper, University of New South Wales, 1992. I am much indebted to this paper in the discussion that follows.

39. James Naremore, *Acting in the Cinema* (Berkeley: University of California Press, 1988), p. 157.

40. Michel Ciment, *Conversations with Losey* (London and New York: Methuen, 1985), p. 78.

41. Gilles Deleuze, *Cinema 2: The Time-Image*, (London: The Athlone Press, 1989), p. 192.

42. Heiner Muller, *Hamletmachine and Other Texts for the Stage* (New York: PAJ Publications, 1984), p. 57.

43. Michel Foucault, *Discipline and Punish: the Birth of the Prison* (London: Penguin, 1977), p. 136.

44. Ibid., p. 152.

45. Critics are very fond of discoursing at length about the many instances in the film where the finger is used as a gun, and of demonstrating via this trope the penis–gun substitution that is operative in the film. Whilst I have no argument with this, it seems to me that its obviousness doesn't yield much of interest, it is a subsitution and an observation that could be made about a good percentage of movies, whereas *Taxi Driver* seems to be doing something more complicated and, perhaps, perverse.

46. In a later sequence we do see the target – a fast montage, alternating between the gun exploding and the target exploding – in the shooting gallery.

47. Carolee Schneeman, 'Kenneth Anger's *Scorpio Rising*', p. 278.

48. There are other ways of reading this which, while also noting the persistence through resurrection, put the emphasis on a more Catholic interpretation: 'Travis Bickle points and shoots – there are no bullets. There is no gun. His sacrificial mission fails. He may have cleansed the city of some of the "scum" but is not able to fully purge himself. He continues to live the life of a "resurrected", albeit still tarnished, hero. He is left in purgatory, to serve out his "living" days in the uncertainty of a future resurrection' (Paul Garcia, 'The Texture of Blood', unpublished paper, University of New South Wales, 1992).

49. Brian Henderson, in '*The Searchers*: An American Dilemma', very convincingly argues that the emotional impact of the film 'becomes explicable only if we substitute black for red and read a film about red–white relations in 1868–1873 as a film about black–white relations in 1956' (p. 19).

50. Gerald Mast (ed.), *The Movies in our Midst: Documents in the Cultural History of Film in America* (Chicago and London: University of Chicago Press, 1982), p. 333.

51. In *Mean Streets* Charlie fantasises about a black woman whom he eventually asks out and then stands up, his desire directly implicated in his racism.

52. Richard Corliss, 'The Hollywood Screenwriter: Take 2', *Film Comment*, vol. 14, no. 4, July–August 1978, p. 46.

53. Sigmund Freud, *Inhibitions, Symptoms and Anxiety* (1925–26), PLF 10, p. 277.

54. Sigmund Freud, *Totem and Taboo*, PFL 13, pp. 128–9.

55. Joan Mellen, *Big Bad Wolves: Masculinity in the American Film* (London: Elm Tree Books, 1978), pp. 309–11.

56. Brian Henderson argues that to some extent Ethan Edwards functions like the white Southerner – as a scapegoat for our own racist fears and desires. See '*The Searchers*: an American Dilemma', p. 22.

57. Referring to *Peeping Tom*, SoS, p. 20.

58. In 'The Scandal of *Peeping Tom*' Ian Christie documents the critical reception of the film. See Ian Christie (ed.), *Powell, Pressburger and Others* (London: British Film Institute, 1978), pp. 109–16.

59. SoS, p. 18.

60. Carol Clover, *Men, Women, and Chainsaws*, p. 68.

61. Kaja Silverman, *The Acoustic Mirror: The Female Voice in Psychoanalysis and Cinema* (Bloomington: Indiana University Press, 1988), p. 32. See also Linda Williams, 'When the Woman Looks', in *Re-vision: Essays in Feminist Film Criticism*, Mary Anne Doane, Patricia Mellencamp and Linda Williams, eds, American Film Institute Monograph Series (Frederick, Md: University Publications of America, 1984). She suggests that *Peeping Tom* 'lays bare the voyeuristic structure of cinema and that structure's dependence on the woman's acceptance of her role as narcissist' (p. 92). Clover, Silverman and Williams are all interested in the way that *Peeping Tom* reveals the structure of cinema as a structuring of gendered subjectivity. Silverman, for instance says, 'it permits the female viewer to see what her voice and image have been made to conceal, and so to adopt a different position in front of the cinematic "mirror" from that prescribed for her by Hollywood' (*The Acoustic Mirror*, pp. 40–1).

62. Pauline Kael, 'Underground Man', p. 185.

63. *The Woman in the Window* is the title of a film noir made by Fritz Lang in 1944, a film that revolves round projection, representation and murder.

64. Carol Clover, 'The Eye of Horror', in *Men, Women, and Chainsaws*, pp.166–230.
65. Kaja Silverman, *The Acoustic Mirror*, p. 41.
66. See Linda Williams, 'When the Woman Looks', p. 92.
67. Laleen Jayamanne, 'They are becoming us or they are becoming other – they are at a dangerous point', in Catriona Moore (ed.), *Dissonance: Feminism and the Arts* (Sydney: Allen & Unwin, 1994), pp. 169–194.
68. Ibid., p. 189.

Chapter 4

1. Quoted in Mary Pat Kelly, *Martin Scorsese: A Journey* (London: Secker & Warburg, 1992), p. 186. He is describing Scorsese on the set of *After Hours*.
2. Salman Rushdie, *The Wizard of Oz* (London: British Film Institute, 1992), p. 23.
3. A tale told by a friend – an obsessive movie-watcher – about his first visit to the pictures. The film was *Lassie Come Home*.
4. 'Home' and 'work' are equivalent in *After Hours*. After leaving work Paul is shown briefly at home in his apartment, a place as sterile as the work environment and clearly somewhere he wants to get away from. Joseph Minion develops this preoccupation with the yuppie confusion of work and home in another bizarrely brilliant script, *Vampire's Kiss*, and the almost subliminal theme of regression finds its apotheosis (or goes completely off the rails) in *Motorama* , a road movie featuring a precocious kid.
5. The Munchkin who drives the horse and carriage that transports Dorothy and friends to the Wizard introduces the 'horse of a different colour'. It changes colour in each successive shot – from purple to orange to gold. These changes were brought about by covering it in a variety of shades of powdered Jell-O. Salman Rushdie provides this information in *The Wizard of Oz,* p. 14. In his turn, Rushdie is indebted to Aljean Harmetz's *The Making of The Wizard of Oz* (New York: Doubleday/Dell, 1989).
6. The words are from 'Stormy Weather'. The voice I hear is Judy Garland's. Fragments from the song are trailed through *Dead Letters*, a radio piece by Gregory Whitehead (1985), and another voice comments: 'You can feel those "O's" when she says, "Can't go on," tremendously opening up out into space.' See Gregory Whitehead, '*Dead Letters*', *Performing Arts Journal*, vol. 14, no. 2, 1992, pp. 71–86.
7. Griffin Dunne quoted in Mary Pat Kelly, *Martin Scorsese: A Journey*, p. 186.
8. *SoS*, pp. 101–2.
9. Ibid., p. 4.
10. Paul Schrader, Introduction: 'Interview with Martin Scorsese', *Taxi Driver* (London: Faber & Faber, 1990), p. xi.
11. Ibid., p. xvi.
12. Edgar Allen Poe, *The Unknown Poe: An Anthology of Fugitive Writings by Edgar Allan Poe* (San Francisco: City Lights, 1980), pp. 60–1.
13. Christian Metz, 'Story/Discourse: Notes on Two Kinds of Voyeurism', in *Psychoanalysis and Cinema: The Imaginary Signifier* (London: Macmillan, 1982), p. 93.
14. Ibid., p. 96.
15. Edgar Allan Poe, *The Unknown Poe*, p. 61.
16. Carol J. Clover, *Men, Women, and Chainsaws: Gender in the Modern Horror Film* (London, British Film Institute, 1992), and Philip Brophy, 'Horrality: the Textuality of Contemporary Horror Films', *Screen*, vol. 27, 1986, pp. 2–13. Reprinted from *Art and Text*, Spring 1983.
17. Carol Clover, *Men, Women and Chainsaws*, p. 41.
18. Ibid.
19. Philip Brophy, 'Horrality', p. 11.
20. *SoS*, p. 20.
21. I am referring here specifically to 'The Imp of the Perverse', not to the complete Poe œuvre and all its ramifications.
22. André Green, *On Private Madness* (London: Hogarth, 1986).

23. Christian Metz, 'The Passion for Perceiving', in *Psychoanalysis and Cinema: The Imaginary Signifier*, p. 59.
24. James Truman, 'Martin Scorsese', *The Face*, no. 82, February 1987, p. 80. Truman introduces this interview by referring to *After Hours* as 'an untypically light-weight farce'.
25. Salman Rushdie, *The Wizard of Oz*, p. 57.
26. Ibid., p. 27.
27. Some critics argue that Paul is redeemed or that he has learnt how to survive. For instance, Bill Van Daalen: 'He is being put through an initiation ritual, a trial by fire for the old self so that a new, more mature one can take its place.' See '*After Hours*', *Film Quarterly*, vol. 16, no. 3, 1988, pp. 31–4. Timothy Corrigan in his chapter entitled 'Illegible Films: Texts without Secrets', argues that Paul escapes 'when he learns to perform himself as a changing identity' and when he understands that survival in contemporary life 'means having a performative relationship with the contingencies that overtake any sense of control'. See *A Cinema Without Walls: Movies and Culture after Vietnam* (New Brunswick, NJ: Rutgers University Press, 1991), pp. 96–97. Michel Cieutat sees *After Hours* as a descent into some sort of Baudelairian hell and he refers to Paul's 'spiritual journey'. See *Martin Scorsese* (Paris: Rivages, 1986), p. 207. Pam Cook, on the other hand, concludes her review thus: 'It is disappointing that it finally draws back from the challenge it offers into a bleak acceptance, perhaps even a celebration, of life's vicious circles.' See '*After Hours*', *Monthly Film Bulletin*, vol. 53, 1986, p. 166.
28. Minion's original script had a different ending. Scorsese has talked a lot about how they arrived at the current conclusion: almost at the eleventh hour, during production, with everyone – from Thelma Shoonmaker, Amy Robinson and Michael Powell to Steven Spielberg – throwing in ideas. The most interesting discussion is in an interview in *Cahiers du Cinéma*, in which Scorsese dwells at length on the ending. His account is primarily descriptive; it details the various options, why they were rejected, and so on. His approach is not analytical and so doesn't lend support in any obvious way to either my reading or the approaches that favour a 'salvation' wrap-up; but the account is fascinating for the sense of struggle and play and panic it conveys, and there is immense relief when finally he says: 'We had a continuity, a circular structure, and that had a funny side.' I find it intriguing for the way it conveys the process of fiction, the way the unconscious speaks not necessarily in psycho-blabber, but through patterns, rhythms, structures. It is as though the film had set in process a structure and was resistant to 'inappropriate' or premature conclusions; but at the same time the ending had to emerge out of the process of the fiction, was not lying in wait as a *deus ex machina*. See Bill Krohn, 'Into the Night', trans. Francine Arakelian, *Cahiers du Cinéma*, no. 383–384, May 1986, p. 93.
29. Timothy Corrigan does an excellent job of placing these films ('illegible films', he calls them) historically and institutionally, within a critical context of production and reception. See *A Cinema Without Walls*, pp. 76–7.
30. Scorsese in an interview with James Truman. See James Truman, 'Martin Scorsese', p. 80.
31. Ivars Peterson, *The Mathematical Tourist: Snapshots of Modern Mathematics* (New York: W. H. Freeman & Co., 1988), p. 17.
32. Ibid., p. 39.
33. Not unlike the pure void that functions, in Lacanian theory, as the object-cause of desire, the zero borrowed from number theory that serves to both inaugurate transference and terminate analysis. Slavoj Zizek discusses this in terms of Hitchcock's McGuffin and distinguishes it from another kind of Hitchcockian object – 'an object of exchange circulating among subjects' – such as the key in *Notorious*. See *The Sublime Object of Ideology* (London: Verso, 1989), p. 182. Keys of this sort, I would argue, always signify a double inscription: they circulate within the diegetic drama, and within the drama of interpretation that takes place in the encounter between text and viewer. In the case of *Notorious* the viewer is reflexively implicated in a diegetic drama that conjoins interpretation with masculinity- as-suspicion. In *Meshes of the Afternoon* the key similarly

(though to different ends) implicates the viewer in interpretation as a dangerous enterprise, and links the danger to questions of gender. Something quite different is going on in another contemporary text that is concerned with allusion and filmic quotation – in Brian De Palma's *The Untouchables* the exchange of keys (analogous to the exchange of guns) serves to consolidate and celebrate, in a quite unproblematic way, male lineage.

34. Indicating, perhaps, a bug in the system. In his reading of the film, David Wills argues that 'most obviously, a psychoanalytic reading of *Blue Velvet* is disturbed by the bugs'. See Peter Brunette and David Wills, *Screen/Play: Derrida and Film Theory* (Princeton, NJ: Princeton University Press, 1989), p. 155. 'If the bugs escape the spaces of narrative, of thematics, and of readings like psychoanalysis that rely on such structured spaces,' he writes, 'it is perhaps because they inhabit the space of the ear, the severed ear lying open-ended in the grass' (p. 157). He sees the severed ear as a breach within the circuit of language, an opening onto writing in the Derridean sense.

35. Barbara Creed lists a number of these psychoanalytic tropes in 'A Journey Through *Blue Velvet*: Film, Fantasy and the Female Spectator', *New Formations*, no. 6, Winter 1988, pp. 97–117.

36. Shoshana Felman, *Writing and Madness* (Ithaca, NY: Cornell University Press, 1989), p. 228.

37. One way of reading *Blue Velvet* is as a post-modern remake of *Bringing Up Baby*, where the wanting or the fantasy is neither repressed nor mobilised narratively, but rather explicitly articulated and acted out in the form of a slapstick – or lipstick – routine (and where the pet leopard, that is 'Baby' from the earlier film, is heard roaring on the soundtrack).

38. The shaft of light and stream of words are combined in Simone Martini's *Annunciation*. Thank you Anne Freadman for locating this image.

39. Comparing *The Wizard of Oz* and *Blue Velvet*, in 'Down the Yellow Brick Road: Two Dorothys and the Journey of Initiation in Dream and Nightmare', James Lindroth elaborates the notion of castration and refers to the 'phallic witch' (*Film/Literature Quarterly*, vol. 18, no. 3, 1990, pp. 160–6).

40. In the Hans Christian Andersen fairy tale of 'The Red Shoes' the girl is eventually driven to beg the executioner to cut off her feet. He says, 'Surely thou knowest not who I am. I cut off the heads of wicked men, and my axe is very sharp and keen.' To which the girl replies, 'Cut not off my head! For then I could not live to repent of my sin; but cut off my feet with the red shoes.'

41. *The Wizard of Oz*, p. 57.

42. Sigmund Freud, *Inhibitions, Symptoms and Anxiety* (1926), PFL 10, p. 274.

43. Marlene Dietrich declares the existence of 'a foreign legion of women too' as she starts walking into the North African desert wearing spiky stilettos. She is following her man and thus in a sense 'going home', that is – taking up her proper feminine place. Yet she is heading into alien territory, to become a foreigner, a stranger at home. There is something unhomely (*unheimlich*) or uncanny about this image.

44. Salman Rushdie, *The Wizard of Oz*, p. 44.

45. Sigmund Freud, *Totem and Taboo* (1913), PFL 13, p. 130.

46. Jean-Philippe Domecq, in *Martin Scorsese: Un rêve italo-americain*, sees these scenes as moments of respite (Lausanne: Five Continents, 1989, p. 129). Certainly there is a sense of Paul retreating, searching for an escape, but after *Taxi Driver* such 'cleansing' respites can surely only be seen ironically.

47. Gilles Deleuze, 'Francis Bacon: The Logic of Sensation', *Flash Art*, no. 112, May 1983, p. 101.

48. See Francois Roustang, 'How do You Make a Paranoiac Laugh?', *Modern Language Notes*, vol. 102, no. 4, September 1987, pp. 707–18.

49. Jacqueline Rose, in 'Paranoia and the Film System,' argues that 'paranoia could be said to be latent to the structure of cinematic specularity in itself' (*Screen*, vol. 17, no. 4, Winter 1976–7, p. 89). I am not proposing such an argument, but her detailing of the way in

which aggressivity is released in *The Birds* is useful for its attention to a certain cinematic articulation of paranoia.

50. Sigmund Freud, *Some Neurotic Mechanisms in Jealousy, Paranoia and Homosexuality*, PFL 10, pp. 200–1.
51. Sigmund Freud, *Inhibitions, Symptoms and Anxiety*, PFL 10, pp. 324–5.
52. I would not want to posit an isomorphism between genres or narrative tendencies and 'neuroses', for in fact there is no telling how a variety of factors will come together in any particular instance. This is merely a generalisation, or speculation about tendencies. It is worth bearing in mind that where anxiety is generated in the movies it is generally, though not invariably, converted. The musical and various forms of comedy are exemplary for the way they both generate and convert anxiety.
53. Sigmund Freud, *Inhibitions, Symptoms and Anxiety*, PFL 10, p. 326.
54. Ibid., p. 297.
55. Samuel Weber, 'Laughing in the Meanwhile', *Modern Language Notes*, vol. 102, no. 4, September 1987, p. 692.
56. Sigmund Freud, *The 'Uncanny'*, PFL 14, p. 376. The example is from Nestroy's farce *Der Zerrissene (The Torn Man)*.
57. Ibid., p. 359.
58. Thus imaging the balletic red shoes whose uncanniness lies in their demonic animation, the fact that they have a life of their own.
59. Sigmund Freud, Inhibitions, *Symptoms and Anxiety*, PFL 10, p. 327.
60. Dana Polan, 'Being and Nuttiness: Jerry Lewis and the French', *Journal of Popular Film and Culture*, vol. 12, no. 1, 1984, p. 46.
61. Sigmund Freud, *Beyond the Pleasure Principle*, PFL 11, p. 293.
62. Edgar Allen Poe, 'The Black Cat', in *The Portable Poe* (Harmondsworth: Penguin, 1986), pp. 299 ff.
63. A very funny exchange takes place about the value of art – 'a stereo's a stereo, but art is forever' – reminiscent of *A Bucket of Blood*'s send-up of the beatnik art scene and its artistic pretensions.
64. Jean Laplanche and J.-B. Pontalis, 'Wild Analysis', in *The Language of Psychoanalysis* (New York: W. W. Norton, 1973), p. 481.
65. Melanie Klein, 'Notes on Some Schizoid Mechanisms', in *The Selected Melanie Klein*, (London: Penguin, 1988), p. 182.
66. William Gass, *On Being Blue: A Philosophical Inquiry* (Boston, Mass.: David R. Godine, 1976), p. 4.
67. Although Laura Mulvey, in a fascinating account of 'The Oedipus Myth', suggests that Frank erupts in the film with all the force of the primal and repressed pre-Oedipal father. See *Visual and Other Pleasures* (London: Macmillan, 1989), pp. 198–9.
68. Carolee Schneeman, 'Kenneth Anger's *Scorpio Rising*', in P. Adams Sitney (ed.), *Film Culture Reader* (New York: Praeger, 1970), p. 277.
69. Patricia Mellencamp, in *Indiscretions: Avant-Garde Film, Video, and Feminism* (Bloomington: Indiana University Press, 1990), writes of a tradition of avant-garde film-making set in place by Cocteau, Smith and Anger, that there is 'on one hand, a confusion of roles and a scandalous challenge to conventions of representation, codes of censorship, and heterosexuality; on the other hand, the structuration is adolescent, involving youthful liberation and rebellion, centering, literally, on the phallus' (p. 22).
70. William Gass, , *On Being Blue*, p. 82.
71. Friedrich Nietzsche, *On the Genealogy of Morals* (New York: Random House, 1967), p. 61.
72. Gregory Whitehead, '*Beyond the Pleasure Principle*: Excerpts from a Radio Play', *Lusitania*, vol. 1, no. 2, 1988, p. 36.
73. Keir Elam, *The Semiotics of Theater and Drama* (New York: Methuen, 1980), pp. 26–7.
74. David Bordwell, in *Narration in the Fiction Film* (Wisconsin: University of Wisconsin Press, 1986), considers the issue briefly, but concludes that 'film narration does not possess features akin to deixis, those linguistic signals of the context of utterance' (p. 77). On the other hand, Paul Willemen's analysis of Raoul Walsh's *Pursued* identifies a

number of features in the film that do operate as shifters; see Phil Hardy (ed.), *Raoul Walsh*, Edinburgh: Edinburgh International Festival, 1975.

75. Roman Jakobson, *Essais de linguistique générale* (Paris: Minuit, 1963), ch. 9.
76. Noel Carroll distinguishes between anticipation and suspense, but does not discuss anticipation at any length. I also would make the distinction, but my emphasis is on aligning expectation with a sense of the indefinite, with a lack of object, in fact with anxiety. See 'Toward a Theory of Film Suspense', *Persistence of Vision*, no. 1, 1984, pp. 65–89.
77. Mary Pat Kelly, *Martin Scorsese: A Journey*, p. 185.
78. Pascal Bonitzer, 'Mâchoires', *Cahiers du Cinéma*, no. 383–4, May 1986, p. 43.
79. VèVè A. Clark, Millicent Hodson and Catrina Neiman (eds), *The Legend of Maya Deren: a Documentary Biography and Collected Works*, Vol. 1, Pt 2: *Chambers (1942–1947)* (New York: Anthology Film Archives/Film Culture, 1988), p. 78.
80. Andrew Sarris, 'Stranded in SoHo's Mean Streets', in *The Village Voice*, 17 September 1985, p. 54.
81. This was the film that launched the Hammer cycle. 'I'll never forget going to a midnight screening at the New York Paramount of *The Curse of Frankenstein* in 1957, the day before it opened. The audience loved it, and there was a graphic quality to it that was totally uncalled for and was extremely endearing to us at about the age of fifteen' (*SoS*, p. 103).
82. Samuel Weber, *The Legend of Freud* (Minneapolis: University of Minnesota Press, 1982), p. 134. This is my reading of Weber's argument; he himself doesn't use the phrase 'acting out'.
83. Tania Modleski, *The Women Who Knew Too Much: Hitchcock and Feminist Theory* (New York: Methuen, 1988), p. 92.
84. Sarah Kofman, *The Enigma of Woman* (Ithaca, NY: Cornell University Press, 1985), p. 56.
85. See Stephen Heath, '*Jaws*, Ideology, and Film Theory', in Bill Nichols (ed.), *Movies and Methods* (Berkeley: University of California Press, 1985), Vol. 2, pp. 510–14.
86. Gilles Deleuze, 'Francis Bacon: The Logic of Sensation', p. 102.
87. Of Molière's *Don Juan*, Michel Serres writes, 'The quintessential ladies' man is a man of ideas, the first hero of modernity.' See *Hermes: Literature, Science, Philosophy* (Baltimore, Md.: Johns Hopkins University Press, 1982), p. 3. Like Paul Hackett, Jerry Lewis, quintessentially in *The Ladies' Man*, presents a highly parodic representation of this 'quintessential ladies' man.'
88. Compare Teri Garr's performance here with her performance in Coppola's *One from the Heart*, a film that is in many ways breathtaking to watch but also a bland and insipidly consoling romance, relying on Kleenex acting, a kind of tarted-up naturalism.
89. Mary Pat Kelly, *Martin Scorsese: A Journey*, p. 188.
90. Paul Willemen cites this instance of 'burn out' in 'Cinematic Discourse: The Problem of Inner Speech', in his book *Looks and Frictions* (London: British Film Institute, 1994), p. 31.
91. Roland Barthes, *A Lover's Discourse: Fragments* (New York: Farrar, Strauss & Giroux/Hill & Wang, 1978), p. 23.

Chapter 5

1. Raul Ruiz, discussing how he came to make a film from Pierre Klowssowski's novel *The Suspended Vocation*. See Raul Ruiz, transcription of a forum presentation at the Australian Film Institute, *Agenda*, no. 30–31, May 1993, p. 53.
2. Martin Scorsese, *Dialogue on Film: Martin Scorsese*, Dialogue on Film Series (Washington, DC: American Film Institute), vol. 4, no.7, April 1975, p. 6.
3. Ibid.
4. Ibid.
5. From the 1943 film *Hello, Frisco, Hello*.
6. Martin Scorsese, *Dialogue On Film*, p. 6
7. William Carlos Williams, 'The Red Wheelbarrow,' in *Penguin Modern Poets*, no. 9 (Harmondsworth: Penguin, 1971 [1938]), p. 84.

8. For an extremely detailed analysis of a credit sequence (the opening of *The Most Danger-ous Game*) see Thierry Kuntzel, 'The Film-Work, 2', *Camera Obscura*, no. 5, Spring 1980, pp. 6–69. He writes: 'For the analyst, what is fascinating about beginnings is the fact that, in the space of a few images, a few seconds, almost the entire film can be con-densed', and 'much more than "meaning" it is the fluttering of meaning that concerns me. The beginning, although inscribed within a certain ideologically determined system (the flattening-out of the signifying volume by narrative), is nevertheless the most "mod-ern" – the most plural – in comparison to the other segments of the film' (p. 24). He does not consider the industrial/ideological dimension of the credits. See also Paul Willemen's comments about credit sequences summarising the coming film in his analysis of Roger Corman's films in Mike Wallington, David Will and Paul Willemen (eds), *Roger Cor-man: The Millennic Vision* (Edinburgh: Edinburgh International Film Festival, 1970.)

9. Raoul Ruiz and Jean Louis Schefer, 'L'Image, la mort, la mémoire', *ça Cinéma*, special issue no. 2, 1980, p. 32. See also Raul Ruiz, 'Object Relations in the Cinema', trans. Jill Forbes, *Afterimage*, no. 10, Autumn 1981, pp. 87–93.

10. Maureen Turim, *Flashbacks in Film: Memory and History* (New York: Routledge, 1989), p. 5.

11. Ellen Burstyn tells of how a happy ending gets imposed on them: 'Marty and I were disgusted. The end they wanted was a movie ending, not a real ending, which was why Marty had everybody in the restaurant applaud [when the Kristofferson character pro-poses to Burstyn], because that was his way of acknowledging that this was the movie ending.' See Mary Pat Kelly, *Martin Scorsese: A Journey* (London: Secker & Warburg, 1992), p. 84.

12. Eisenstein, talking about colour movement, what happens on a plastic plane, about 'emotional colouring'. See Sergei Eisenstein, 'Colour Film: from *Notes of a Film Direc-tor*', in Bill Nichols (ed.), *Movies and Methods* (Berkeley: University of California Press, 1976 [1948]), pp. 381–8. The article was written as a letter to L. Kuleshov.

13. Gérard Genette points out that this is the most persistent function of recalls in *Remem-brance of Things Past*. See Gérard Genette, *Narrative Discourse: An Essay in Method* (Oxford: Basil Blackwell, 1980), p. 56.

14. Thank you, Anne Rowe, for drawing my attention to *Lancelot*.

15. See, for instance, Raymond Durgnat and Scott Simmon, *King Vidor, American* (Berke-ley: University of California Press, 1988).

16. David Thomson, *A Biographical Dictionary of Film* (New York: William Morrow, 1981), p. 628.

17. *Cahiers du Cinéma*, no. 48, 1955, p. 14. Cited by Stuart Cunningham in *Featuring Aus-tralia: the Cinema of Charles Chauvel* (Sydney: Allen & Unwin, 1991), p. 159.

18. See Jodi Brooks, 'Fascination and the Grotesque: *Whatever Happened to Baby Jane?*', *Continuum: The Australian Journal of Media and Culture*, special issue: *Film – Matters of Style*, vol. 5, no. 2, 1992, pp. 225–34.

19. *Alice* was made at a time when feminist consciousness was creating pressure for believa-ble and well rounded female characters and I suspect that this might have resulted in the loss of a potentially cutting and abrasive edge. There was an implicit embargo on bad girls (like Jane and Blanche) though this strain does surface with the kids, in the perform-ances of Jodie Foster and Alfred Lutter, and in the female sidekicks, Dianne Ladd and Lane Bradbury.

20. In this connection it is interesting to note that experimental cinema frequently – more in the past than now – does away with credits altogether, presumably not because they would detract from the illusion of fiction (because these works are seldom narrative) but because they would detract from the status of the product as art by drawing attention to money and to a production context and division of labour that might undermine the aura of the artist-creator.

21. Thanks to Ruth Vasey for drawing my attention to this.

22. David Bordwell, Janet Staiger, and Kristin Thompson, *The Classical Hollywood Cinema: Film Style and Mode of Production to 1960* (London: Routledge, 1988 [1985]), pp. 312–3.

23. Claire Johnston and Paul Willemen (eds), *Frank Tashlin* (Edinburgh: Edinburgh Film Festival, 1973), p. 58.
24. See Jacques Derrida, *The Truth in Painting* (Chicago: University of Chicago Press, 1987).
25. Paul Willemen (ed.), *Pier Paolo Pasolini* (London: British Film Institute, 1977), p. 64.
26. Robert Phillip Kolker, *A Cinema of Loneliness: Penn, Kubrick, Coppola, Scorsese, Altman* (New York: Oxford University Press, 1980), p. 254.
27. Super 8 film-making was instituted in Mozambique after independence (in 1975) in a major project, initiated by the newly formed National Film Institute and the University of Maputo with Jean Rouch co-ordinating. In this instance, super 8 was envisaged not as a form of home-movie-making, but, within a revolutionary context, as a mode of public writing, or to use Rouch's term, as *carte postale*. The first feature made by a Mozambican was *Mueda: memoria e massacre* (Ruy Guerra, 1979), an extraordinary historical dramatisation, deploying memory and re-enactment to recover and transform the past. The white regime did leave surprisingly well equipped studios and labs (after a ten-year war) but few trained personnel and no tradition of, or expertise in, fictional film-making since the government production house had been dedicated exclusively to propaganda. A number of the Zimbabweans now making films acquired their skills through working as actors, extras and even stuntmen on international feature films shot on location in Zimbabwe.
28. Dambudzo Marechera, *Dambudzo Marechera: 1952–1987* (Harare: Baobab Books, 1988), p. 25. Marechera was probably Zimbabwe's best-known writer, as well as being a flamboyant and iconoclastic figure, when he died in 1987.
29. Paul Virilio, *War and Cinema: The Logistics of Perception* (London: Verso, 1989 [1984]), p. 69.
30. Sergei Eisenstein, 'The Dynamic Square', in Jay Leyda (ed.), *Film Essays and A Lecture* (New York: Praeger, 1970), pp. 48–65.
31. He argues this in a witty and persuasive reading of *It's Always Fair Weather*, *Widescreen Cinema* (Cambridge, Mass.: Harvard University Press, 1992) p. 224.
32. André Bazin, 'Beauté d'un Western', *Cahiers du Cinéma*, no. 55, January 1956, p. 35. Quoted by David Bordwell in David Bordwell, Janet Staiger, Kristin Thompson, *The Classical Hollywood Cinema*, p. 361.
33. Sergei Eisenstein, 'The Dynamic Square', p. 59.
34. Many of the arguments about the efficacy of widescreen revolve around questions of realism, and how appropriately the wide screen can carry out the realist destiny of the cinema. Probably the best-known argument for widescreen from a realist point of view is found in Charles Barr, 'CinemaScope: Before and After', *Film Quarterly*, vol. 16, no. 4, Summer 1963, pp. 11–20. Although Bordwell stresses Bazin's cautious welcoming of widescreen as a move away from montage-based cinema, in fact Bazin's position was ambivalent and contradictory (as he himself notes); he also wrote, 'I would not go so far as to say that paradoxically the wide screen is unsuitable for westerns or that it adds nothing to them, but it seems to me already an accepted fact that CinemaScope will add nothing decisive to this field.' See André Bazin, 'The Evolution of the Western', in *What is Cinema?* (Berkeley: University of California Press, 1972), Vol. 2, p. 157. Rivette, on the other hand, argued that with widescreen the director 'will unburden the image, no longer fearing holes or imbalances, and will multiply compositional violations the better to obey the truths of cinema'. See Jacques Rivette, 'L'Âge des metteurs en scène', *Cahiers du Cinéma*, no. 31, January 1954, p. 48.
35. Raymod Durgnat, in *Seeing in the Dark: A Compendium of Cinemagoing* (London: Serpent's Tail, 1990), p. 12.
36. Walter Benjamin uses the phrase 'the optical unconscious' in his essay 'A Small History of Photography'. He remarks that photography shares with medicine and other technology the capacity to reveal in detail the structural and detailed aspects of things. 'Yet at the same time,' he says, 'photography reveals in this material the physiognomic aspects of visual worlds which dwell in the smallest things, meaningful yet covert enough

to find a hiding place in waking dreams, but which, enlarged and capable of formulation, make the difference between technology and magic visible as a thoroughly historical variable.' See *One Way Street and Other Writings* (London: New Left Books, 1979), pp. 243–4.

37. My intention here is not to argue that television *caused* the film industry recession: it was one of a number of factors which included anti-trust legislation, a move to the suburbs, the development of a range of competing leisure-time activities, not to mention the argument that Hollywood never in fact recovered from the Depression (assuming, that is, that the wartime figures are a false indication of recovery). For such an argument, see Joel W. Finler, *The Hollywood Story* (London: Octopus, 1988).

38. For the former, see Fredric Stuart, 'The Effects of Television on the Motion Picture Industry', in Gorham Kinder (ed.), *The American Movie Industry* (Carbondale: Southern Illinois University Press, 1982), pp. 257–307. For the latter, see Tino Balio, 'Introduction to Part 1', in *Hollywood in the Age of Television* (Boston, Mass.: Unwin Hyman, 1990), pp. 20–1.

39. *SoS*, p. 4.

40. Tino Balio, *Hollywood in the Age of Television*, pp. 17 and 36.

41. James L. Baughman, 'The Weakest Chain and the Longest Link: The American Broadcasting Company and the Motion Picture Industry, 1952–60', in Tino Balio (ed.), *Hollywood in the Age of Television*, p. 104.

42. Raymond Bellour, with Lea Bandy (ed.), *Jean-Luc Godard: Son + Image 1974–1991* (New York: Museum of Modern Art, 1992), p. 149.

43. Quoted in Timothy Corrigan, *A Cinema Without Walls: Movies and Culture After Vietnam* (New Brunswick, NJ: Rutgers University Press, 1991), p. 121.

44. The notion of independence in this context is of course highly anomalous. Douglas Gomery, in *Shared Pleasures: a History of Movie Presentation in the United States* (Madison: University of Wisconsin, 1992), argues that Hollywood has more of a monopoly and more power than ever before. Timothy Corrigan, at the other extreme, in *A Cinema Without Walls*, downplays Hollywood in positing a radical heterogeneity in contemporary movie production and, more particularly, consumption. The entanglement of film and television in America does not in fact account for modes of realignment that have occurred in Europe (including Britain) and elsewhere (for instance, it certainly doesn't account for patterns of distribution and reception in Third World countries). Any extensive discussion of this entanglement would need to take into account the work in television (both writing and production) of figures such as Alexander Kluge and Jean-Luc Godard.

45. Time Inc. (of which HBO was a subsidiary) purchased Warners Communications Inc. in 1989. In addition to financing scores of independent productions, HBO had interests in Tri-Star Pictures and Orion Pictures. See Tino Balio, *Hollywood in the Age of Television*, p. 265.

46. Martin Scorsese, *SoS*, p. 49. In *Dialogue on Film* he also mentions John Ford's *Tobacco Road* and Kazan's *East of Eden* as influential. Thompson and Christie have a footnote explaining William Cameron Menzies (1896–1957): 'One of Hollywood's most respected art directors (*The Thief of Bagdad*, 1924) before he took up direction as well in the thirties. His most prestigious projects of the thirties were Korda's spectacular *Things to Come* (1936), which he directed and part-designed, and *Gone with the Wind* (1939) for which he was art director. But his later low-budget science fiction movies have a cult following – especially *Invaders from Mars* (1953), in which both adult world and a flying saucer invasion are seen from a child's point of view' (*SoS*, p. 67). Russell Metty was a cinematographer associated with many major directors and films, such as *Touch of Evil* (Orson Welles, 1958) and a number of Douglas Sirk widescreen Technicolor films, including *Written on the Wind* (1956). Scorsese has endeavoured to work with a number of veterans from the studio era. As David Ehrenstein points out, Boris Leven, who had designed the sets for *The Silver Chalice*, *The Shanghai Gesture*, *Anatomy of a Murder* and *West Side Story*, was chosen when 'Scorsese needed to recreate the glamour

of the set-bound films of the studio era for *New York New York'*. See David Ehrenstein, *The Scorsese Picture: The Art and Life of Martin Scorsese* (New York: Birch Lane Press, 1992), p. 158.

47. This is the case in *Alice* but not invariably the case – Scorsese uses the frame-within-a-frame device quite often and though it always evokes a *différance* (not just a difference, but a degree of incommensurability or untranslatability), it doesn't always refer to the relation between the Academy ratio of studio pictures and the wide screen. At the end of *Italian American* the frame shrinks to a square in the centre of the rectangle – within the inner frame an image of his mother is frozen and sepia-tinted. Michael Bliss notes: 'Given *Italian American*'s wonderful evocation of the Scorsese family's past, which is visually captured in family stills, this metamorphosis of Catherine Scorsese into yet another family portrait brilliantly situates her in the familial context as a chromo of Italian-American life.' See Michael Bliss, *Martin Scorsese and Michael Cimino* (Metuchen, NJ.: The Scarecrow Press, 1985), p. 91.

48. In Gregory L. Ulmer, *Applied Grammatology Post(e) Pedagogy from Jacques Derrida to Joseph Beuys* (Baltimore, Md.: Johns Hopkins University Press, 1985), p. 111.

49. Although there were occasional one-offs (which meant that a few films received early television exposure) such as CBS's 1956 acquisition of *The Wizard of Oz* (it would of course have been seen in its entirety in black and white). See William Lafferty, 'Feature Films on Prime-Time Television', in Tino Balio (ed.), *Hollywood in the Age of Television*, p. 242.

50. John Belton, *Widescreen Cinema*, p. 216.

51. William Lafferty, 'Feature Films on Prime-Time Television', p. 252.

52. Cited by John Belton, who comments: 'With *Cape Fear* (1991), however, which was filmed in Panavision, Scorsese has finally made a 'Scope film, encouraged, no doubt, by the success of some of his colleagues in releasing their widescreen films on video in the letterbox format.' See *Widescreen Cinema*, p. 225. In fact, in Australia anyway, it has not been letterboxed on video; although it is available on videodisc.

53. Douglas Gomery, *Shared Pleasures*, p. 261.

54. Thelma Schoonmaker, who worked on *Who's That Knocking at My Door?*, and has cut all Scorsese's features since *Raging Bull*, tells how she stumbled into a film job after college, with 'an old hack who was butchering the films of Fellini and Truffaut' for TV broadcast. See Stephan Talty, 'Invisible Woman', *American Film*, vol. 16, September–October 1991, p. 44.

55. For a very interesting discussion of these issues see Richard Maltby and Ruth Vasey, 'The International Language Problem: European Reactions to Hollywood's Conversion to Sound', in David W. Ellwood and Rob Kroes (eds), *Hollywood in Europe: Experiences of a Celluloid Hegemony* (Amsterdam: Amsterdam University Press, 1994), pp 68–93.

56. *SoS*, p. 6.

57. Robert Gustafson, '"What's Happening to Our Pix Biz?" From Warner Bros. to Warner Communications Inc.', in Tino Balio (ed.), *The American Film Industry*, revised edition (Madison: The University of Wisconsin Press, 1985 [1976]) p. 583.

58. Giuliana Bruno, 'Ramble City: Postmodernism and *Blade Runner*', *October,* no. 41, Summer 1987, pp. 61–74; and Kaja Silverman, 'Back to the Future', *Camera Obscura,* no. 27, September 1991, pp. 109–132. Fredric Jameson sets out the terms for a discussion of *Blade Runner* under this rubric in his essays 'Postmodernism, or The Cultural Logic of Late Capitalism' and 'Nostalgia for the Present' in *Postmodernism, or, The Cultural Logic of Late Capitalism* (Durham, NC: Duke University Press, 1991).

59. Raymond Bellour (ed.), *Godard: Son + Image 1974–1991*, p 159.

60. Timothy Corrigan, for instance, takes this very terrain as the subject matter of *A Cinema Without Walls*. He examines the way in which changing social and technological conditions have 'massively altered how those movies are received by viewers and, *as a consequence of those new patterns of reception*, how those movies now address their audiences' (p. 1). His book is extremely interesting in charting these changes and for situating film readings in the context of usage – how films are watched, how meanings circulate in the social. There is, however, a major divergence between our approaches –

he assumes (and it is a not uncommon assumption of certain post-modern postulates) a correlation between the proliferation of viewing contexts and the fracturing of subjectivity. With the VCR and the 'remote control' viewers are able to position and control the movie much as it used to position and control the viewer, and 'simultaneously, they are reflected in that experience as always *potentially* a discontinuous or fragmented subjectivity without a centered or stable position, a discursively mobile identity' (p. 29). I do not see how the one postulate entails the other, how one infers fragmented subjectivity (as though there were once a certainty of viewing position) from a remote control device. Similarly, to posit the walls that have collapsed as authoritarian is one thing, but to deduce from that a contemporary dramatisation of multiple self-identities strikes me as fanciful to say the least. I certainly do agree that changes in modes of perception are associated with changes in exhibition, and also that the parameters of possibility, in terms of representation, are redrawn; but I am sceptical about approaches which seem to assume that viewers are now caught, in general, in some jubilant crisis of subjectivity.

61. The original theatrical sequence survives, however, in the laserdisc edition because, Dante says, 'Laser disc consumers are into letterboxing and are basically interested in recreating the theatrical experience at home'. See Tim Lucas, 'Joe Dante', *Sight and Sound*, vol. 3, no. 6, June 1993, p. 9.

62. 'Colour Problem', *Sight and Sound*, vol. 50, no. 1, 1980–1, p. 12.

63. Sue McNab, in *Seeing in the Dark*, p. 156.

64. See John Halliday, *Sirk on Sirk* (London: Secker & Warburg/BFI, 1971), p. 119.

65. Gilles Deleuze, *Cinema 1: The Movement–Image* (Minneapolis: The University of Minnesota Press, 1986), p. 118. The Ollier reference is given as *Souvenirs écran*, pp. 211–18. The Godard 'formula' was given in an interview with *Cahiers du Cinéma* when the interviewers remarked, 'There is a good deal of blood in *Pierrot*.' See Jean-Luc Godard, *Godard on Godard* (London: Secker & Warburg, 1972), p. 217.

66. Ibid., p. 119.

67. Albert Namatjira was the key figure and best-known artist of the Aranda watercolour school – very popular, but ignored until recently by the art history establishment in part because it was seen as too European, as 'inauthentically' Aboriginal, and at the same time viewed as a kind of kitschy primitivism. For an article that maps out the art history debates and the cultural and political ramifications see Ian Burn and Ann Stephen, 'Traditional Painter: The Transfiguration of Albert Namtjira', *Age Monthly Review*, vol. 6, no. 7, November 1986.

68. Walter Benjamin, 'A Berlin Chronicle', in *Reflections: Essays, Aphorisms, Autobiographical Writings* (New York: Schocken, 1986), p. 25.

69. He also mouths a song in silence: 'Love me Tender Love me True'. I do not attempt here to deal with the role that Jimmy Little plays in the film, but see Laleen Jayamanne, 'Love Me Tender, Love Me True, Never Let Me Go . . . A Sri Lankan reading of Tracey Moffat's *Night Cries: A Rural Tragedy*', in Anna Yeatman and Sneja Gunew (eds), *Feminism and the Politics of Difference* (Sydney: Allen & Unwin, 1993), pp. 73–84. Jayamanne approaches his 'meaning' via the notion of assimilation and looks at the way in which assimilation figures in the film not only as a thematic but also as an aesthetic strategy. See also Ingrid Periz, '*Night Cries*: Cries from the heart', *Filmnews*, vol. 20, no. 7, August 1990, p. 16.

70. Michel de Certeau, *The Practice of Everyday Life* (Berkeley: University of California Press, 1985), p. 88.

71. Gayatri Chakravorty Spivak, 'Can the Subaltern Speak?', in Cary Nelson and Lawrence Grossberg (eds), *Marxism and the Interpretation of Culture* (Urbana: University of Illinois Press, 1988), p. 296.

72. Peter Wollen, 'Cinema and Technology: A Historical Overview', in Teresa De Lauretis and Stephen Heath (eds), *The Cinematic Apparatus* (New York: St Martin's Press, 1980), p. 24. This is actually from the discussion following the conference presentation of his paper.

73. Dudley Andrew, 'The Post-War Struggle for Colour', in Teresa De Lauretis and Stephen Heath (eds), *The Cinematic Apparatus*, p. 67.

74. For a history of Technicolor Inc. see Fred E. Basten, *Glorious Technicolor* (London: A.S. Barnes, 1980).
75. Gorham Kindem, 'Hollywood's Conversion to Color: The Technological, Economic, and Aesthetic Factors', in Gorham Kindem (ed.), *The American Movie Industry* (Carbondale and Edwardsville: Southern Illinois University Press, 1982), pp. 152–3.
76. Scott MacQueen, 'Technicolor and the True Believer', *The Perfect Vision*, Spring 1991, p. 25.
77. Dudley Andrew, 'The Post-War Struggle for Colour', in *The Cinematic Apparatus*, p. 68.
78. Gorham Kindem, 'Hollywood's Conversion to Colour', p. 156.
79. Ed Buscombe, 'Sound and Colour', in Bill Nichols (ed.), *Movies and Methods* (Berkeley: University of California Press, 1985), Vol. 2, pp. 83–92.
80. For an account of how different histories of colour could be written according to different ideological perspectives see Edward Branigan, 'Colour and Cinema: Problems in the Writing of History', in *Movies and Methods*, Vol. 2, pp. 121–43.
81. Brad Chisholm, 'Red, Blue, and Lots of Green: The Impact of Colour Television on Feature Film Production', in *Hollywood in the Age of Television*, p. 217.
82. For Natalie Kalmus's own comments and prescriptions see the following: John K. Newman, 'Profile of Natalie Kalmus', in John Huntley (ed.), *British Technicolour Films* (London: Skelton Robinson, 1949); Natalie Kalmus, 'Colour', in Stephen Watts (ed.), *Behind the Screen* (London: Arthur Barker, 1938); Natalie Kalmus, 'Color Consciousness', *Journal of SMPTE*, vol. 25, no. 2, August 1935; Roderick T. Ryan, *A History of Motion Picture Color Technology* (New York: Focal, 1977).
83. Julia Kristeva, *Desire in Language: A Semiotic Approach to Literature and Art* (New York: Columbia University Press, 1980), p. 221.
84. Steve Neale, *Cinema and Technology: Image, Sound, Colour* (London: BFI/Macmillan, 1985), p. 158. I should point out that this is an odd and somewhat uncharacteristic remark in a work which is remarkably clear and thoughtful in bringing together questions of technology and ideology.
85. Peter Wollen, 'Cinema and Technology: A Historical Overview', in *The Cinematic Apparatus*, p. 22.
86. Although as Scott MacQueen points out, the famous transition from monochrome Kansas to colour Munchkinland 'does not play today as it should (or as it did in 1939). The moment of transition occurs in the first shot of Reel Three: Dorothy moves to the door of her house and opens it onto the land of Oz, as the camera dollies past her into the opening of the door. The shot was made with the three-strip camera, but only the area seen through the door was printed in dye-transfer. Dorothy and the inside of her farmhouse, printed seperately, remained in sepia-platinum' ('Technicolor and the True Believer', p. 28).
87. David Ehrenstein, *The Scorsese Picture*, p. 116.
88. Between 1935 and 1955 three-colour feature films gradually increased from less than 1 per cent to more than 50 per cent of the total US. output. Between 1955 and 1958 it dropped to 25 per cent, picking up again in the mid-60s and by 1970 it was 94 per cent. See Gorham Kindem, 'Hollywood's Conversion to Colour', pp. 146 and 156.
89. Gorham Kinder, ibid., recounts: 'One such promotion took the form of a short film in which a popular television star (Red Skelton) talked about the advantages of motion pictures over television as he emerged from a corner of the screen inside a small box in black-and-white to fill the entire screen in color.'
90. Even John Izod, in a book published in 1988, well after the campaign for colour preservation had been initiated and much publicised, writes: 'A further breakthrough in colour production occurred in 1949 when Eastman-Kodak brought out a cheaper and readily available photochemical film which could be run through a conventional movie camera. Eastman-Kodak had a major advantage over Technicolor: the massive resources required to back further research into photochemical colour and to capitalise mass production and distribution' (*Hollywood and the Box Office 1895–1986*, Basingstoke: Macmillan, 1988, p. 138).

91. Quoted in 'Colour Problem', p. 12.
92. Mary Pat Kelly, *Martin Scorsese*, p. 125.
93. This and the three following quotes are from Scott MacQueen, 'Technicolor and the True Believer', pp. 24, 33, 37–8 and 34.
94. Jodi Brooks, 'The Amorous Subject of the Cinema: The Collector and Humour', unpublished paper, University of New South Wales, 1993.
95. Steve Howard, 'The Making of *Alice Doesn't Live Here Anymore*: An Interview with Martin Scorsese', *Filmmakers Newsletter*, vol. 8, no. 5, March 1975, p. 26.
96. Don DeLillo, *White Noise* (New York: Viking Penguin, 1985), p. 13.
97. Michel de Certeau, *The Practice of Everyday Life*, p. 86.
98. Walter Benjamin, 'A Berlin Chronicle', in *Reflections*, p. 25–6.
99. Adrian Martin, 'Raul Ruiz: The Comedy of Exile', programme note, in *The Cinema of Raul Ruiz* (Sydney: Australian Film Institute, 1993), p. 10.
100. Corrigan, for instance, in *A Cinema Without Walls*, and Charles Eidsvik talk of the 'glance aesthetics' that have, in contemporary culture, replaced 'gaze aesthetics'. See Charles Eidsvik, 'Machines of the Invisible: Changes in Film Technology in the Age of Video', *Film Quarterly*, vol. 42, no. 2, Winter 1988–9, pp. 18–23
101. Roger Corman, with Jim Jerome, *How I Made a Hundred Movies in Hollywood and Never Lost a Dime* (New York: Random House, 1990), p. 82.
102. James Monaco, *American Film Now* (New York: Oxford University Press, 1979), p. 51.
103. Calderón's classic seventeenth-century play concerns a prince, Segismundo, who is incarcerated from birth by his father, the king, in order to avoid the tragic fate which has been predicted. He is eventually released but told that he is dead and dreaming. As the play progresses it becomes increasingly difficult to unravel the threads of dream, fantasy, reality; and increasingly difficult to ascertain who is mad and who is dreaming – 'to live is to dream and therefore to awaken is to be dead, to be dead is to be awake.' One can see how the allegorical dimension would appeal to Ruiz, the elaboration of a political discourse that is densely detailed, but detailed by elements that are embroidered on gossamer. *Life Is A Dream* could serve as a perfect dramatisation of Lacan's idea that there is someone more mad than the beggar who thinks he's a king, and that's a king who thinks he's a king – that is to say, someone who identifies with a symbolic position.
104. Adrian Martin, 'Raul Ruiz: The Comedy of Exile', p. 15; AFI programme note.
105. Sigmund Freud, '"A Child is Being Beaten" A Contribution to the Study of the Origin of Sexual Perversions)', PFL 10, pp. 159–193. Freud analysed this common childhood fantasy by beginning with its characteristic lack of specification. To questions concerning who, where, why, the patient could only reply, 'I know nothing more about it: a child is being beaten.' Freud proceeded to break the phantasy down into several phases, or levels of meaning, and suggested a verbalisation for each phase.
106. Walter Benjamin, *Illuminations* (London: Collins/Fontana, 1973), p. 91.
107. Walter Benjamin, *One Way Street and Other Writings*, pp. 71–2.

Chapter 6

1. John Conomos and Raffaele Caputo, '*Bedevil*: Tracey Moffatt Interviewed', *Cinema Papers*, no. 93, May 1993, p. 31.
2. A familiar trope since *Carrie* and *Halloween*.
3. Peter Biskind, 'Slouching Toward Hollywood', *Premiere*, vol. 5, no. 3, November 1991, p. 73.
4. Walter Benjamin, 'A Berlin Chronicle', in *Reflections* (New York: Schocken, 1986), p. 26.
5. Catherine Clément, *Opera, or the Undoing of Women* (Minneapolis: University of Minnesota Press, 1988), p. 139.
6. I am grateful to Thomas Reiner for helping me to listen to the score.
7. For interesting accounts of *Cape Fear*'s indebtedness to low-budget horror and slasher movies, such as Abel Ferrara's *Ms 45* (aka *Angel of Vengeance*), see Pam Cook, 'Scorsese's Masquerade', *Sight and Sound*, vol. 1, no. 12, April 1992, pp. 14–5; Jim Hoberman,

'Sacred and Profane', *Sight and Sound*, vol. 1, no. 10, February 1992, pp. 8–11; Jenny Diski, 'The Shadow Within', *Sight and Sound*, vol. 1, no. 10, February 1992, pp. 12–3.

8. Catherine Clément, *Opera, or the Undoing of Women*, p. 118.

9. Moylan C. Mills, 'Charles Laughton's Adaptation of *The Night of the Hunter*', *Literature/Film Quarterly*, vol. 16, no. 1, 1988, p. 56.

10. Jack Ravage, '*The Night of the Hunter* [On Videotape]', *Film Quarterly*, vol. 42, no. 1, Fall 1988, p. 44. Ravage also points out that it sunk at the box office at least partly because 'United Artists seemed to wish that audiences would simply overlook what it thought of as a momentary lapse of control over their own "story department"'. Stephen King includes *The Night of the Hunter* on a list of the twenty scariest movies of all time. See Stephen King, *Danse Macabre* (New York: Berkley, 1983), p. 181.

11. These quotations are assembled, with others, by Jacques Goimard, following his article, 'Plus noir que vous ne pensez', *Avant-Scène*, no. 202, February 1978, pp. 4–6. For Truffaut's review see Simon Callow, *Charles Laughton: A Difficult Actor* (London: Methuen, 1987), p. 236.

12. This novel (1957) has been reissued under the title *Cape Fear* (Melbourne: Penguin, 1991). This retitling of books in the wake of film adaptations (another example is the change of *Schindler's Ark* to *Schindler's List*) is interesting in terms of a recasting of originality. It is as though the film becomes the origin and the novel a derivation. In remakes also it is usually the original novel, story or script that is the 'property' purchased, copyrighted, not the original film.

13. Thomas Leitch points out that this is a common device in remakes which face the dilemma that they cannot risk invoking memories of the earlier film too fervently and yet are limited in the kinds of novelty they can introduce: 'Remakes most often address this problem by adding a twist to their exposition, teasing knowing audiences as they bring new audiences up to their level of background knowledge.' See Thomas M. Leitch, 'Twice-Told Tales: The Rhetoric of the Remake', *Literature/Film Quarterly*, vol. 18, no. 3, 1990, p. 140.

14. And I in turn am reminded of this question in *Thriller* by Patricia Mellencamp, 'Haunted History: Tracey Moffatt and Julie Dash', *Discourse*, vol. 16, no. 2, Winter 1993–4, p. 129.

15. Beth Spencer, 'Fatal Attraction in Newtown', in Helen Daniel and Drusilla Modjeska (eds), *Picador New Writing 2* (Sydney: Picador Macmillan, 1994), p. 118.

16. Richard Gere, in the remake of *Breathless*, also wears a tattooed heart over his own heart. It is as though these 'remade' men wear their hearts on their skin as a sign of heartlessness.

17. Gilles Deleuze and Felix Guattari, *Anti-Oedipus: Capitalism and Schizophrenia* (Minneapolis: University of Minnesota Press, 1983), pp 144–5.

18. It is Freddie Francis who is reminiscing here, cited by Kevin Jackson in 'Gothic Shadows', *Sight and Sound*, vol. 2, no. 7, 1992, p. 40. Illusion Arts of Los Angeles was the name of a company that Francis had used before shooting *Cape Fear*.

19. Leo Bersani, *A Future for Astyanax: Character and Desire in Literature* (New York: Columbia University Press, 1984), p. 13.

20. Ibid. p. 286.

21. Peter Biskind, 'Slouching Toward Hollywood', p. 73.

22. Luce Irigaray, *Marine Lover of Friedrich Nietzsche* (New York: Columbia University Press, 1991), p. 123.

23. In his essay, 'The Body of the Divinity Captured by Signs', Louis Marin argues that the sentence 'This is my body' is a paradigmatic utterance, that it operates as the matrix of all signs, the model for all significations. Furthermore, it could be said 'to mark the emergence of the body within the functioning of language and of bodily practices within linguistic exchanges' (p. 14). He focuses on Antoine Arnauld and Pierre Nicole's *The Port Royal Logic* (1662), wherein 'the Eucharist makes the problem of language appear to be a particular instance of a general problem surrounding the signifying body and the word as an efficacious force by means of which things may be brought to articulation and transformed'. See Louis Marin, *Food for Thought* (Baltimore, Md: Johns Hopkins University Press, 1989 [1986]).

24. Scorsese in an interview with Amy Taubin, 'Blood and Pasta', *New Statesman and Society*, 9 November 1990, p. 14.

25. Walter Benjamin, *Reflections*, p. 66–7.

26. Gilles Deleuze, *Cinema 2: The Time–Image* (London: Athlone Press, 1989), p. 59–60. This is in the context of discussing the notion of an 'implied dream' where 'we would say that the optical and sound image extends into movement of the world . . . Characters do not move, but, as in an animated film, the camera causes the movement of the path on which they change places, "motionless at a great pace". The world takes responsibility for the movement that the subject can no longer or cannot make. This is a virtual movement, but it becomes actual at the price of an expansion of the totality of space and of a stretching of time.'

27. Paul Hammond, 'Melmoth in Norman Rockwell Land . . .', *Sight and Sound,* vol. 48 no. 2, Spring 1979, p. 109. The reference to the Big Bad Wolf does not actually appear in the film, but its import nevertheless registers. This sense of a mixing of genres, a navigation on the frontiers of the human and non-human, brings to mind again *The Last Temptation of Christ* and Serge Toubiana's comparison of the film with *Who Framed Roger Rabbit?*. See Serge Toubiana, 'L'Ultime Tentation du cinéma', *Cahiers du Cinéma,* no. 412, October 1988, p. 18.

28. Beth Spencer, 'Fatal Attraction in Newtown', p. 120.

29. '1914: One or Several Wolves', in Gilles Deleuze and Félix Guattari, *A Thousand Plateaus: Capitalism and Schizophrenia* (London: Athlone Press, 1988), p. 26. When an earlier translation of this article appeared in *Semiotexte* it was accompanied by an illustration of lots of little Doggy Freuds sitting in the branches of a tree – that is, wolf/dog bodies and Freud head, replete with spectacles and cigar. See 'May 14, 1914. One or Several Wolves?', *Semiotexte,* vol 11, no. 3, 1977, p. 137.

30. Roberta E. Pearson, *Eloquent Gestures: The Transformation of Performance Style in the Griffith Biograph Films* (Berkeley: University of California Press, 1992), p. 21.

31. This transition is also discussed by Tom Gunning in *D. W. Griffith and the Origins of American Narrative Film* (Urbana: University of Illinois Press, 1991), p. 228.

32. Cited by Pascal Bonitzer, 'Hitchcockian Suspense', in Slavoj Zizek (ed.), *Everything You Always Wanted to Know about Lacan (But Were Afraid to Ask Hitchcock)* (London: Verso, 1992), pp. 16–7. Morin dates the transition later, between 1915 and 1920.

33. This is not quite, I think, what Deleuze means when he writes (of *L'Amour fou*): 'Rivette invents a theatricality of cinema totally distinct from the theatricality of the theatre (even when cinema uses it as a reference).' See Gilles Deleuze, *Cinema 2: The Time–Image,* p. 194. In chapter two *The Red Shoes* and *Raging Bull* are both situated within this invention of a theatricality of cinema. Although I would indeed consider both these films to be histrionic, they are also thematically concerned with performance, with a ceremonialising of the everyday, with a staging. Histrionic cinema is not invariably bound by such thematic concerns – though an interest in acting out often means that storytelling and fictionality is highlighted, as can be seen in the *The Night of the Hunter* and the two *Cape Fears.*

34. Geoffrey Macnab, 'Caught in the Act', *Sight and Sound,* vol. 4, no. 4, April 1994, p. 61; Laurence Olivier commented about Laughton: 'I only know that whether you liked it or not something extraordinary happened while he was acting and it was always well garnished with fabulous touches of originality. I often think of these, copy them and shall probably go on doing so, as I have no shame about being a copycat' – quoted in Charles Higham, *Charles Laughton: An Intimate Biography* (New York: Doubleday, 1976), p. 215

35. Jack Ravage, *'The Night of the Hunter* [On Videotape]', pp. 45–6.

36. François Regnault, 'Plaidoyer Pro Niro', *Cahiers du Cinéma,* no. 286, March 1978, p. 51.

37. Bertold Brecht, *Brecht on Theatre: The Development of an Aesthetic* (London: Eyre Methuen, 1973), p. 194.

38. Ibid., pp. 165–6.

39. Bertold Brecht, Foreword to *The Life of Galileo* (London: Methuen, 1964), p. 13.

40. *Brecht on Theatre*, p. 163.

41. Simon Callow, *Charles Laughton: A Difficult Actor* (London: Methuen, 1987), p. 177.

42. David Thomson, *A Biographical Dictionary of Film* (New York: William Morrow, 1981), 2nd edn, p. 332.

43. Yann Tobin, '*La Nuit du chasseur*', *Positif*, no. 254–5, May 1982, p. 56.

44. Charles Higham, *Hollywood Cameramen: Sources of Light* (London: Thames & Hudson in association with the British Film Institute, 1970), p. 99.

45. Gilles Deleuze, *Cinema 2: The Time–Image*, p. 60.

46. In a 1938 interview, reprinted in Simon Callow, *Charles Laughton*, pp. 142–3.

47. George E. Turner, 'Creating *The Night of the Hunter*', *American Cinematographer*, December 1982, p. 1274.

48. Quoted in Charles Higham, *Hollywood Cameramen*, p. 114–15.

49. Scorsese, quoted in David Morgan, 'A Remake That Can't Miss: *Cape Fear*', *American Cinematographer*, no. 72, October 1991, p. 34.

50. In the Criterion videodisc commentaries on *Taxi Driver* and *The Tales of Hoffman* (1951) respectively. Francis was also camera operator on Powell and Pressburger's *The Small Back Room* (1948) and *Gone to Earth* (aka *The Wild Heart*, 1950).

51. David Morgan, 'A Remake That Can't Miss', p. 34.

52. Freddie Francis in David Morgan,'A Remake that Can't Miss', p. 40.

53. Ibid., p. 38.

54. Alexander Walker, *Stardom: The Hollywood Phenomenon* (Harmondsworth: Penguin, 1974), p. 59.

55. I am particularly grateful to the class on Histrionics for discussion of this film in relation to the two *Cape Fear*s. Martin Vaughn called my attention to the *Mother Courage* association and Rachel Brebach made the connections with *Whatever Happened to Baby Jane?* and the wicked witch from *The Wizard of Oz*.

56. It was supposedly Hedda Hopper who dubbed Gish the 'steel butterfly'. See Moylan C. Mills, 'Charles Laughton's Adaptation of *The Night of the Hunter*', p. 51.

57. Jean-Louis Comolli, 'Historical Fiction: A Body Too Much', *Screen*, vol. 19, no. 2, Summer 1978, pp. 43 and 46. Comolli's topic is historical fiction, but this is a wonderful piece of writing on the relation between fiction and the cinematic body.

58. Marguerite Duras, '*La Nuit du chasseur*', *Cahiers du Cinéma*, no. 312–13, 1980, pp. 60–1

59. Béla Balázs, for instance, writes: 'For the pantomime is not only a silent art, it is the art of being silent, expressing what rises from the depths of silence. The gestures and mimickry of pantomime are not an accompaniment to words which have been spoken and which we cannot hear, but the expression, by means of gestures, of the profound experience of music, the music that lives in the depths of silence.' See Béla Balázs, *Theory of the Film: Character and Growth of a New Art* (New York: Dover, 1970 [1948]), p. 71.

60. Harlan Kennedy, 'Mitchum' (interview), *Film Comment*, vol. 28, no. 4, July–August 1992, p. 35.

61. 'No slouch', *Sight and Sound*, vol. 53, no.4, 1984, pp. 275–6.

62. James Naremore, *Acting in the Cinema* (Berkeley: University of California ress, 1988), p. 63.

63. Michel Ciment, *Conversations with Losey*, p. 78. Simon Callow remarks: 'The interesting thing is that Laughton, normally ill at ease with uniformly masculine men, was very comfortable with Mitchum, and that Mitchum's performance in *Night of the Hunter* is to a striking degree delicate, seductive, soft-eyed.' See Simon Callow, *Charles Laughton*, p. 232.

64. Jacques Goimard, 'Plus noir que vous ne pensez', p. 5. Leo Braudy, *The World in a Frame: What We See in Films* (Garden City, NY: Anchor Press/Doubleday, 1976), p. 234.

65. Stein quoted by Virgil Thomson, 'Words and Emotions into Music', *Unmuzzled Ox*, no. 26, 1989, p. 45.

66. Graham Fuller, 'Martin Scorsese', *Interview*, vol. 21, no. 11, 1991, p. 18

67. Foster Hirsch (in an otherwise rather pedestrian study) speaks of Brando's Corleone as a vaudevillian performance that Olivier might have given. See *A Method to Their Madness: The History of the Actors Studio* (New York: Da Capo, 1984), p. 302.

68. As James Naremore, in one of the best accounts of Method acting in Hollywood, points out, 'The Method was articulated in terms of "essences", but audiences looked at surfaces; for them, the much-talked-about new technique was associated with behavioral tics and a star image.' See James Naremore, *Acting in the Cinema*, p. 212 (in Chapter 11: 'Marlon Brando in *On the Waterfront*'). Andrew Higson discusses this phenomenon in terms of narrative excess. In discussing a *Screen* day school at the NFT he writes: 'As an example of the way in which an acting style may produce quite unintended effects, [John] Caughie pointed to the way in which the Method school of naturalist film acting may in fact drift into self-reflexivity, signifying a power of presence and inner truth which may actually exceed the requirements of narrative. Thus, the gestures of Marlon Brando in *The Godfather* tend to exceed narrative motivation – to exceed that which is narratively required of character' ('Film acting and Independent Cinema', in Jeremy G. Butler (ed.), *Star Texts: Image and Performance in Film and Television* (Detroit, Mich.: Wayne State University Press, 1991), p. 158; reprinted from *Screen*, vol. 27, nos 3–4, May–August 1986, pp. 110–32.

69. Bazin is very instructive on these differences. He points to a certain interiority in Bogart's acting style, but differentiates it from that of Brando and Dean or the 'Kazan style' which, he says, 'is postulated upon anti-intellectual spontaneity. The behaviour of the actors is intended to be unforeseeable, since it no longer translates the profound logic of the feelings but externalised immediate impulses whose link with the inner life cannot be read directly. Bogart's secret is different. It is of course a case of Conrad's prudent silence . . . Bogey is a stoic.' See 'The death of Humphrey Bogart', trans. Phillip Drummond, in Jim Hillier (ed.), *Cahiers du Cinéma: The 1950s: Neo-Realism, Hollywood, New Wave* (Cambridge, Mass.: Harvard University Press, 1985), p. 100.

70. Jacques Rivette, 'Notes sur une révolution', in John Caughie (ed.), *Theories of Authorship* (London: Routledge & Kegan Paul, 1981), p. 41; reprinted from *Cahiers du Cinéma*, no. 54, Christmas 1955. Rivette is actually speaking of the new Hollywood auteurs, including Nicholas Ray.

71. Eric Rohmer, 'Ajax or the Cid?', in Jim Hillier (ed.), *Cahiers du Cinéma: The 1950s*, p. 114.

72. Hal Hinson, 'Some Notes on Method Actors', *Sight and Sound*, vol. 53, no. 3, Summer 1984, p. 203.

73. Virginia Wright Wexman, *Creating the Couple: Love, Marriage, and Hollywood Performance* (Princeton, NJ: Princeton University Press, 1993), p. 179.

74. Simon Callow, in discussing Brecht's interest in Laughton, remarks: 'His performances never console nor do they sedate.' See *Charles Laughton*, p. 169.

75. Robert De Niro, 'Dialogue on Film', *American Film*, vol. 6, no. 5, March 1981, p. 45.

76. In 'Plaidoyer Pro Niro', François Regnault talks of an 'inner jubilation' in De Niro, expressed in this declaration: 'I like to act.' He shows what he knows, what skills he has learned (and therefore what he hasn't learned). This demonstration of acting as a skill inspires in the audience a sense that 'I too can be an actor.' Regnault, in this article, delineates perfectly what I would call histrionic acting.

77. 'A Dialogue About Acting', cited by Jeremy G. Butler in *Star Texts*, p. 7.

78. J. Hoberman, 'Sacred and Profane', p. 11.

79. Jenny Diski, 'The Shadow Within', p. 13.

80. Bruno Bettelheim, *The Uses of Enchantment: The Meaning and Importance of Fairy Tales* (London: Penguin, 1991 [1976]), p. 176.

81. Ibid., p. 176. Bettelheim is describing Doré's illustration of the fairy tale.

82. *Three Essays on the Theory of Sexuality*, PFL 7, and *Totem and Taboo*, PFL 13.

83. This phrase, and some of the ideas on cannibalism that are developed here, were originally inspired by Jacques Derrida's seminar, 'Rhetorics of Cannibalism', University of California, Irvine, 1990.

84. Carol J. Clover, *Men, Women, and Chainsaws: Gender in the Modern Horror Film* (London: British Film Institute, 1992), p. 232.

85. Ibid., p. 12.

86. Luce Irigaray, *Marine Lover*, p. 123.
87. Philip Brophy, in an interesting article, 'Read My Lips', discusses this kind of quotation and the difficulties of writing about it: 'The role of "quoting" when voiced becomes more complex than the linear text-referencing invoked by literary discourse. When the written becomes spoken, a whole range of potential clashes arise between the act of enunciation, the role of recitation and the effect of utterance, in that, for example, one can vocally "italicise" an earnest statement, just as one can compassionately "underline" a self-deprecating quip. Script, character and performance become fused because there is a confounding lack of distinction between the possible orientation of the quote (i.e. not where it comes from, but where it must go).' See Philip Brophy, 'Read My Lips: Notes on the Writing and Speaking of Film Dialogue', *Continuum*, no. 5, 1992, p. 260.
88. Pam Cook, 'Scorsese's Masquerade', p. 15. Angela McRobbie writes, 'The excesses of the Max Cady character are hardly tolerable in the light of increasing cultural acceptance of sexual politics, no matter how many quotes from Nietzsche or Henry Miller are thrown in.' See Angela McRobbie, '*Cape Fear*', *Sight and Sound*, March 1992, p. 40.
89. Walter Benjamin, *One Way Street and Other Writings* (London: New Left Books, 1979), p. 100.
90. Jane Goodall, *Artaud and the Gnostic Drama* (Oxford: Oxford University Press, 1994), p. 130.
91. Scorsese describes Ed McDonald, the FBI agent who interviews the Hills in *GoodFellas*, as 'wearing a terrifying tie'. See Kathleen Murphy, 'Made Men', interview, *Film Comment*, September–October 1990, p. 69.
92. Luce Irigaray, *Marine Lover*, p. 123.
93. Gertrud Koch, 'Alexander Kluge's Phantom of the Opera', *New German Critique,* no. 49, Winter 1990, p. 81. Koch writes: 'Kluge believes that opera and film correspond to different needs; whereas opera invokes the Feeling for irreparable tragedy, the majority of films imagine themselves obliged to offer a happy ending.'

Chapter 7

1. Maya Deren, 'Ritual In Transfigured Time', *Dance Magazine,* December 1945.
2. Maya Deren, 'A Study in Choreography for Camera' [1945], Clark *et al.*, *The Legend of Maya Deren*, p. 629.
3. Referring to *At Land*, *The Legend of Maya Deren*, p. 263. Reprinted from *Film Culture*, no. 39.
4. Leo Bersani, *A Future for Astyanax: Character and Desire in Literature* (New York: Columbia University Press, 1984).
5. 'Martin Scorsese Interviewed by Gavin Smith', *Film Comment*, vol. 29, no. 6, November–December 1993, p. 19.
6. John Berger, *G* (London: Penguin, 1972), pp. 190–1.
7. 'Martin Scorsese Interviewed by Gavin Smith', p. 21.
8. 'Choreography for the Camera', *The Legend of Maya Deren*, p. 265. Reprinted from *Dance Magazine*, October 1945.

Filmography

Index of Films Cited